About the volume:

This book examines the urban activities of the medieval institutional Church – parish and diocese, monastery and cathedral – which did so much to shape the origins and development of medieval towns. That influence is evident in buildings and town plans, in urban law and marketing of products, but also in conflict and negotiation between secular and Church authorities.

The contributors to this valuable collection of essays take examples from towns in many parts of the British Isles, and examine problems from a variety of academic viewpoints, to build on earlier work and to suggest new perspectives.

About the editors:

T.R. Slater is Reader in Historical Geography at the University of Birmingham. Gervase Rosser is Senior Tutor at St Catherine's College, University of Oxford.

The Church in the Medieval Town

The Church in the Medieval Town

Edited by

T.R. SLATER and GERVASE ROSSER

Ashgate
Aldershot • Brookfield USA • Singapore • Sydney

© T.R. Slater, Gervase Rosser and the contributors, 1998

All rights reserved. No part of this publication may be reproduced, stored in a retrieval system, or transmitted in any form or by any means, electronic, mechanical, photocopying, recording, or otherwise without the prior permission of the publisher.

Published by
Ashgate Publishing Limited
Gower House
Croft Road
Aldershot
Hants
GU11 3HR
England

Ashgate Publishing Company
Old Post Road
Brookfield
Vermont 05036-9704
USA

The authors have asserted their moral right under the Copyright, Designs and Patents Act, 1988, to be identified as the authors of this work.

British Library Cataloguing in Publication Data

The Church in the Medieval Town.
 1. Church history—Middle Ages, 600–1500. 2. Cities and towns, Medieval—Religious aspects—Christianity. 3. Cities and towns, Medieval—England. 4. England—Church history—1066–1485.
 I. Slater, T.R. II. Rosser, Gervase.
 282.4'2'0902

ISBN 1-84014-213-8

Library of Congress Cataloging-in-Publication Data

The church in the medieval town/edited by T.R. Slater and Gervase Rosser.
    p. cm.
  Includes index.
  ISBN 1-84014-213-8 (hc)
    1. City churches—England—History. 2. City churches—Ireland—-History. 3. Cities and towns—England—History. 4. Cities and towns—Ireland—History. 5. England—Church history—1066–1485. 6. Ireland—Church history—600–1500. 7. England—Economic conditions—1066–1485. 8. Ireland—Economic conditions.
  I. Slater, T.R. II. Rosser, Gervase.
  BR750.C475 1998
  274.2'05'091732—dc21   97-27229
                                                             CIP

ISBN 1 84014 213 8

This book is printed on acid free paper

Typeset in Sabon by Manton Typesetters, 5–7 Eastfield Road, Louth, Lincolnshire, LN11 7AJ and printed in Great Britain by Galliard (Printers) Ltd, Great Yarmouth.

Contents

List of Tables and Figures	vii
Notes on Contributors	xi
Preface Nicholas Brooks	xiii
Introduction T.R. Slater and Gervase Rosser	1
1 Status and Class in the Medieval Town Rodney Hilton	9

2 Conflict and Political Community in the Medieval Town:
     Disputes between Clergy and Laity in Hereford
     Gervase Rosser
	20

3 The Church and the Jews in English Medieval Towns John Edwards	43

4 Trade, Towns and the Church: Ecclesiastical Consumers and
     the Urban Economy of the West Midlands, 1290–1540
     Christopher Dyer
	55

5 The Origin and Early Development of the London
     Mendicant Houses
     Jens Röhrkasten
	76

6 Urban Rectories and Urban Fortunes in Late Medieval
     England: the Evidence from Bishop's Lynn
     R.N. Swanson
	100

7 The Town and the Monastery: Early Medieval Urbanization
     in Ireland, AD 800–1150
     B.J. Graham
	131

8 Benedictine Town Planning in Medieval England: Evidence
     from St Albans
     T.R. Slater
	155

9 Trading Places: Monastic Initiative and the Development of
     High-Medieval Coventry
     Keith D. Lilley
	177

10	The Origins of Urban Parish Boundaries *Nigel Baker and Richard Holt*	209
11	Medieval Parishes and Parish Churches in Canterbury *Tim Tatton-Brown*	236
12	Clerical Communities and Parochial Space: the Planning of Urban Mother Churches in the Twelfth and Thirteenth Centuries *John Blair*	272

Index 295

List of Tables and Figures

Table

4.1	Ecclesiastical institutions in the West Midlands with evidence of expenditure	56

Figures

4.1	Places mentioned in the text in Warwickshire and Worcestershire	57
5.1	Location of mendicant houses in London, 1230–1320	78
6.1	Tithes of Bishop's Lynn, 1370–1428	111
6.2	Tithes of Bishop's Lynn, 1429–1536	112
6.3	Oblations of Bishop's Lynn, 1370–1428	114
6.4	Receipts of St Margaret's Church, Bishop's Lynn, 1429–1536	115
6.5	Receipts of the chapels of St Nicholas and St James, Bishop's Lynn, 1429–1536	118
7.1	The morphology of Kells (County Meath)	137
7.2	The medieval morphology of Duleek (County Meath)	138
7.3	A simplified contemporary street plan of Armagh	145
7.4	The comparative context: Toulouse in the early thirteenth century	146
7.5	Clonmacnoise (Co. Offaly)	148
8.1	Borough and parish boundaries in St Albans	162
8.2	Plot patterns and defences in St Albans	165
9.1	A plan analysis of Coventry	180
9.2	Plan-unit X: the priory precinct	184
9.3	Plan-unit XI: the market area	186
9.4	Market infill: suggested topography of Butcher Row, Little Butcher Row and Cross Cheaping in *c.*1410	188
9.5	Plan-units XII and XIV: Bishop Street and Cook Street	192
9.6	Plan-unit XX: Far Gosford Street	195
9.7	Coventry and its hinterland, *c.*1450	197
10.1	The historic parishes of Worcester	214
10.2	Worcester: a reconstruction of the Anglo-Saxon *burh*	216

10.3	Worcester: historic city parishes with extramural territory	217
10.4	Worcester: hypothetical parish boundaries determined by the 'nearest-church-door' principle	219
10.5	The historic city parishes of Gloucester	222
10.6	Gloucester: hypothetical parish boundaries determined by the 'nearest-church-door' principle	223
10.7	A model of parish formation in minster towns with numerous churches	231
11.1	Town plan of Canterbury *c.*1500	237
11.2	Structural analysis of St Alphege's and St Martin's churches	240
11.3	St George the Martyr: archaeological evidence and structural analysis, late eleventh to early fourteenth century	242
11.4	St Mary Bredin: archaeological evidence	243
11.5	Structural analysis of St Mary Northgate and St Andrew's	244
11.6	Early nineteenth-century view of the chancel of St Mary Northgate from the south (demolished, 1830)	245
11.7	Structural analysis of All Saints' and St Peter's churches	247
11.8	Structural analysis of St George the Martyr, fifteenth century to 1942	248
11.9	Structural analysis of Holy Cross and St Mildred's churches	249
11.10	Mid-eighteenth-century engraving of All Saints' Church from the south-east	250
11.11	Structural analysis of St Paul's Church	251
11.12	Drawing of St Mary Bredman from the north-east in 1788, by Francis Grose	253
11.13	Structural analysis of St Margaret's and St Dunstan's churches	254
11.14	Late eighteenth-century engraving of Holy Cross Church from the north-east	257
11.15	Structural analysis of St Mary Bredman and St Mary Magdalen churches	258
11.16	Town plan of Canterbury *c.*1050	264
12.1	Crediton, Devon: the later medieval development of a cruciform collegiate church originally built *c.*1160	273
12.2	Bampton, Oxfordshire, in 1317	276
12.3	Non-cruciform collegiate churches (pre-1250 features only)	278

12.4	A selection of cruciform churches, monastic, collegiate and parochial, based on the 'austere' plan (pre-1200 features only)	280
12.5	Two cruciform collegiate churches in their later medieval state	284
12.6	Wimborne Minster, Dorset (pre-1250 features only)	286
12.7	Faringdon, Berkshire, as existing *c.*1250	287

Notes on Contributors

Nigel Baker is a freelance archaeologist based in Shropshire. He was Research Fellow for the 'English Medieval Towns and the Church' project.

John Blair is Lecturer, The Queen's College, University of Oxford.

Nicholas Brooks, FBA, is Professor of Medieval History and Head of Department in the School of History, University of Birmingham. He was co-director of the 'English Medieval Towns and the Church' project funded by the Leverhulme Trust, 1988–93.

Christopher Dyer, FBA, is Professor of Medieval Social History in the School of History, University of Birmingham.

John Edwards retired as Reader in Spanish History in the School of History, University of Birmingham.

B.J. Graham is Professor of Geography in the School of Environmental Studies, University of Ulster at Coleraine.

Rodney Hilton, FBA, is Professor Emeritus of Medieval History in the University of Birmingham and a member of the Institute for Advanced Studies in the Humanities.

Richard Holt is Lecturer in the School of History, University of Birmingham. He was Research Fellow for the 'English Medieval Towns and the Church' project.

Keith D. Lilley is British Academy Research Fellow in the Department of Geography, Royal Holloway, University of London.

Jens Röhrkasten is Lecturer in the School of History, University of Birmingham.

Gervase Rosser is Senior Tutor at St Catherine's College, University of Oxford. He was co-director of the 'English Medieval Towns and the Church' project.

T.R. Slater is Reader in Historical Geography in the School of Geography, University of Birmingham. He was co-director of the 'English Medieval Towns and the Church' project.

R.N. Swanson is Reader in Medieval Church History in the School of History, University of Birmingham.

Tim Tatton-Brown is an architectural historian and freelance archaeologist based in Salisbury.

Preface

The Church permeated the life of medieval towns. Many towns were founded by churches or had a great church as their chief landlord, property developer or court-holder. The Church was also the creator and administrator of urban parishes, the focus for the religious devotion of the laity – often for its social organization as well – and the inspiration for the town's most important buildings. How can the urban role of the medieval church be best understood? Modern research into the development of towns in Britain, as in Europe, has raised questions which can only be answered by interdisciplinary collaboration. All too often promising early work on urban morphology by geographers or archaeologists had lacked a secure foundation in the study of that town's written documentation; all too often historians had delved into the archival riches of a town's records to illuminate its political history or its economic fortunes but had shown minimal interest in understanding the constraints imposed by the physical development of the townscape.

The University of Birmingham was fortunate in having a group of outstanding urban historians, geographers and field archaeologists interested in collaborative work at the very time that the Leverhulme Trust announced its intention to sponsor a series of major interdisciplinary research projects in the Humanities. The Trust's generous support for a five-year project on 'English Medieval Towns and the Church' enabled two Research Fellows, Dr R.A. Holt and Dr N.J. Baker – a historian and a geographer/archaeologist – to work on a collaborative and comparative study of West Midland towns, with a particular concentration upon Worcester and Gloucester. The overall co-ordination of the project and of the meetings of the group of Birmingham scholars to whom the Fellows reported their findings was my responsibility, but the detailed direction of the work on the historical and morphological and cartographic sides fell chiefly upon Dr A.G. Rosser and Dr T.R. Slater respectively. An essential component in the evolution of the project's strategy was the group of contributing scholars: Dr S.R. Bassett, Professor C.C. Dyer, Professor R.H. Hilton, Dr R.N. Swanson and Professor J.W.R. Whitehand who were later joined by Dr J. Röhrkasten and by a research student, Dr K.D. Lilley, working on the borough of Coventry.

The dialogue between the Research Fellows and the wider body of scholars both in Birmingham and beyond has been carried through to the project's final publications. We hope to fulfil the aims of collaborative research that the Leverhulme Trust sought to promote by showing how understanding of the planning and growth of our medieval towns and of the varied roles of the Church in the town is transformed by effective interdisciplinary and co-operative research. My particular thanks go to the successive directors of the Leverhulme Trust, Sir Rex Richards and Professor B. Supple, for their support and interest throughout the project, to Professors C.N.L. Brooke and P.D.A. Harvey who refereed our initial application and maintained interest in our progress thereafter, to Mr H. Buglass, Mrs A. Ankorn and Mr N. Mudie for their superb cartography which graces this volume and has always been an essential precondition for understanding and visualizing the church in the town, and finally to Alec McAulay of Scolar Press for his keen interest and patient determination that the eventual publication should meet the highest standards of the different disciplines involved.

Nicholas Brooks
University of Birmingham

Introduction

T.R. *Slater and Gervase Rosser*

This volume derives from a major research project funded by the Leverhulme Trust at the University of Birmingham designed to explore the interaction of church and town in the medieval period in England. Part of the organizational framework of the project was a group of advisory researchers drawn from the history, geography and archaeology departments within the University of Birmingham who met at regular intervals to discuss the progress of the research and to add their particular expertise towards resolving the questions under investigation. In the final year of the project a research seminar was organized to expose the research methodology and preliminary results to a wider scrutiny from outside the University of Birmingham. It was always our intention to publish some of the papers from that seminar as one of the outcomes from the 'English Medieval Towns and the Church' project. As is often the case, intention has taken some time to reach fruition. None the less, the editors believe that the wait has been worth while and that this volume will be welcomed as reflecting some of the major themes under investigation by historians of the medieval town. The chapters fall neatly within the bounds of two major themes. The authors of Chapters 1 to 6 explore the social and economic dimensions of the interaction between church and town; in Chapters 7 to 12 the emphasis moves to the spaces and built forms of towns and their church buildings.

Society and economy

In Chapter 1 Rodney Hilton takes a broad view of contemporary class and status distinction in the urban context. Historians long ago reached a consensus that rural medieval society had, inbuilt, a conflict between landowners and the peasantry which was essentially a class conflict. This periodically manifested itself in popular discontent and physical violence. However, Hilton claims, the status and class dimensions of the population of towns are less well defined than for the countryside and historians have been slower in exploring the relationship between merchants and craftworkers; between landowners (including the Church) and both merchants and the poor. Hilton presents some of the evidence that can be gleaned from contemporary documentation in Britain and

France on these relationships and the ways in which they were manifested in status groups, dress codes and public ceremony and ritual. It was in this last that tension and conflict was contained, but also occasionally overflowed into riot. One such conflict, the 'Gladman' insurrection of 1443 in Norwich, is used to exemplify the actors involved.

Gervase Rosser develops this theme in much more detail in Chapter 2. He is concerned to examine the ways in which the inequalities in the social structure of towns are manifested in the realities of the political process; in particular, the ways in which the political élite needed to mobilize popular opinion in order to uphold their position. One of the most common types of dispute was that between the merchant élite and the clerical authorities in particular cities. Rosser takes the city of Hereford as his case study and examines in some detail the ways in which quarrels over ecclesiastical liberties in the city were important in affirming the identities of both town and church there. The separate jurisdictions of the king's fee, governed by a mayor and his aldermen since the grant of the fee farm in the twelfth century, the fee of the cathedral dean and chapter, and the bishop's fee were an inevitable source of conflict and negotiation. What is especially interesting is the way in which disorder was used by one side or the other to strengthen their negotiating position but that, always, there was the expectation that there would have to be a negotiated compromise. Relationships were deliberately engineered to crisis point so that particular problems could be reviewed and principles re-established. History was almost always appealed to, and the collective memory of the townspeople was regularly called to witness. Again, ritual processions on feast days, where town and church were supposedly demonstrating the unity of the city, were often the place in which orders of precedence demonstrated the levels of authority of different protagonists. The detailed evidence from Hereford is then used to make some comparisons with other cathedral cities in southern England.

This evaluation of conflict within the urban community is also a feature of John Edwards's Chapter 3, an analysis of Jewish–church relationships in British cities up to the expulsion of the Jews from England by Edward I, in 1290. The Jewish presence in England was mainly an urban one from the Norman invasion onwards, but it was also a dispersed one since nearly 60 towns in England and Wales had one or more Jewish families resident whereas only six cities had sufficient Jewish residents to make a visible community. Their principal function was to provide financial services to the Crown, the Church, townspeople and the barons in the shires. Edwards takes the well-known cases of the so called 'ritual murder' of young boys, beginning with William of Norwich, to explore the growing antagonism and violence between the Christian and Jewish communities in these larger cities. This culminated in the slaughter of many of the Jewish community in London and York, as well as many smaller towns, on the accession of Richard I. A full study of the attitudes of the various social groups in England towards the Jewish community has yet to be made but this chapter goes some way towards that study by exploring the attitude of the Church, both locally and in a European context. Edwards shows that it was not until the reign of Henry III that papal canons restricting the contact between Christians and Jews were given effect in secular law. Important, too, at this time was the growth of the Dominican and Franciscan friars who sought to give practical effect to the edicts of the Third Lateran Council of 1179, that converting Jews should be welcomed. Houses of converts were established in Southwark, London and Oxford in the thirteenth century.

Christopher Dyer has made the study of the medieval urban economy very much his own. In Chapter 4 he examines from where, and from whom, the Church in the West Midlands purchased its goods and services. The urban hierarchy in the West Midlands has been subject to more investigation than any other region and it should be possible, says Dyer, to pose questions about the places of purchase of common everyday items and luxury or specialist items of consumption. Many monastic houses were at least partly self-sufficient, of course, but even they needed money for building works and gifts which involved people outside the monastic community. Dyer shows that the wealthiest churchmen made most of their purchases from outside the region altogether. London was the favoured centre for the Bishop and the Prior of Worcester, whilst the easy links with Bristol meant that other major purchases could be made there, most notably of wine and spices. Despite the overland journey, Boston was a favoured source of fish and cloth for these prelates. Worcester itself seems to have supplied relatively few of the needs of the cathedral priory. In smaller towns, adjacent monasteries often held the town in lordship and there was a much closer relationship economically. Grain, animals and foodstuffs were bought and sold in the local market but specialist services, such as painters, glaziers and goldsmiths were only found in the medium-sized towns. The hierarchical nature of this commercial network is shown to reflect that of society in general in this period. Clergy were an important sector of society, but they did not necessarily dominate or distort the economy of the towns which they patronized.

Despite the loss of the English mendicant order's archives, in Chapter 5 Jens Röhrkasten reviews the early development of friaries in London using a wide variety of sources so as to discern something of their initiators and early supporters. Friaries, of course, are essentially urban institutions and the answers to these questions therefore tell us something of the religious stance of certain sectors of the urban élite in the thirteenth century. Within 70 years, eight mendicant orders had established friaries in London, more than almost any other city in Europe. Despite modest beginnings, they had a profound effect on the topographical development of the city, or more particularly its suburbs, as houses and land were acquired for their convents. In almost all cases, the early support of some of the most prominent ecclesiastics and aristocrats in London was significant in their foundation, but gifts from wealthy citizens and merchants quickly followed and the support of the Crown was constant in these early years, with gifts of both building materials and alms.

In Chapter 6, Robert Swanson takes a different sector of the urban church, the ordinary parish churches, and explores another topic in which archival sources are in short supply, namely the finances of these institutions in late medieval England since this might reasonably be expected to reflect something of the economic vicissitudes of the urban community at this time. Urban parish churches constitute an enormously complex set of institutions which vary significantly in their circumstances from place to place. The revenues of a single urban parish church with an extensive rural hinterland are clearly very different from a small, wholly urban church in a multi-parish town, whilst the appropriation of most of the revenues of many churches by monastic institutions and the like is also significant in any comparative assessment. The first part of Swanson's chapter explores something of this variety, and of the variety of income in cash and kind, that the limited sources reveal. The second part of his chapter concentrates on the financial records of the benefice of St Margaret's, Bishop's Lynn which survive for the period from the 1370s to the 1530s. This relatively long run of statistics is carefully analysed for the light it sheds on the fluctuating economy of the town. Generally, when all the complexities of different sources of income have been considered, the trend reflects a slow decline in the economy of this particular town.

Topography and built forms

The 'monastic town' has entered the literature as the distinctive contribution of Ireland to the re-establishment of urbanism in post-Roman Europe. In Chapter 7, Brian Graham attempts to resolve the paradox of having a separate theory of early medieval urbanization in Ireland by suggesting that monasteries and towns there can be understood as evolving with the emergence of a feudal society in exactly the same way as elsewhere. Ireland was, of course, different from the rest of western Europe in having no Roman towns to provide a location for dioceses. Graham argues that early medieval monasteries in Ireland were as much secular as ecclesiastical institutions, and that the administration of both church and state was inextricably bound up in these sites from the eighth century onwards. Evidence for urban plot patterns (reflecting property laws) and for urban administration is lacking in all the monastic towns, and Graham's argument therefore focuses upon the form and function of urban defences. He takes as his model the division of early French cities into defended *cité* and merchant *bourg*, a variant on the 'urbs–suburbium' model of central-European writing. The principal morphological characteristic of the Irish monastic town is the double elliptical earthwork enclosure. The inner enclosure was reserved for the churches and monastic community as a spiritual sanctuary. However, Graham argues, there is little evidence to suggest that most of these enclosures date from the monastic foundation, many may well derive from the ecclesiastical reorganization of the twelfth century, following the Anglo-Norman invasion. The second morphological element of the monastic town model, the outer, secular enclosure is based on even less certain evidence as to chronology and, in some cases, their very existence. Consequently, Graham argues, it is inaccurate to talk of 'monastic towns' with a supposition of causative links between monastery and urbanism; rather, most of these places could have been defended towns where marketing, secular administration and the Church coalesced in the same way as elsewhere in Europe.

If there was nothing to distinguish the Irish monastic town from towns elsewhere in Europe then, clearly, this is also true about monastic towns in England. Terry Slater's chapter on the evidence for planning in towns dominated by monasteries of the Benedictine order affirms this. They, too, were places which were towns first and foremost, but in which the dominating building and institutional landholder was a monastery. He uses the example of St Albans, which is of crucial significance in the history of English urban development, since it is one of the few places in Britain where the common European phenomenon of a town developing around the shrine of a Christian burial in a Roman cemetery can be firmly established; in this instance, the tomb of the proto-martyr Alban. It is also a place in which the evidence from the later abbey chronicle suggests that the Benedictine community was engaged in a major exercise in town founding and town planning in the tenth century. Slater uses the evidence from town-plan analysis to suggest that the record of the chronicle can be accepted, but that the early town was not the simple tight-knit town around the triangular market space that earlier interpretations have suggested. This complexity of physical development in a medieval planned town was characteristic of all towns, whether monastic or not, and, like Graham, Slater would see this example of town planning as fitting a European-wide development of towns and urban functions in the twelfth and thirteenth centuries.

Keith Lilley provides another example of the development of a Benedictine town in Chapter 9; in this instance the enigmatic case of Coventry. Enigmatic because the sudden rise of that city in the urban hierarchy in the twelfth century has never been satisfactorily explained. Once more it is the evidence of plan analysis that has provided the key to a model of the city's development which suggests that it was the founding of the Benedictine monastery in 1043 by Earl Leofric of Mercia which explains the beginnings of the town's development as well as the well-known tenurial division which was to become the focus of later-medieval disputes. The centre of the monastic-founded town was a large triangular market-place. This was later deliberately infilled by the cathedral priory as a way of increasing its rent roll. Similarly, the prior developed a new street in the growing city to provide a ceremonial way to the priory cathedral which did not involve passing through the earl's fee to the south and, later still, suburban land was developed on one of the major approach roads to the city. All this begins to make sense of the forged charters by which the priors attempted to rebuff the legal challenges to their successfully developing town made by the holders of the secular earl's fee.

The topographical theme pursued in Chapter 10 by Nigel Baker and Richard Holt is the origin of urban parish boundaries. Their studies of the topographical development of the cities of Worcester and Gloucester raised many questions about the development of this little-discussed plan element and, eventually, some answers to those questions. In both places the seventh-century minsters (St Peter's Abbey in Gloucester and the cathedral in Worcester) did not have a monopoly in the pastoral care of the townspeople even before the tenth century. The new parish churches of these two towns, however, were not provided by private citizens, as was often the case elsewhere, but by the Crown or the minsters themselves. The early parishes in both Worcester and Gloucester provide some support for Rogers's hypothesis that such parishes are recognizable from their large areas of extramural territory; however, this is only so for churches which were on the fringe of the contemporary urban area. There was another group of early churches wholly within the town. For this group, the archaeological evidence shows that parish boundaries were far from fixed by the twelfth century and that small-scale adjustments continued to be made well into the later medieval period and, in some cases, even beyond. There is also some support, especially in Worcester, for Keene's suggestion that, in Winchester and London, parishes had been determined by a 'nearest church door' principle. But there are also significant anomolies from the expected pattern, some of which remain inexplicable, and there is more limited support for this hypothesis in the parish boundaries of Gloucester, other than those which were established in the twelfth century or later. An especially well-documented property in Gloucester provides a window on later medieval parochial boundary adjustment.

Another cathedral city provides the exemplar material in Chapter 11. Here Tim Tatton-Brown uses the building evidence of the parish churches of Canterbury to examine the changing ecclesiastical provision made for the people of that city and the changing fashions in urban parish church design. Given the enormous literature on the architectural history of English parish churches it is surprising that full surveys of urban churches are notable for their almost complete absence. Tatton-Brown's chapter, with its careful melding of architectural, archaeological, art historical and documentary evidence demonstrates why such a task, at least in those cities characterized by a multiplicity of small parish churches, has been so rarely undertaken. Only five of Canterbury's 22 medieval churches are still in ecclesiastical use, and only 11 survive in whole or in part above ground; for seven nothing is known other than their site. The evidence marshalled by Tatton-Brown shows how frequently the high medieval churches of the city were rebuilt in whole or in part, occasionally on completely new sites. Only two were demolished following the depredations of the plague. The post-medieval history of the churches is sketched in and then their parochial geography is considered. Tatton-Brown sees close analogies between the pattern in Canterbury and that in London as proposed by Brooke.

Finally, in Chapter 12, John Blair discusses the planning of minster church buildings in the twelfth and thirteenth centuries. He makes the link between the survival of the pattern of communal or collegial life and large cruciform churches being built or enlarged in the mid-twelfth to late thirteenth centuries. These churches had a typical plan of aisleless nave, double length chancel, crossing, and transepts with eastern chapels, in imitation of the greater churches of the regular monastic communities. The communities served by these former minster churches were very frequently urban because of the central-place functions attached to minsters and, consequently, the liturgical problems which had to be accommodated in the thirteenth century were those associated with the conflicting needs of the laity and the ecclesiastical communities for worship within a single architectural space. The increasing elaboration of the long chancel and crossing for the clerics, and of lesser altars in the transepts served by them for particular lay groups was one part of the pattern. This left the nave, with its rood under the west crossing arch, and the later nave aisles as the principal secular spaces. This was a pattern which was to be reflected later in smaller country churches and in elaborate late-medieval urban churches with other patterns of collegiality.

The primary emphasis of these essays is upon the urban activities of the medieval church as a set of institutions: the parish, the diocese, the monastery, and the liberty. In these various institutional roles, the Church did much to shape both the origin and the development of the medieval town. Its influence is evident in architectural forms and in the topography of town plans; in structures of marketing and in the development of urban law. In each of these areas, as the various chapters in this volume demonstrate, the relationship of church and town could be at once mutually beneficial and a source of conflict. In exploring these fundamental themes, however, the contributors to the book shed light in addition on the vexed questions of secular attitudes to the Church and of the perceived role of Christianity in structuring, validating and, in various ways, disturbing, the lives of the Church's town-dwelling lay members. Despite their variety of academic viewpoints and the wide geographical spread of their exemplars, these chapters provide much material that both builds on earlier work and encourages reflection on some of the problems that are at the centre of the wider research project with its intensive investigation of the West Midland cities of Worcester and Gloucester, and which will be presented in a second volume.

CHAPTER ONE

Status and Class in the Medieval Town

Rodney Hilton

Medieval social theorists, who recognized that society was differentiated into social strata with unequal access to wealth and power, nevertheless insisted on the allegedly harmonious interrelationship of these strata. Their respective and particular functions were necessary for the survival of the whole, even though the different degree of 'honour' ascribed to each status group indicated a strict social hierarchy. In view of the fact that medieval society was riven by social conflict, peasant rebellions in particular, the social doctrine of status harmony can only be regarded as ideological rather than descriptive. As Georges Duby argues in his fundamental work, *Les trois ordres ou l'imaginaire du féodalisme*, the concept was not a reflection of reality but a project for acting upon it.[1] And although a few historians have copied their medieval intellectual predecessors in interpreting medieval society as composed of interrelated status groups, most have recognized it as a class society, in which the conflict between landowners (both lay and ecclesiastical) and the peasantry was a permanent feature. A similar perception of class division and class conflict in the urban context is, however, less generally accepted and here, oddly enough, status rather than class tends still to be seen as defining social differentiation.

Theorists and preachers continued to the end of the Middle Ages, and beyond, to insist on the tripartite concept (prayers, warriors, workers). The social context of the scheme was essentially agrarian, but it had some relevance to towns. The higher churchmen and nobility were often lords of towns, and among the great range of town-dwellers were numerous clergy serving the parishes, chantries and fraternities, in addition to the gentry with town houses. The remaining townspeople were more difficult to fit into the conventions of the three orders. For example, merchants were scarcely workers in the normal sense, but nor can they be regarded easily as belonging with the aristocratic warriors. Moralists who identified the duties and delinquencies of different social groups were nevertheless obliged to bring in urban classes. Merchants appear as early as the twelfth century in the *Livre des Manières* of Étienne de Fougères, Bishop of Rennes and chaplain to Henry II

Plantagenet. Their faults and virtues are listed here and in later treatises, where they, and other urban classes, including artisans and journeymen, are integrated into the estate concept of social hierarchy.[2] This is well illustrated in the *Vox Clamantis* of John Gower, a late fourteenth-century English writer who was also a Kentish landowner with London connections. *Vox Clamantis* begins with a bitter attack on the rebels of 1382, expressed in a dream in which peasants are symbolized as animals failing to do their duties, such as asses refusing to carry their sacks to the city and oxen refusing to be yoked to the plough. It also includes a section which sketches the traditional tripartite model of the social orders and their duties: 'We know that there are three estates within which everybody lives as is customary ... ' He continues with the traditional description of knights, clergy and peasants, but adds other social groups. Merchants are favourably presented, being necessary for the distribution of goods, even though fraud and usury in urban society is condemned. Gower includes artisans as lesser citizens who must live in agreement with the greater citizens, the merchants, for all to go well.[3]

An important aspect of modern historians' advocacy of 'estate' theory is that any manifestation of social discontent is dismissed as irrational, since its proponents assume that social classes, defined in economic terms, with genuinely conflicting interests, do not exist. As I have suggested, most agrarian historians do now in fact accept that the landowner–peasant confrontation was a class conflict. How is the problem of status and class confronted by historians of the medieval town?

Medieval urban society may not be as clearly identifiable as that of medieval agrarian society as one divided into classes with conflicting interests. A long tradition of historical writing emphasizes the antagonism between towns and landlords, parallel to the relationships found in the countryside between lords and peasants. Church landlords, and in particular monastic landlords, were especially prone to dispute with the towns over which they ruled.[4] As far as concerns relations among the townspeople themselves, however, a trend among historians of French and English towns rejects class analysis, and therefore tends to assume the irrationality of any form of rebellious action. Historians vary in their emphasis. Susan Reynolds, for example, realizes that conflicting class interests existed. However, she considers that the class antagonisms, that we may think their rational interests required, did not manifest themselves because they had faith in consensus and reconciliation. Others are more dismissive of popular discontent. Bernard Chevalier states that popular violence was simply due to the emotions of the poor. There was no class conflict, nor any idea of change. The poor were simply angry because they thought that the rich were not doing their social duty. Jacques Rossiaud is equally dismissive of rebellion. For him, urban revolts were irrational violence provoked by rumour, and usually manipulated from above. Having acknowledged these views, it may be well to consider briefly whether an analysis of medieval urban society in terms of class structure is feasible.[5] In practice, even some urban historians who are doubtful about class analysis provide useful descriptions of urban class structures. Philippe Wolff does this, in his work on social movements in fourteenth-century Languedoc, even while he attempts to dismiss concepts of class conflict by declaring that there were rich and poor in every social class.[6] Urban class structures are not, in fact, difficult to define, even though analysis of inter-class relations is more problematical than in the case of agrarian society.

An economic definition of the main producing class of the medieval town, the manufacturing artisans, is relatively straightforward. The basic unit of production was the family household, generally nuclear but sometimes extended to include close collaterals. This would be enlarged as the master craftsman employed apprentices and journeymen, seldom more than two or three (and the latter tended to be non-resident), additional to family members. Even though many urban artisan households might have small plots of land[7] they did not, as did most of the peasantry, produce their own means of subsistence. Their production was entirely for the market, whether they sold direct to the final consumer or through merchant intermediaries. Urban artisans paid rent, but rent was not so important an item in the incomes of urban rulers as it was of rural landlords.[8]

The artisan households did not by any means include the whole of the working population of the medieval town. Apart from retail traders, a not easily definable group, there was a considerable population of unskilled workers outside the structures of the craft workshops, such as labourers in the building trades. Some might have a reasonably stable existence, but they also shaded off into a fluctuating class of marginals, difficult to define, which – especially in the bigger towns – included transient immigrants from the countryside.

Urban ruling classes, though complex in composition, are not hard to define. In both France and England there existed landowners with both urban as well as rural property. Before the thirteenth century, indeed, these were often more important in the ruling structures of urban society than the merchants. Such land-owning knights were prominent, for example, in the towns of Provence and Languedoc in the twelfth century, but in the thirteenth they were being joined and even superseded by merchants. The land-owning element was, of course, not peculiar to southern France in the early period. The twelfth-century patricians of Arras were originally landowners, as were those of twelfth-century London.[9] But in most English towns there was already by the twelfth century a distinct mercantile element, with some political strength, as was manifested in their *gilde mercatorie*.[10] From the thirteenth century onwards, in both countries, the mercantile element became generally predominant among the bourgeoisie, even where feudal land-owning interests remained influential.

Class relationships in the towns did not seem so clearly exploitative as in the countryside, where the manor or *seigneurie* was the focus of power. There were, of course, centres of feudal power in towns, such as the castles, urban houses and estates of the lay aristocracy, but especially the jurisdictional enclaves of the ecclesiastics, by which bishops, monasteries and friaries claimed special privileges within sections of the larger towns. But as far as urban merchants were concerned, their economic relationship with the class of manufacturing craftsmen was expressed in market terms. As always in such relationships, exploitation, where it existed, was covert. Merchants fixed the terms of trade, as putters-out of raw material and sellers of the finished product, as middlemen, or as urban rulers who exercised control over the market. More overt clashes between classes were those concerning wages and hours of work which opposed craft masters and journeymen, whose hopes of becoming masters themselves declined in both France and England from the fourteenth century onwards.

We do not, however, leave urban revolt behind once we have considered the economic grievances mentioned so far. There was also an element of class conflict which, in some ways, was analogous to peasant protest against rent increases. This class conflict, from the twelfth century onwards, consisted of numerous episodes, ranging from peaceful protest to violent and concerted action, provoked by what was seen as unjust and corrupt taxation. Urban tax was a levy on artisan households not unlike the levy of rural rent and, in view of the effective exclusion of the artisans from genuine participation in town government, could readily be perceived as arbitrarily imposed. From the rebellion in London led by William FitzOsbert in the 1190s through to the late fourteenth- and fifteenth-century tax rebellions in French towns, it is clear that taxation was a major issue in urban social politics over a wide area and a long period. These conflicts have been well documented and described by French and English historians, even though they have by no means always been identified as class conflicts.[11]

If urban classes, and merchants in particular, were represented in moralizing literature as 'orders', was this perception of the social hierarchy adopted by the urban élites themselves? One of the most interesting ways in which status, as distinct from class, was expressed was the hierarchical description which emphasized, not the real hierarchy of wealth and power, but a hierarchy of moral worth. Urban administrative documents in both English and French towns are full of such designations, and this way of describing the upper end of the urban social hierarchy was used by the English royal chancery from the thirteenth century.[12] Almost universally in medieval English towns, the ruling groups of merchants were referred to as *probi homines* or *prud'hommes*, that is, 'worthy men'. Similar terminology was equally widespread in French towns. Other designations in use were analogous, such as 'the more worthy citizens' of Lincoln and Winchester, the 'best of the citizens' of Newcastle under Lyme, the 'better sort' in Hereford. The ruling élite at Lyons were described as the 'greater and better'; at Tours they were the 'honourable men'. The *probi homines* of Avignon 'were truly honourable and lived like knights'. The wardens of some craft-guilds in Languedoc were sometimes referred to as *probi homines*, but in general, and especially in French towns, the rest of the population was described as 'the lesser people' *le menu peuple*. In thirteenth-century Canterbury, they were described as the 'lesser and weaker (*infirmior*)' part, as against the 'greater and healthier (*sanior*)', that is, the mercantile élite. When the 'greater people' of Shrewsbury fled to the countryside at the time of the Black Death, the 'lesser people' who took over the government of the town were referred to as *animales viles*.[13]

Status designations in terms of moral rather than material distinction were symbolically reinforced in England at the national level by the sumptuary regulations issued by the king's government. The statute of 1363 which attempted, without success, to impose the rule of 'one man, one trade', in order to deprive urban craftsmen of the right to engage in commerce as well as manufacture, also contained a typical set of sumptuary regulations. These laid down what garments people might wear, and even what food they might eat, according to their status. They were not effective, indeed the statute was repealed, but similar regulations were repeated as late as 1464.[14] They also provide a scale of status equivalences between town and country which are of some interest. Ordinary servants, whether of country lords or of urban merchants and master craftsmen, were not to eat meat and fish more than once a day, and were to consume other victuals, such as milk and cheese, 'according to their estate'. Their wives and daughters could only wear veils below a certain price. Craft journeymen were allowed to wear a slightly more expensive cloth, but not silk, silver cloth, girdles, knives, garters, brooches and so on. Their wives and daughters should not wear veils of silk but only of native fabric. No furs of higher status than sheep, rabbit, cat and fox were allowed. Merchants and master craftsmen who had chattels worth the high sum of £500 or more were allowed to wear the same apparel as gentry who had incomes of £100 a year. If they had chattels worth £1,000 they could dress like esquires with £200 a year. (It hardly needs saying that craftsmen with £1,000 worth, or even £500 worth, of chattels would be very rare.) But the king's sumptuary legislation was merely echoing the contemporary emphasis on status, which is made explicit in the theorizing about the orders of society in the moralistic literature and sermons.

Another theoretical concept which emphasized the theme of harmony within divergence and the divinely ordained functions of the various social strata was the ancient analogy between the social order and the human body. It was reiterated in the twelfth century by John of Salisbury, Bishop of Chartres, in his *Policraticus*. It was used again in a sermon by Thomas Brinton, Bishop of Rochester (1373–89). As usual, kings are represented by the head and peasants, and labourers by the feet. Unlike John of Salisbury, Brinton introduces the urban classes. The left hand represents merchants and the faithful artisans. The heart, being in the centre of the body, represents the citizens and burgesses.[15] It was a sufficiently common, not to say banal, image to be enunciated in a royal order of 1267 banning unauthorized meetings in London on the grounds that 'all persons of the city, rich as well as poor, should be, as it were, one body and one man, faithfully and in fealty to maintain the peace'.[16] By the end of the fourteenth century, the image of the city as a body corporate had become widespread and was the essence of much civic ceremony.

Ceremony, whether associated with feasting and rejoicing or with solemn ecclesiastical ritual, was clearly recognized in medieval towns as a means of promoting social cohesion. The celebration of Corpus Christi, invented as one of the year's holy celebrations and saint's days in the early fourteenth century, provided a useful form of civic ceremony, in which the analogy between the civic body and the body of Christ was emphasized. Many English urban governments organized processions composed of mercantile and craft-guilds, often associated with the performance of pageants representing stages in universal Christian history, from the Creation to the Last Judgement.[17] Guild processions on Corpus Christi day emphasized both hierarchy and unity. At Coventry, typically, the most humble – the poor fishmongers – led the way, and the rich drapers brought up the rear. Although the Corpus Christi processions most obviously emphasized the unity of the civic body, other ceremonial processions performed essentially the same function. The sequence of processions following the election of London's mayor at the end of October began with a journey, in which he was accompanied by representatives of the guilds, through the city streets to the exchequer at Westminster. From there they returned to the cathedral of

St Paul, and visited other city churches on subsequent feast days. Similar ceremonies followed the election of the mayor of Bristol in September, linked with the elections of the masters of the craft-guilds: the mayor and sheriff distributed gifts of wine to the 21 crafts.[18]

Presents of wine and other such diversions were evidently regarded as an essential feature of civic ceremony in French towns, too, especially on the occasions of the 'joyous entries' of kings, queens and dukes. Free wine flowed from the fountains of Paris on the occasion of Isabel of Bavaria's entry in 1389. When the dukes of Brittany entered Breton towns, minstrels were hired for the entertainment of the people, 'to give them a relief from an otherwise difficult existence'. Even the carnivals and the *fêtes des fous* of the thirteenth century, which started as spontaneous demonstrations of 'the world turned upside down' by young men and low-ranking clerics, were, by the fourteenth and fifteenth centuries, taken over by the civic authorities. They were allowed to retain their festival aspect and even some elements of ridicule, but in practice were cleverly manipulated by the ruling urban élites as harmless ways of 'letting off steam'.[19]

On the other hand, in spite of the generally successful containment of carnival within civic ceremonies acceptable to urban authorities, some forms of popular ceremony remained potential vehicles for disruption of the social order. This is illustrated by an episode in the cloth-manufacturing city of Norwich in the middle of the fifteenth century.[20] In 1377, Norwich was the fifth largest town in England; by 1523 it had become the second largest. In addition to being a cathedral city and county town, its manufacture of woollen and worsted cloth was of great importance. By the middle of the fifteenth century, the city itself had acquired county status, and was ruled by a mercantile oligarchy: a mayor, two sheriffs and a council of 24 aldermen or *probi homines*. The less important common council of 60 freemen was also merchant-dominated, admitting only a few master craftsmen as members. Mercers were overwhelmingly predominant among the ruling élite, and were closely linked with local feudal landowners, such as the Earl of Suffolk and many landed gentry. This alliance was expressed in the Guild of St George, founded in 1385, an essentially mercantile fraternity but one which included members from the local gentry and nobility. It became so closely identified with the dominant elements in the ruling élite that it was integrated into the governing body of the city from 1452. The mayor automatically became alderman of the guild for a year after completing his term of office. All aldermen were automatically members. The guild excluded craftsmen from its membership. When, in 1463, a shoemaker was elected to the common council, it was decided that it would be a dishonour to the city and the Guild of St George if a person of such a craft should be admitted.

Norwich politics did not simply reflect a division between the craft and mercantile interests, however. In the mid-fifteenth century there were rival factions within the mercantile body itself. One of these was associated with the county nobility and gentry, many of the latter, as we have seen, being members of the Guild of St George. This faction was also favourably inclined to the ecclesiastical landowners who held property in and near the city. The other, although occasionally (and unsuccessfully) appealing for help to the Duke of Gloucester, was hostile to the feudal, and especially to the ecclesiastical, landowners. It was associated with a somewhat obscure 'Bachery' (bachelors') guild and tended to seek allies among the city craftsmen, who were also hostile to the feudal presence in the city. Aristocratic politics were also involved: the 'popular' party's hostility to the 'Lancastrian' magnates, such as the Earl of Suffolk, eventually led them to become supporters of the 'Yorkist' party and to benefit from the arrival of the Yorkist dynasty in 1461.

The troubles of the 1440s focused on antagonisms between the majority of the townspeople and the feudal–ecclesiastical interests within the city.[21] The Benedictine cathedral priory was not only a wealthy landowner and appropriator of parish churches throughout East Anglia, but had privileges and jursidiction within the city of Norwich. It had lordship over extensive parts of the city, and over the two Tombland fairs (at Whitsun and Trinity Sunday), deriving from them a considerable profit. The nearby nunnery of Carrow held and profited from a September fair, as did the Magdalen Hospital from another in July. Jurisdictional conflicts also arose with two other ecclesiastical corporations, the abbeys of Wendling and St Benet of Hulme. The antagonism between the city and these ecclesiastical corporations was made even worse when the Crown was persuaded to declare that the priory had never been part of the city, and to take the suburbs, where some of the ecclesiastical property was situated, away from city jurisdiction by pronouncing them to be part of the county.

Early in 1443, an extraordinary procession made its way through the streets of Norwich, led by one John Gladman. This ceremony seems to have focused much of the tension which underlay relations between the city and the ecclesiastical interests. Ceremonies were organized on a regular basis in Norwich, as in Coventry and elsewhere, no doubt as a way of dampening down lower-class antagonism to the city's rulers. The evidence for the elaboration of Corpus Christi processions and guild plays in Norwich comes from the late 1440s and the 1450s: perhaps significantly a period of serious social and political tension in the city. The nature of the Gladman ceremony, however, is not entirely clear, except that it was perceived by a hostile jury in the aftermath as a subversion of due hierarchy and civic harmony. Gladman is said to have been a merchant. He rode, however, as a king, his crown, sword and sceptre carried before him, accompanied by 24 mounted men wearing the badge of a crown, and armed like true yeomen of the Crown (*valetti corone*). Three only of these 24 were identified but, significantly, the jury stressed their low status: a shoemaker, an ostler and a cutler, of whom only the cutler is otherwise recorded as a freeman of the city. The mayor, allegedly lending encouragement to the procession, was said to have ordered a hundred others to follow Gladman's procession on horseback. According to the jury, the procession itself was followed by a violent attack upon the priory by the mayor and the commonalty. The monks of the priory were forced to surrender documents which provided evidence of the previous surrender to the priory of areas of civic jurisdiction. The town gates being closed, as if Norwich had declared war against the king, the Duke of Norfolk, the Earl of Oxford and other royal officials were excluded from the city.

Gladman's defenders claimed that he had simply been disporting himself with his neighbours on 'Fastyngong Tuesday', his horse being 'trapped' with tinsel for the annual Shrove Tuesday or carnival celebrations. He was crowned, they said, 'King of Christmas' (*sic*) in token that all mirth should end with the 12 months of the year. He was preceded by men representing each month, also disguised as their respective seasons. The one representing Lent was clad in white with red herring skins, and his horse 'trapped' with oyster shells in token of sadness and absence of mirth. They rode about the streets of the city with others, also disguised, 'making mirth and disport and plays'. Unfortunately for the chronology of this defence, the hostile jury had already sat to discuss the incident over a week before Shrove Tuesday. Nevertheless, we need not disallow Gladman's procession as a subversive ceremony contradicting those official occasions which stressed hierarchy and civic harmony. The actual date of the procession, according to the original jury, was 25 January, the date of the conversion of St Paul. This itself was an important feast day, and could well have provided the occasion for a demonstration in what was already a politically charged atmosphere. The Gladman insurrection should not be underestimated as an irrelevant, if amusing episode, for it led to the imprisonment in London of the mayor, as the leader of what may be described as the 'popular' party, together with his supporters, and to a four-year suspension of the city's liberties.

To sum up, feudal lordship provided the essential background to social relations in towns. Often lordship was wielded by church landlords who either ruled over the whole town, or more often (as in the case of Norwich) claimed jurisdiction over part of the urban space, and thereby aroused bitter resentment among at least a section of the townspeople. The Gladman insurrection developed out of conflicting attitudes towards the cathedral priory and other monastic landowners in Norwich. The church had a general and indirect influence also over the means by which social unity and antagonisms were displayed in the towns, because the Christian calendar determined the pattern of rituals and processions which punctuated the civic year. The complexities of social and political conflict in mid-fifteenth-century Norwich were exhibited in public displays, and the events show that ceremony, so often used to assert the hierarchy of status, could also undermine the social order.

Notes

1. G. Duby, *Les trois ordres ou l'imaginaire du féodalisme* (Paris, 1978); trans. as *The Three Orders: Feudal Society Imagined* (Chicago and London, 1980).
2. C.V. Langlois, in *La Vie en France de la fin du XIIe siècle au milieu du XIVe siècle d'après les moralistes du temps* (Paris, 1926), has transcribed a number of these moralizing treatises.
3. John Gower, *Vox Clamantis*, in E.W. Stockton (ed.), *Major Latin Works of John Gower* (Seattle, 1962).
4. N.M. Trenholme, *The English Monastic Boroughs* (Columbia, 1927); M.D. Lobel, *The Commune of Bury St Edmunds* (1935); D. Knowles, *The Religious Orders in England*, vol. 1 (1948), ch. 22; R.N. Swanson, *Church and Society in Late Medieval England* (1989), chs 2, 5 and 6. Recent discussions include D. Postles, 'The Austin canons in English towns, c.1100–1350', *Historical Research*, **66** (1993); C. Dyer, 'Small-town conflict in the later middle ages; events at Shipton-on-Stour', *Urban History*, **19** (1992), 183–210.
5. S. Reynolds, *An Introduction to the History of English Medieval Towns* (1977), 139; B. Chevalier, *Les Bonnes villes de France du XIVe au XVIe siècle* (Paris, 1982), 299–302; A. Chédeville, J. Le Goff and J. Rossiaud, *Histoire de la France urbaine, 2: La ville médiévale* (Paris, 1980), 524.
6. P. Wolff, 'Les luttes sociales dans le Midi français', in his *Regards sur le Midi médiévale* (Toulouse, 1978).
7. A. Higounet-Nadal, 'Les jardins urbains dans la France médiévale', *Flaran*, **9** (1989), 115–44.
8. R. Hilton, 'Some problems of urban real property in the middle ages', reprinted in his *Class Conflict and the Crisis of Feudalism* (1985).
9. J. Lestocquoy, *Patricians du moyen âge: les dynasties bourgeoises d'Arras* (Arras, 1945); S. Reynolds, 'The rulers of London in the twelfth century', *History*, **57** (1972), 337–57.
10. C. Gross, *The Gild Merchant* (1890).
11. R. Hilton, 'Révoltes rurales et révoltes urbaines au moyen âge', in *Révolte et société*, vol. 2, *Actes du XIVe Colloque d'histoire au présent*, 1988 (Paris, 1989).
12. J. Tait, *The Medieval English Borough* (1936), 244, refers to the early use of the term *probi homines* in royal chancery documents.

13. R. Hilton, *English and French Towns in Feudal Society: a Comparative Study* (1992), 113–17.
14. *Statutes of the Realm*, vol. 1 (1810), 379f.; *Rotuli Parliamentorum*, vol. 5 (1783), 504–5.
15. E. Lewis, *Medieval Political Ideas*, 2 vols (1954), vol. 1, 225 (John of Salisbury); M.A. Devlin (ed.), *The Sermons of Thomas Brinton, Bishop of Rochester (1373–1389)*, 2 vols, Camden Society, 3rd series, 85 (1954), xxiii, 111.
16. H.T. Riley (ed.), *Chronicles of the Mayors and Sheriffs of London* (1863), 103.
17. C.V. Phythian-Adams, 'Ceremony and the citizen: the communal year at Coventry 1450–1550', reprinted in R. Holt and G. Rosser (eds), *The English Medieval Town, A Reader in English Urban History 1200–1540* (1990); M. James, 'Ritual, drama and social body in the late medieval town', *Past and Present*, 98 (1983), 3–29; M. Rubin, *Corpus Christi: the Eucharist in Late Medieval Culture* (1991), ch. 4.
18. H.T. Riley (ed.), *Munimenta Gildhallae Londoniensis. Kiber Albus*, Rolls Series (1859), 24–5; L. Toulmin Smith (ed.), *The Maire of Bristowe his Kalendar*, Camden Society, 2nd series, 5 (1872); E.W.W. Veale (ed.), *The Great Red Book of Bristol*, pt i, Bristol Record Society, 2 (1931).
19. J. Heers, 'Les métiers et les fêtes médiévales en France du Nord et en Angleterre', *Revue du Nord*, 55 (1973), 193–206; J.P. Leguay, *Un réseau urbain au moyen-âge: les villes du Duché de Bretagne* (1981), ch. 19; M. Grinberg, 'Carnaval et société urbaine', *Ethnologie française* (1974).
20. The following account is based on the documentation in W. Hudson and J.C. Tingey (eds), *Records of the City of Norwich*, 2 vols (1906). More recent work includes P.C. Maddern, 'The legitimation of power: riot and authority in fifteenth century Norwich', *Parergon*, 6 (1988); *idem, Violence and the Social Order: East Anglia, 1422–1442* (Oxford, 1992), 196–205; B.R. McRee, 'Religious gilds and civic order: the case of Norwich in the later middle ages', *Speculum*, 67 (1992), 69–97; *idem*, 'Peacemaking and its limits in late medieval Norwich', *English Historical Review*, 109 (1994), 831–66.
21. Such conflicts are also discussed by Gervase Rosser in Chapter 2 of the present volume.

CHAPTER TWO

Conflict and Political Community in the Medieval Town: Disputes between Clergy and Laity in Hereford

Gervase Rosser

It is an axiom of virtually all historical writing about medieval English towns that effective power within them was concentrated in the hands of a relatively tiny minority of the population. A wealthy élite, it has been generally argued or assumed, automatically inherited either *de facto* or constitutional power to control urban affairs. Recent scholarship, while adding complexity to the model by drawing distinctions between varieties of 'oligarchy', has at the same time re-emphasized the received picture.[1] Clearly, there is truth in this conventional view. The existence of mercantile élites in medieval towns is not in dispute. What deserves closer analysis, however, is the extent to which economic pre-eminence could be translated into political control. After all, the distribution of wealth in late twentieth-century Britain is not dissimilar to the pyramid, broad at the base and narrowly tapering at the apex, of the late-medieval towns.[2] If 'angels [coins] worked wonders' in the earlier period no less than 'money talks' today, it should nevertheless be evident that in neither case is there a simple correlation between personal fortune and political influence. Of course, rich medieval townsmen occasionally defended such a direct equivalence on practical grounds also invoked by Aristotle in vindication of aristocracy: wealth implied both experience of the world and leisure to devote to applying this in the interest of the polity at large. So far as it goes this justification deserves, and may in the Middle Ages have received, more credit than historians have tended to allow.[3] But the economic imbalance was in any case never the whole story. Concentration on the inequalities of the social *structure* may unduly distract attention from the realities of the political *process* in medieval towns. To an extent which has not yet been fully recognized, that process regularly involved not merely enfranchised citizens – themselves, naturally, never more than a minority – but also the wider body of the townspeople.

During much of their lives, medieval town-dwellers below the ranks of the mercantile or propertied aristocracy may have recognized little in politics to interest them. Nevertheless certain issues, and certain political circumstances, could be guaranteed to trigger the formulation and expression of opinion across a broad social spectrum. The perennial issues alluded to here include the fixing of basic commodity prices – a means of indirect taxation which affected most directly the very poorest elements in the urban population – and the regulation of both large- and small-scale production and commercial activity. The particular circumstance which most commonly precipitated wide-ranging debate on such issues was a division within the political élite. The rhetoric of disputants in clashes within the urban aristocracy often evinced a perceived need to appeal to, and to mobilize, a wide band of popular opinion, as a means of demonstrating the moral superiority of a certain political position. Such clashes took many forms, but none was more common than that between the clerical and the lay authorities within a particular city. The ubiquitous presence in the medieval town of the Church, with its variable package of rights and immunities, was virtually bound to generate fissures within the ruling class as prelates and merchants vied for control of resources. The present chapter, which takes for illustration disputes of this kind occurring in the cathedral town of Hereford in the late Middle Ages, aims to underline how readily such issues were broadened, drawing the population at large into a debate about the history, identity and purpose of the urban community. Of course, the rhetoric of these arguments should not be confused with reality. The significant point, however, is that quarrels over ecclesiastical liberties helped to stimulate widespread awareness and discussion both of practical issues affecting the population at large and, to a degree, of the principles underlying the identity of the town.

On a Saturday in October 1519, the recently retired former mayor of Hereford was stepping out from a house in that town into Castle Street when his attention was drawn by the noise of an affray.[4] Beyond the gate at the end of the street, within the cemetery of the cathedral, one of the cathedral canons, Nicholas Walwe, was arguing with another man named William Hill. The observer saw the canon seize his interlocutor and pummel him with his fist, crying out that he was 'a whoreson' and 'a knave' and then, snatching from the other a pewter pint pot, strike him violently with it about the head. At this point, according to other witnesses, blood was drawn, which as it fell polluted the holy ground. In a short space the current mayor, Nicholas Hayes, was on the scene with his aldermen behind him. As he arrived Hayes announced with gusto that, since the privileged sanctity of the place had been desecrated by the bloodshed, he and his men could now freely break the heads of others within the cathedral close.[5] The mayor's zeal seems to have been directed less in the cause of peace than towards the exploitation of a welcome excuse to invade the normally immune franchise of the dean and chapter. The situation encapsulated in this incident was characteristic of many towns before the early nineteenth century. From the point of view of the mayor, the existence within 'his' town of protected spheres of rival jurisdiction was a thorn in the side of rational government. The secular urban administration of Hereford had been recognized by royal grant of a fee farm in the twelfth century and its chief officer dignified by the title of 'mayor' in the late fourteenth, yet even by Mayor Hayes's day it had not quelled the competing claims of the bishop, dean and chapter to extensive powers of jurisdiction within the town.[6] Indeed, until the 1835 Municipal Reform Act, in Hereford and in many other towns, the existence of a plurality of claimants to the exercise of local government was not a temporary inconvenience to be simply ironed out, but a permanent condition.[7] The question at once arises: How might the primacy of either one or other of these competing authorities be vindicated?

An answer might appear to be provided by the Customs of Hereford: an unequivocal normative statement issued by the secular power. The Customs survive in a manuscript of 1486, during the mayoralty of John Chippenham, by whom they were edited.[8] The long text is infused with a sense of civic pride – 'this city is the chief of all market towns from the sea to the banks of the Severn' – and of the responsibility borne by the mayor and his officers for the community as a whole. All the principal aspects of urban life are treated in the Customs: the appointment of public officers, administration of justice, control of trade, recovery of debts, protection of property and inheritances, provisions for security in time of war. The superficial impression given by this as by sets of customs from other towns is of a coherent, well administered community. Yet a closer reading reveals the cracks which the Customs attempt to paper over. Although the town is declared to be as one (*unum sumus*) in the defence of its collective rights, this sentiment is vitiated by the pronouncement that not all the townspeople were 'of the same condition'. The rights to trade toll-free and to hold civic office were confined to the restricted body of the citizens. Admission to this privileged group was reserved to those who inhabited houses within 'the king's fee' in the town and whose eligibility was allowed by a meeting of 'the better sort' among the community. The king's fee was that part of the town for which the fee farm rent was paid annually to the Crown. Ownership of property here, in so far as it entailed contributions to the fee farm, was recognized by the mayor as a material commitment to the citizen community. Those who lived in houses not on the king's fee but belonging to other lords, among whom the dean and chapter of the cathedral were the most prominent, remained perforce townsmen of different status. The Customs also set out at length the elaborate diplomacy of relations between officers of the city government and those of other authorities; again the chief object of concern was the cathedral's sphere of jurisdiction. Yet, despite its heroic attempt to proclaim these complexities resolved for all time in a single code, the Hereford custumal of 1486 marked no more than one stage in a continuing process of disputes and settlements. No final solution was ever arrived at during the medieval period, with the result that the issue remained a perpetual catalyst of political debate.

The text of the Customs as set down in 1486 contains summaries of earlier treaties between the civic and the cathedral authorities. Quarrels had been endemic since the first half of the thirteenth century; in successive incidents a variety of means had been employed to restore temporary peace. The first recorded troubles, of the 1230s and 1240s, reveal the bishop and the secular bailiffs disputing the former's claim to exclusive jurisdiction throughout the entire town during the annual six-day fair which opened on the feast of St Ethelbert (20 May), and to tolls at all times of the year.[9] Although both sides appealed to the crown for judgement, experience proved this to be mutable and consequently of no more use than as one means among several to be employed in the continuing debate.[10] In fact, one of the most serious clashes ever recorded in Hereford, in 1262, elicited from the participants themselves a negotiated settlement more lasting in its effect than any verdict of the king's justices. The occasion of this settlement was a major riot in the town. Peter Aquablanca, then Bishop of Hereford, was one of Henry III's unpopular foreign appointees and a man of daunting temper; his character doubtless exacerbated the problem of local administration, although the specific catalyst of conflict on this occasion is unknown. At the signal of their common bell, the townsmen armed themselves and blockaded the cathedral precinct. The bishop and his canons and household were prevented from passing in or out and were denied supplies of victuals. While the melodrama of the record in such cases needs always to be heard with caution, it would appear that more participants were recruited to this protest than the leading citizens alone. The demonstration was successful in winning from the clerical body an agreement to negotiate: at this critical juncture the bishop, dean and chapter on the one hand and all the citizens (*tota communitas predicte civitatis*) on the other, together drew up a pragmatic composition (*composicio*).[11] Bishop Peter (confident in the backing of the crown) secured a face-saving gesture: 12 elected citizens, in the name of the whole community of the city (*in animis totius illius communitatis*) swore to honour thenceforth the privileges of the cathedral church. Yet this *ad hoc* agreement is less one-sided than a pervasive tone of clerical indignation might imply; in a tense situation, both sides were prepared to compromise. A fundamental threat to stability hitherto had been the continual growth of the Church's territory in Hereford, at the expense of the king's part of the city, as a result of the gifts and sales of properties made by the townspeople to the cathedral. By the composition of 1262 this process of creeping enlargement of the cathedral fee was halted; property might thereafter be acquired by the Church for its fiscal value but this would not affect rights of jurisdiction.[12] Peace had been restored on a new basis worked out by negotiation between the disputants themselves. Although its authors asked that the *composicio* be enrolled in the king's records for a permanent witness, it was itself a product, not of authoritative judgement, but of adaptive co-operation at the local level.

The composition of 1262 provided a fixed point of reference for subsequent debate; it did not, however, remove all occasion for future discord.[13] In fact, although medieval town-dwellers naturally did not regard endemic disorder as a good thing, particular conflicts seem to have been consciously generated with intent to bring about renewed discussion of wider issues. From time to time in Hereford (as in 1262 and again later on) one party or the other seems to have deliberately sought a major trial of strength, involving maximum public ventilation of the principles at stake, with the intention of forging from the contest a newly revised *modus vivendi*. Thus in the last quarter of the fourteenth century the citizens of the king's fee mounted a concerted campaign to consolidate their powers. Their earlier charters were confirmed by the king in 1378; in 1383 they were permitted to call their chief bailiff 'mayor' and to appoint their own coroner for the town; and in 1393 royal sanction was granted for the purchase of a house to be used as a council chamber and town hall.[14] These successive assertions of their position by the leaders of the citizen body brought renewed confrontation ever closer. The precipitant issue chosen was symbolic. The dean and chapter in 1389 acquired a royal licence permitting them to enclose the cathedral cemetery.[15] Their action, although publicly justified on minor practical grounds, appears to have been designed primarily as a demonstration on the part of the cathedral body of its separate status. This inference is given weight by the fact that the dean and chapter simultaneously secured a confirmation from the Crown of their judicial rights.[16] The significance of this ritual wall-building was recognized in the town, where it was seized upon as an act of provocation. As soon as the new barrier was erected it was torn down by the citizens. Having thus precipitated a public crisis, the disputants jointly chose two arbitrators, the bishop and the Herefordshire knight and Member of

Parliament John Clanvowe, to whose decision (*arbitrium*) they agreed to submit.[17]

At each moment of conflict the parties drew up catalogues of their respective grievances. While the extant draft petitions were prepared for presentation to successive arbitrators, their language betrays an additional concern to recruit the sympathies of a wider audience.[18] Throughout the later Middle Ages the character of the complaints altered very little. The claims of the dean and chapter were founded on the premise that 'the said city is divided into several liberties [of which their own was one of the two most substantial] so that the citizens [sc. the mayoral council] have by the king's grant but the moiety of the city'.[19] It was provocatively asserted, moreover, that no inhabitant of the cathedral fee owed respect to any ordinance made by the mayor.[20] Notwithstanding this separate status, the dean and chapter declared that their tenants ought nevertheless to enjoy the same privileges as those of the king's fee; the cathedral's men 'should freely buy and sell within the said city and *should have community within the same*'.[21] In other words the cathedral authorities, as part of the defence of their own jurisdictional liberty, were bidding for the support of their tenants by claiming on the latter's behalf the privileges enjoyed by other townsmen, in addition to the legal immunities attaching to the ecclesiastical estate. The desire of the dean and chapter to be perceived as acting in the interests of others rather than themselves thus broadened their debate with the mayor. This mobilization of the cathedral's tenantry, and invocation of their alleged rights as members of the wider society of the town, gave them (*tertius gaudens*) a recognition and even, potentially, a voice which was otherwise denied by their disadvantaged political status.

The claimed rights of the Church's tenants, both rich and poor, had been contravened by the mayor, who had made enjoyment of full citizen status conditional upon possession of freehold property on the king's fee and attendance at the mayoral courts. Thus 'such persons of [the dean and chapter's] fee as desire to be promoted to worship within the said city' were blackmailed into moving house and taking oaths of loyalty to the mayor.[22] That officer was even accused with his bailiffs of calling on cathedral tenants and luring them with friendly overtures (*sub colore amoris et pacis*) into the public street, where they were promptly arrested and hauled off to prison until they would change their allegiance.[23] The dean's own officers were said to be treated so roughly by the mayor that no person of suitable substance would undertake the job of bailiff or sergeant in the cathedral fee 'for fear of disfranchising'.[24] Other alleged tyrannical acts by the mayors around 1400 included arrests made in houses within the Church's fee (or before their doors; whereas the franchise of a property extended to the middle of the street), fines extorted for the release of cathedral tenants from arbitrary imprisonment, and the anticlerical blackmail of cathedral clergy by threat of public disclosure of moral misdemeanours.[25]

Particular incidents were deliberately blown up to become *causes célèbres*, dramatizing the broad issues at stake. Such was the unfortunate case of Brother William Bradley and the stolen stockfish. William was a Benedictine monk who had strayed from his impoverished abbey at Alcester in Worcestershire, and who inhabited the precinct of Hereford cathedral, where he taught children. In May 1407 he was interviewed by officers of the mayor in connection with certain stockfish which had gone missing from the market. Gaining admission to the monk's chamber the mayor's sergeant professed himself aggrieved (*multum doluit*) to discover the fish in question, together with a dagger he identified as one lately lost by a townsman and a bow and arrows which he also confiscated.[26] The mayor's man had allegedly been instructed to behave with discretion, in order to avoid causing embarrassment either to Brother William or to the Church.[27] Yet the latter institution resolutely protested, making an issue of this invasion of the sanctuary, although to little practical effect.[28] The dean and chapter three years later, in 1410, however, trumpeted their triumph in the case of the abduction of a canon's horse. One Henry Nevill had 'trespassed' within the cathedral close in order to distrain upon one of the canons for rent overdue from a house elsewhere in the town. In lieu of the rent Nevill had on his own initiative ridden away on a horse belonging to the canon, an act of bravado he lived to regret. After judgement, he was compelled in penance to carry a candle before the cathedral procession on six successive Sundays. To publicize and commemorate their victory the canons compiled a neatly transcribed dossier of the case which was made up into a small book. This manuscript concludes with an awesome warning to future violators of the religious sanctuary.[29] The record itself, thus portentously elaborated, acquired its own symbolic power, which could be invoked in subsequent disputes.

In the past, the officers of both fees had consented to collaborate in apprehending criminals who ingeniously hoped to evade justice by moving from one jurisdiction into the other.[30] But around 1410 the need was evidently felt for a fresh major statement of mutual relations on this matter. Again arbitration was sought. The role of peacemaker was now accorded to a former dean of Hereford who in 1407 had moved to the deanery of York and who in addition held royal office as Keeper of the Privy Seal. John Prophet clearly commanded widespread respect in Hereford.[31] On the invitation both of the dean and chapter and of the mayor and citizens, he attempted to assist the two parties by establishing once for all the precise limits of their respective authorities. Prophet's arbitration (*arbitrium*) reveals the full extent of the problem which underlay all the disputes. The two fees, of the Crown and the dean and chapter respectively, had never been clearly defined in terms of geography. The Church's early acquisitions of property and concomitant jurisdiction – although doubtless originating in a coherent primary core – had increasingly been scattered in haphazard fashion throughout the town. The composition of 1262 had arrested (in theory at least) the judicial extension of the cathedral fee; but the situation by the time of this freeze was already chaotic, as the arbitration of *c.*1410 reveals. Prophet tried to list all the houses in the town about which there had been controversy: this house was in the king's fee, that one next door in the dean and chapter's; a certain tenement was subject to one jurisdiction, the shop in front of it to another. The possibilities for contention were obviously numberless, as, by the same token, were the reasons for private tenants of all degrees to concern themselves with the political issues involved. It was hoped that such a catalogue would enable boundaries to be observed; good fences make good neighbours. Prophet appended further reconciliatory measures and directed that the text of his arbitration should be read out publicly each year in the cathedral and other churches of the city to the furtherance of lasting peace (*tranquillitatem perpetuam*).[32] But these measures were no more conclusive in achieving their ends than any of the others.[33] They did, however, raise popular consciousness of the debate about political power in the town.

From these illustrations of what has been seen to be a permanent condition of latent strife within the city, certain general and interrelated features stand out. Four of these deserve particular emphasis: the deliberate precipitation of crises by the participants, with a view to forcing discussion; their use of history; the perceived significance of ritualized public events; and the frequent involvement of a large proportion of local society. The last point is crucial, and underlies the other three. Each will be considered briefly in turn. A stratagem repeatedly employed by the disputing parties was that of deliberately bringing relations to a crisis, thereby rendering unavoidable a fresh review and publication of general principles. The controlled discussion of problems of secondary importance offered a forum for the airing of views on more fundamental questions which might otherwise have boiled dangerously beneath the surface. A particular issue, such as the arrest of vagabonds in various parts of the town, would be made the occasion for a public debate on the responsibilities of the various component elements of the town: 'There has been disagreement ... but now it has been agreed by the whole community of all the liberties that, etc.'[34] Out of a specific quarrel, the parties were thus able to bring a clear public statement of the city's essential unity. Recognized prodedures were available at each juncture. In a particular crisis, a truce would be declared for a few months or weeks or even hours, pending a more lasting resolution.[35] When, in October 1464, an arrest was made in the cathedral precinct by the mayor's sergeant of a cutpurse caught red-handed during the celebrations of the feast of St Thomas Cantilupe, a bond was signed and sealed by the mayor and the dean whereby the former undertook to return the prisoner to the latter's charge within six hours. After three days in the cathedral gaol the thief was to be handed back into the custody of the mayor. Face was thereby saved on both sides, and a major disturbance avoided.[36] In such circumstances the king's law could provide neither a clear nor a speedy solution, and was relatively rarely invoked, preference being shown for constructive dialogue between the disputants. This dialogue might be direct, but the resort to one or more arbitrators was normal. It is, indeed, becoming increasingly clear that, in medieval Europe at large, such relatively informal means of dispute settlement operated alongside and in conjunction with the better-documented processes of litigation.[37] The role of arbitrators was not to judge on the basis of legally conceived and immutable rights, but to assist the quarrelling parties to reach a negotiated compromise. What is particularly striking about the kind of dispute under consideration here is that representations made in the course of negotiation were couched in terms less of legal precision with respect to some higher authority than of public utility with respect to the urban population as a whole.

A second characteristic of these interminable negotiations is the regular appeal to the past. Popular notions of Hereford's history were a valuable potential support for either party in a dispute. In the quarrels among the town's élite, therefore, the collective memory of the wider population was regularly called to witness. The invocation of civic history reached its apogee in a document of the later fifteenth century in which both parties set out, in parallel columns, their cases regarding the secular courts of the town. Each body claimed the greater antiquity. The mayor's argument that the cathedral fee had originated in gifts of the townspeople in Henry I's reign was at once trumped by the extravagant counter-claim that 'the dean and canons were founded before time of mind and out of time of mind and before had great possessions, franchises and liberties in the said city'.[38] Apart from such traditions, the text is peppered with citations from specified sources: 'the book of the Customs of the said city ... diverse court rolls ... a charter of Edward the Confessor ... a book of the Exchequer ... the book of Domesday ...' John Prophet's arbitration.[39] For all the disputants' declared intentions to establish an ideal situation which had supposedly existed in the past, in fact conditions had never been either simple or clear. The idea of an urban society living in perfect harmony was a necessary myth required by the actuality of current disputes. This myth was located in the past and confused with historical reality, so that in the course of their eternal wrangling the citizens and the cathedral body simultaneously appealed to and further encouraged popular notions about the history of the city and the source of its present greatness: 'for this city is the chief of all market towns from the sea to the banks of the Severn'. Such historical reflections, therefore, although born of a particular conflict, paradoxically promoted among the wider urban society a sense of the city as a whole, with a character and a destiny of its own. In non-literate societies conceptions of the past tend to be fluid, susceptible to renewal and alteration in each generation; the same is true of such a partially literate society as that under discussion, in which not so much is readily available in writing as to constrict the historical imagination.[40] By a creative act of the memory, the past is adjusted to suit present circumstances. It is precisely the conflict generated by changed circumstances which gives occasion for such revision of the past. In the competing appeals to the remembered past by the dean and chapter and the townsmen of Hereford, the wider public memory can be seen in the process of regeneration and readjustment.

A third trait evinced by the protagonists in these disputes was a keen sense of the importance of public display. 'Ritual' in medieval towns has been partially misunderstood, in so far as it has been conceptualized as standing outside the quotidian processes of social and political relations. On the contrary, it is more helpful to view the dramatic collective behaviour of medieval townspeople, more or less consciously manipulated as it was by its participants, as a continuation of those same processes – strengthened by the effects of enlarged participation and heightened visibility.[41] Events of negligible significance in themselves, such as the apprehension of a pickpocket or a scuffle in the cemetery, would be seized upon as pretexts for pointed and pompous displays – displays whose intended audience, once again, was by no means confined to the political élite.

The *locus classicus* of this concern with ritualized behaviour was the civic procession made on feast days in the cathedral close. On the feasts of St Ethelbert and St Thomas Cantilupe, Hereford's patrons, and on other high days of the year, the unity of the city was represented in the ideal harmony of a public procession. It was ironical yet inevitable that these events should be used to play out, in the order of precedence observed, differing views of the due hierarchy of authority within the town. In 1495 an enquiry was conducted in an attempt to establish, as usual, what had been the supposed ideal practice in the past.[42] Those who gave evidence revealed once more that the conduct of the procession had never been straightforward. A man who had been a sergeant in the mayoralty of John Chippenham recalled one such occasion on which a fellow sergeant had been so angered by the dean's officers who pushed in behind their master and before the mayor, that he had led a countercharge of the mayor's retinue and with his staff of office struck the dean's servant on the backside so that he fell forward, smiting the dean with his head in the back. One of the canons conveyed all the sense of self-importance with which these processions were imbued when he referred scornfully to the mayor's officers as 'men in torn hose and broken shoes'. Clearly these occasions, purportedly formal demonstrations of the city's dignity and unity, brought into the open feelings less than perfectly fraternal. The necessity for constantly revised pragmatic solutions is illustrated once again by the deposition of another witness who had held office successively under both mayor and dean. It was remarked that once Mayor Monington and Dean Pede, anticipating trouble in the procession, had dined together the same day and agreed on a compromise to defuse mounting tension.[43] Such contact and compromise, however, themselves helped to promote consciousness of the idea of a more lasting unity. Such ceremonial enables conflicts to be aired in a context whose nature claims for the outcome an enhanced status.[44] At the same time, this kind of ritualized behaviour is not merely a reflection of current social relations; by periodically restating the terms on which people are to live together, it plays a creative role (though the model be never imitated with complete success) in generating a conception of society as a unity.[45] Like the processes of arbitration and the evolving sense of history, public shows in medieval towns were capable of manifesting conflict and at the same time of facilitating discussion of their resolution. All three derived their particular force from their engagement with a relatively extensive body of the townspeople.

For finally, and crucially, these problems of negotiation, history, and ritualized activity were all fought out in the wide arena of urban society at large. The question of franchises was in the first instance a matter of dispute between members of the civic élite, associated respectively with the cathedral and the town hall. But as each party claimed public sanction for its position, the mass of less privileged townspeople was mobilized and drawn into the debate. Public meetings and the organization of large-scale demonstrations (such as the siege of the cathedral close in 1262), the orchestration of formal displays on occasions when the whole city held holiday, and publicized contention over the history of the town, were all ways in which the feud within the élite was broadened to admit a large measure of popular involvement. Moreover, each of the rival factions evinced a desire for active public support, which led to the airing of popular concerns not always identical with those preoccupying the primary disputants themselves. The issue which in all towns was most likely to politicize the mass of the unenfranchised was that of indirect taxation through the fixing of prices of basic provisions. Thus the cathedral authorities made a representation on behalf of vintners and their customers throughout the town adversely affected by the mayor's artificial inflation of the price of wine, which benefited only the powerful merchants who supplied the drink in bulk, while uncooperative taverners were forced to shut their shops.[46] Petty chapmen operating near the cathedral in Cabbage Lane were also given a voice in the case against the mayor, who was alleged to have pulled down their stalls.[47] For his part, the mayor's constant appeal to the need for public order (which the existence of ecclesiastical liberties undermined) while, of course, expressing an immediate concern of his own with social control, was at the same time addressed to, and calculated to appeal to, the majority of ordinary townspeople, whose private anxieties about vagrancy and crime were doubtless real.[48] The communal dimension to the franchise dispute was emphasized by the regular publication of its results: for example, the annual rehearsal in all the city churches of the arbitration of $c.1410$, and the similar twice-yearly proclamation, on the occasions of mayoral general inquests, of customs of the city relating to trade in the different fees.[49]

The details of Hereford's experience were, of course, unique, but the general themes which have been drawn out were universal. Brief comparison with other towns will further clarify the picture. At Exeter, for instance, the mayor had to contend with no fewer than seven distinct fees within the city, among which the chief outside the mayoral jurisdiction were the fees of the bishop ('St Stephen's') and the dean and chapter ('St Sidewell's').[50] Exeter, like Hereford, witnessed continual disputes over franchises, the earliest recorded arbitration, between the town and the cathedral chapter, taking place in 1249. Relations between the mayoral and episcopal authorities entered their stormiest period in the 1440s. Here, as in Hereford, a formal procession to high mass in the cathedral in 1445 provided occasion for an airing of the conflict. John Vousleghe, a servant of one of the canons, was accused by Mayor Shillingford of provocation: 'Which John Vousleghe of purpose setting a black hat on his head dressed himself straightly between the wall and the said mayor, visaged him and shouldered him almost into the canell [sc. gutter], in despite of the said mayor and commonalty and contempt of our sovereign lord the king.' The canons' yeomen and grooms then aggravated the offence, 'of purpose pushing them[selves] between the procession and the said mayor and between the said mayor and the sergeants bearing the king's mace, dressing their back parts even into the mayor's lap, and ever visagingly'.[51] At this time the bishop successfully upheld his franchise, but in 1447–48 Mayor Shillingford returned to the fray with an ambitious campaign to win the favourable arbitration of the royal chancellor. The grievances listed by Shillingford all find parallels in Hereford. The church fees, as at Hereford, were not concentrated in coherent blocks but scattered. Yet when the mayor's officers entered any house belonging to the cathedral to call up the city watch they were warned off with threats of breaking of their heads. Malefactors evaded justice by 'taking the church', resorting to the ecclesiastical franchises so that the king's laws were frustrated, 'for now almost every man takes colour by my lord [sc. the bishop]'.[52] Particularly galling for the civic officers was the uncontrolled trade conducted within the cathedral precinct in 'dishes, ornaments and jewels', evidently serving the clerical and pilgrim markets.[53] The Exeter close was also said to harbour unlicensed drinking-houses of such evil repute that neighbours had complained to the mayor and, since he was powerless, threatened (so he alleged) to leave the town altogether.[54]

In challenging the ecclesiastical franchise Mayor Shillingford, like the protagonists in the Hereford disputes, appealed to history. He referred to Exeter's origins, long before the cathedral was moved there in the mid-eleventh century, in the city of Penholtkeyre, 'the most, or one of the most, ancient cities of this land'. The city had had walls and even a suburb before the time of Christ – and so before churches had begun to irritate civil jurisdiction – and had withstood a siege by Vespasian (although Jerusalem itself had subsequently fallen to that emperor). In support of this stirring account the mayor called general knowledge to witness, citing 'old chronicles' and a public inscription, 'as it is written in an old table [sc. board] the which hangeth in [the] choir of the said [cathedral] church'. When the chapter claimed to the contrary that St Stephen's fee was older than the secular government of the city, the mayor's characteristic remark was: 'If so be, it is hard to answer. It asketh many great ensearches; first, in our treasury at home, among full many great and old records; afterwards at Westminster, first in the Chancery, in the Exchequer, in the Receipt and in the Tower.'[55] Again as at Hereford, arbitrators were appointed to bring an end to hostilities. The award in Shillingford's campaign (which was given largely in favour of the Church) was the result, not of deliberation in Chancery, but of the arbitration of two local magnates, the Earl of Devon and Sir William Bonvil, who were called in at the express prayer of the citizens after other dealings had broken down.[56]

When comparisons are drawn between different cities the chronology of these disputes takes on significance. In almost all cases of quarrels over church franchises in towns the earliest recorded incidents occurred in the early or mid-thirteenth century. This was precisely the period in which citizen bodies first established their distinct communal authorities. Prior to this, the jurisdictional rights inherent in land ownership, and therefore enjoyed by private individuals in their separate holdings, had hindered the development of municipal jurisdiction.[57] Doubtless private legal rights had not prevented the occasional meeting of town assemblies to discuss public matters; but it was in the late twelfth century that the more precocious urban governments first attempted to transcend this mêlée of individual lordships. The novelty of this period was not the collective political action, but the growing independence of the communes. The counter-claims pressed by ecclesiastical bodies in the next century to extensive urban lordships of their own were probably made in direct response to this challenge. Thus the Archbishop of Canterbury appropriated to himself the western suburb of Canterbury around 1200, and in 1231 Bishop Peter des Roches of Winchester consolidated his soke within his own episcopal city.[58] The early disturbances recorded in thirteenth-century Hereford and Exeter, and others at York where similar trouble broke out in the 1220s, may be seen in this light as the product of jockeying for position between competitors for a new kind of power.[59] So, too, in Norwich the famous riot of 1272, during which the townsmen set fire to the cathedral, was provoked by the prior's attempt 'to draw away men of the franchise from the commons of the city, in order that they might be of his own jurisdiction and severed from the commons'.[60]

The struggles for power in the thirteenth-century towns should doubtless be seen, together with the rapid evolution of the communal governments themselves, as the products of urban economic expansion and prosperity in this period. Some at least of the later medieval conflicts, on the other hand, were cast in a different light, conditioned by a contracted economy. So when the townsmen of Salisbury complained in 1406 that two-thirds of the city was in the hands either of the Church or of other 'alien' lords, the burden of their grievance was that, given their own diminished resources, royal taxes were becoming unbearably onerous.[61] The secular authorities of Winchester at the same period made meticulous note of franchisal boundaries in the town, as the cost of the fee farm bore more heavily upon them.[62] Competition for control of material resources (whether these were expanding or diminishing) was, however, only one of a complex mesh of issues which might be at stake in a particular struggle. Manifest contentions were often deflected battles, indirectly expressive of other, more deep-seated concerns. The objective of a party in raising a small storm over an incident relatively insignificant in itself was less likely to be outright legal victory in the particular case (usually, as has been seen, a difficult end to achieve, even were it desired) than to raise the issue of general principle.

The mayoral council in Hereford was quick to seize an opportunity provided by the dean and chapter for a portentous exhibition of its own idea of right order in the town. When, in 1505, the dean enclosed a meadow outside the town previously used in common by the townspeople, the mayor armed the ritual number of 12 of his councillors with billhooks and knives, whereupon all processed solemnly to the field in question, 'and the grass there growing mowed and cast down'.[63] At Bristol, likewise, the city fathers in 1519 inflated a minor event into an occasion for ceremonious demonstration of their challenge to the franchise of St Augustine's Abbey in the western suburb of the city. Upon the flight of a wanted offender into the franchise, the mayor promptly appeared on the green before St Augustine's, escorted by his officers and by a large crowd of armed citizens (to the number of 500 according to one probably over-excited witness) in impressive and menacing array.[64] There was an economic aspect to the case. But the mayors of Hereford and Bristol by these stage-managed scenes were concerned to make, before a wide audience, a statement of broader significance, and to enrol popular opinion for their cause. Their emphasis on the importance of unity in their respective cities, and their claim to govern in the recognized interests of the urban population at large, were evidently designed to meet perceived expectations of the townspeople. It may also be inferred that such shows had the additional effect of further stimulating awareness of, and debate about, urban political issues.

To the mass of citizens who participated in the larger clashes these demonstrations offered the opportunity to express common concerns. Occasionally such expression was given a focus by the identification of a minority construed as a threat to the harmony of the whole. The readily identified group most commonly cast in the role of subverter of social peace was the clergy, whose personal and institutional franchises could (particularly when exacerbated by social tensions) credibly be blamed on this count. Canterbury in 1327 provides another instance of a jurisdictional quarrel between civic ruling groups which was evidently encouraged by its instigators to develop into a popular protest, tinged with more than a hint of anticlericalism. The prior of the cathedral having resisted the attempt of the city government to impose a levy on his tenants, the citizens' response was to convene a public meeting in the churchyard of the Dominican house in the town. There the crowd passed a series of melodramatic resolutions, each more extravagant than the last. If the convent persisted, the townsmen declared that they would break the windows of its houses in Bargate and drive its tenants from their houses; would wreck the conventual mills and place an embargo on the supply of provisions to the monastery; would arrest any monk daring to come out and force pilgrims entering to swear to make no offerings to the Church; and would dig a deep trench around the entire precinct. Finally, all present announced that they would have from the treasure of St Thomas's shrine a gold ring for a finger of each hand.[65]

It would be wrong to interpret such outbursts as expressive of widespread hostility to the churchmen as pastors, but it seems certain that such continuing tensions over legal rights facilitated the Dissolution of the monasteries in the sixteenth century.[66] Nevertheless, until the Crown for other reasons turned against the religious houses, local hostilities were generally contained within manageable limits. Contemporaries were not, of course, disposed to regard high levels of physical violence as functional and consequently tolerable but, in fact, violence tended to be minimal. Gathering tension was almost always defused before reaching its logical conclusion in fighting. Even in the most notorious incidents, very few injuries were recorded.[67] Confrontations nearly without exception stopped short at the stage of noisy posturing, behaviour which may itself have played a cathartic role in directing and releasing pent-up hostilities. Thus a mob at Gloucester in 1512 turned from vandalism to jollification. Here, as at Hereford in 1505, an outburst was triggered over the question of pasturage. The Abbot of Gloucester's cattle were driven from a meadow outside the west gate of the city, and a great ditch was dug there to deny him further access. Then the jubilant townsmen declared a holiday, 'going forth in the morning and coming home at night with tabors and horns blowing and piping; and also set barrels of ale at the High Cross, there drinking and eating with great shouts and cries in manner of triumph'.[68]

Despite the dissensions, the persistent and fundamental truth was that the different elements in these towns perceived a need for one another. Urban society was, of course, hierarchically divided; wealth and formal political rights were unequally distributed. Yet the office-holding minority did not have an entirely free hand. The importance to the élite of being perceived as truly representative of the interests of the town as a whole is apparent in the language and conduct of public disputes. On these occasions the reliance of the city's ruling groups upon a broad base of popular support was most clearly manifested. Meanwhile, awareness of the mutual interdependence of clerical and lay communities also helped to prevent the irredeemable collapse of order. The local economies of Hereford, Gloucester, Canterbury and the rest were heavily reliant upon the needs of the urban religious communities, and for this reason alone their final destruction was unlikely to be in the townsmen's financial interests.[69] Moreover, loyalties cut across one another in more complex ways. Family, parish or trade associations made their own demands on an individual which might pull counter to that of a particular fee. Such competing allegiances added complexity to any disputes, but at the same time the instinct for self-preservation of each affinity created a desire for a peaceable resolution.[70] The balance of relationships within the town, however, underwent changes over time in each case, necessitating revisions of the *modus vivendi*. These moments of readjustment offered the opportunity for the various elements in society, and not only those enjoying the right to a constitutional vote, to express themselves on subjects of immediate concern.

Conflict was inherent in medieval towns, where it was by no means regarded as an unmitigated blessing. Yet it frequently played a creative role, providing occasion for the controlled airing of views on matters which, if ignored or suppressed, might fatally rend society. Processes of negotiation and arbitration were employed whereby accommodation and compromise were constantly, and publicly, renewed. By promoting awareness and public discussion of the diversity of social groups making up the urban community as a whole, of the town's history and of the meaning of public ceremonies, these very processes of dispute settlement themselves acted as a catalyst of the idea of the urban community. Although unrealizable in practice, that image of the urban population as a community was consequently made available as a point of reference, against which perceived present failings were judged. The recurrent internal strife which characterized the urban élite – and which was most commonly precipitated by the presence of the Church – demonstrably acted as a stimulus both to the creation of a language of shared identity and purpose, and to a significant measure of popular participation in urban politics.

Acknowledgements

For their comments on an earlier version of this essay I am grateful to Julia Barrow, Chris Dyer, Jane Garnett, Rodney Hilton, Geoffrey Martin and Susan Reynolds. For their hospitality and assistance I am also most grateful to the former officers of the Hereford Cathedral Archive and Library, the late Miss Meryl Jancey and the late Miss Penelope Morgan.

Notes

1. Useful discussions, with references to the older literature, are S. Rigby, 'Urban "oligarchy" in late medieval England', in J.A.F. Thomson (ed.),

Towns and Townspeople in the Fifteenth Century (1988), 62–86; and J.I. Kermode, 'The formation of oligarchies in late medieval England', in ibid., 87–106.
2. In the UK in 1970, 1 per cent of the adult population owned almost 30 per cent of the total personal wealth of the country, and 5 per cent of the population owned 51.9 per cent of the total personal wealth. Royal Commission on the Distribution of Incomes and Wealth, *Report No. 7* (1979), 93: Table 4.4. For comparable statistics from English towns in the 1520s (derived from royal subsidy assessments), see e.g. W.T. MacCaffrey, *Exeter 1540–1640. The Growth of an English County Town*, 2nd edn (Cambridge, Mass., 1975), 248, 250; D.M. Palliser, *Tudor York* (1979), 136; A.D. Dyer, *The City of Worcester in the Sixteenth Century* (1973), 175.
3. See the valuable remarks of Susan Reynolds in 'Medieval urban history and the history of political thought', *Urban History Yearbook* (1982), 14–23.
4. There is no serious modern study of medieval Hereford, apart from the good short introduction by M. D. Lobel in M.D. Lobel (ed.), *The Atlas of Historic Towns*, vol. 1 (1969).
5. 'Asseruit ... quod libere potuerunt frangere capita aliorum in cimiterio sine pollucione eiusdem pro eo quod per dictum sanguinis effusionem cimiterium erat pollutum' (Hereford Dean and Chapter Muniment [hereafter HDCM] 1164).
6. *Rotuli Chartarum*, pt i, 53, 212–13; *Calendar of Charter Rolls, 1226–57*, 25; ibid., *1300–26*, 240–1; ibid., *1327–41*, 52, 55, 212; *Calendar of Patent Rolls, 1377–81*, 134; ibid., *1381–85*, 333. See also E.M. Jancey, *The Royal Charters of the City of Hereford* (1973).
7. 'Frequently there are precincts locally situated within the limits of the corporate authority, but exempted from its jurisdiction' (Commission on Municipal Corporations, *First Report* (1835), 31 (no. 31); see also 42 (no. 103), and Appendix 2, 724, 843, 905. See further below; for the several jurisdictions within Hereford, see note 19.
8. Of two English versions of the medieval Customs of Hereford, made respectively in the seventeenth and the eighteenth century, the earlier was printed in 1871, although the published text has been little noticed since. W.H. Black and G.M. Hills, 'The Hereford municipal records and the Customs of Hereford', *Journal of the British Archaeological Association*, 27 (1871), 453–88. The existence at Belmont Priory near Hereford of the Latin text from which both translations derive was noticed in 1871 (ibid., 456) and again by M. Bateson in 'The laws of Breteuil', *English Historical Review*, 15 (1900), 303, but has never attracted serious attention. The Latin MS is now in the Hereford Public Library, Hill MSS, vol. VIII. *Pace* Bateson (who described the MS as 'probably Elizabethan', 'The laws of Breteuil', 303) the hand of the Latin document appears to be contemporary with the date of its redaction, 1486, given in a concluding note. The original Latin text has been used here in preference to its erratic postmedieval derivatives. The two English versions are now, respectively, in Hereford and Worcester Record Office, Hereford Branch, Hereford Corporation Records, vol. 1; and Hereford Public Library, Hill MSS, vol. 4, 79–139.
9. *Curia Regis Rolls*, vol. 15, 512 (no. 1990); ibid., vol. 16, 19 (no. 82), 30 (no. 114); and see *Calendar of Close Rolls, 1237–42*, 123.

10. *Curia Regis Rolls*, vol. 16, 346–7 (no. 1727); *Calendar of Charter Rolls, 1226–57*, 256–7, 259; *Calendar of Patent Rolls, 1258-66*, 208. See also later complaints concerning royal charters conceded to one party which patently conflicted with previous royal grants to the other. Public Record Office (hereafter PRO), MS SC8/251/12518 (petition of the mayor and citizens, *c*.1400); HDCM 2963 (similar petition, *mutatis mutandis*, of the bishop, dean and chapter, early fifteenth century).
11. PRO, MS JUST1/1191, mm. 3–4, 6; *Calendar of Patent Rolls, 1258–66*, 232; W.W. Capes (ed.), *Registrum Thome de Cantilupo*, Canterbury and York Society, 2 (1907), 91–3. For Aquablanca's poor contemporary reputation, see Matthew Paris, *Chronica Majora*, Rolls Series, 7 vols, (1872–83), vol. 4, 403, vol. 5, 422.
12. On the increasingly suspicious attitude of urban governments towards the appropriation of town property by the Church in the thirteenth century, see C. Gross, 'Mortmain in medieval boroughs', *American Historical Review*, 12 (1907), 733–42.
13. The citizens of Hereford played a violent and rebellious part in the baronial revolt of 1265 which may well have been directed in part against the episcopal authority. PRO, MS C145/12/11; *Calendar of Patent Rolls, 1258–66*, 644–5; *Calendar of Close Rolls, 1264–68*, 165. In 1275 the bishop appealed once again to the civic authorities to respect the cathedral. *Registrum Thome de Cantilupo*, 5–6. Further incidents, in the early fourteenth century, are recorded at PRO, MS JUST1/302, mm. 40, 43 *dors*, 81 *dors*; JUST1/303, m.63; and SC1/25/103. From the late thirteenth century civic hostility became increasingly focused upon the dean and chapter, while the bishops, whose material stake in the town was less substantial and whose presence less continuous, played a more detached role.
14. *Calendar of Patent Rolls, 1377–81*, 134; ibid., *1381–85*, 333; ibid., *1385–89*, 213. PRO, MS C81/483/3012, the Chancery warrant for the issue of the grant that the bailiff should be denominated mayor, gives no further information as to the preceding petition.
15. HDCM 2227; *Calendar of Patent Rolls, 1388–92*, 160. The royal letters patent were not issued until 21 November 1389 – *after* the fence had been erected and torn down (see below).
16. *Calendar of Patent Rolls, 1388–92*, 160. The pattern occurred elsewhere; see C. Coulson, 'Hierarchism in conventual crenellation: an essay in the sociology and metaphysics of medieval fortification', *Medieval Archaeology*, 26 (1982), 69–100.
17. HDCM 1491 and 2946: agreement by the citizens to accept the bishop and Sir John Clanvowe as arbitrators in the dispute (or a third person appointed by these two if they failed to reach an accord), dated 18 October 1389; HDCM 2944, dated 6 December 1389: suspension of hostilities between the parties until Christmas, while agreement was reached; HDCM 2943, dated 22 December 1389: bond of the mayor and citizens to abide by the arbitrators' settlement; HDCM 2954: the arbitration (incomplete, and lacking date) of Bishop John Trefnant and Sir John Clanvowe. For Clanvowe see K.B. Macfarlane, *Lancastrian Kings and Lollard Knights* (1972), 199–206, 230–32.
18. The opening years of the fifteenth century witnessed a spate of such publicized disputations; another marked the last two decades before 1500.

The evidence for these disputes is preserved among the records of Hereford cathedral. It comprises a considerable body of draft petitions and memoranda relating to the views of both parties in the disputes. Many of the documents are undated; some are fragmentary. Their present numeration in the archive (the result of recataloguing in the present century) does not assist their explication. Nevertheless it is possible to recover the approximate chronology of events. See the following notes for references.

19. HCAL, MS 2936. In addition to the courts of the chapter and of the mayor separate courts were held for the smaller fees of the bishop, of the priory of St John of Jerusalem and of the priory of Llanthony; certain of the cathedral canons had the right to hold further secular courts for the districts of their canonries. Some records of the bishop's Hereford courts, *temp*. Edward IV, are in the British Library, MSS Additional Rolls, 27290–310. Some mayor's court rolls are in Hereford and Worcester Record Office, Hereford Branch, MS X/72. A rental of 1505 indicating the extent of the St John's Hospital fee is in the same archive, MS A63/III.
20. HDCM 2956B.
21. HDCM 2960 (emphasis added).
22. HDCM 2962.
23. HDCM 2934.
24. HDCM 2960. See an earlier complaint of the bishop, dean and chapter in the late fourteenth century that 'les bailliefs du dite ville ount fet et fount de jour en jour tielz manasses a borgoys du dite cite qui sount de la fee du dit decane et chapitre qu'ilz n'osent estre bailiefs du decane et chapitre quant ils sount eleus a celluy office' (PRO, MS SC8/116/5756). In *c*.1495 the dean's bailiff bore witness to the truth of this claim, having, as he averred, been imprisoned by the mayor simply for exercising his office. PRO, MS C1/217/22 (1493 X 1500). Again in 1511 it was alleged that the spiritual courts of justice were subverted, because the bishop's sergeants 'be often tymes unliefully entreted, vexed and troubled for the same by [the mayor] and [his] officers' (A.T. Bannister (ed.), *Registrum Ricardi Mayhew*, Canterbury and York Society, 27 (1921), 135–6).
25. HDCM 2968.
26. HDCM 1154. William is described as 'monachus monasterii de Alsedr". As such, his position in the close at Hereford was presumably irregular. For Alcester Abbey's indigent position at this period see *Transactions of the Birmingham Archaeological Society*, 64 (1941–42), 38.
27. HDCM 1154: 'Idem maior misit dictum Ricardum [sc. constabulum suum] tanquam amicum dicti Willelmi monachi ut inquireret secrete de ipsis piscibus et conservaret in quantum posset honorem ipsius Willelmi monachi et ecclesie Herefordensis.'
28. J.H. Parry (ed.), *Registrum Ricardi Mascall*, Canterbury and York Society, 21 (1917), 96–103; HCAL, MS 2847.
29. HDCM 3209.
30. HDCM 2950; see also 2948–9, 2951.
31. For John Prophet see J.H. Wylie, *History of England under Henry IV*, 4 vols (1884–98), vol. 2, 484n.; T.F. Tout, *Chapters in the Administrative History of Medieval England*, 6 vols (1920–33), vol. 3, 466–7, vol. 5, 95, 97n.
32. HDCM 2935: the date is approximately fixed by 2937. There exists a cartulary of the Hereford cathedral chapter of *c*.1300, which indicates the

group of Hereford properties acquired by that date (they were concentrated in Castle Street and Cabbage Lane, close to the precinct; but on their full distribution see above). Oxford, Bodleian Library, MS Jones 23. The clearest statement of historical knowledge of the Church in Hereford before the Conquest is M. Gelling, *The West Midlands in the Early Middle Ages* (1992), 159–64.

33. For late fifteenth century resolutions see HDCM 2961. For a set of proposed reforms drafted in the early seventeenth century, optimistically designed to resolve the problems of the fees, see HDCM 2964. For continuing disputes on the same subject in the eighteenth century, see HDCM 6.D.i, 21 ff.
34. 'Discordia fuit . . . super quo concordatum fuit per totam communitatem omnium libertatum.' HDCM 2951B; also in the city Customs, cited above, note 9.
35. HDCM 2944 (1389), 2937 (1409).
36. HDCM 2945.
37. E. Powell, 'Arbitration and the law in England in the later Middle Ages', *Transactions of the Royal Historical Society*, 5th series, 33 (1983), 49–67; D.J. Clayton, 'Peace bonds and the maintenance of law and order in late medieval England: the example of Cheshire', *Bulletin of the Institute of Historical Research*, 58 (1985), 133–48. See also M.T. Clanchy, 'Law and love in the Middle Ages', in J. Bossy (ed.), *Disputes and Settlements: Law and Human Relations in the West* (1983), 47–67, for the relevant point that in medieval England 'law' is well documented but negotiation is not. In general see S. Roberts, 'The study of disputes: anthropological perspectives', in Bossy, *Disputes and Settlements*, 1–24.
38. No source is proffered for the latter assertion; a fact which suggests that traditions about Hereford's Mercian past were no longer current in the later Middle Ages.
39. Oxford, Bodleian Library, MS Herefordshire Rolls, 36.
40. M.T. Clanchy, 'Remembering the past and the good old law', *History*, 55 (1970), 165–76.
41. C. Bell, *Ritual Theory, Ritual Practice* (1992), *passim*; G. Rosser, 'Myth, image and social process in the English medieval town', *Urban History*, 23 (1996), 5–25.
42. HDCM 2957–8.
43. Ibid.
44. For comparison, see e.g. P. Borsay, '"All the world's a stage": Urban ritual and ceremony, 1660–1800', in P. Clark (ed.), *The Transformation of English Provincial Towns 1600–1800* (1984), 228–58, esp. 242–3. On the significance of medieval urban Corpus Christi processions as potent images of social integration (whether or not such integration could be realized in practice), see M. James, 'Ritual, drama and the social body in the late medieval English town', *Past and Present*, 98 (1983), 3–29.
45. V.W. Turner, *The Drums of Affliction: a Study of Religious Processes among the Ndembu of Zambia* (1968), 6 and *passim*.
46. HDCM 2960 (*c*.1400).
47. Ibid.
48. This theme runs, e.g., through the Customs of Hereford (above, note 9).
49. See above; and the city custumal cited in note 9.
50. For jurisdictional disputes in Exeter see S.A. Moore (ed.), *Letters and*

Papers of John Shillingford, Mayor of Exeter 1447–50, Camden Society, 2nd series, 2 (1871); A.S. Green, *Town Life in the Fifteenth Century*, 2 vols (1894), vol. 1, 338–68; M.E. Curtis, *Some Disputes between the City and the Cathedral Authorities of Exeter*, History of Exeter Research Group, Monograph No. 5 (1932); and M. Kowaleski, 'Local markets and merchants in late fourteenth-century Exeter', PhD thesis, University of Toronto (1982), 52–67.

51. Cit. Curtis, *Exeter*, 25n.
52. Moore, *Letters and Papers of John Shillingford*, 53.
53. 'As at Wells, Salisbury and other places.' Ibid., 93–5. For similarly contested stalls in the close at Lincoln see J.W.F. Hill, *Medieval Lincoln* (1948), 265–7.
54. Moore, *Letters and Papers of John Shillingford*, 89–91.
55. Ibid., 58, 75–7, 105; see also ibid., 10, 17. For public boards or 'tables' displaying the history of particular places or institutions see G.H. Gerould, '"Tables" in medieval churches', *Speculum*, 1 (1926), 439–40; A. Gransden, *Historical Writing in England*, vol. 2, *c.1307 to the Early Sixteenth Century* (1982), 495; C. Richmond, 'Hand and mouth: information gathering and use in the later Middle Ages', *Journal of Historical Sociology*, 1 (1988), 233–52, at 246–7 n. 5.
56. See Curtis, *Exeter*, ch. 2.
57. F.W. Maitland, *Township and Borough* (1898), 71–4 and *passim*; and see references cited in the following note.
58. D. Keene, *Survey of Medieval Winchester*, Winchester Studies, 2 (1985), 72–3. On the sokes of London see F.M. Stenton, 'Norman London', reprinted in D.M. Stenton (ed.), *Preparatory to Anglo-Saxon England* (1970), 23–47: 'The distinctive feature of London justice in the Norman age is the influence of such private liberties, the sokes ... These sokes presented a most formidable obstacle to the growth of any ubiquitous city jurisdiction' (33–4). See also G.H. Martin, 'Domesday Book and the boroughs', in P.H. Sawyer (ed.), *Domesday Book: A Reassessment* (1985), 143–63, at 161.
59. For the case of York see E. Miller, 'Medieval York', in *The Victoria County History of Yorkshire: the City of York* (1961), 25–116, at 38–40; and for the major settlement of contentions there in 1275, F. Drake, *Eboracum* (1736), 553–7.
60. 'Prior extraere a Communa Civitatis homines de libertate nitebatur, ut essent sub dominio suo, separati a Communa' (T. Stapleton (ed.), *De Antiquis Legibus Liber* (1846), 145). See also W. Rye, 'The riot between the monks and citizens of Norwich in 1272', *Norfolk Antiquarian Miscellany*, 2 (1880), 17–89; W. Hudson and J.C. Tingey (eds), *The Records of the City of Norwich*, 2 vols (1908–10), vol. 2, 269–71; N. Tanner, *The Church in Late Medieval Norwich, 1370–1532*, Pontifical Institute of Mediaeval Studies, Studies and Texts, 66 (1984), 141–54. The earliest recorded outbreaks of this kind in Norwich occurred in the reign of John; Rye, 'The riot', 17–18, 72. At Worcester by the late Middle Ages, to counter the attractions of the liberties, it was ordained by the city government

> that every citizen and every inhabitant within the said city, or citizens foreign, being tenant, servant or bondman to the bishop of Worcester [should] take no benefice in any action

commenced or to be commenced against him, before the bailiffs of Worcester, by that though he or they be the said bishop's tenants, upon pain of disfranchising'. (Ordinances of Worcester, printed in L. and J. Toulmin Smith, *English Gilds*, Early English Text Society, original series, 40 (1870), 406).

61. 'Due partes civitatis predicte in manibus spiritualium et forinsecorum et vix tertia pars in manibus civium ibi existentium [sunt], per quod iidem cives onera colleccionum et subsidiorum infra eandem civitatem absque eorum gravi deterioracione sustinere nequeant, ut asserunt' (cit. F. Street, 'The relations of the bishops and citizens of Salisbury (New Sarum) between 1225 and 1612', *Wiltshire Archaeological and Natural History Magazine*, 39 (1915–17), 185–257, 319–67, at 228).
62. Keene, *Winchester*, 75.
63. PRO, MS STAC1/1/19.
64. Details of the long-standing conflict between St Augustine's abbey and the mayor and commonalty of Bristol were carefully preserved by the civic officers in a specially allocated volume: E. Ralph (ed.), *The Great White Book of Bristol*, Bristol Record Society Publications, 32 (1979), 2–3, 17–67.
65. Historical Manuscripts Commission, *Ninth Report: Appendix* (1883), 98. The choice of the mendicant house as the place of convention may reflect additionally upon the relations of the friars with the cathedral priory. The troubles at Canterbury in 1381 were a different case, relating less to problems specific to the urban community than to social changes affecting town and country together; the same is probably true of other towns affected by the revolt. See A.F. Butcher, 'English urban society and the revolt of 1381', in R.H. Hilton and T.H. Aston (eds), *The English Rising of 1381* (1984), 84–111, at 102–4.
66. Cf. D.A. Eltis, 'Tensions between clergy and laity in some western German cities in the late Middle Ages', *Journal of Ecclesiastical History*, 43 (1992), 231–48; W. Eberhard, 'Klerus- und Kirchenkritik in der spätmittelalterlichen deutschen Stadtchronik', *Historisches Jahrbuch*, 114 (1994), 349–80.
67. At Norwich in the 1272 disturbances the exceptional number of thirteen 'clerks and laymen' (but no monks) died; more typically, in 1443 (when Gladman's ritual protest succeeded upon the failure of arbitration by the Earl of Suffolk to win acceptance) there were no fatal casualties. Rye, 'The riot', 12 and Appendix 12; Tanner, *Church in Late Medieval Norwich*, 151–2; and on the later incident see also P.C. Maddern, 'The legitimation of power: riot and authority in fifteenth-century Norwich', *Parergon*, new series, 6 (1988), 65–84. The same point could be sustained in respect of the monastic boroughs notoriously riven by such disputes, such as St Albans and Bury St Edmunds. For these see N.M. Trenholme, *The English Monastic Boroughs*, University of Missouri Studies, 2(3) (1927), where, however, it is arguable that too bloody a picture is drawn.
68. W.H. Hart (ed.), *Historia et Cartularium Sancti Petri Gloucestriae*, Rolls Series, 3 vols (1863–67), vol. 3, xxxix–xlvii.
69. See e.g. R.B. Dobson, 'Cathedral chapters and cathedral cities: York, Durham and Carlisle in the fifteenth century', *Northern History*, 19 (1983), 15–44; P. Rixon, 'The medieval town of Reading', Oxford University D.Phil. thesis (forthcoming).
70. Cf. M. Gluckman, *Custom and Conflict in Africa* (1956), ch. 1.

CHAPTER THREE

The Church and the Jews in English Medieval Towns

John Edwards

> A word must be said about the relationship between the Jews and the Church. From the religious point of view, of course, some degree of antagonism was natural, and occasionally individual churchmen were seized with a desire to proselytize which resulted in a certain amount of discomfort and possibly even in massacre ... Apart, however, from antagonism on the religious side, which was in the circumstances natural and only to be anticipated, the relations between the Jews and the Church, especially in commercial transactions, were on the whole friendly and harmonious.[1]

Thus wrote F. Ashe Lincoln in 1939, in his history of the Hebrew *starrs*, documents which recorded dealings between English Jews and their neighbours in the period between 1070 and 1290. In 1908, before an earlier world war, Albert Hyamson took a less sanguine, and in terms of what was to follow during this century, a more prophetic, view of the Jewish experience in medieval England:

> The history of the Jews in England is the history in miniature of the Diaspora. Since the opening of the Christian era the story of the Jews has everywhere been the same – continual alternations of prosperity and persecution. With nations as with individuals the wheel of fortune ever revolves, but with the Jews its progress seems to have been more rapid, for the alterations have been more numerous than with any other race.[2]

Here, in brief, is the problem which faces the historian of medieval English Jewry, and of its abrupt end in the national expulsion, at the orders of Edward I, in 1290. How is it possible to understand, and even perhaps to explain, the ambivalent attitudes towards their Jewish neighbours of English rulers, churchmen and townspeople?

It is quite clear that Jewish settlement in Norman, Angevin and Plantagenet England was a primarily urban phenomenon, in the sense that Jews who settled in the kingdom in that period were either invited in by rulers or else found a living in centres of governmental activity. Whatever Jewish settlement may have occurred in the British Isles in the Roman and Anglo-Saxon eras, medieval Jewish life in England, together with relatively minor extensions into English-occupied north Wales[3] and Ireland, was certainly the result of the importation of Ashkenazi Jews from Normandy, in or after 1066. To say that Jews in England were primarily townspeople is not necessarily to imply, however, that they were concentrated in few, and large, communities. Although, in the period between the Norman Conquest and the expulsion in 1290, Jews are recorded as resident, whether permanently or temporarily, in over 50 towns in England, and nine in north Wales, only a few of these towns contained, at any stage during the period, more than a single-figure number of Jewish families.[4]

When it comes to trying to establish the numerical strength of the English Jewish population at any time during the period of medieval settlement, the normal problems intrinsic in medieval demography are accentuated by the fact that Jews were taxed by the crown as a religious and social group, and not even by household. This was, of course, the result, in England as in the rest of western Europe at the time, of their being regarded legally as the property of the crown, or *servi Cameræ*.[5] However, Kenneth Stow has pointed out, in the case of the Rhineland at the time of the first Crusade and the resulting massacres, that this sense of communal responsibility was not by any means unnatural to Jews, for religious as well as social reasons. 'All were supposed to pay a fair share of taxes, and every community member was equally "obligated" to study [the Torah, or Law of Moses]'.[6] In any case, in the vast majority of places of Jewish settlement in England between 1066 and 1290, with an overall population numbered in hundreds or, at the most, a few thousand, there was no practical need or possibility of forming a 'ghetto' (to use the later Venetian expression[7]), even though any group of orthodox Jews, however small, has always needed to seek the services necessary to fulfil its religious duties, including dietary requirements. Only in a few places, such as London, York, Norwich, Lincoln, and the university cities of Oxford and Cambridge, would a numerically large Jewish presence have been visible. None the less, as various incidents in the period were graphically to demonstrate, a low demographic profile did not necessarily save Jews from the conspicuous attention of their gentile neighbours.

From the beginning of royally sponsored Jewish settlement in the mid-eleventh century, Englishmen were most likely to encounter Jews in towns and, most probably, in some form of economic transaction. The studies which have accumulated during the last century, which are being continued and developed, for example, by Joe Hillaby, have revealed that, not only were Jews involved in tax payments to the Crown, and the provision of loans to successive kings,[8] but they also engaged in the provision of a wide range of financial services to townspeople, to ecclesiastical institutions, and to knights and barons in the shires.[9] Recent research, much of it in the Public Record Office, has also revealed criminal links between Jewish and Christian townspeople, particularly in thirteenth-century Norwich.[10] It was in this same East Anglian cathedral city that anti-Jewish feeling first showed itself in a public, indeed spectacular, manner, in what became known as the 'ritual murder' of 'St' William of Norwich. One result of that child's death was to be a steady growth in the number of violent incidents involving Christians and Jews, which took place in English towns

On the Monday of Holy Week, 20 March 1144, a small Norwich boy apparently went, with his mother's consent, to work with a cook in the archdeacon's kitchen. He was not seen again alive, but was found dead in the nearby Thorpe wood, on the following Holy Saturday.[11] Initially, the case seems to have been treated as a sad, but all too normal, child murder but, as late as 1150, the story began to gain credence that young William had been murdered by Jews, who had attempted to re-enact the sufferings which their ancestors had supposedly inflicted on Jesus himself. Thereafter, a cult of the supposed martyr began to take shape, with the active assistance of the chronicler Thomas of Monmouth, who proceeded both to accuse the Jews and to provide a hagiography.[12] By 1155, the chronicler of Peterborough abbey knew about the accusation that the child had been crucified, while, in 1168, a similar cult started at Gloucester abbey, after a boy named Harold was found dead beside the River Severn.[13] In 1181, a child called Robert supposedly suffered a similar fate in the abbey town of Bury St Edmunds[14] while, two years later, a supposed serial crucifier of Christian boys was found in Bristol.[15] In the mean time, the story had spread to the Continent, appearing in Blois, in 1171,[16] and lasting throughout the rest of the medieval period up to the notorious case of Simon of Trent,[17] in 1475, and that of the 'Holy Child' of La Guardia, in Spain, which helped to prepare the way for the expulsion of the Jews from Castile and Aragon in 1492.[18]

As far as England is concerned, the most notorious subsequent case was that of 'little' Hugh of Lincoln, supposedly murdered after torture, and dropped into a cistern by Jews in that city, on a disputed date in the summer of 1255. There had, by then, been a lull of some decades in the establishment of 'ritual murder' cults, both in England and on the Continent, indeed, not only had the 1183 Bristol story failed to develop in that way, but so had similar accusations in Winchester, in 1192, 1225 and 1232, and in Lincoln in 1202. In Norwich, however, where the cult of St William was well established, a number of Jews were tried for circumcising a Christian child, apparently as a preparation for crucifixion, and possible 'ritual murder'. Contemporary sources, the Bury St Edmunds chronicle and Matthew Paris, state that four Jews in the city were dragged through the streets at horses' tails, and then hanged, in 1240, apparently as a result of this case. It thus appeared that, as the middle of the thirteenth century approached, interest in such accusations was reviving. In 1244, a Christian child was buried by the canons in St Paul's churchyard, after converted Jews [see below] claimed that he had been violently abused and ritually murdered.[19] The distinctive feature of the 1255 Lincoln case, however, was that King Henry III intervened personally, believing the truth of the tale. He arrived in the city at the beginning of October of that year, and entrusted the investigation to the knight, John of Lexington, brother of the then bishop of Lincoln. A Jew named Copin 'confessed' to the murder, 91 other Jews (there was a major social gathering going on in the city at the time) were taken to the Tower of London, and 18 of them were hanged before the slaughter was stopped, apparently at the request of the friars.[20] This was the first case in Europe in which a reigning monarch explicitly endorsed the charge of 'ritual murder' of Christian boys by Jews, but it reflected a deterioration in Jewish–Christian relations in English towns which had begun some time before.

The accession of Richard I to the English throne, in 1189, appears to have precipitated a series of violent attacks by Christian townsmen on their Jewish neighbours. Thanks to the fact that, as Barrie Dobson has remarked, the events of 1189–90, culminating in the York massacre, coincided with 'perhaps [the] most prolific of all periods in the history of chronicle writing in this country',[21] a fairly good idea may be gained of the bloody events which greeted the new sovereign's arrival in his kingdom. Many of these sources were included by Joseph Jacobs, together with commentary by Jews, in his valuable late nineteenth-century collection,[22] and they reveal a sorry story, in the words of writers such as Ralph de Diceto, Dean of St Paul's in London, the Winchester monk, Richard of Devizes, Roger of Howden and, above all, William of Newburgh. In brief, Jews who had gathered on 3 September 1189 to greet their new sovereign and direct lord, but had been excluded from the coronation, were attacked in Westminster Hall. The survivors fled to the City of London, where further killings, woundings, arson, looting and forced conversion took place, then and on the following day. Although royal and corporation officials eventually succeeded in restoring order, and the king immediately sent instructions to his sheriffs and other officers throughout the kingdom, forbidding any further violence against Jews, these orders were not obeyed. As provincial Jews fled home from London, they were attacked once again in a succession of smaller towns, including Stamford, York, Lincoln, Lynn, Norwich, Bury St Edmunds and Colchester. It is important to note that these were not, generally speaking, attacks and massacres carried out in the heat of the moment. The killings were still going on in February and March of the following year, and culminated in the notorious massacre, forced conversion and mutual suicide of Jews in York on the night of 16 March 1190, which has been analysed so brilliantly by Barrie Dobson.[23]

Although an openly Jewish life was still to be legally possible in England up to Edward I's expulsion order of 18 July 1290, similar more localized moves had begun, even before the violence of 1189–90, and were to be repeated during the remainder of the existence of Jewry in medieval England. In a chapter mainly devoted to the purchase by the abbey of Bury St Edmunds of the manor of Mildenhall, in 1190, Jocelin of Brakelond somewhat laconically records the expulsion of the Jews from the adjoining town:

> The abbot asked the king for written permission to expel the Jews from St Edmund's town, on the grounds that everything in the town and within the *banleuca*[24] belonged by right to St Edmund: therefore, either the Jews should be St Edmund's men, or they should be banished from the town. Accordingly, he was given permission to turn them out, but they were to retain their movable possessions and also the value of their houses and lands. When they had been escorted out and taken to various other towns by an armed troop, the abbot directed that in future all those who received back Jews or gave them lodging in St Edmund's town, were to be excommunicated in every church and at every altar.[25]

It should be noted that, according to Ralph de Diceto, 57 Jews had been massacred in Bury, the day before the expulsion.[26] It was in the thirteenth century, though, that such local expulsions took place. In 1231, Simon de Montfort, Earl of Leicester, decreed that all Jews should be removed from that town, but the intercessions of his aunt, and of the then archdeacon, Robert Grosseteste, later Bishop of Lincoln, persuaded him to delay until Grosseteste was dead, in 1253. Other examples occurred, generally without such exalted intercession, in Newcastle upon Tyne, in 1234, High Wycombe in 1235, Southampton in 1236, Berkhampstead in 1242, Newbury in 1244, Derby in 1261, and Bridgnorth in 1274. In the following year, 1275, Jews were expelled from all the towns held, since 1236, by Queen Eleanor of Provence, mother of Edward I, that is, Worcester, Bath, Gloucester, Cambridge and Huntingdon. Not apparently envisaging, at this stage, a general expulsion of Jews from his kingdom, Edward, in this same ordinance of 16 January, decreed that the Jews in question should be deported, under the supervision of county sheriffs, to neighbouring towns: those of Marlborough to Devizes, those of Gloucester to Bristol, those of Worcester to Hereford, and those of Cambridge to Norwich.[27] As Dobson has suggested, it may well be that the initiative, in this case, came not from the queen mother, but from the king himself, who wished, like his

Capetian neighbours in France,[28] and his successors, the Catholic monarchs, Ferdinand and Isabella, in Spain,[29] to try out partial and local expulsions, as in Gascony in 1288, before a more general effort, such as that in England in 1290. Both techniques left a precedent for later European rulers, leading to the almost total eviction of Jews from western Europe by 1520.[30]

The current state of historiography in relation to Edward I's decision to complete the expulsion of Jews from his realm is well summarized by Zefira Entin Rokeah:

> A full study of the various factors that brought about the expulsion of the Jews from England has not yet been made. As a rule, historians have concentrated on the economic aspects of the problem – primarily the impoverishment of the Jews and their replacement in economic life by Italian bankers. There is no question that the attitudes of various groups in English society must be studied, including the lords, the knights, the townsmen, and clergymen of all ranks, before we can begin to understand the many-faceted background of the expulsion.[31]

Such a wide-ranging approach is indeed necessary, but the main purpose of what follows will be to highlight one social category among those mentioned by Rokeah, that is, the clergy, as well as the institution for which they worked, the Catholic Church. The surviving sources offer some justification for regarding the relationship between English Jews and the Anglo-Norman and Angevin monarchies as having been primarily economic. In the thirteenth century, however, things seem to have changed. Looking at the question of Jewish–Christian relations in Catholic Europe as a whole, it seems undeniable that the fate of English Jews became increasingly subject, as the thirteenth century went on, to the application or otherwise of policies which were, at least in their appearance, religious in nature. The question of whether there was in fact a shift in the Church's policy, in the period up to and succeeding the Fourth Lateran Council called by Innocent III in 1215, is still controversial,[32] and in such a case, it may be necessary, before looking at the particular situation in England, to go back to the 'basics' of Christian scripture.

Although the history and interpretation of the texts which have come to form the 'canon' of the Bible are extremely controversial, it does still seem safe to make two general points. In the first place, there are a number of texts in the New Testament, for example in the gospels and in the letters of Paul, which easily lend themselves to an anti-Jewish interpretation.[33] Second, whatever additional regulations for Jewish life and relations between Jews and Christians may have been introduced in the thirteenth century, they not only had to be based on these scriptural texts (which even Innocent III could not change), but also could, by the very nature of papal legislation, be no more than repetition or development of much earlier conciliar canons.[34] In any case, whatever measures the Lateran fathers enacted were inevitably to be brought to England in some form and at some time. The basic principles of this legislation were that Jews might retain basic religious freedom but their religious buildings were not to be as ostentatious as those of Christians, and Jews were never to exercise authority over Christians. As Canon 69 of Lateran IV, *Etsi judæos*, put it, 'It is too absurd for a blasphemer of Christ to exercise the force of power over Christians'.[35] Thus the status of English and other Jews as *servi cameræ* was confirmed. The other preoccupation of the Lateran fathers, as of their predecessors, was to reduce to a minimum, and if possible prevent, all social contact between Jews and Christians. Thus Christians should not be servants in Jewish households, in order to prevent 'continuous conversation and assiduous familiarity'.[36]

As to the application of this and succeeding canon law in England, the overall impression is that the English bishops, like many of their Continental brethren, notably in the Iberian peninsula, were not especially preoccupied with Jewish questions or Christian–Jewish relations. J.A. Watt notes that, of the 36 sets of canons issued by English councils or synods between 1205 and 1290, only 11 concern themselves with Jews at all, and many of these were re-issues of earlier material, such as those in Winchester in 1219, 1220 and 1240. None at all were issued in the province of York.[37] However, the Oxford council of 1222 did apply Lateran IV decrees to English Jews. Jews were not to build synagogues in places which they had not previously settled; they were not to remain in England at all unless they had financial means and guarantors; they were not to make excessive noise while worshipping, and they were not to have Christian women as their servants. Jews were not to buy or eat meat during Lent, they were not to disparage Christianity or debate religious matters with Christians, they were not to have sex with Christians and, to avoid such outcomes, they were to wear identifying badges. Jews were not to enter churches, or persuade their co-religionaries against converting to Christianity. They were not to move to new places of settlement without a licence.[38] Although this set of provisions seems draconian, to say the least, and was followed up by a series of more local enactments and reissues during the period up to the expulsion in 1290, it was, significantly, not until 1253 that they were incorporated into the secular law, in a statute of Henry III. Rokeah blames this measure on the king's lack of understanding of Christianity, and the excessive influence on him of his mother, Eleanor of Provence, whose expulsion policy in her particular domain has already been noted.[39]

However, the legislation of Innocent III's successors, and in particular that of Gregory IX, indicate that Henry was the very opposite of being out of touch with current papal thinking.

It is true that only 30 out of nearly 2 000 decretals in Gregory IX's collection concerned Jews, yet, by his support of the orders of Dominican and Franciscan friars, which had been recognized by his predecessors, Innocent III and Honorius III, as well as his effective foundation of the Papal Inquisition in 1230–1233, his reign was to have a considerable effect on Jewish life throughout western Europe.[40] Although his campaign against rabbinical Judaism, in the form of the collection of works known as the Talmud, seems not to have had resonance in England, any more than did the Inquisition, Zefira Rokeah was undoubtedly right to observe that 'unfortunately, there has not yet appeared a serious study of the influence of the Franciscans and Dominicans on the attitude of the English to the Jews'.[41]

Some response to this challenge may be given by means of a discussion of the activity in England of the newly arrived orders of friars in attempting to answer papal concern that Jews should be converted to Christianity, so that, in their adherence to Judaism, they should not attract Christians in the opposite direction. The Third Lateran Council, in 1179, set out the Church's attitude to Jews who sought to become Christians:

> If, under divine inspiration, Jews were to be converted to the Christian faith, no one should dispossess them, since it is fitting that converts to the faith should be in a better position than they enjoyed before conversion. If anyone treats them otherwise, we order princes and local authorities, under pain of excommunication, to ensure restitution of their inheritance, and of their own property.[42]

This policy was supported by the Fourth Lateran Council, and was implemented in England, with increasing effect, as the thirteenth century advanced. The approved method was to set up a 'House of Converts', in which converts from Judaism might both be instructed in the Christian faith, and 'protected' from Jewish attempts to regain them for their ancestral faith. A pioneering institution seems to have been set up in Southwark, in 1213, and another by the Dominicans in Oxford, in 1221, but the most significant foundation proved to be that established by Henry III, in 1233, on part of the Chancery Lane site of the Public Record Office. Despite the official expulsion of Jews from the kingdom in 1290, the London House managed to retain its existence long enough to have Mr Secretary Thomas Cromwell as its warden in 1534.[43]

The provision for converted Jews in houses such as that in Chancery Lane was modelled on 'corrodies', annual payments made by monasteries in kind, for example food, drink, clothing and accommodation.[44] Explicit conversion campaigns were rare under Henry III, though more frequent under his successor, between 1275 and 1290. None the less, the London House of Converts had apparently reached full capacity by the 1250s, so that, for example, in the year of the Hugh of Lincoln case, 1255, about 150 converted Jews were scattered among religious houses of at least seven orders throughout the kingdom, and this practice continued up to 1290.[45] As for the genuineness of the conversions, it is still impossible to make a judgement. Under the rules established by Innocent III, it was difficult to find release from baptism, when it was imposed under pressure: only physical resistance at the time would do. Concern was expressed, in a royal ruling in England in 1236, that the children of mixed-religion couples should have freedom of religious choice, but the impression remains that English legislators of the thirteenth century, whether lay or ecclesiastical, were more preoccupied with possible 'impurities' which might be gained from contact with those who remained Jews, than with the subsequent fate of those who experienced the waters of baptism.[46] It might fairly be suggested that the inclusion of 'converted' Jews in the corrody system, whether in a central 'House of Converts' or in individual religious houses, was simply an extension of the, by then traditional, practice of admitting lay brothers, or *conversi*, to monasteries.[47] The importance of these English precedents was to be amply demonstrated, when much larger numbers of Jews were baptized in Spain, after 1390.

Notes

1. F.A. Lincoln, *The Starra. Their Effect on Early English Law and Administration* (1939), 25.
2. A.M. Hyamson, *A History of the Jews in England*, 2nd edn (1928), vii preface to the first edition, 1908.
3. It is questionable whether Jews actually settled in the Edwardian boroughs of Rhuddlan and Flint (1277), Harlech, Caernarfon, Conwy and Criccieth (1283). Beaumaris and Newborough, in Anglesey, although often mentioned as having Jewish settlers, did not become boroughs until five years after the expulsion. R.R. Davies, *The Age of Conquest: Wales, 1063–1415* (1991), 372. The book was first published, in 1987, as *Conquest, Co-existence and Change: Wales, 1063–1415*.
4. Hyamson, *Jews in England*, 17, and the slightly incomplete and inaccurate map of settlement in P. Fletcher Jones, *The Jews of Britain. A Thousand Years of History* (1990), 70. The map does not include settlements, or residence, in Bridgnorth, Tewkesbury, Royston and Chesterton (apparently that now attached to Cambridge). For Wales, see note 3 above.
5. Hyamson, *Jews in England*, 24. For the equivalent French case, see Gavin I. Langmuir, '*Tanquam servi*: the change in Jewish status in French law

about 1200', in M. Yardeni (ed.), *Les Juifs dans l'histoire de France* (Leiden, 1980), 25–54, reprinted in revised form in G.I. Langmuir, *Toward a Definition of Antisemitism* (Berkeley, Los Angeles and London, 1990), 167–194.

6. K.R. Stow, 'The Jewish family in the Rhineland in the High Middle Ages: form and function', *American Historical Review*, 92 (1987), 1107–9, and 'Sanctity and the construction of space: the Roman ghetto as sacred space', in M. Mor (ed.), *Jewish Assimilation, Acculturation and Accommodation: Past Traditions, Current Issues and Future Prospects, Proceedings of the Second Annual Symposium of the Philip M. and Ethel Klutznick Chair in Jewish Civilization*, Studies in Jewish Civilization, 2 (Lanham, New York and London, 1989), 57–8.

7. J. Edwards, *The Jews in Christian Europe, 1400–1700*, 2nd edn (1991), 83–4; B. Pullan, *Rich and poor in Renaissance Venice. The Social Institutions of a Catholic State, to 1620* (1971), 489.

8. The burden of royal financial demands on English Jews, which increased steadily after the establishment of the specialized 'Exchequer of the Jews' by Richard I in 1194, has been extensively studied and discussed. Older works on the subject include Hyamson, *Jews in England*; C. Roth, *A History of the Jews in England* (1964); H.G. Richardson, *The English Jews under the Angevin Kings* (1960), and, on the exchequer of the Jews in particular, A.C. Cramer, 'The Jewish Exchequer: an inquiry into its fiscal functions', *American Historical Review*, 45 (1940), 327–37; *idem*, 'The origins and functions of the Jewish Exchequer', *Speculum*, 16 (1941), 226–9; C.A.F. Meekings, 'Justices of the Jews, 1218–1268: a provisional list', *Bulletin of the Institute of Historical Research*, 28 (1955), 173-188. A more recent study is R. Mundill, 'Anglo-Jewry under Edward I: credit agents and their clients', *Jewish Historical Studies [Transactions of the Jewish Historical Society of England]*, 31 (1988–90), 1–21.

9. More recent studies of local Jewish communities, and their financial activities, include: C. Roth, *The Jews of Medieval Oxford*, Oxford Historical Society, new series, 9 (1951); V.D. Lipman, *The Jews of Medieval Norwich and the Hebrew Poems of Meir of Norwich* (London, 1967), and 'Jews and castles in medieval England', *Transactions of the Jewish Historical Society of England*, 28 (1981–82), 1–19; R.B. Dobson, *The Jews of Medieval York and the Massacre of March 1190*, Borthwick Papers no. 45 (1974); *idem*, 'The Jews of medieval Cambridge', *Jewish Historical Studies*, 32 (1990–92), 1–24; and, more generally, *idem*, 'The role of Jewish women in medieval England', in *Christianity and Judaism [Studies in Church History, 29]* (1992), 145–68; D. Stephenson, 'Colchester: a small medieval English Jewry', *Essex Archaeology and History*, 16 (1974–75), 48–52; J. Hillaby, 'A magnate among the marchers: Hamo of Hereford, his family and clients, 1218–1253', *Jewish Historical Studies*, 31 (1988–90), 23–82; *idem*, 'The Worcester Jewry, 1158–1290: portrait of a lost community', *Transactions of the Worcestershire Archaeological Society*, 12 (1990), 73–122; *idem*, 'London: the thirteenth-century Jewry revisited', *Jewish Historical Studies*, 32 (1990–92), 89–158.

10. Z.E. Rokeah, 'The Jewish church-robbers and host desecrators of Norwich', *Revue des Etudes Juives*, 141 (1982), 331–62; *idem*, 'Money and the hangman in late thirteenth-century England: Jews, Christians and

coinage offences alleged and real', *Jewish Historical Studies*, **31** (1988–90), 83–109 and **32** (1990–92), 159–218.

11. These events seem to have taken place in Holy Week, and not Easter week, as is misleadingly stated by G.I. Langmuir, in his otherwise excellent discussion and analysis of the case in 'Thomas of Monmouth: detector of ritual murder', *Speculum*, **59** (1984), 822–46, reprinted in *idem*, *Toward a Definition of Antisemitism* (see note 5, above), 209–36.
12. Thomas of Monmouth, *The Life and Miracles of St William of Norwich*, trans. and ed. A. Jessop and M.R. James (1896).
13. Langmuir, 'Thomas of Monmouth', 234; W.W. Hart (ed.), *Historia et cartularium monasterii Sancti Petri Gloucestriae*, Rolls Series, **33** (1863–67), i, 20–21.
14. Jocelin of Brakelond, *Chronicle of the Abbey of Bury St Edmunds*, trans and eds D. Greenway and J. Sayers (1989), 15.
15. For the extraordinary case of Samuel, a Jew of Bristol, see M. Adler, *Jews of Medieval England* (1939), 185–6 (though the story may have been fabricated after the expulsion).
16. R. Chazan, 'The Blois incident of 1171', *Proceedings of the American Academy of Jewish Research*, **36** (1968), 13–31.
17. R. Po-Chia Hsia, *Trent, 1475. A Ritual Murder Trial* (New Haven and London, 1992).
18. F. Fita, 'La verdad sobre el martirio del Santo Niño de La Guardia, o sea el proceso y quema (16 noviembre 1491) del judío Juçe Franco en Avila', *Boletín de la Real Academia de la Historia*, **11** (1887), 7–134; H.C. Lea, 'El Santo Niño de la Guardia', *English Historical Review*, **4** (1889), 229–50; M. Kriegel, 'La prise d'une décision: l'expulsion des Juifs d'Espagne en 1492', *Revue Historique*, **260** (1978), 83–5; J. Edwards, 'Why the Spanish Inquisition?', *Christianity and Judaism* [*Studies in Church History*, 29(1992)], 234–5.
19. Z.E. Rokeah, 'The State, the Church and the Jews in medieval England', in S. Almog (ed.), *Antisemitism through the Ages* (1988), 106–9, 120–22 nn.
20. See the exemplary analysis of the case, and of its use by Chaucer, in Langmuir, 'The knight's tale of young Hugh of Lincoln', *Speculum*, **47** (1972), 459–82, reprinted in Langmuir's *Toward a Definition of Antisemitism*, 237–62.
21. Dobson, *Jews of Medieval York*, 22.
22. J. Jacobs (ed.), *The Jews of Angevin England* (1893).
23. Dobson, *The Jews of Medieval York*. For a selection of contemporary sources, in translation, for the events of 1189–90, see Jacobs, *The Jews of Angevin England*, 99-131.
24. The area subject to the abbey's jurisdiction.
25. Jocelin, *Chronicle*, 41–2.
26. Jacobs, *The Jews of Angevin England*, 112.
27. Hyamson, *Jews in England*, 57; Dobson, 'Jews of medieval Cambridge', 16–17.
28. For a full discussion of the vacillating policies of French monarchs see W.C. Jordan, *The French Monarchy and the Jews: from Philip Augustus to the Last Capetians* (Philadelphia, 1989).
29. For the similar process in late fifteenth-century Spain, see Edwards, 'Why the Spanish Inquisition?', 234.

30. For an outline of the process and its results, see Edwards, *Jews in Christian Europe*, 11–12.
31. Rokeah, 'The State, the Church and the Jews', 116. For other examples of such economic expulsions, see: G.H. Leonard, 'Expulsion of the Jews by Edward I. An essay in explanation of the exodus A.D. 1290', *Transactions of the Royal Historical Society*, new [second] series, 5 (1891), 103–46; B.L. Abrahams, 'The expulsion of the Jews from England in 1290', *Jewish Quarterly Review*, 7 (1895), 75–100, 236–58, 428–58; P. Elman, 'The economic causes of the expulsion of the Jews in 1290', *Economic History Review*, 7 (1937), 145–54; S.A. Singer, 'The expulsion of the Jews from England in 1290', *Jewish Quarterly Review*, 55 (1964), 117–36.
32. For the change is J. Cohen, *The Friars and the Jews: the Evolution of Medieval anti-Judaism* (Ithaca and London, 1982), while against it is R. Chazan, *Dagger of the Faith. Thirteenth-Century Christian Missionizing and Jewish Response* (Berkeley, Los Angeles, London, 1989); see also Edwards, *Jews in Christian Europe*, 1991 edn, esp. 12–18.
33. A selection of such texts (Matthew 27:22–6; John 8:42–5; Romans 11:1–2, 11–24) is included and analysed in J. Edwards, *The Jews in Western Europe, 1400–1600* (1994), 5–8, 27–30.
34. Edwards, *Jews in Christian Europe*, 16.
35. Decretales 5.6.13, in J.A. Watt, 'Jews and Christians in the Gregorian decretals', *Studies in Church History*, 29(1992), 95–105.
36. Decretales 5.6.8, in Watt, 'Jews and Christians', 98.
37. J.A. Watt, 'The English episcopate, the State and the Jews: the evidence of the thirteenth-century conciliar decrees', in P.R Coss and S.D. Lloyd (eds), *Thirteenth-century England*, vol. 2. (1988), 137–47. These sources are in (eds) F.M. Powicke and C.R. Cheney, *Councils and Synods with Other Documents Relating to the English Church*, vol. 2, part 1 (1205–65) and part 2 (1265–1313), (1964).
38. *Councils and Synods*, 1, 473–4 (see note 36); Rokeah, 'The State, the Church and the Jews', 114–15.
39. Rokeah, 'The State, the Church and the Jews', 115.
40. Watt, 'Jews and Christians', 94.
41. Edwards, *Jews in Christian Europe*, 19–20; Rokeah, 'The State, the Church and the Jews', 116.
42. Decretales 5.6.8, in Watt, 'Jews and Christians', 98.
43. Hyamson, *Jews in England*, 107–11; M. Adler, 'The history of the Domus Conversorum', in *Jews of Medieval England* (1939) 279–379; N.C. Vincent, 'Jews, Poitevins and the bishop of Winchester, 1231–1234', *Studies in Church History*, 29(1992), 125 and note.
44. R.N. Swanson, *Church and Society in Late Medieval England* (1989), 236–7; J. Greatrex, 'Monastic charity for Jewish converts: the requisition of corrodies by Henry II', *Studies in Church History*, 29(1992), 133–43.
45. Greatrex, 'Monastic charity', 137.
46. Watt, 'Jews and Christians', 99–100, 143.
47. C.H. Lawrence, *Medieval Monasticism. Forms of Religious Life in Western Europe in the Middle Ages*, 2nd edn (1989), 153–4, 158–9, 178–81; and, for the extension of the practice to the orders of friars, *idem*, *The Friars. The Impact of the Early Mendicant Movement on Western Society* (1994), 45–6.

CHAPTER FOUR

Trade, Towns and the Church: Ecclesiastical Consumers and the Urban Economy of the West Midlands, 1290–1540

Christopher Dyer

The contribution of the Church to the economy of the medieval town is a large and complex problem, involving questions of government, jurisdiction, tenure and even morality, but this chapter is concerned to clarify one aspect: the Church's purchase of the goods and services provided by towns. In enquiring where, and from whom, the clergy acquired foodstuffs, manufactured goods, imported products and craftsmen's services, we can learn about the interaction between landed society and the commercial world.[1] We can explore more fully the function of the towns, the variations between towns according to size and type, and their trading relationship with different sections of society.[2] A study of the part played in trade by the clergy will help to locate them in their own society, and see to what extent they were set apart, or at least differed in economic behaviour, from the laity.

The region, its religious institutions, and its towns

The West Midland region is ideal for this enquiry. Evidence survives in the form of accounts drawn up for a wide range of institutions, from the very wealthy bishopric and priory of Worcester, and the rich Benedictine abbey of Pershore, through the moderately well-endowed monastic houses of the new orders – Bordesley, Merevale and Halesowen, and the collegiate church of Warwick, to the relatively poor priory of Maxstoke and the nunnery at Westwood near Droitwich. In addition there are accounts and other evidence for the spending of parish clergy, churchwardens and fraternities (see Table 4.1). Most of the institutions in our sample were located in or near towns, either because towns had grown up at their gates, often planned or encouraged by the clergy, or because (in the case of the new orders of the twelfth or thirteenth

Table 4.1 Ecclesiastical institutions in the West Midlands with evidence of expenditure

Institution	Type	Annual income in pounds
Tewkesbury Abbey	Benedictine monastery	1 598
Worcester Cathedral Priory	Benedictine monastery	1 290
Worcester bishopric	Bishopric	986
Evesham Abbey	Benedictine monastery	1 183
Pershore Abbey	Benedictine monastery	643
Bordesley Abbey	Cistercian monastery	388
St Mary's Warwick	Collegiate church	334
Halesowen Abbey	Premonstratensian monastery	280
Merevale Abbey	Cistercian monastery	254
Bishop's Cleeve rectory	Rector of parish church	84
Maxstoke Priory	Augustinian house of canons	81
Westwood Priory	Nunnery of the Order of Fontrevault	75
Guild of the Holy Cross, Stratford-upon-Avon	Fraternity	46
Halesowen parish church	Churchwardens	3 12s. 0d.*
Burton Dassett parish church	Churchwardens	2 14s. 8d.†

Notes:
* median calculated for years 1497–1515
† 1529

Sources: for income: all are based on *Valor Ecclesiasticus*, in D.M. Knowles, *Medieval Religious Houses* (1971), except for Bishop's Cleeve rectory: *Valor Ecclesiasticus*, 2, 444; Stratford guild: *VCH Warwicks*, 3, 31–2: churchwardens: F. Somers (ed.), *Halesowen Churchwardens Accounts (1487–1582)*, Worcestershire Historical Society (1952–7); British Lib., Stowe 795, fo. 6.

centuries) an urban site was thought to be appropriate. Only the Cistercians shunned such proximity and did not found new towns. The bulk of the evidence is drawn from the counties of Worcestershire and Warwickshire (see Figure 4.1), though some attention will be paid to accounts from adjoining areas, given that the flow of trade crossed county boundaries.

The urban hierarchy of the West Midlands has been more fully investigated than that of any other English region.[3] Coventry at the beginning

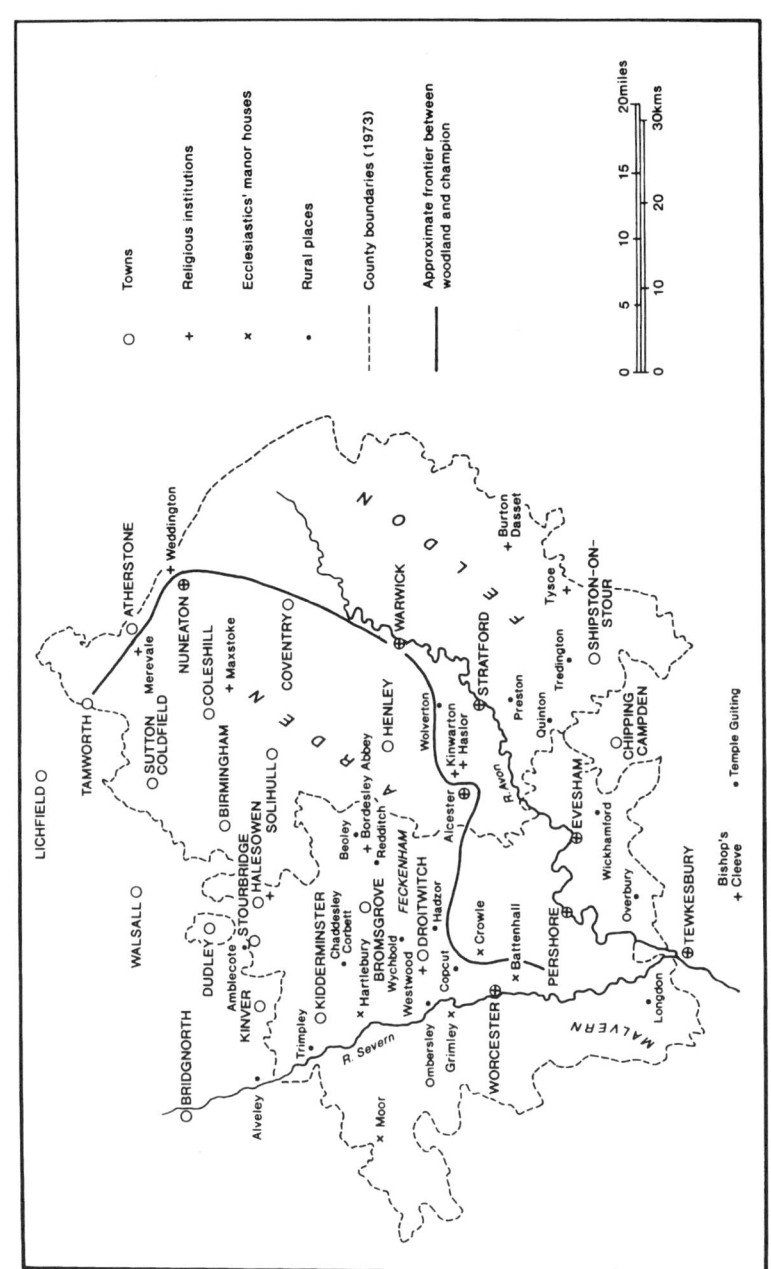

4.1 Places mentioned in the text in Warwickshire and Worcestershire

of our period with a population of perhaps 5 000 was larger and richer than Worcester, with 2 000–3 000 inhabitants, and comparable with Gloucester.[4] During the fourteenth century Coventry rose to become the undoubted capital of the region with a population of 10 000, and retained its primacy in spite of its decline in the later fifteenth and early sixteenth century.[5] Lichfield, the largest town in Staffordshire, came close behind Worcester. Then we can identify a group of towns with populations in the region of a thousand or two, including Birmingham, Droitwich, Evesham, Kidderminster, Pershore, Stratford, Walsall and Warwick. And below them were at least another 20 small market towns in Warwickshire and Worcestershire alone, such as Alcester, Atherstone, Coleshill, Dudley, Halesowen, Nuneaton, Shipston-on-Stour and Solihull.[6] The River Severn provided the single most important communication route through the region, giving easy access to another regional capital, Bristol. But the road system of the region should not be underestimated. The Gough map of *c.*1360 shows the precursor of the modern A38 running north up the Severn valley and turning eastward through Droitwich and Birmingham to Lichfield, and four major roads converging on Coventry.[7] Long-distance routes joining the region with the outside world included the important drove roads from north Wales, and the connections to the east coast ports and south-east to London.[8] The many minor roads included those linking the wooded north and west of the region – the forests of Arden and Feckenham, and Malvern Chase – with the 'champion' areas of the vale of Evesham and the Warwickshire Feldon. The woodlands produced a surplus of animals, cheese, fuel and timber, and tended to contain important rural industries, while the champion villages practised sheep and corn husbandry, with an emphasis on cereal cultivation.[9]

Before turning to the purchases of the region's clergy, we ought to consider their spending power. We are often encouraged to regard monastic economies as self-contained, supplying the needs of the monks, canons or nuns from the resources of the house. Indeed, all of our institutions had their own endowments of manors or tithes, and often gained at least part of their food directly from their estates. The best example of self-sufficiency is that of Maxstoke Priory in 1345–46 (a few years after its foundation as an Augustinian house).[10] All of the grain consumed by the canons, their servants and their visitors came from three manors (in fact appropriated rectories) at Maxstoke itself, nearby Shustoke, and Long Itchington in the south-east of Warwickshire. Just over 383 quarters of wheat, maslin (wheat/rye mixture), peas, beans and malt provided the convent with its bread, pottage and ale. In the same way the priory's larder was filled with cattle, pigs and sheep from the estates. The 1 300 heads of garlic consumed in the household were grown in the prior's garden, and candles were made from the tallow left over from the kitchen. Merevale Abbey in the 1490s employed its own full-time craftsmen, including a cooper and cartwright, and other monasteries engaged in industrial production – Halesowen in 1366 and Tewkesbury 20 years later had their own tanneries, and the monks of Bordesley built and maintained within their precincts a forge and metal-working shop in which some of the operations were powered by a water-mill.[11] Almost every monastic establishment in the two counties invested in ponds for fresh-water fish.[12] Churchmen and wealthy laymen exchanged gifts, of game or fish in many cases, which again reduced their dependence on markets.[13]

But this 'natural' economy should not be overemphasized. Even at Maxstoke the priory laid in stores of preserved fish and spices worth nearly £12, and in many weeks sent out for a few shillings worth of fresh fish, dairy produce and joints of meat. Of course, manufactured goods such as clothing, and work on the monastic buildings, had to be paid for in cash. At the other extreme, the dean and canons of St Mary's Warwick in the fifteenth century had most of their assets (again, appropriated rectories) at farm, and received an income almost entirely in money.[14] The larger monasteries changed their management over time, not always moving away from direct consumption of estate produce to a cash income. Worcester Priory bought most of its grain in the 1290s, but was obtaining a great deal from its manors in 1326. The bishopric of Worcester was supplying the household on a large scale from its manors as late as the 1370s.[15] In the early fifteenth century Coventry Priory arranged for the farmers of its manors to pay rents in kind, reminiscent of the foodfarms of the period before 1200.[16] But in general churchmen were as well integrated into the market economy as their secular counterparts. They obtained a high proportion of their income in rents, and sold much of their demesne produce. After 1400 most of their manorial demesnes were farmed for cash. They expected to buy a high proportion of the food consumed by the convent, and almost all of their manufactured goods and services. Their ventures into industry were designed to make a saleable surplus. Nor were deer parks and fishponds outside the market economy: they cost a great deal of wage labour to maintain. Really impressive gifts needed money too: when in 1444–45 the Prior of Worcester wished to win the 'friendship' of Lady Margaret Beauchamp, he spent £5 on a gold brooch decorated with gems.[17] But our main concern here is not with the clergy as producers and extractors of wealth, but with their role as consumers.

Patterns of consumption

The wealthiest churchmen took their custom outside the region entirely. William More, who was provided with a household quite separate from the Cathedral Priory of Worcester of which he was prior, lived for most of his time in office (1518–35) in his rural manor houses of Battenhall, Crowle, Grimley and Moor (in Lindridge).[18] He made purchases regularly in London. His silverware and sumptuous vestments came from a London goldsmith called John Cranck, and many other items were also provided by Londoners, notably pewter, books (including the works of St Augustine), cloth, linen, carpets, spices, saddles and harness. He even bought two cades (casks) of sprats there. Sometimes visits to the capital on official business were combined with shopping expeditions. More's attendance at the chapter of the Black Monks in 1519 provided the occasion for a £100 spending spree including the purchase of cloth of gold at 66s. 8d. per yard (good woollen cloth could be had for 2s. per yard).[19] Smaller quantities of goods such as spices came occasionally from London to More's household by carrier. The bishops of Worcester also obtained their more expensive purchases in London, where they kept a great house on the Strand. In 1435–36 Thomas Bourgchier, setting himself up in his new episcopal style, went to a London mercer, a tailor, a skinner, a shoemaker and a goldsmith for his 'wardrobe' and plate, at a cost exceeding £100.[20] Although we lack detailed accounts from Evesham Abbey, its chronicle recounts the monastery's acquisition of property in London in the 1360s and, at about the same time, boasts of the purchases of silver plate and elaborate ecclesiastical vestments, no doubt to the benefit of London merchants.[21]

The attraction of London was not just the wide choice of goods being sold by its numerous merchants, or the better price that could be obtained by bulk purchases direct from the importer, or the convenience of magnates who visited the law courts or Parliament regularly, but also that a very large city contained suppliers of specialisms unobtainable in the provinces. Therefore it was not only the wealthy churchmen like Prior More who bought richly embroidered and bejewelled vestments in the capital, like his mitre which cost £50. The modestly endowed Stratford-upon-Avon fraternity, the Guild of the Holy Cross, also sent to London in 1469–70 for embroideries for the vestments of their chapel for which they paid 56s., and in 1455–56 when the Guild's gold and silver cross needed repair, they sent it to a London goldsmith.[22]

Our consumers were also attracted by other large towns outside the two counties. Pershore Abbey bought spices at Oxford, and Bishop Bourgchier acquired wine and the services of a shoemaker and tailor there.[23] Worcester Priory went to Gloucester for cloth (in 1320–21) and (in 1423–24) for 'great wire' for the cathedral clock – Gloucester handled products made from the iron of the Forest of Dean.[24] But it was to Bristol that the wealthier West Midland churchmen most often turned, because the large size of the town and its busy port made it second only to London for some products – and of course it could be reached by boat down the Severn.[25] Sometimes Bristol merchants sold specialized manufactured goods which would be found only in a large centre, such as the great bell ropes bought there by Pershore Abbey in 1388–89.[26] But its main attraction lay in the high-quality wine that it could provide in large quantities. The cellarer of Worcester Priory, the Prior of Worcester, successive bishops of Worcester, and the rector of Bishop's Cleeve, all obtained their wine from Bristol merchants.[27] Bristol was a centre for the trade in preserved fish, such as barrels of salt salmon and herrings, and also for spices, and these were supplied to the larger ecclesiastical consumers.[28]

The West Midlands looked east as well as west for imported goods and fish, and particularly to the Lincolnshire port of Boston. This town was still enjoying great prosperity in the early fourteenth century when the monks of Worcester sent representatives there, in 1320–1, buying livery cloth for £20 6s. 8d., and spices worth £1.[29] A visit in the previous year was specifically said to be for St Botolph's Fair, and no doubt this major commercial occasion attracted the monks, where they could choose high quality products (the cloth that they bought cost about 3s. per yard) from an extensive range, at the prices which provincial merchants paid before selling them on to customers with an appropriate mark-up.[30] There must have been considerable advantages to outweigh the trouble of the 120-mile journey, and the 20s. charge for the carriage of the goods. Later in the century Worcester Priory ceased its visits to Boston, no doubt contributing to the town's decline, though in 1366 Halesowen Abbey was sending to Boston for preserved fish, spices and pewter vessels. In the late 1350s, Maxstoke Priory also bought 'provisions' at Boston for £12 15s. 0½d., but in the fifteenth century it was using another eastern venue for its fish purchases: Stourbridge Fair near Cambridge.[31]

Finally, Lichfield deserves mention as a town which clearly dominated the trade of south Staffordshire, providing fish, dried fruit, mustard and vinegar among other foodstuffs for the household of the Bishop of Coventry and Lichfield in 1461, and extending its commercial pull into north Worcestershire: Halesowen Abbey bought much of its preserved herring at Lichfield Fair in 1366.[32]

Worcester and Coventry were the largest towns within our two counties. The commercial relationship between Worcester Priory and the city at its gates was not as close as we might expect. We have seen that many of the monks' most expensive requirements came from London, Bristol and Boston. Occasionally a Worcester merchant received a sizeable order for such items – wine worth £11 5s. 0d. in 1320–21, or £20 worth of cloth in 1376–77.[33] But for the fortunate merchants involved, Arnald Moran in the first case, John Edde in the second, such windfalls hardly provided the basis of a steady trade. All too often we find small quantities of wine, fish and spices being bought in Worcester to supplement bulk purchases from further afield. An accounting official would explain that the expense was necessary because visitors had to be entertained. When sweet wines (such as Malmsey) were gaining in popularity in the fifteenth century, the Priory would still buy its red and white wines by the pipe and tun (holding 120 and 240 gallons respectively) while buying odd gallons of sweet wine from Worcester suppliers. In the same way, ale worth a shilling or two would be bought in the town when the priory's brew house could not cope with a surge in demand, and in one year the manors did not send enough butter and some had to be purchased.[34] Perhaps Worcester people noticed their inferior position in the commercial hierarchy. Certainly when Prior More at Christmas 1520 gave a party for the bailiffs and 24 councillors of Worcester (vintners among them, no doubt) he bought 10½ gallons of wine in the town, perhaps because his last hogshead from Bristol was running out, or perhaps it seemed tactful to serve his guests with locally bought drink.[35]

We should not minimize Worcester Priory's contribution to the trade of the city. Even the limited purchases for visitors in many years amounted to £5. Although much of its grain came from the countryside, and little was bought in the town's market, the priory might buy it by treaty from a local merchant – 7 quarters in one year, 20 in another (1293–95).[36] Many of the purchases for which no place or person is mentioned in the documents are likely to have come from the nearest supplier. Nor must we forget that a great deal of the money given in wages to the numerous servants, and much of that spent by the other lay people living in or near the monastery, such as corrodians, would have found its way into the local economy. The monastery also attracted visitors – laymen seeking hospitality, officials and advisers, clergy arriving on church business, pilgrims – all potential spenders in the city. Indeed, it is likely that the traders of Worcester gained more from these indirect benefits than from the cellarer and other priory obedientiaries.

Worcester did not depend on the priory – the city attracted trade from a large number of consumers over a large hinterland. No specialisms are apparent. Worcester's quays, of course, handled the barrels and bales sent up from Bristol; if the purchase had been made from a Bristol merchant, only the labour of the workers unloading boats and loading carts contributed to Worcester's economy. But many Worcester merchants also dealt in imports obtained originally from Bristol – salt fish for Halesowen Abbey and for the monks of Pershore, wine and wax also for Pershore, and spices for the Stratford guildsmen.[37] Worcester held an important fair for livestock, where the rector of Bishop's Cleeve bought sheep in 1397.[38] It also had a reputation for saddlery: the Bishop of Hereford purchased a saddle and bridle for 14s. 3d. in 1290 and Bordesley Abbey had a saddle repaired there.[39] It became an important cloth-making centre, supplying the bishop in 1463–64.[40] The records of Westwood Priory give the impression of the city's miscellaneous range of merchandise: it bought poultry, iron, malt and a horse hide – and secured the services of a carpenter at Worcester.[41] The Stratford guild found venison on sale there.[42] Specialist craftsmen operated from Worcester. From a base in a large town of commercial and administrative importance, potential clients would be likely to hear of their skills. One such was Geoffrey Carver, hired by Bishop John Carpenter to work on the wooden desks and fittings of his newly-founded public library in Bristol in 1463–64.[43]

Coventry, larger than Worcester, had a wider range of merchandise and a more extensive trading area to match. It could serve its local monasteries with miscellaneous goods – Maxstoke Priory and Merevale Abbey found grain, livestock, cloth, leather goods, ironmongery and kitchen equipment there.[44] From further afield Halesowen bought saddlery, and Pershore Abbey fresh sea fish from the east coast.[45] Coventry's fame as a cattle market brought buyers from Owston Abbey (in Leicestershire), a distance of 40 miles, and from Peterborough Abbey, more than 60 miles away.[46] It became especially important as a cloth-making centre, which attracted major purchases by the Bishop of Worcester in the 1460s.[47] Coventry craftsmen were also serving a sufficiently large area to provide specialities for ecclesiastical consumers – window glazing at Worcester Priory in 1396–97, gold wire to mend a vestment for St Mary's Warwick in 1454–55, bell-ropes for the parish church of Halesowen in 1505–06 and a cross (of metal) for the Stratford guild chapel.[48]

Many monasteries and church institutions were sited in small towns, which sometimes – Evesham and Pershore for instance – they had founded. In the case of houses belonging to the new orders the small town was not under their lordship and lay a mile or two distant – Atherstone and Merevale Abbey, Coleshill and Maxstoke Priory, and Droitwich and Westwood are all examples. Whatever the precise tenurial or geographical relationship, we might expect to find strong commercial connections. Monasteries certainly resorted to their local market:

both Maxstoke and Merevale are found selling and buying grain, animals and other goods in their neighbouring small towns. Westwood sold firewood, livestock and hay in Droitwich, and in turn bought wheat and malt, and hired sawyers and smiths. But it also made much use of Worcester, Alcester, Evesham and lesser places; Maxstoke Priory went to traders in Coventry, Nuneaton, Solihull, Sutton Coldfield and Walsall; while Merevale Abbey, besides its purchases at Coventry, bought goods at Northampton, Tamworth and Burton-on-Trent.[49] We are made constantly aware of the wide range of small towns visited by our monastic consumers; they were in no way confined to one place. Even the Stratford guild, with burgesses of the town as its officials, while buying much bread, ale, meat and building materials in Stratford, sometimes found apparently better bargains, or perhaps large enough quantities of goods, in Warwick, Shipston, Henley or the surrounding villages.[50]

The distinctions between towns can be regarded often as a function of size – even at the level of the small towns a place of 1 000 inhabitants would offer much more to the discerning consumer than one with a population of only 500. Halesowen Abbey patronized the brewers of its own very small town, but found ironmongery, pigs and veterinary services (for the abbot's sick grey horse) at Walsall.[51] The same advantage of a larger centre is apparent in the early sixteenth century when the Halesowen churchwardens again went out of their own town for a number of services. Birmingham, then having as many as 2 000 people, could support a goldsmith, an organ-maker and a painter capable of executing a 'Doom'. Dudley provided the skills of a glazier, and Stourbridge a locksmith.[52] Evesham, somewhat larger than nearby Pershore, supplied wine to Pershore Abbey, and the Stratford guild found the cooks, minstrels and plumber that they needed in Warwick rather than in their own town, though here the higher status of Warwick as the county town gave it a superiority in service trades.[53]

Some places had developed specialisms because of advantages in their location or resources. Walsall was well known for its lime; Tewkesbury, because it lay on the Severn, was an important centre both for the sale of grain, and the purchase of wine. Perhaps the nuns of Westwood chose to buy wheat at Alcester because that market served as an outlet for the crops of the Vale of Evesham. Though small towns were likely to provide an ordinary selection of commonplace goods and services, occasionally individual craftsmen became known for their work and travelled beyond the normal marketing zone of the centre in which they lived. A glazier from Alcester worked on Prior More's manor house at Moor; a Kinver (Staffs) carpenter made the ceiling of the Bishop of Worcester's Hartlebury Castle in 1467–68; and the churchwardens of

Burton Dassett found a carver from Henley-in-Arden to work on the 'boarding' around their altars.[54] There were a few small towns which attracted customers from a long distance by the fame of their products. This must explain why Bishop Carpenter of Worcester in 1453–54 bought cloth from Frome in Somerset.[55]

No rational explanation can be given for some of the choices made – why did the Stratford guild buy wine in Henley-in-Arden, or what made Birmingham a suitable place for Halesowen Abbey to buy eels? Why was Evesham the best source of fish for the rector of Bishop's Cleeve? We must suppose that in small towns supplies of anything out of the ordinary were both limited and precarious; consumers anxious to obtain perishables like fish might hear of a delivery in the next town while the local retailers were running short. Perhaps, also, traders became known for particular lines or a local product was developed with desirable characteristics. Maxstoke Priory, for example, in 1475–76 went to John Bell of Solihull for two dozen 'broad arrow heads', and a 'certain man' of Sutton (Coldfield) supplied horse bits.[56] Often the choice of an apparently out of the way small town must be attributed to personal contacts which are usually hidden from view. When the rector of Bishop's Cleeve in 1396–97 recruited a mason from Pershore, 12 miles away, he overlooked dozens of craftsmen in nearer Cotswold villages and towns. The importance of individual recommendation becomes clear when we find that the rector's steward, John Vampage, came from Pershore.[57]

In identifying the places and people who supplied the ecclesiastical consumers we cannot confine our attentions to the towns, because so many goods and services came from the countryside. This is easy to explain in the case of raw materials and agricultural produce, because it was often convenient for these to be bought near to the point of production. Building materials were best obtained straight from the quarry, tile-kiln or wood, and grain could be most conveniently supplied by the peasant, farmer or tithe collector. These were not always local transactions: Cotswold stone slates, for example, only came from places with the right combination of geological conditions and local skills and, accordingly, Pershore Abbey, the Bishop of Worcester, and the Stratford guild bought theirs at Temple Guiting.[58] Similarly Westwood Priory, which used mineral coal for boiling the brine in its Droitwich salt works, had to cart the fuel 14 miles from the mines at Pensnett and Amblecote in Staffordshire.[59] The need for coppice woodland with the right amount of growth for firewood, and with access to the Severn for easy transport, had Worcester Priory searching along the full length of the county, from Longdon in the south to Trimpley near Kidderminster in the north. The rector of Bishop's Cleeve had his fuel carried 40 miles down the river from Alveley in Shropshire.⁶⁰ Grain was often bought directly from the producers, and over surprisingly long distances, considering the fact that it was grown in all parts of the region. It seems that Worcester Priory preferred to obtain its wheat in an area where it was really plentiful (and therefore perhaps cheaper), in the Stour valley near Tredington, and in the lower Avon valley at Overbury. Halesowen Abbey also went to the south to buy its wheat, but no further than Chaddesley Corbett and Hadzor, both in the north of Worcestershire, though the grain was perhaps more extensively cultivated there than in the immediate vicinity of the abbey.

The officials of the Holy Cross Guild at Stratford seem to have had some difficulty in obtaining the foodstuffs for their annual feasts. Messengers were sent to scour the countryside for poultry, pigs and sheep. In 1431–32 the expedition lasted four days, and three years later they had to go as far as Beoley to find enough calves.⁶¹ One notes in this search, as in other records of purchases, reflections of the regional differences in land-use and farming systems. Cattle and fuel came from the Arden and the Worcestershire woodlands, while wheat and barley were to be found in most abundance in the south and east of the region.

As in the case of the small towns, we must suspect slight differences in the variety and quality of produce which attracted buyers. Was it the breed, or the rearing of Quinton pigs which brought them to the notice of the Stratford guild officials? Or perhaps we should take into account the activities of village-based traders, like the 'merchant' of Wickhamford who in 1381–82 bought Pershore Abbey's piglets.⁶² Purchasers may have found that rural entrepreneurs had cornered the market, and could offer quantities of produce, saving, in the case of the pigs, the search for many peasants each with one surplus animal. Among craftsmen, too, there were clearly skills and specialisms in the countryside (and perhaps at lower cost), which satisfied the discerning consumers – the smith of Ombersley who worked for Westwood Priory, for example, or the cooks of Preston-on-Stour and Wolverton who helped prepare a Stratford guild feast.⁶³ Board-makers were to be found in two urbanizing places in the north Worcestershire woodlands, Redditch and Stourbridge, in the latter case attracting the custom (in 1396–97) of Worcester Priory.⁶⁴

General implications

Geographical theory tells us that our ecclesiastical consumers were behaving according to a pattern found in many societies and cultures. They travelled the longest distances to the largest cities to buy the most expensive goods, and they bought cheap everyday requirements in nearby small towns and villages. The wealthiest monasteries and bishops were more likely to patronize the merchants of London or Bristol. In this respect there is no marked difference between clerical and lay households in the region. The earls of Warwick or the Duke of York (during a stay at Hanley Castle in south Worcestershire in 1409–10) have many similarities in their spending patterns with our ecclesiastical magnates. Rich knightly households, like those of Sir William Mountford, Lady Katherine Beauchamp of Powicke, and Sir Hugh Mortimer of Martley can all be compared with Halesowen Abbey or Pershore Abbey in the range and variety of their commercial connections.[65] We have seen that Westwood Priory bought grain at Droitwich: this house's income was equivalent to that of the lower range of knights, and in 1221 complaints were made to the justices in eyre that a new toll would deter 'neighbouring knights' from their usual practice of buying food in Droitwich.[66] Clergy and laity were closely connected – some important clerics, like Bishop Bourgchier, came from aristocratic families. The influential gentry met the monks in their councils to dispense legal and financial advice. They mixed socially, for example when monasteries entertained the local gentry to dinner. It is predictable that they should have gone to the same towns and traders.

Ecclesiastics and laymen alike used similar methods of purchasing. They visited fairs a good deal, often to buy in bulk, including both the large-scale international fairs like Boston and Stourbridge, which (in the case of Boston) tended to diminish in importance in the fourteenth and fifteenth centuries, and the local fairs, at Coventry, Worcester, Pershore, Bridgnorth, Lichfield and Chipping Campden.[67] The last was clearly an important occasion for trade in grain, horses, cattle and other goods, and like a number of these local events, continued to attract buyers and sellers throughout our period. Weekly markets seem to have provided our consumers with less of their needs – they were more likely to make contact with individual sellers, and negotiate the bargain directly. This avoided tolls (Westwood Priory paid 4d. to buy nine quarters of wheat at Alcester in 1332–33) but considerations of choice, quality and convenience were more important reasons for preferring such private treaties.[68] The most troublesome tolls in the region were those collected at Copcut and Wychbold on the main road between Worcester and Bromsgrove which cost Worcester Priory 9s. 8d. in 1294–95.[69] These added to the general costs of transport, generally borne by the buyer rather than the seller. Carriage by water had a considerable cost advantage – the transport of each tun of wine brought up the Severn from Bristol to Worcester in the 1320s and 1330s cost about ½d. per mile, including the hauling of the barrels at each end, while a century later a figure of 3½d.–3¾d. per mile per tun can be calculated for the journey from Worcester to Pershore by road.[70] Prior More's small-scale deliveries from London came by a carrier, who apparently took a cart regularly from Worcester to London and back. In 1521 he charged 20d. for bringing 32½ lbs of spices, or 7 per cent of the price of the goods (23s. 4d.).[71] But costs of individual journeys were usually not counted directly, because the buyer had carts and packhorses available, staffed by full-time employees. Worcester Priory had its own boat.

Ecclesiastical consumers differed from their lay counterparts in two important respects. Lay households focused on the family of the lord or lady, while monasteries, though hierarchical, had a more collective character, with many officials participating in the management of the house. Monks or canons were more likely than lay lords to attend a fair in person, or themselves negotiate directly with a seller. The clergy also were tied more closely to one place. Lay magnates wandered to a succession of castles and manor houses over the whole country, and knights often had more than one residence. Bishops had a style of life like that of earls (though most of their manors were at least confined within their diocese), but monasteries and collegiate churches were fixed, and their manors often lay within a relatively small radius of about 15 miles. Finally, of course, until the Reformation the clerical institutions enjoyed a continuity unknown among the laity, whose lines of succession were constantly broken or diverted by the vagaries of inheritance and marriage.

The peculiar characteristics of churchmen might be expected to have influenced their behaviour as consumers. The proximity of the estates ought to have encouraged self-sufficiency and prolonged the direct transfer of foodstuffs from the manors, and to a limited extent this did happen: the example of Maxstoke Priory has already been quoted (p. 58–9 above). In the case of purchasing, the stability of the religious household might have created a close relationship between customers and merchants, to the point where the monastery regularly dealt with the same supplier, building a degree of mutual dependence. It is often assumed, for example, that a monastic town, such as Evesham or Pershore, was peculiarly tied to its abbey, and went through a crisis in the 1540s after the dissolution of its protector and best customer.

Some churchmen did make frequent use of a single source of supply. For example, Prior More spent much money with a London goldsmith, John Cranck, and was able to make regular small-scale purchases from London through Hugh 'Carrier'. The obvious danger of too much reliance on a single supplier was that the merchant would take advantage. St Mary's at Warwick seems to have developed in the mid-fifteenth century an unhealthy loyalty to a group of Warwick traders – among others, John Martin, Richard Iremonger and John, Richard and Agnes Chapman, the last three no doubt all members of the same family.[72] The dean and canons may not have benefited – on one occasion, in 1432–33, when they bought wax at Coventry, some of it cost 5½d per pound, whereas in the same year Richard Chapman of Warwick charged 6d.[73] Sometimes the choice of supplier can be shown to have been the result of favouritism. Prior More bought wine year after year from Robert Pers of Bristol. Pers clearly regarded him as a valued customer, and in 1521 Robert's wife sent some wine as a gift.[74] The reason for this unusual courtesy becomes clear enough when we find that More's family name was Pers, that Robert was his brother, and the free wine was therefore at least partly a gift from his sister-in-law. Our worst suspicions about the nature of the relationship are confirmed by an incident in 1525, when More abused his official position as surveyor of the estates of the bishopric of Worcester to grant Robert Pers a valuable holding of land on the outskirts of Bristol, provoking a riot among the tenants.[75]

Another characteristic of the clergy may have been their tendency to buy from each other. The rector of Tredington sold grain to Worcester Priory, and the vicar of St Andrew's Pershore supplied wax to Pershore Abbey, for example.[76] But such deals could still have been conducted in a businesslike manner, without disadvantage to the buyer. A proportion of those with goods to sell were bound to be clerics, especially those with surpluses of tithes.

Despite the apparent examples of favouritism and excessive dependence given above, it would be wrong to regard sales to the Church as being generally corrupt or channelled narrowly through a few privileged merchants. The accounts of monastic officials, bishop's household stewards, or others in charge of expenditure were subject to auditing, and consistent overcharging would presumably have been noticed. As we have noted already, there was a marked lack of continuity in purchasing, with the places chosen changing constantly, and in unpredictable ways. St Mary's Warwick was quite exceptional in the degree to which that church's officials bought in their own town. Every other consumer we have studied spread its custom over many places and traders. There is in consequence very little evidence that urban economies were devastated by the removal of the monastery – the population of Evesham, for example, probably increased, and certainly showed no decline after the Reformation.[77]

If urban economies, even those of the 'monastic' towns, were not bound up exclusively with ecclesiastical consumers, we must conclude that towns had the general function of serving a cross-section of society; the churchmen joined with the secular lords and the mass of peasants, artisans and wage-earners to contribute to the trade of towns. The part played by the peasants in the market economy, especially of the smaller towns, has not received sufficient recognition. Though they had limited resources as individuals, cumulatively they wielded considerable spending power. Their surpluses had to be converted into cash for rent and tax payments, and they consumed a good deal of the foodstuffs sold in towns, and textiles, leather goods and ironmongery.

Just as the peasantry tend to be underestimated in the conventional picture of the urban market, so we are in danger of omitting from this survey the bulk of the clergy, that is the rectors, vicars, chaplains and clerks, most of them with modest incomes of well below £20 per annum, who have left us no financial accounts. We can discover them indirectly in the records of the borough courts, where they appear pleading against other clergy, or more often laymen, or being impleaded for debts, trespasses or the detention of chattels. We are rarely given details of the debts, which might have been incurred for the sale of goods or services, but may have arisen from failure to repay loans, wages or rents. Pleas involving clergy account for less than one in fifty of those heard in the courts, but that does not accurately reflect their importance in the urban economy, because we cannot be sure that every clergyman appearing would be identified in the records as *capellanus* or by some other clerical title. A full range of local clergy made their way through the borough courts – successive abbots of Alcester in that town's courts; the prioress of Nuneaton at Nuneaton; and the abbot and individual monks of Merevale at Atherstone.[78] Rectors and vicars of nearby parishes clearly had dealings with their local market centres – the rector of Tysoe at Stratford, the vicar of Weddington at Nuneaton, and the rectors of Haselor and Kinwarton at Alcester. The many chaplains named are likely to have included those belonging to the urban community itself, either where the town was served by a chapel rather than a church, or because the parish church or churches were supplemented by guild and chantry chapels. The sums of money involved in the pleas were in the same order of size as those in most small town transactions – rarely more than a few shillings. A detailed case at Shipston-on-Stour in 1374 shows a clergyman involved in a typical sale – John Doshelme, chaplain, bought an ox from Richard Hobben for 11s. 0d., but did not receive the beast, because Richard claimed that it had been agreed that he could keep it until Whitsun.[79] The lesser clergy, as cultivators of glebes (or of land held in their own right), and as sellers of tithe, as well as consumers, were clearly drawn into the normal routines and the everyday frictions of the economy.

We can conclude that the institutions of the Church and the individual clergy were fully integrated into medieval commercial life. A study of their purchasing behaviour reinforces the belief that a strong correspondence existed between the urban hierarchy and the status and wealth of the consumers. It also shows that the clergy, like their lay equivalents, were discriminating and sophisticated purchasers, travelling long distances and visiting small places to obtain the best advantage in terms of quality and price. They were also fallible human beings, capable of apparently idiosyncratic choices based on personal preference. The range of facilities offered by towns diminished at the lower levels of the urban hierarchy, though even small towns could provide some surprising specialities. Towns did not monopolize commercial life, and many sales were negotiated in the countryside. The clergy did sometimes arrange their purchases in ways appropriate to their style of life, but this did not include a close domination of the trading activity of the towns in which they were sited, and in general did not differ greatly in their consumption habits from laymen with equivalent incomes. Towns served the whole of society, of which the clergy formed a significant section.

Acknowledgements

I am grateful to Dr R. Holt, Dr J. Greatrex and Dr A. Watkins for help in collecting information for this essay. The last has allowed me to use his unpublished thesis. Dr Holt gave helpful criticisms. Mr R. Stratton and Dr B. Benedikz gave me access to documents from Worcester Cathedal Library.

Notes

1. These issues have been examined also in C. Dyer, 'The consumer and the market in the later middle ages', *Economic History Review*, 2nd series, **42** (1989), 305–27.
2. These theoretical problems of urban functions and hierarchies are surveyed in P. Bairoch, *Cities and Economic Development: from the Dawn of History to the Present* (1988), 142–52.
3. R.H. Hilton, *A Medieval Society*, 2nd edn (1983), 168–207; C. Phythian-Adams, *Desolation of a City. Coventry and the Urban Crisis of the Late Middle Ages* (1974), 7–30; T.R. Slater, 'The urban hierarchy in medieval Staffordshire', *Journal of Historical Geography*, **11** (1985), 115–37; C. Dyer, 'The hidden trade of the middle ages: evidence from the West Midlands of England', *Journal of Historical Geography*, **18** (1992), 141–57.
4. P.R. Coss (ed.), *The Early Records of Medieval Coventry*, British Academy Records of Economic and Social History, new series, **11** (1986), xlii;

C.M. Barron, 'The fourteenth century poll tax returns for Worcester', *Midland History*, 14 (1989), 7; R. Holt, 'Gloucester in the century after the Black Death', *Transactions of the Bristol and Gloucestershire Archaeological Society*, 103 (1985), 149.
5. Phythian-Adams, *Desolation of a City*, 34–9.
6. R.H. Hilton, *The English Peasantry in the Later Middle Ages* (1975), 76–94; idem, 'The small town and urbanisation – Evesham in the Middle Ages', *Midland History*, 7 (1982), 1–8; idem, 'Lords, burgesses and huxters', *Past and Present*, 97 (1982), 3–15; idem, 'Small town society in England before the Black Death', *Past and Present*, 105 (1984), 53–78; idem, 'Medieval market towns and simple commodity production', *Past and Present*, 109 (1985), 3–23; R. Holt, *The Early History of the Town of Birmingham*, Dugdale Society Occasional Paper, 30 (1984); A. Watkins, 'Society and economy in the northern part of the Forest of Arden, Warwickshire, 1350–1540', PhD thesis, University of Birmingham (1989), 301–24; idem, 'The development of Coleshill in the Middle Ages', *Warwickshire History*, 5 (1983–4), 167–84; C. Dyer, 'Small town conflict in the later Middle Ages: implications of events at Shipston-on-Stour', *Urban History*, 19 (1992), 1–28.
7. E.J.S. Parsons (ed.), *The Map of Great Britain circa A.D.1360 known as the Gough Map* (1958), 18.
8. B.P. Hindle, 'Roads and tracks', in L. Cantor (ed.) *The English Medieval Landscape* (1982), 193–217.
9. J.B. Harley, 'The settlement geography of early medieval Warwickshire', *Transactions of the Institute of British Geographers*, 34 (1964), 115–30; C. Dyer, *Warwickshire Farming 1349–c.1520*, Dugdale Society Occasional Paper, 27 (1981); A.D. Dyer, *The City of Worcester in the Sixteenth Century* (1973), 67–73.
10. PRO, SC6/1258/7.
11. PRO, E315/283; Society of Antiquaries Library, MS.535; T. Wakeman, 'On the Kichener's roll of Tewkesbury Abbey', *Journal of the British Archaeological Association*, 15 (1859), 321; G. Astill, 'Monastic research designs: Bordesley and the Arrow Valley', in R. Gilchrist and H. Mytum (eds), *The Archaeology of Rural Monasteries*, British Archaeological Reports, British Series, 203 (1989), 285–7.
12. M. Aston and C.J. Bond, 'Warwickshire fishponds', and 'Worcestershire fishponds', in M. Aston (ed.), *Medieval Fish, Fisheries and Fishponds in England*, British Archaeological Reports, British Series, 182 (1988), pt. ii, 417–55.
13. For example, Lady Katharine Beauchamp staying mostly at Alcester in 1421–22 received numerous gifts of game, fish, spices and fruit from neighbours, including the abbot of Evesham, who sent fresh salmon: Hereford and Worcester County Record Office (henceforth, HWCRO), ref. 705:99 BA 5540/2.
14. D.M. Styles (ed.), *Ministers' Accounts of the Collegiate Church of St Mary, Warwick*, Dugdale Society, 26 (1969).
15. J.M Wilson and C. Gordon (eds), *Early Compotus Rolls of the Priory of Worcester*, Worcestershire Historical Society (1908), 22, 31; S.G. Hamilton (ed.), *Compotus Rolls of the Priory of Worcester*, Worcestershire Historical Society (1910), 69–74.
16. PRO, E 164/21 (Coventry Priory cartulary with surveys of manors, 1411).

17. Worcester Cathedral Library (henceforth, WCL), C396.
18. E.S. Fegan (ed.), *Journal of Prior William More*, Worcestershire Historical Society (1914).
19. Fegan, *Journal*, 101–4.
20. HWCRO, ref. 009:1, BA 2636/175.
21. W.D. Macray (ed.), *Chronicon Abbatiae de Evesham*, Rolls Series (1863), 301–2.
22. [W.J. Hardy (ed.)], *Stratford-on-Avon Corporation Records, the Guild Accounts* (n.d.), 34, 43.
23. F.B. Andrews, 'The compotus rolls of the monastery of Pershore', *Transactions of the Birmingham Archaeological Society*, 57 (1933), 36; HWCRO, ref. 009:1, BA 2636/175 (Bourgchier may have bought goods in Oxford because his position as Chancellor of the University led him to visit the town).
24. WCL, C55, C425.
25. E.M. Carus-Wilson, 'The overseas trade of Bristol in the fifteenth century', in E.M. Carus-Wilson, *Medieval Merchant Venturers*, 2nd edn, (1967), 1–97.
26. Andrews, 'The compotus rolls', 58.
27. WCL, C55, C57, C59; Fegan, *Journal*, 75, 78, 123, 130, 149; HWCRO, ref. 009:1, BA 2636/166, 168, 174; Corpus Christi College, Oxford (henceforth, CCC), B14/2/3/6.
28. HWCRO, ref. 009:1, BA 2636/175; Wakeman, 'On the Kichener's roll', 322; PRO, SC6/1074/1; Society of Antiquaries Library, MS. 535.
29. WCL, C55.
30. WCL, C693; E.W. Moore, *The Fairs of Medieval England: an Introductory Study* (Toronto, 1985), 85–6.
31. Society of Antiquaries Library, MS. 535; PRO, SC6 1040/9; Shakespeare's Birthplace Trust Record Office (henceforth, SBT), DR 37/114; Bodleian Library, Oxford, Trinity College MS. 84, fo. lx.
32. Staffordshire County Record Office, D 1734/3/3/264; Society of Antiquaries Library, MS. 535.
33. WCL, C55; Hamilton, *Compotus Rolls*, 15.
34. Wilson and Gordon, *Early Compotus Rolls*, 37 (the year was 1313–14).
35. Fegan, *Journal*, 145.
36. Wilson and Gordon, *Early Compotus Rolls*, 22, 31.
37 Society of Antiquaries Library MS. 535; Andrews, 'The compotus rolls', 77, 80; PRO, SC6/1074/1, 1072/26; [Hardy], *Guild Accounts*, 16
38. CCC, B/14/2/3/6
39. J. Webb (ed.), *A Roll of the Household Expenses of Richard de Swinfield, Bishop of Hereford*, Camden Society, 59 (1854), 182; HWCRO, ref. b 705:128, BA 1188 (cellarer's account dated to the reign of Edward III).
40. HWCRO, ref. 009:1, BA 2636/175.
41. Birmingham Reference Library (henceforth BRL), Hampton 311, 312, 315, 317 (accounts dating from the period 1379–c.1390).
42. [Hardy], *Guild Accounts*, 20.
43. HWCRO, ref. 009:1, BA 2636/175.
44. Watkins, 'Society and economy', 390; Bodleian Library, Oxford, Trinity College MS. 84.
45. Society of Antiquaries MS. 535; Andrews, 'The compotus rolls', 36.
46. R.H. Hilton, *The Economic Development of some Leicestershire Estates*

in the 14th and 15th Centuries (1947), 137: J. Greatrex (ed.), *Account Rolls of the Obedientaries of Peterborough*, Northamptonshire Record Society, 33 (1984), 181, 195.
47. HWCRO, ref. 009:1, BA 2636/174, 175.
48. WCL, C479; Styles (ed.), *Ministers' Accounts*, 55; F. Somers (ed.), *Halesowen Churchwardens' Accounts (1487–1582)*, Worcestershire Historical Society (1952–57), 26; [Hardy], *Guild Accounts*, 26.
49. Watkins, 'Society and economy', 378, 381; SBT, D37/114; Bodleian Library, Oxford, Trinity College MS. 84; A. Watkins, 'Merevale Abbey in the late 1490s', *Warwickshire History*, 9 (1994), 99–100; PRO, E315/283; HWCRO, ref.705:349, BA 3875/10, ix; B.R.L., Hampton 311–17.
50. [Hardy], *Guild Accounts*, 21, 23, 24, 27, 30.
51. Society of Antiquaries Library MS. 535; T.R. Nash, *Collections for the History of Worcestershire* (1782), II, appendix, xxxiii–xxxiv.
52. Somers, *Halesowen Churchwardens' Accounts*, 23, 29, 33.
53. Andrews, 'The compotus rolls', 86; [Hardy], *Guild Accounts*, 16, 30, 42.
54. Fegan, *Journal*, 139; HWCRO, ref. 009:1, BA 2636/176; British Library, Stowe 795, fo. 6r.
55. HWCRO, ref. 009:1, BA 2636/168.
56. SBT, D37/114.
57. CCC, B/14/2/3/6; C. Dyer, *Lords and Peasants in a Changing Society* (1980), 384.
58. Andrews, 'The compotus rolls', 33; HWCRO, ref. 009:1, BA 2636/158; [Hardy], *Guild Accounts*, 35.
59. BRL, Hampton 311, 314.
60. CCC, B/14/2/3/6.
61. [Hardy], *Guild Accounts*, 23.
62. Andrews, 'The compotus rolls', 32.
63. BRL, Hampton 313, 314; [Hardy], *Guild Accounts*, 37.
64. BRL, Hampton 313; WCL, C479. The rector of Bishop's Cleeve bought boards in Bristol: CCC, B/14/2/3/6.
65. Longleat MS 96779; Northamptonshire Record Office, Westmorland (Apethorpe), 4xx4; SBT, DR 37/73; HWCRO, ref. 705:135, BA 2566 no. iv.
66. D.M. Stenton (ed.), *Rolls of the Justices in Eyre for Lincolnshire, 1218–19 and Worcestershire 1221*, Selden Society, 53 (1934), 565.
67. On the persistence of local fairs, D.L. Farmer, 'Marketing the produce of the countryside', in E. Miller (ed.), *The Agrarian History of England and Wales*, vol. 3 (1971), 339–47.
68. HWCRO, ref. 705:349, BA 3835/10 (ix).
69. WCL, C54.
70. WCL, C55, C57; Andrews, 'The compotus rolls', 80, 84. The price of transport rose after the Black Death because of rising labour costs but these figures still imply a considerable differential between water and road transport, much more than that proposed in J. Masschaele, 'Transport costs in medieval England', *Economic History Review*, 46 (1993), 266–79
71. Fegan, *Journal*, 134.
72. Styles, *Ministers' Accounts*, 25–8, 49–51.
73. Ibid., 8.
74. Fegan, *Journal*, 130.

75. Dyer, *Lords and Peasants*, 161; R.A. Houlbrooke, 'Women's social life and common action in England from the fifteenth century to the eve of the Civil War', *Continuity and Change*, 1 (1986), 178.
76. Wilson and Gordon, *Early Compotus Rolls*, 40; Andrews, 'The compotus rolls', 70.
77. Hilton, 'The small town and urbanisation', 4; Phythian-Adams, *Desolation of a City*, 8; suggest a population of between 800 and 1,200 in 1524 (121 taxpayers) and 1 200–1 400 in 1563 (311 families). Pershore had 78 taxpayers in 1524 and 216 families in 1563.
78. These generalizations are based on the borough court records of Alcester: Warwickshire County Record Office, CR 1886/141–66; Bromsgrove: A.F.C. Baber (ed.), *The Court Rolls of the Manor of Bromsgrove and King's Norton*, Worcestershire Historical Society (1963), 42–62; Shipston-on-Stour: WCL, E1–E91; Stratford-upon-Avon: SBT, DR 75/4,7,8. Also comments on this aspect of the Atherstone and Nuneaton borough court rolls, kindly communicated to me by Dr A. Watkins.
79. WCL, E25.

CHAPTER FIVE

The Origin and Early Development of the London Mendicant Houses

Jens Röhrkasten

Almost from their very beginning the mendicant orders focused on the towns as centres for their activities. The connection between friars and urban life arose as a consequence of the tasks the mendicants set themselves: to work and preach among the population, and to give an example through their attempt to live the apostolic life. This could best be done in an urban environment where it was not only possible to approach a large number of people but, as the Dominican prior general Humbert of Romans put it: ibi sunt plura peccata [here, there are more sins].[1] The orders' economic restrictions, resulting from their observance of collective poverty, equally required them to hold close contacts with the urban population, on whose support they had to rely to a large extent. Modern historians have come to regard the connections between friars and towns as so close that the study of a region's urban development has been attempted by locating mendicant convents.[2] In order to explore the mendicants' role in urban life and development in a more systematic way, a number of questions have been raised, concerning their social and religious influence and also aspects of their foundation and early history: who initiated the foundation of the houses? Who gave support and what forms did this support take? How did the convents' location relate to the towns' topography?[3]

The most serious obstacle in the pursuit of these questions is the fact that in many towns the individual convents can be traced for the first time only decades after their foundation, whereas the study of the early years is essential to the understanding of the friars' success. The London friaries are an exception to this pattern, and thus a promising subject for such a study, despite the almost total loss of the English mendicant archives. Not only is it possible to rely on frequent references to London in the account of the Franciscan Thomas's 'De adventu fratrum minorum in Anglia', there is also material among the records of the exchequer and the chancery relating to the early history of the London convents. Even though it may not be possible to provide conclusive answers to the whole range of questions on the list, the application of these methods in the case of London should at least be attempted.

In the thirteenth century London was one of the cities with the largest number of friaries in Europe (see Figure 5.1). The Dominicans and Franciscans came in the 1220s and from the middle of the century onwards, the members of six other mendicant orders arrived, each group settling in its own convent. In this chapter I intend to analyse the process of integration of these orders in the city, a development which began with their arrival and ended when they had become part of the ecclesiastical establishment towards the end of the thirteenth century.

The Dominicans who landed at Dover in August 1221 were the first mendicants to come to England.[4] The group passed through London on their way to Oxford where they built their first house in England. The Dominican convent in London was established at some time between 1222 and August 1224.[5] The exact date cannot be established but it must have been prior to September 1224 because in this month they provided shelter for four Franciscans who had just arrived in London, members of the first group of the Friars Minor in England. After two weeks the Greyfriars formed an independent community in a house in Cornhill. In the following year they moved to the site of their future convent, still during their founder's lifetime.

Dominicans and Franciscans had been living in London for more than 20 years when they were joined by the Carmelites. There is hardly any information on the early history of the London Whitefriars and it is not even possible to establish the exact date of their arrival. According to Stow, who based his account on the order's own historiography, the London Carmelite convent was founded in 1241,[6] after Richard of Cornwall's return from the crusade, the patron being Sir Richard de Grey, one of the knights who had accompanied him.[7] The year 1253 has been suggested as an alternative date.[8] More recent research has shown the Carmelite historical tradition to be a fabrication of a later date, the only contemporary source being a brief remark by Thomas of Eccleston. Following his custom of avoiding dates, the Franciscan chronicler does indeed say that the first Carmelites were brought to England by Sir Richard de Grey[9] but this cannot have been before January 1242, the date of the crusaders' return. At this time a settlement in an urban environment would have been unthinkable because the order was still firmly fixed in its eremitical tradition and this is reflected in the location of their first houses which were at Hulne in Northumberland and at Aylesford in Kent. Only profound changes in their rule, authorized by Pope Innocent IV in September 1247, in the wake of their general chapter at Aylesford, opened the way into the towns.[10] The London convent was the first foundation after these changes and it is likely that it took its origin in that year.[11]

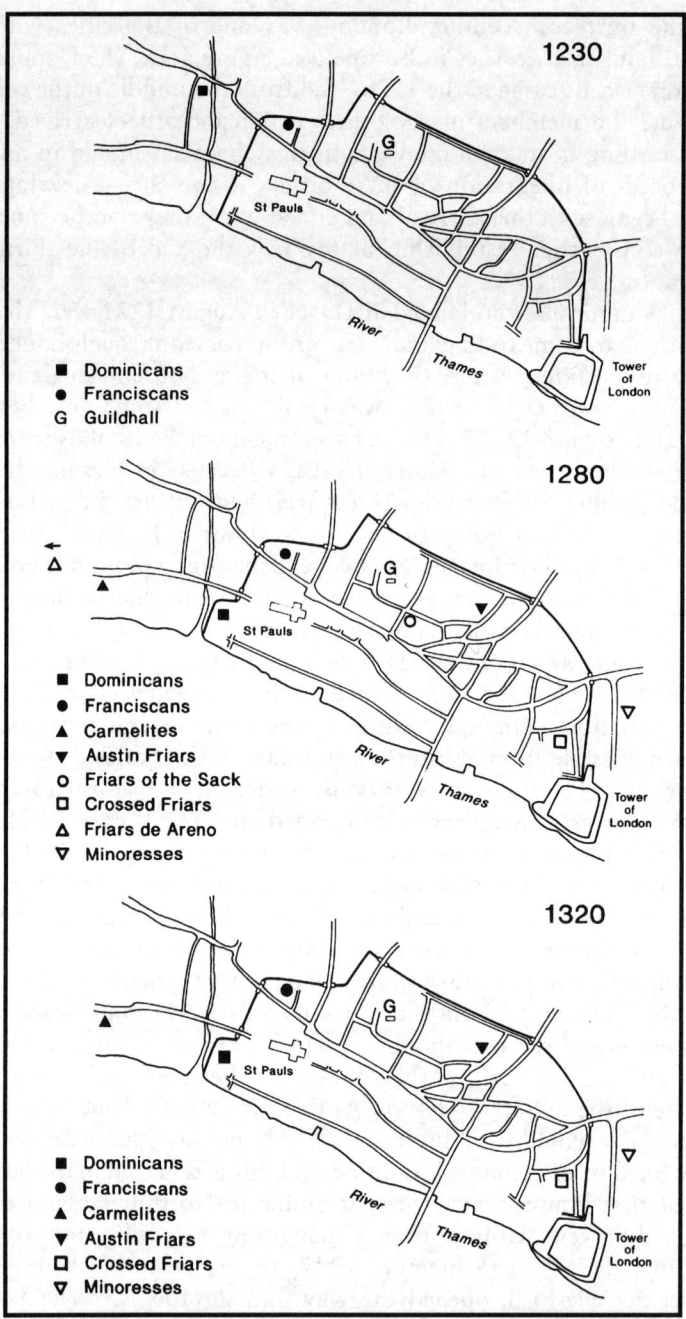

5.1 Location of mendicant houses in London, 1230–1320

The house of the Hermits of St Augustine, according to Stow, was established six years later, in 1253, three years before the 'magna unio Augustiniana' which created the order of Austin Friars.[12] This date has been accepted because Augustinian hermits had been in England since 1249, when they were welcomed by Henry III and taken under his protection.[13] They most likely belonged to the Friars Hermits of the Order of St Augustine of Tuscany, a congregation which itself had only been formed a few years earlier, in 1244, when hitherto independent groups of hermits in Tuscany had been brought under a common organization. This was the future order's most active group and its expansion can be traced also to other parts of Europe.[14] By 1277 the construction of their London convent was well under way (see Figure 5.1).[15]

Members of yet another mendicant order arrived in London in 1257, new friars who had not been seen before, as Matthew Paris reports.[16] The Fratres de Poenitentia Jesu Christi, or Friars of the Sack, as they came to be popularly known because their habits were made from coarse material, enjoyed royal support from the beginning. Henry III granted them 100 marks for the purchase of a site in London.[17] This new order had been created in 1248 by a citizen of Hyères in Provence, Raimund Attanulfi, whose hopes to join the Franciscans had remained unfulfilled. At the time of its official confirmation, by Pope Innocent IV in 1251, 12 houses had already been founded in Provence and Languedoc.[18] In the following decade it experienced a vigorous expansion so that representatives from the provinces of Provence, Spain, France and England convened for the general chapter at Paris in 1258. The order was still expanding when it was suppressed at the Second Council of Lyon.

This fate was shared by a smaller and lesser known order the Fratres B. Mariae Matris Christi, which had originated in the south of France shortly before 1257, when they received papal approval.[19] Members of the order can be traced in England in 1267, when Henry III gave them authority to found a convent.[20] Their house near London was founded in this year or shortly afterwards.

The Friars of the Holy Cross (Ordo S. Crucis) present an even more difficult case because there were a number of different groups under similar names whose origins are obscured by their own historiographical tradition.[21] Mendicant friars of the cross, to be distinguished from the 'Crossed Friars' of a hospital in Colchester, came to England in 1244, making their first appearance at a synod of the Bishop of Rochester.[22] Members of another order 'fratres de ordine Crucis' seem to have come forward shortly afterwards, obtaining royal protection in October 1249.[23] They may have belonged to the friars who in the previous year had been approved by the Bishop of Liège in whose diocese they had a convent at Clairlieu. This official recognition, based on a papal command, gave the friars the rule of St Augustine and institutions modelled on those of the Dominicans.[24] This may well be the first reference to the 'Crutched Friars' in England but their initial attempts to find support were unsuccessful, the Franciscans also reacted in a hostile manner and nothing more is heard of them until 1265, when they were granted royal protection again.[25] According to Stow, their London convent was founded in 1298, but already in 1269 Henry III had given financial support for the construction of an oratory which was still being built in 1273 (see Fig. 5.1).[26]

The Clarisses were the last order of mendicants to arrive but the foundation of their London monastery occurred before 1293, the date of origin commonly accepted.[27] Already on 9 October 1281, Pope Martin IV had granted indulgences to those who on certain days visited the convent, which is described as being 'extra muros'.[28] Therefore the activities of Edmund of Lancaster and his wife Blanche of Castile who brought nuns from France in 1293 have to be regarded as a second foundation. Whereas nothing is known of the earlier convent, the later Minoresses followed a rule originally intended for the monastery of Longchamp near Paris which had been drawn up at the request of Isabella, sister of King Louis IX of France and foundress of Longchamp. According to this rule the possession of property was not prohibited.[29] Thus their economic basis was very different from that of the city's other mendicant houses.

According to this survey the London friaries had been founded over a period of about 70 years. Consequently they were all at different stages of completion in the thirteenth century, just as the orders themselves were in different phases of their development during that time. This needs to be kept in mind when the following three points are discussed:

1. What impact did the friars have on London in the thirteenth century?
2. How was the friars' success in London achieved?
3. How important was London for the mendicants?

As the realm's most important centre of population and commerce, its spheres of influence even extending beyond the Channel, medieval London was a metropolis without rival in the country.[30] The exchequer and royal justices in regular session had been based in Westminster since at least 1156 and 1178 respectively. The city had the most important mint, and the chancery, though still mobile, was beginning to have repositories there.[31] London was also an important religious centre, seat of a bishopric with a large number of religious houses in its vicinity or within the walls.

On a city of these dimensions the arrival of small groups of friars had no impact at all, whatever the Londoners' first response to this new form of spiritual life may have been. The first Dominicans stayed only for some days and the first Franciscans were few in number.[32] The Greyfriars' first independent habitation was a house in Cornhill which had to be adapted to the religious community's purposes by very primitive means.[33] But while the Franciscans were spending the winter of 1224–25 in temporary accommodation, the process which was to bring noticeable alterations to London's topography had already begun: the Dominicans had obtained a house of their own, situated outside the city walls in the parish of St Andrew Holborn, to the west of the Fleet river and south of Holborn Bridge.[34] A few years later adjacent land was acquired to enlarge the convent, marking the beginning of a long process of extension, described in detail by Hinnebusch.[35] The provision of timber for the construction of conventual buildings and a church in 1235 and 1237 indicates that building had already made important progress by then.[36] The gradual acquisition of further land coincided with the construction of a monastery with a church, additional buildings, and its own water supply. The work took a long time, suggesting that it was not continuous and not always under the Dominicans' own control, depending on the arbitrary provision of funds and building materials. The water-pipes were laid between 1259 and 1260 and in a subsequent phase, in 1262–63, the dormitory was built.[37] The convent was probably not quite finished when the friars moved to another site between 1275 and 1286.

The Franciscans on the other hand were to remain at the place procured for their use in 1225 until the Dissolution. There were already a number of houses on the plot of land they took over in the parish of St Nicholas Shambles just inside the walls, situated to the north-east of Newgate. The precise location of this first property which was to be the nucleus of their monastery is not known[38] but it might well have been opposite the parish church of St Nicholas in Stinking Lane. Within a few years adjacent plots were acquired to enlarge the site and the same process of gradual extension of the precinct, lasting into the first years of the fourteenth century and largely coinciding with the construction of the conventual buildings, can also be observed in this case. Building was well under way in 1229,[39] and about ten years later a chapel was being built and other edifices, including an infirmary, were erected.[40] A water supply, possibly the model for that of the Dominicans, was added in 1256, and from 1269 new building activity, including a larger church, a chapter house, dormitory and refectory can be traced.[41] Eventually the precinct, which also included a garden, extended as far north as the town wall.⁴²

London's first two mendicant houses were located in the western part of the city or in the suburbs just outside. As yet there is no detailed study of the area's social composition at that time but there are indications that in the case of both friaries artisans were strongly represented in the neighbourhood. Tanning was one of the main occupations along the Fleet river but crafts of the building trade were also represented. A number of apparently local witnesses of charters for the Dominicans had the surname 'carpentarius'; far more numerous were the tilers.⁴³ According to this evidence the Dominicans' neighbours were largely artisans, some of them owning messuages which were eventually added to the precinct. Richard, servant of the Fleet prison, also appeared in one of the witness lists.⁴⁴ The proximity of the Abbot of Cirencester's inn to the south, and the Bishop of Lincoln's inn to the west, may be taken as an indication that the area's social composition was mixed to a certain degree. In 1286 the conventual buildings were sold to Henry de Lacy, Earl of Lincoln, who converted them into his London residence.

The Franciscan convent was situated in the butchers' quarter. It has been emphasized that the Greyfriars found themselves in an area with serious disadvantages, not unlike Franciscans in other English towns.⁴⁵ There certainly were problems with sanitation around their monastery but the land was accepted without complaint. This may be accorded with the early Franciscans' principle to accept whatever was offered provided it was genuinely needed,⁴⁶ but there may have been other reasons. The area also had advantages. In fact the site was well chosen for an order following a spiritual ideal based on the apostolic life, and the same can be said for the location of the Dominican friary. Both convents, near Newgate, and near Holborn Bridge, were close to major routes into the city and thus ensured that the friaries were easily accessible.

The location of these two convents corresponds to a pattern observed in many other towns. It was quite common for mendicant houses to be situated in the suburbs, near a gate or the town wall, close to a main road.⁴⁷ These places emerged as the most prominent topographical focus points among factors like proximity to the river, the main markets or the harbour. In a number of Tuscan and Umbrian towns (e.g. Siena, Todi but also in Palermo) standard distances to the cathedral or other religious houses were observed when the convents were planned. On the town map the lines connecting these houses take the shape of regular triangles, the point of intersection focused on the town's central square.⁴⁸ While these particular aspects have so far only been discovered in Italy the other features appear in all regions and can be observed in towns of very different size and nature.⁴⁹ Therefore it has to be assumed that the orders were pursuing a long-term strategy and that the availability of space was not the only factor. This suggests the possibility of planning, although the orders' own official documents are silent on the subject. Without doubt, the orders' general expansion followed a careful strategy. The creation of new provinces required thorough deliberation, energetic and capable friars had to be chosen, and the future field of activity had to be studied as well. The Dominicans proceeded very methodically and the foundation of new convents had to be licensed in a lengthy procedure by the general, as well as the provincial chapter, even though the formalities were not strictly adhered to. The fact that the first Franciscan houses in Italy were equidistant, about a day's march apart from each other, leads to the same conclusion.⁵⁰ Therefore there may have been planning on a local level as well, including deliberation on the suitability of a possible site, but the resulting discussion may never have been recorded.⁵¹ Planning was certainly required if a rule laid down by Pope Clement IV in 1265 was to be observed which fixed the minimum distance between two friaries at 300 'cannae' (c.500 metres), but by that time many mendicant houses had already been built and the order does not seem to have been very effective.⁵²

Information on the early history of the other London friaries – with the exception of the Minoresses – is far more limited; in some cases even a precise location is impossible. Not all of them were affected by this topographical arrangement but on the whole they appear to have fitted largely into the pattern mentioned above. The Carmelite convent was situated in Fleet Street on the main land connection between London and Westminster, between the New Temple and the Bishop of Salisbury's inn.⁵³ Although no documents concerning its foundation survive, one can assume that development was similar to that of the Dominican and Franciscan precincts, the original grant consisting of a small plot which was gradually enlarged.⁵⁴ Here, too, the construction of conventual buildings took a long time; various deliveries of timber between 1267 and 1299 point to the last decades of the thirteenth century as the main building phase.⁵⁵ The house of the Austin Friars in Broad Street Ward was not very far from Bishopsgate. Nevertheless, it was neither located on a main thoroughfare nor was it sufficiently close to the gate to provide convenient access to passers-by. In this respect it differs from the other three friaries and it has to be assumed that other factors than the ones mentioned above influenced its location. Possibly the friars took over the parish church of St Olave Bread Street; without doubt the plot of land where the parish church used to be and the 'pertinentiis' became part of the precinct in 1271.⁵⁶ Since there are very few traces of early building activity – the first reference to the construction of a church dates from 1354[57] – an existing church building may well have formed the original part of a convent which eventually was to expand almost to the town wall, making it the largest of the London friaries in area.

During their short presence of about 50 years, the Friars of the Sack constructed a convent and even moved to another site; however, neither of the two places can be located with certainty. Their first friary was situated in the city's north-western suburb, outside Aldersgate, where they had several houses.[58] This area was sold or exchanged in 1270 for one, possibly two, plots of land in Coleman Street Ward.[59] The accumulation of friaries in one area may have been a cause for this move towards the city centre but it remains unknown whether practical reasons, a papal order issued several years before, or other motives gave the impetus. Because they claimed to be disturbed by the Jews in the synagogue adjacent to their new house, they were granted the 'scola iudeorum' in 1272, which was consecrated to become their chapel.[60]

Even less is known about the location of the Friars de Areno. Upon their arrival they were provided with property in the parish of Holy Innocents (St Mary le Strand) on the main road between London and Westminster.[61] Since two messuages and a chapel could be taken over, new buildings were not required.[62] Further land was added but very little else about the precinct or the house in general is known. By 1317 only one of the friars was still alive.[63] The last of the male orders to found a convent in London, the Friars of the Cross, pose different problems. There are very few sources on their early history, but there is no doubt about the convent's location, which was situated in the eastern part of the city, in the parish of St Olave Hart Street, not far from the Tower. Since there is no indication that they moved to another site, their first oratory was very likely constructed in this place from 1269 onwards.[64] Although the precinct was extended in the late thirteenth and fourteenth centuries, the house was to remain the smallest of the surviving five male friaries in London.[65]

Whereas the arrival of small groups of friars in London was of no consequence, their importance grew with the foundation and development of their convents. In almost all cases large precincts were created out of a number of small plots of land, some convents even encroaching upon or enclosing roads.[66] The Franciscan house was enlarged until it was positioned directly behind the city's defences,[67] and the relocation of the Dominican monastery was to leave an even greater mark. From 1275 onwards the Black Friars began to develop a second site, within the walls, in the western corner of the city, which eventually required the rebuilding of a part of the town wall further west, on the bank of the Fleet river.[68] The reasons for this move are not known but it is possible that the Dominicans wanted to be within the walls and closer to the Thames.[69] They had also attracted criticism because by extending their first site they had blocked one of the approaches to the Fleet.[70] After the Friars of the Sack, the Dominicans were the second of the London mendicant houses to exchange their site but their move was on a much larger scale. Apart from taking over the sites of Baynard's Castle and the tower of Montfichet, they extended their precinct to the west, thus changing the city's shape. Although the construction of the new friary proceeded quickly, the city adapted only slowly to the changes: the new wall along the Fleet was still being built in 1315.[71] Another aspect needs to be taken into account: at least two of the friaries had their own water supply systems, a small but nevertheless significant improvement of the city's infrastructure.

The transformation of small communities into prospering religious houses within a few decades could only be achieved with outside help. This assistance came from different social groups and took different forms; generally, however, it was motivated by the friars' new spirituality. Although only a few details about the early friars' activities and their poor living conditions are known,[72] the effects of their efforts can be measured by the conversion of prominent clerics who joined the Franciscans and Dominicans[73] as well as by the number of novices who joined in the early years. Given their initial lack of influence it is surprising to see how well the two orders coped with the task of mobilizing support. In a very short time connections with the highest circles in London, as well as in the kingdom at large, were established. The first Dominicans on their way to England encountered Peter des Roches returning from his pilgrimage to Santiago de Compostella. The bishop not only gave them transport across the Channel, he also introduced them to Stephen Langton in Canterbury.[74] Quickly aware of changes in political power they enlisted the support of Hubert de Burgh, the founder of their London convent.[75] The Black Friars were not the only aristocratic foundation. The houses of both the Carmelites and the Austin Friars had a similar origin.[76] The Minoresses, possibly refounded, certainly richly endowed by Edmund of Lancaster and his wife Blanche, also fall into this category.[77] Apart from Hubert de Burgh, the Dominicans received support from William Marshall in the form of timber for the new buildings.[78] Ela Longespee, Countess of Warwick, together with her second husband Sir Philipp Basset provided further land in Holborn in 1262.[79] The Greyfriars, to whom she gave two plots of land, also profited from her benefactions.[80]

The leading urban groups contributed on at least a similar scale. Their role may have been even more important because their representatives were more numerous. Already, by the 1220s, the Dominicans had received their first land grant from a wealthy London citizen, William le Veill.[81] Alice la Brune, possibly a relative of Walter Brun, who had been sheriff in 1202 added further land[82] and similar donations were made by Ralph Eswy and Richard Renger, who both held high offices. Both purchased land adjacent to the precinct from third parties which was subsequently made over to the Blackfriars.[83] After Renger's death which occurred probably while he was still mayor in 1338, it turned out that not only Eswy but also Friar Walter, prior of the Dominicans were among his executors.[84] The support given by the urban élite to the Franciscans was of even greater significance, aristocratic involvement in their development occurred only at a later stage. Their first provisional accommodation in Cornhill was provided by John Travers, one of the sheriffs, in 1224–25. A number of other officeholders, Joceus Fitzpiers, who had been sheriff in 1211, William Joynier, who concluded his career as mayor, and other members of prominent London families, can be found among those who provided money and land.[85] Therefore it may not be unexpected that the city of London nominally held the property of which the Franciscans had the use.[86]

The London friaries grew fast – in 1233, 100 pairs of shoes were bought for the Dominicans and 350 yards of cloth for the Franciscans[87] – and from about the mid-thirteenth-century onwards with the arrival of six new groups, their numbers increased further. Consequently, apart from the large-scale support in the form of land grants, or the financing of building activity, help of a different nature was needed as well: the friars' economic basis had to be secured and their routine activities had to be financed. In addition to the costs of subsistence, rents were due from many of the newly acquired lands – the grants by the draper Ivo de Mortlake in 1262 may serve as an example – they added an annual financial burden of £1 6s. 6¼d. to the Dominicans' expenses.[88] It has to be assumed that large sections of London's population helped to cover these demands by providing a constant flow of small donations. No traces of this help survive in the records but their importance is underlined by an episode in 1255 when the Dominicans and Franciscans tried to intervene against public hysteria about the alleged ritual killing of a Christian boy by Jews in Lincoln. Having incurred popular hostility the doors were shut in the friars' faces and they had to go hungry for several days.[89]

While the friars' support by the population at large is as difficult to assess as their influence on Londoners, another important source of constant assistance is well documented: the involvement by the king and the royal family. All the London friaries benefited from royal support during their first phase of development. This help took different forms and was not distributed evenly. Several groups of friars received royal protection upon their arrival in England or at a later stage.[90] Three of the London convents can be regarded as royal foundations: the Friars of the Sack received 100 marks for the purchase of a house in 1257[91] and royal interest in their progress continued. Queen Eleanor may have particularly favoured this order which had originated in her home country of Provence. Their lands in Colchurchstreet were taken under her protection and other signs of royal favour could also be due to her.[92] In contrast to this large sum, Henry III gave just 20 marks to the Friars of the Cross for the construction of an oratory.[93] To the Friars de Areno he gave lands and buildings near Westminster in 1268, after a general permission for the purchase of a plot had been issued in the previous year.[94]

During the long building process repeated gifts of timber and other materials were made. The first to profit from this type of royal help were the Franciscans in 1229[95] but seen over a longer period the Dominicans were the main recipients who sometimes also profited from the fabric at Westminster Abbey. Timber, lead, stones and lime from various locations reached the friary in Holborn at irregular intervals.[96] The Friars of the Sack, the Carmelites and the Austin Friars obtained some, but by no means as many, donations of this kind.[97] The construction process was also supported financially, the Dominicans again being the main beneficiaries. In 1240, they were given £10 for the building of their church and until 1261 at least another £83 6s. 8d. was disbursed to them for similar purposes.[98] With the exception of the Friars of the Sack all other orders received considerably less or nothing at all. This included even the Franciscans whose buildings were largely financed by London citizens, until an ambitious reconstruction programme was begun by Queen Margaret, Edward I's second wife, at the beginning of the fourteenth century. The prominent role of the Dominicans as recipients of royal support continued after their move to the new site near Ludgate. In 1278 they were granted all deodands collected during general eyres for the following three years.[99] This income, which also came to include amercements, amounted to at least £160 10s. 8d.[100] as well as movables, for example, in one instance, a boat.[101] Together with the revenues from the sale of their Holborn convent to the Earl of Lincoln (550 marks), continuing grants of building material,[102] and further financial assistance,[103] the new, larger site could be regarded as a royal foundation.[104] After Queen Eleanor's death Edward I promised a further 1 000 marks to the convent where her heart was buried and at least a part of this sum was actually paid.[105]

In addition to these contributions, both Henry III and Edward I provided substantial help for the friars' maintenance. Numerous royal donations of fuel, clothing and food helped to sustain the increasing numbers of friars in the city from 1233 onwards.[106] Donations were made to individual convents on certain feast days, for example, to the Franciscans on the day of St Edward or St Francis,[107] in the context of general donations to the poor[108] and, usually, to all houses on the monarch's arrival at his Westminster palace. Again, the Dominicans appear among the principal recipients. Without doubt they were extremely influential. From Henry III onwards members of the order were royal confessors until the reign of Henry IV[109] and the assistance provided in the crisis of 1258 by the first of these confessors, the London prior John Derlington, may have been considerable.[110] However, it has to be kept in mind that royal alms were often assessed on the number of friars in the convent and their house was the oldest and largest of the London mendicant houses. Until the end of the thirteenth century information on royal pittances to the London friaries survives for 11 years.[111] According to these sources – which in themselves are not entirely complete – the mendicants received subsistance payments totalling £312 8s. 7½d. during that time. The Franciscans (£93 0s. 6d.) and the Dominicans (£89 13s. 4d.) obtained the largest share, followed by the Austin Friars (£42 11s. 6d.), the Carmelites (£33 12s. 8d.), the Friars of the Cross (£20 6s. 5½d.), the Friars de Areno (£17 3s. 8d.) and the Friars of the Sack (£15 13s. 6d.).[112] Despite the gaps in the evidence it can be assumed that such payments were made on a fairly regular basis. The royal contribution, therefore, was of major importance to the convents' development.

Two other forms of royal assistance need to be mentioned. Both concern the orders' own administration. Regular payments were made towards the cost of general and provincial chapters, some of which were held in London. On a different level, the royal administration gave help to maintain discipline within the orders. Apostate and vagabond friars were outside their orders' control. Petitions for their arrest through royal officials were handed in from various orders; apparently the city was also a favoured place of refuge for apostates.[113]

Apart from these sources of direct support, the mendicants also appear to have come to an arrangement with the local church, in particular with other religious houses. Although there are hardly any examples of immediate help,[114] there were businesslike relationships about rents and rights with a number of local priories and hospitals which contributed to the friars' integration in the city.[115]

A common feature of the London friaries is the time of their foundation, which – with the exception of the Minoresses – was right at the beginning of their expansive phase. Dominic had just died, Francis was still alive when their followers arrived in the city. Nevertheless, London's importance for the orders appears to have developed only gradually, especially in the case of the Dominicans and Franciscans. Gilbert of Fresney and his 12 confrères came to England with a specific purpose in mind: the foundation of a convent in Oxford. Their aim was to forge a link with the university. This was part of the order's policy to attract as large a number of able academics as possible, an idea generated by St Dominic and vigorously pursued by Jordan of Saxony.[116] When Jordan visited the English province, he actually stayed in London but on his mind was the recruitment of novices in Oxford, the anticipation of which he expressed in a letter to the Dominican sisters in Bologna, a text in which London was not even mentioned.[117] To the Franciscans, London equally was not the main goal at the beginning. They followed a strategy which had already been employed during the order's expansion in Germany: they split up into smaller groups which pursued separate itineraries. Five of the first nine friars in England remained in what was to become their province's first convent at Canterbury, while four proceeded to London. Two of these later went to Oxford and other small groups founded convents at Northampton and Cambridge. Again London was not the centre which was given immediate preference. It has already been mentioned above that the Carmelites and Austin Friars – for different reasons – also avoided London initially.

The change occurred only gradually and was partly due to the success of the London friaries and to internal changes in the orders themselves. Initially, the Franciscans and the Dominicans had concentrated on Italy, France and Germany. The Black Friars regarded Bologna as their capital[118] and Paris as their major link to the academic world, a fact reflected in the location of their general chapters which alternated between the two cities from 1220 to 1244. This pattern was first broken in 1245 when the gathering was held in Cologne. London was the venue in 1250 and its increasing importance is underlined by the chapter's return to the city in 1263.[119] This indicates increasing attention to the English Dominican province and also goes to show that the Holborn convent was capable of housing large numbers of friars.[120] Although no Franciscan general chapters were held in England, the English Franciscan province gained increasing importance from the late 1230s onwards, a fact underlined during Albert of Pisa's visitation in 1236. The first Franciscan provincial chapter was held in London in 1238; another followed three years later.[121] In the following decades other venues were chosen, but the Franciscans returned possibly in 1287,[122] certainly in 1297, and in 1302.[123] London's importance is underlined by the general pattern; the Carmelites held their general chapter here in 1291[124] and out of 51 known venues for provincial chapters until the end of Edward I's reign, London was chosen 17 times. The Friars de Areno still held a general chapter in the city in 1306.[125]

The development of the London friaries needs to be seen in its context. First, existing religious houses also relied on the public's attention to some degree. The priory of Holy Trinity Aldgate was particularly prosperous in the years 1222–1248, at a time when the first London mendicants were also attracting significant funds.[126] Henry III's main concern in this respect was the rebuilding of Westminster Abbey, and together with many members of the aristocracy he maintained close links with the Templars, in particular with the Temple in London.[127] Secondly, other religious houses and hospitals were founded in London in the thirteenth century, partly by prominent citizens like the Hospital of St Mary Bethlehem (1247), aristocrats, like the Hospital of St Thomas of Acon, or the king, like the Domus Conversorum.[128] After the Dominicans had enjoyed the deodands for three years these revenues were granted to the Domus Conversorum by Edward I.[129] Londoners were confronted with other demands on their charity, especially after the rebuilding of London Bridge. The first two friaries had apparently been received with enthusiasm, the integration of the others may well have been more complicated as new orders representing other facets of apostolic life arrived. Nevertheless, London could easily cope with this expansion and obviously provided good conditions for the friars – the two convents affected by the suppression order of the Second Council of Lyon survived well into the fourteenth century.

Within less than a century the houses of the Dominicans and Franciscans had developed from modest beginnings, even provisional accommodation into important topographic landmarks. After not quite 30 years other orders arrived and more convents were founded until the mendicants were represented in all areas of the city and its suburbs. The friaries' location corresponds to a pattern which can be observed in many other towns, they were close to important roads, town gates, in the suburbs, near the wall. However, it is not possible to determine whether the friars chose these sites or whether they had to accept whatever was available. Two of the convents, the Dominicans and the Friars of the Sack, had first obtained sites outside the wall and later moved inside the town defences, a relocation which can be observed also in many other towns.[130]

The development of the houses and precincts coincided with and depended on the growth of the orders' importance in several other areas, the establishment of connections with leading families and office-holders including mayors, and a close relationship with the urban authorities. Close links were also established to a number of aristocratic families. In addition, both Henry III and Edward I as well as other members of the royal family took great interest in the convents' development and prosperity. The speed with which this network of support was created or came into being may be the standard with which to measure the success of the early London mendicants.

Acknowledgement

I should like to thank the British Academy for its support towards the research of this article.

Notes

1. G. Barone, 'L'ordine dei predicatori e le città', *Mélanges de l'Ecole Française de Rome* (hereafter *MEFR*) **89/2** (1977), 611.
2. J. Le Goff, 'Apostolat mendiant et fait urbain dans la France médiévale: L'implantation des ordres mendiants', *Annales Economies, Sociétés, Civilizations* (hereafter *Annales ESC*), 23 (1968), 335–48. *Idem*, 'Ordres mendiants et urbanisation dans la France médiévale', *Annales ESC*, 25 (1970), 924–46.
3. A. Vauchez, 'Introduction. Les ordres mendiants et la ville en Italie centrale', *MEFR*, **89/2** (1977), 561–2.
4. T. Hog (ed.), *Nicholai Triveti Annales* (1845), 209; W.A. Hinnebusch, *The Early English Friars Preachers*, Institutum Historicum FF. Praedicatorum Romae ad S. Sabinae, Dissertationes Historicae, 14 (Rome, 1951), 2.
5. Hinnebusch, *English Friars Preachers*, 20, gives 1224 based on Palmer's date, R. Palmer (ed.), 'Monumenta Conventus S Mariae et S Ioannis Baptistae Londinensis', *Analecta Sacri Ordinis Fratrum Praedicatorum*, 5–6 (1897–98), 286–306, but the first surviving charter can only be dated by Richard Renger's mayoralty (1222–27), G. Williams, *Medieval London: From Commune to Capital*, University of London Historical Studies, **11** (1963), 329. The London Dominican foundation occurred at the most seven years after the foundation of the Preachers' house in Paris (1217), R.W. Emery, *The Friars in Medieval France. A Catalogue of French Mendicant Convents 1200–1350* (New York and London, 1962), 109; M. Heimbucher, *Die Orden und Kongregationen der katholischen Kirche*, 2 vols (Paderborn, 1980), vol. 1, 476, and only briefly after the arrival of the first Dominicans in Cologne (1221), M. Groten, 'Köln (Mittelalter)', in *Lexikon des Mittelalters* (Munich and Zurich, 1990), vol. 5, col. 1256–61; G.M. Löhr, *Beiträge zur Geschichte des Kölner Dominikanerklosters im Mittelalter*, Quellen und Forschungen zur Geschichte des Dominikanerordens in Deutschland, **16, 17**, 2 vols (Leipzig, 1920–22), vol. 1, 1–2.
6. J. Stow, *A Survey of London*, ed. C.L. Kingsford, 2 vols (1908), vol. 2, 46; K.J. Egan, 'The establishment and early development of the Carmelite order in England', PhD thesis, Cambridge University (1965), 1–8.
7. G.C. Cockayne, *The Complete Peerage*, 13 vols (1910–40), vol. 6, 126–7.
8. S.E. Rigold, 'Two Kentish Carmelite houses – Aylesford and Sandwich', *Archaeologia Cantiana*, 80 (1965), 1–28.

9. A.G. Little (ed.), *Fratris Thomae vulgo dicti de Eccleston Tractatus de Adventu Minorum in Angliam* (1959), 102; Egan, 'Establishment', 1.
10. Egan, 'Establishment', 50; H.J. Schmidt, 'Karmeliter', in *Lexikon des Mittelalters* (Munich and Zurich, 1991), vol. 5, col. 998–1000.
11. D. Knowles and R.N. Hadcock, *Medieval Religious Houses. England and Wales* (London and New York, 1971), 235. If this is the case, the Carmelites had settled in London before they had come to Cologne (1256), Groten, 'Köln', col. 1257. In 1259 the Cologne Carmelites were forbidden to maintain a school for boys which has led Koch to date the foundation of the convent to 1256, H.H. Koch, *Die Karmeliten-Klöster der Niederdeutschen Provinz, 13.–16. Jahrhundert* (Freiburg im Breisgau, 1889), 12, 29; or Paris (1258), Emery, *Friars*, 109.
12. Stow, *Survey*, vol. 1, 177; F. Roth, *The English Austin Friars, 1249–1538*, Cassiciacum, 6, 7, 2 vols (New York, 1961–66), vol. 1, 286.
13. Roth, *English Austin Friars*, vol. 2, no. 2, 5.
14. K. Elm, 'Eremitengemeinschaften des 12. und 13. Jahrhunderts. Studien zur Vorgeschichte des Augustiner-Eremitenordens', in *L'Eremitismo in Occidente nei secoli XI et XII*, Miscellanea del Centro di Studi Medioevali, 4 (Milan, 1962), 491–559, E.A. van Moé, 'Recherches sur les Ermites de Saint-Augustin entre 1250–1350', *Revue des questions historiques*, 60 (1932), 275–316, at 285–6. However, doubts about Stow's information may still be justified: Although royal protection for the Augustinians was again granted in 1255, *Calendar of Patent Rolls* (hereafter *CPR*) *1247–58*, 403, and they were paid royal alms in the following year, it is not absolutely certain that these sources refer to their London convent: *Calendar of Liberate Rolls* (hereafter *Cal.Lib.R.*) *1251–60*, 274. Since in the same entry the London Franciscans are specifically mentioned, Roth, *English Austin Friars*, vol. 1, 286, had no doubt that the money was intended for the London Austin Friars. However, this entry may well refer to the royal grant of a chapel dedicated to St Lawrence on the way to Clayhanger (Middlesex) to the Austin Friars, which was prepared in the same year by an inquisition 'ad quod damnum'. The jurors' verdict on 20 February, London PRO, C143/1/38, five days later the payment was authorized. In fact Austin Friars were not mentioned when royal alms were paid to the mendicant convents in London – the Dominicans, Franciscans, Carmelites and Friars of the Sack – as well as to a number of other regular institutions in and around London in Lent 1260, *Calendar of Close Rolls* (hereafter *CCR*) *1259–61*, 238–9.
15. *CCR 1272–79*, 388. Even though the foundation's precise date is unknown, the Austin Friars' arrival – like the Carmelites they had initially avoided the towns – coincided with that of their confrères in Paris, Strasbourg, Cologne and Zurich: Paris (1259), Emery, *Friars*, 102; Strasbourg (1257), F. Rapp, 'Die Mendikanten und die Strassburger Gesellschaft am Ende des Mittelalters', in K. Elm (ed.), *Stellung und Wirksamkeit der Bettelorden in der städtischen Gesellschaft* (Berlin, 1981), 88–100; Cologne (1264), Groten, 'Köln', col. 1257.
16. H.R. Luard (ed.), *Matthaei Parisiensis, Monachi sancti Albani, Chronica Majora*, Rolls Series, 57, 7 vols (1872–83), vol 5, 621.
17. London, PRO, E403 15A m 1.
18. R.W. Emery, 'The Friars of the Sack', *Speculum*, 18 (1943), 323–34; R.I.

Burns, 'Penitenza di Gesù Cristo, Frati della', in *Dizionario degli Istituti di Perfezione* (Rome, 1980), vol. 6, col. 1399; M. de Fontette, 'Les mendiants supprimés au 2e Concile de Lyon (1274). Frères Sachets et Frères Pies', in *Les mendiants en pays d'Oc au XIIIe siècle*, Cahiers de Fanjeaux, **8** (1973), 193–216.

19. K. Elm, 'Fratres B. Mariae Matris Christi', in *Lexikon des Mittelalters* (Munich, 1989), vol. 4, col. 851–2; R.W. Emery, 'The Friars of the Blessed Mary and the Pied Friars', *Speculum*, **24** (1949), 228–38.
20. *CPR 1266–72*, 122.
21. K. Elm, 'Kreuzherren', in *Lexikon des Mittelalters* (Munich and Zurich 1991), vol. 5, col. 1500–1502.
22. H.F. Chettle, 'The Friars of the Holy Cross in England', *History*, **34** (1949), 204–20; 'Chronica majora', vol. 4, 393/4. Although this group of 'fratres ordinis S. Mariae de ordine Cruciferorum' received royal protection in the same year they were antagonized by Robert Grosseteste, *CPR 1232–47*, 435; A.G. Little (ed.), *De Adventu* (1959), 103.
23. *CPR 1247–58*, 51.
24. H. Russelius, *Chronicon Cruciferorum* (Cologne, 1635), 52–3; C.R. Hermans (ed.), *Annales Canonicorum Regularium S.Augustini Ordinis S.Crucis*, 3 vols (s'Hertogenbosch, 1858), vol. 2, 68–9; M. Vinken, 'Croisiers', in *Dictionnaire d'histoire et de géographie écclésiastiques* (Paris, 1956), vol. 13, col. 1044.
25. *CPR 1258–66*, 456.
26. Stow, *Survey*, vol. 1, 147; M. Reddan, 'Friaries', in W. Page (ed.), *Victoria History of the Counties of England* (hereafter *VCH*) (London, 1909), 514; Knowles and Hadcock, *Medieval Religious Houses*, 209; *Cal.Lib.R. 1267–72*, 81; also in: London PRO, E 403 1226 m 5. Further royal grants towards the building were made in 1273: London PRO, E 404/1/2 no. 1.
27. Stow, *Survey*, vol. 1, 125–6; *VCH London*, 516.
28. We are not dealing with a failed foundation attempt because in 1291 the possessions of the Minoresses were subject to taxation. C. Eubel (ed.), *Bullarii Franciscani Epitome* (Quaracchi, 1908), 153; A. Potthast (ed.), *Regesta Pontificum Romanorum*, 2 vols (Berlin, 1875), vol. 2, no. 21801; A.F.C. Bourdillon, *The Order of Minoresses in England* (1926), 12–13; *Taxatio Ecclesiastica Angliae et Walliae auctoritate P. Nicholai IV circa 1291*, Record Commission (1802), 247, 311. It has to be kept in mind, though, that these entries were made in the margin of the document.
29. G. Duchesne, *Histoire de l'Abbaye Royale de Longchamp (1255–1789)* (Paris, 1906), 31–45.
30. D. Keene, 'Medieval London and its region', *London Journal*, **14** (1989), 99–111.
31. R.L. Poole, *The Exchequer in the Twelfth Century* (1912), 179; W. Stubbs (ed.), *Gesta Regis Henrici Secundi Benedicti Abbatis*, Rolls Series **49**, 2 vols (1867), vol. 1, 207; T.F. Tout, *Chapters in the Administrative History of Medieval England: the Wardrobe, the Chamber and the Small Seals*, Publications of the University of Manchester, Historical Series, **34, 35, 48, 49, 57, 64**, 6 vols (1920–33), vol. 1, 96–7; H.C. Maxwell-Lyte, *Historical Notes on the Use of the Great Seal of England* (1926), 9–10; F.M. Powicke, *The Thirteenth Century* (1953), 65; N. Denholm-Young, *Richard of Cornwall* (1947), 59; T.F. Tout, 'The beginnings of a modern capital: London and Westminster in the

fourteenth century', in T.F. Tout, *Collected Papers*, 3 vols (1934), vol. 3, 249–75.
32. Hog, *Triveti Annales*, 209.
33. Little, 'De adventu', 9; K. Esser, *Anfänge und ursprüngliche Zielsetzung des Ordens der Minderbrüder*, Studia et Documenta Franciscana, 4 (Leiden, 1966), 136.
34. It is likely that the friars found one or more buildings in existence here although the earliest surviving document gives no information on this. It just mentions 'placeam illam cum pertinentiis', London PRO, DL 27 59; also in Palmer, 'Monumenta', 286.
35. London PRO, DL 25 143; Palmer, 'Monumenta', 286–7; Hinnebusch, *English Friars Preachers*, 23–7.
36. *CCR 1234–37*, 71, 97, 457.
37. *CCR 1259–61*, 10, 130, 244; Hinnebusch, *English Friars Preachers*, 27; *CCR 1261–64*, 169, 194.
38. J.S. Brewer (ed.), *Monumenta Franciscana*, Rolls Series, 4, 2 vols (1858), vol. 1, 494; C.L. Kingsford, *The Grey Friars of London* (1915), 146; M.B. Honeybourne, 'The extent and value of the property in London and Southwark occupied by the religious houses, the inns of the bishops and abbots and the churches and churchyards before the dissolution of the monasteries', MA thesis, University of London (1929), 143.
39. *CCR 1227–31*, 169.
40. Little, 'De adventu', 21; Kingsford, *Grey Friars*, 34; *Cal.Lib.R. 1240–45*, 122.
41. *Cal.Lib.R. 1251–60*, 274; Kingsford, *Grey Friars*, 158–9; *CPR 1266–72*, 339.
42. London, British Library (hereafter BL), MS Add. 7966A fol. 66 v; Honeybourne, 'Extent', 154.
43. Geoffrey Joppe 'tannator' London PRO, DL 27 65; Richard Lungejambe, tanner, owns messuage adjacent to the Dominicans, later added to the convent, London PRO, DL 25 131, DL 25 132; Bartholomew Parmentarius, Lucas Parmentarius London PRO, DL 25 142; Serlo Parmentarius London PRO DL 27 65; Gervasius 'tannator', London PRO DL 27 64; Henry 'tannator', London PRO, DL 25 131; Ralph Carpentarius London PRO, DL 25 141; Richard Carpentarius London PRO, DL 25 140; William Carpentarius had owned land which eventually was to form part of the precinct London PRO, DL 25 137; Cecily wife of Adam Tiler, Margery wife of Henry Tiler, Roger Tiler London PRO, DL 25 140, DL 25 141; Geoffrey of Holborn, tiler owned land which later became part of the Dominican precinct London PRO, DL 25 140; Stephen Tiler London PRO, DL 27 65; Robert Tiler London PRO, DL 25 132; DL 25 135; DL 25 134; DL 25 136; DL 25 140; DL 25 141; DL 25 148; DL 27 65; DL 27 66; Gilbert Tiler London PRO, DL 25 132; DL 25 134; DL 25 136; DL 25 141; DL 25 143.
44. London PRO, DL 25 140.
45. E.g. Exeter, A.G. Little and R.C. Easterling, *The Franciscans and Dominicans of Exeter*, History of Exeter Research Group, 3 (1927), 15.
46. Their role as 'minores' was underlined by this just as much as by the architecture of their first conventual buildings. Albert of Pisa intervened during the construction of what must have been their dormitory and had the stone walls replaced by those made from mud, Little, 'De adventu',

44. The same happened at Shrewsbury, ibid., 23 and Southampton, ibid., 79.
47. A.W. Clapham and W.H. Godfrey, *Some Famous Buildings and their Story* (n. d.), 243; L. Butler, 'The houses of the mendicant orders in Britain: recent archaeological work', in P.V. Addyman and V.E. Black (eds), *Archaeological Papers from York Presented to W.M. Barley* (1984) 124–36; E. Guidoni, 'Città e ordini mendicanti. Il ruolo dei conventi nella crescità e nella progettazione urbana del XIII e XIV secolo', *Quaderni medievali*, **4** (1977), 69–106.
48. J.-C. Schmitt, 'Où est l'enquête 'ordres mendiants et urbanisation dans la France médiévale?', in K. Elm, *Bettelorden*, 13–18; Guidoni, 'Città e ordini mendicanti', 86–103.
49. A. Benvenuti Papi, 'Ordini mendicanti e città. Appunti per un' indagine, il caso di Firenze', in D. Maselli (ed.), *Da Dante a Cosimo I* (Pistoia, 1976), 122–45; B. Neidiger, *Mendikanten zwischen Ordensideal und städtischer Realität. Untersuchungen zum wirtschaftlichen Verhalten der Bettelorden in Basel* (Berlin, 1981), 137; N. Hecker, *Bettelorden und Bürgertum. Konflikt und Kooperation in deutschen Städten des Spätmittelalters* (Frankfurt am M. 1981), 55–60; H.-J. Schmidt, *Bettelorden in Trier* (Trier, 1986), 43–7; E. Isenmann, *Die deutsche Stadt im Spätmittelalter* (Stuttgart, 1988), 220.
50. L. Pellegrini, 'Insediamenti rurali e insediamenti urbani dei francescani nell' Italia del secolo XIII', *Miscellanea Francescana*, **75** (1975), 197–210.
51. G.R. Galbraith, *The Constitution of the Dominican Order 1216–1360*, Publications of the University of Manchester, Historical Series, **44** (1925), 48; B. Reichert (ed.), *Acta Capitulorum Generalium Ordinis Praedicatorum*, Monumenta Ordinis Fratrum Praedicatorum Historica, 3, 4, 8, 9, 4 vols (Rome, 1898), vol. 1, 30; M.-H. Vicaire, 'Le développement de la province dominicaine de Provence (1215–1295)', in *Les mendiants*, 35–77. The Franciscans had a similar attitude as e.g. the persistence in their attempt to settle in Bury St Edmunds demonstrates, A. Gransden (ed.), *The Chronicle of Bury St Edmunds 1212–1301* (1964), 23–4, 27–8.
52. It was renewed several times, H.-J. Schmidt, *Bettelorden*, 43.
53. Honeybourne, 'Extent', 171; Egan, 'Establishment', 161; L.C. Sheppard, *The English Carmelites* (1943), 27.
54. The area was extended in the fourteenth century, A.W. Clapham, 'The topography of the Carmelite Priory of London', *Journal of the British Archaeological Association*, new series, **16** (1910), 15–32.
55. *CCR 1264–68*, 321/2; *CCR 1268–72*, 482; *CCR 1272–79*, 279; *CCR 1296–1302*, 249. Construction of the church 1270–72: *Cal.Lib.R. 1267–72*, 113, 220; *CCR 1268–72*, 206; *CCR 1272–79*, 261.
56. Roth, *English Austin Friars*, vol. 2, 27–8.
57. A grant of timber in 1277, *CCR 1272–79*, 388; Roth, *English Austin Friars*, vol. 1, 287.
58. *CCR 1264–68*, 433.
59. *CPR 1266–72*, 406.
60. *CCR 1268–72*, 522; Gransden, *Chronicle of Bury St Edmunds*, 53; Stow, *Survey*, 287. The problem of the location of this second convent is due to the fact that there were either two sites in the same area or – as

seems more likely – because 'Colemanesstrete' was inadvertently substituted for 'Colechurchestrete': Colemanstreet: 'capella ... que dudum fuit synagoga Judeorum' (there was a synagogue in Colchurchstreet) London PRO, C 143/45/10. Reference to two parishes, St Olave Jewry and St Margaret Lothbury in R.R. Sharpe (ed.), *Calendar of Letter Books of the City of London*, Letter Book C (1901), 61–2; London Corporation of London Record Office (hereafter CLRO), Liber Horn fol. 285r–v. Later documents point to a site in Colchurchstreet: London CLRO, Bridge House Deeds B 69, C 37; J. Stow, *A Survey of London* (1908), vol. 1, 277.
61. R.W. Emery, 'The Friars of the Blessed Mary', 232 'in Westminster'.
62. *Calendar of Charter Rolls* (hereafter *Cal.Chart.R.*), vol. 2, 89.
63. *CPR 1266–72*, 447. London PRO, C62 56 m 2 refers to a claim by the widow of William de Aldenham to her dower, part of which is a rent owed by the Friars de Areno for their convent. This may point to yet another donation in the last years of Henry III's reign. London, Library of the Society of Antiquaries, MS 120 fol. 10 r.
64. CCR 1267–72, 81; London PRO, E 404/1/2 no. 1.
65. A. Povah, *The Annals of the Parishes of St. Olave Hart Street and Allhallows Staining in the City of London* (1894), 1–2; Honeybourne, 'Extent', 216.
66. 'Dicunt etiam quod fratres minores fecerunt purpresturam de quadam venella obturata ... que vocatur Stigandeslane ... fratres predicatores obturant quandam venellam in Sholand ... ', *Rotuli Hundredorum*, Record Commission, 2 vols (1812–18), vol. 1, 429; the Carmelites enclosed 'Crockerelande' in 1349, H.A. Harben, *A Dictionary of London* (1918), 625; London PRO, C 143/2/17.
67. This location was not entirely uncommon for Franciscan houses, B.E.J. Stüdeli, *Minoritenniederlassungen und mittelalterliche Stadt*, Franziskanische Forschungen, **21** (Werl, 1969), 36; J.B. Freed, *The Friars and German Society in the Thirteenth Century*, The Mediaeval Academy of America, **86** (Cambridge, Mass., 1977), 50.
68. Palmer, 'Monumenta', 299; R.R. Sharpe, *Calendar of Letter Books of the City of London*, Letter Book B (1900), 56.
69. The Dominican convent in Zürich had initially been outside the walls, and was later relocated within, M. Wehrli-Johns, *Geschichte des Zürcher Predigerkonvents, 1230–1524. Mendikantentum zwischen Kirche, Adel und Stadt* (Zurich, 1980), 11; and the same development can be observed in Strasbourg, Freed, *Friars and German Society*, 36. A quay was part of the new convent, CCR 1288–96, 373.
70. London PRO, SC5/London/Tower/1 m 2, m 3: 'Fratres Predicatores London, Abbas Colecestre et Fratres sancti Egidii extra London incluserunt regiam stratam que ducere debet et ducere consuevit de aqua de Flete usque Sholane'.
71. R.R. Sharpe (ed.), *Calendar of Letter Books of the City of London*, Letter Book E (1903), 63.
72. A number of anecdotes illustrate the early Franciscan adherence to their founder's ideals, e.g. Friar Salomon, guardian of London, refuses to prepare accounts; or the primitive conditions in their house in Cornhill, Little, 'De adventu', 7–9.
73. 1233: canons from Dunstable join the Franciscans, H.R. Luard (ed.),

Annales Prioratus de Dunstaplia, Annales Monastici, Rolls Series, 36, 5 vols (1864–69), vol. 3, 133–3; 1235: The Abbot of Osney joins the Franciscans, *Annals of Tewkesbury*, Annales Monastici, 1, 98; 1238: Ralph Maidstone, Bishop of Hereford joins the Franciscans, *Annales Monasterii de Waverleia*, Annales Monastici, 2, 320; *Chronica XXIV Generalium*, Analecta Franciscana, 3 (Quaracchi, 1898), 26; 1245: Walter Mauclerk, Bishop of Carlisle joins the Dominicans, *Annales Monasterii de Waverleia*, Annales Monastici, 2, 337.

74. I should like to thank Dr Nicholas Vincent (Cambridge) for his information on the bishopric of Winchester's pipe rolls.
75. He also made large bequests and was later buried there, Hinnebusch, *English Friars Preachers*, 20–21; London PRO, DL 27 59; *CCR 1247–51*, 251/2.
76. While the Carmelites were founded by de Grey of Codnor, as was mentioned above, the convent of the Austin Friars was a foundation of the Bohun family. Both families were still closely connected to these friaries in the second half of the fourteenth century, Roth, *English Austin Friars*, vol. 1, 287; Egan, 'Establishment', 195.
77. *Calendar of Papal Registers* (hereafter *Cal.Pap.Reg*), vol. 1, 522, 560, 562, 575; London PRO, C 143/22/26.
78. *CCR 1234–37*, 71, 97.
79. London PRO, DL 25 138.
80. Kingsford, 'Grey Friars', 150–51.
81. London PRO, DL 25 143.
82. T. Stapleton (ed.), *Cronica maiorum et vicecomitum Londoniarum*, Camden Society, 34 (1846), 2; London PRO, DL 25 131.
83. London PRO, DL 25 132; DL 25 135.
84. London BL, Harl. Ch. 55 G 12.
85. Little, 'De adventu', 21.
86. The role played by the urban upper classes and knightly families is underlined if the information available on novices joining the Franciscans is taken into account. The mercer John Iwun, described as 'dominus' by Thomas of Eccleston, not only was the first to provide land for the convent near Newgate, he also later joined the order. Thomas of Eccleston's anecdote of Friar Salomon who deeply embarrassed his sister when he appeared as a beggar at her door or another of his stories, about John Gobiun, son of a Northampton knight who provoked his father's resentment when he became a novice support this impression. It is also noteworthy that some instances of direct speech quoted by Eccleston are in French, in Little, 'De adventu', 12, 37.
87. *Cal.Lib.R. 1226–40*, 233/4. This may not represent the total number of inmates, but the members expected to join in the near future, cf. B. Gratien, *Histoire de la fondation et de l'évolution de l'Ordre des Frères Mineurs au XIIIe siècle* (Paris, 1928), 72–3.
88. London PRO, DL 25 137.
89. Luard, *Chronica Majora*, vol. 5, 516; Hinnebusch, *English Friars Preachers*, 29; *CPR 1247–58*, 457.
90. *CPR 1232–47*, 435; *CPR 1247–58*, 51, 403, 493; *CPR 1258–66*, 351, 456.
91. London PRO, E 403 15A m 1. This was twice the amount originally

intended. The cancelled entry for the payment of 50 marks in E 403 14 m 1.
92. London CLRO, Liber Horn fol. 285r; Sharpe, 'Letter Book C', 61–2; *CCR 1264–68*, 433; *CCR 1268–72*, 456, 522; *CPR 1266–72*, 406.
93. London PRO, E 404/1/2 Nr. 1. £10 were still due in 1273.
94. *Cal.Chart.R.*, vol. 2, 89; *CPR 1266–72*, 122.
95. *CCR 1227–31*, 169.
96. E.g. *CCR 1234–37*, 459; *CCR 1237–42*, 80; *CCR 1254–56*, 366; *CCR 1256–59*, 73, 379; *CCR 1259–61*, 347, 359, 372; *CCR 1261–64*, 34; *Cal.Lib.R. 1226–40*, 275–6; *Cal.Lib.R. 1240–45*, 122.
97. E.g. *CCR 1268–72*, 206, 340, 456, 482; *CCR 1272–79*, 388; *CCR 1264–68*, 433; London PRO, C 62 49 m 4.
98. *Cal.Lib.R. 1240–45*, 48, 87; *Cal.Lib.R. 1251–60*, 484; *Cal.Lib.R. 1260–67*, 16, 50; London PRO, E 403 18 m 1.
99. *CCR 1272–79*, 515; London PRO, E 159 53 m 6d.
100. London PRO, E 159 54 m 1, m 21; E 159 55 m 5, m 12; E 159 57 m 11d; E 159 59 m 26d; *CCR 1272–79*, 74, 448, 508–9; possibly also 551.
101. *CCR 1279–88*, 2.
102. *CCR 1288–96*, 373; *CCR 1296–1302*, 451.
103. London PRO, E 403 59 m 1.
104. Hinnebusch, *English Friars Preachers*, 83.
105. London PRO, C 62 67 m 4; C 62 68 m 5; E 403 64 m 1; E 403 72 m 1.
106. *CCR 1231–34*, 214; *Cal.Lib. R. 1226–40*, 233–4.
107. *CCR 1247–51*, 331; London PRO, C47/4/4 fol. 42 v.
108. *CCR 1242–47*, 279; *Cal.Lib.R. 1240–45*, 324; A.K. Warren, *Anchorites and their Patrons in Medieval England* (Berkeley, 1985), 159; *CCR 1259–61*, 238–9.
109. C.F.R. Palmer, 'The king's confessors', *Antiquary*, **22** (1890), 114–20; 159–61; 262–6, **23** (1891), 24–6.
110. *CCR 1256–59*, 317/8. He was one of those elected for the king's party in the Provisions of Oxford, W. Stubbs (ed.), *Select Charters and other Illustrations of English Constitutional History* (1913), 379.
111. 1240, 1241, 1245, 1252, 1256, 1259, 1278, 1285, 1289, 1290, 1297.
112. The Minoresses had the smallest portion by far with only 7s. but they appear in just one account because they were the last of the convents to arrive and were endowed by another branch of the royal family. These figures are based on: *Cal.Lib.R. 1226–40*, 501; *Cal.Lib.R. 1245–51*, 16; *Cal.Lib.R. 1251–60*, 39, 274, 456/7; London PRO, E 403 1 m 2; E 403 3 m 1; E 403 3115 m 2; C 62 54 m 1; C 47/4/1 fols. 8 v, 19 r, 20 r, 23 v, 24 r, 24 v, 44 v, 45 v, 50 r, 50 v; C 47/4/2 fols 26 v, 27 r, 27 v; C 47/4/4 fols 38 r, 39 r, 42 r, 42 v, 43 r, 43 v; BL, MS Add. 7965 fol. 9 r.
113. London PRO, C81/1793/5; C 81/1793/10, C81/1793/12 (Carmelites), C81/1794/8 (Austin Friars),C81/1794/24, C81/1794/25 (Friars de Areno).
114. *CCR 1247–51*, 289–90.
115. Franciscans: Priory of Clerkenwell, Kingsford, *Grey Friars*, 149, 152, 155–6; Priory Haliwell, ibid., 149–50, 151–2; St Bartholomew's Hospital, ibid., 150; Priory S. Bartholomew, Crutched Friars: Priory Holy Trinity, *Catalogue of Ancient Deeds* (hereafter *Cat.Anc.Deeds*), vol. 2, 107.
116. A. Walz (ed.), *Beati Iordani de Saxonia Epistulae*, Monumenta Ordinis Praedicatorum Historica, **23** (Rome, 1951), letters no. VII (novitiis bonis

et idoneis), VIII, XX, XXI (omnes sunt viri honesti et competenti litteraturae), XXVI, XXXII, XL, LVI.
117. Ibid., no. XVI, 19–20; Little, 'De adventu', 12–13.
118. Walz, *Beati Iordani de Saxonia Epistulae*, no. V, 8.
119. Reichert, *Acta Capitulorum*, vol. 1, 48, 117.
120. Hinnebusch, *English Friars Preachers*, 30–31.
121. *Cal.Lib.R. 1226–40*, 331; *CCR 1237–42*, 294; *Cal.Lib.R. 1240–45*, 48.
122. London PRO, E 403 55 m 1.
123. London BL, MS Add. 7965 fol. 9 v; PRO, E 101/365/10 m 6d.
124. London PRO, C47/4/4 fol. 46 r. L. Saggi, 'Constitutiones Capituli Londinensis Anni 1281', *Analecta Ordinis Carmelitarum*, 2 (1950), 203–45.
125. London PRO, E 101/369/11 fol. 7 v.
126. G.A.J. Hodgett (ed.), *Cartulary of Holy Trinity Aldgate*, London Record Society, 7 (1971), xv–xvi, xix.
127. J.B. Williamson, *The History of the Temple*, (1925), 20; A. Sandys, 'The financial and administrative importance of the London Temple in the thirteenth century', in A.G. Little and F.M. Powicke (eds), *Essays in Medieval History Presented to T.F. Tout* (1925), 147–62, at 149.
128. E.G. O'Donoghue, *The Story of Bethlehem Hospital from its Foundation in 1247* (1914), 10.
129. *CCR 1279–88*, 107.
130. Pellegrini, 'Insediamenti', 206–7; M. d'Alatri, 'I più antichi insediamenti dei mendicanti nella provincia civile di Campagna', *MEFR*, **89/2** (1977) 575–85; S. Lesur, 'Le Couvent des Grands Carmes de Toulouse au XIIIe siècle', in *Les Mendiants en pays d'Oc au XIIIe siècle*, Cahiers de Fanjeaux, **8** (Toulouse, 1973), 101–11. In the case of the Carmelites this move was also due to the order's changing character, ibid., 103.

CHAPTER SIX

Urban Rectories and Urban Fortunes in Late Medieval England: the Evidence from Bishop's Lynn

R.N. Swanson

A noticeable gap in the debate on the fortunes of late medieval English towns is any detailed assessment of the Church's urban role, and how its analysis might contribute to development of the issues.[1] The Church has not been ignored: the extensive building and repair are often cited; and the discussion of changing rent levels is often based on records of clerical urban institutions like the vicars choral of York Minster and the varied ecclesiastical bodies in Winchester. But the precisely church origins of the evidence are not seen as significant: church-building is put alongside the building of guild-halls, town walls, and other projects; rents paid to ecclesiastical bodies are treated just like those of lay individuals and institutions.[2] Yet evidence of the financial fate of urban churches may usefully expand the analyses of the changing fortunes of English towns between the Black Death and the onset of the Reformation.

Crucial to this would be the financial history of the urban parochial benefices. As a church received a lot of money from its parishioners, for varied purposes, the urban parish's changing fortunes should reflect the changing fortunes of the town. While that may be the ideal, investigating the reality is not straightforward. Much depends on the status of the benefice, on the relationship between parish and town, and on the source material.

The term 'urban parish' is shorthand. There was not always one parish per town, or one town per parish. Nor was there always a clean and abrupt break between town and country which was marked by parochial boundaries. Nor, further, was there a neat break between 'ecclesiastical' and 'secular' worlds: ecclesiastical institutions were often the lords of unchartered boroughs, as at Stratford-upon-Avon, Beverley, Evesham, Bury St Edmunds, and St Albans, the first two controlled by the officials of the Bishop of Worcester and the Archbishop of York, the others dominated by their abbeys: clearly here the Church also had a special interest.[3]

URBAN RECTORIES AND URBAN FORTUNES 101

Given the uncertainties, any attempt to generalize about England's late medieval urban parishes faces many obstacles. This chapter considers some of the economic contexts of the parochial evolutions, bearing in mind the varying types of provision which might exist. Then, rather than pursue an argument through the patchwork of evidence which is available, attention focuses on one decidedly urban parish which both offers the required run of evidence and shows some of the complications which were generated during the period.

Urban parishes and their revenues

Identity

Urban parishes exhibited a complex variety.[4] A town might be only part of a much larger parochial organism, contributing only some of the full parochial revenues. This clearly applies to a place like Longbridge Deveril (Wiltshire), whose main settlement seemingly fell on the borderline between 'town' and 'village', or even to Scarborough in Yorkshire. Both parishes had a rural component, which paid its own type of dues. The extant Longbridge Deveril accounts suggest that any 'urban' contribution was minor;[5] at Scarborough the extant benefice accounts focus on the urban income, and omit agrarian tithes, although it is inconceivable that the parish's large rural area was not being farmed.[6]

In contrast, there were parishes which were only parts of towns. Many English towns contained a multitude of parishes, some of these necessarily very small. The precise number varied over time, but late medieval London had almost 100 parishes within its walls (and more in the extramural areas under the city's jurisdiction), Norwich and York over 40, Worcester ten, and Cambridge just as many.[7] Even without such fragmentation, a town might be divided between two or three parishes, as at Salisbury.[8] Some of the parishes might include the town fields, and be large, drawing considerable rural revenues. Even so, in general (and particularly within a town's walls) the more the parishes, the smaller they were: some in York contained only a few acres, with populations correspondingly small.[9] There were also towns consisting of a single parish, covering only the town and the area under its jurisdiction. This was the case at Westminster, where parish and vill were effectively coterminous.[10] On the assumption (perhaps overgenerous) that evidence of market activity reveals urban functions at their most basic, and considering all the permutations of urban and parochial boundaries, in the pre-Reformation centuries some 20–25 per cent of English parishes may at some time have derived some income from 'urban' sources, no matter how small the amount. On the eve of the Reformation, the proportion receiving such revenues probably stood at 10–15 per cent.[11]

The status of the parochial benefices in towns also requires comment. By 1500 many English parishes had been appropriated, transferring the greater tithes to undying corporations which retained the rectories, monasteries, collegiate churches, university colleges and hospitals. The parish revenues were usually divided, and the living converted into a vicarage, generally endowed with only part of the income.[12] Nevertheless, for a total assessment of parish revenues, the money which passed to the appropriator (and was thus often withdrawn from the local economy) must be taken into account. While many towns fell within parishes which had become vicarages, and some of the smaller urban parishes had been appropriated, those which were not were still numerous.[13]

Income

How far any one of these groups gives a realistic picture of the fate of English towns obviously varies. Before considering the evidence, it must be emphasized that the concern is solely with the revenues received by the urban parish as a benefice (or in some cases, combination of benefices). The normal division of fiscal responsibilities in English parishes, with the churchwardens and laity overseeing the nave and churchyard, while the tithe-holder was liable for maintenance of the chancel, could result in major differences between the revenues received by either half of the arrangement.[14] In some urban cases, the laity effectively took over the whole administration of the parish, as at Ludlow, where in 1432 the rector was reduced to the status of a pensionary while the laity rebuilt the parish church according to their own plans.[15] Where churchwardens were responsible for the hiring and supervision of chantry priests and other stipendiaries within a church, caring for the endowments, and so on, the incumbent might have little scope for independent action; spiritual provision might thus be effectively withdrawn from his hands. Energetic urban governments might also seek to dominate and control their local churches and clergy, as at Hull.[16]

The most serious problem in tackling urban parishes and their incomes is the nature of the evidence. Only two general surveys give the overall revenues of English parishes (urban or rural): the *Taxatio* of Pope Nicholas IV of 1291 and, in 1535, the more detailed *Valor Ecclesiasticus*. While both may be used, they have major defects as sources and as full reflections of the revenues of the parishes they cover.[17] Between these two dates, there is partial coverage in the *Inquisitiones Nonarum* of 1342, but the purpose of that was to record tithes of sheaves, lambs, and wool; its utility for treatment of urban parishes is limited. Moreover, there is some doubt about its usefulness and how far it reflects real parochial incomes in 1342.[18] Other sources also reveal parochial incomes (mainly tax returns from the early sixteenth century), but they rarely give detailed analyses of the revenues, and so are of limited use.[19]

While basic figures for total incomes between 1291 and 1535 might be compared – or, indeed, the occasional milestones in between these dates to suggest the overall economic development of urban benefices during the period – such a comparison would be very blunt. In particular, it could not reveal the changing nuances of urban parochial revenues in response to the period's economic and social changes (assuming for the present that these would be reflected in such figures). What is needed is a relatively long run of accounts which can be analysed, and which might offer a model for developments elsewhere. Such survivals are few, indeed rare. Most extant statements of spiritual receipts from urban sources survive because the parish had been appropriated to a monastery or collegiate body within the town, the full revenues going to the major institution rather than split between the appropriator and a beneficed vicar. In such a situation, the pastoral provision would be arranged by hiring a stipendiary. These, and the stipendiaries on short-term contracts, received only a fraction of the total revenues. Thus, at Selby in 1416–17, the town curate received only a stipend of £4 13s. 4d. from the extensive income taken by the abbey.[20] Some appropriated urban parishes did have fully incumbent vicars. Sometimes these operated merely as stipendiaries, and so differed from the unbeneficed only in the security of their tenure. Others were endowed with a portion of the revenues, thus entailing some division in the accounts. Where a vicarage covered a complete town, or a parish with both rural and urban elements, this was not necessarily detrimental – Scarborough comes immediately to mind. In other cases it is hard to see the justification for the arrangements, especially those involving small intramural parishes. At first glance these possessed few fiscal attractions for an appropriator, unless the church had sufficient property endowment to give a decent return from rents.

Divided towns are singularly underrepresented in the extant material which details parochial revenues. Even where statements survive, they are likely to be isolated examples, like those for Warwick.[21] Such losses are particularly regrettable, for they would add major contrasts to the picture to be presented later. They would also add complications: such parishes are likely to show the differences between appropriated parishes with ordained vicarages, and those where the revenues remained undivided. Evidence of the differential development of the individual parishes in places like Oxford, Cambridge, Worcester, York, London and Norwich would enhance the current debate on 'urban decline'. Given the factors affecting the contraction of settlement in towns, for which Winchester provides the best evidence,[22] differences could certainly be expected, with some parishes losing wealth or inhabitants, while others maintained or perhaps increased both.

The difference between unified and fragmented towns is clear from a comparison of the *Valor Ecclesiasticus* entries for two of the most highly taxed towns of the early 1500s. Norwich heads W.G. Hoskins's ranking list of English towns based on the taxations of 1523–27; Newcastle upon Tyne has third place.[23] However, there is a marked difference in the relative wealth of their parochial incumbents. At Newcastle, even though the living was an ordained vicarage, the vicar was still returned as receiving a clear income of £50 in 1535. In serving the cure, he could presumably also call on the chaplains of the chantries in the town's four churches (but he may have had to pay the chaplains of those chapelries, thus reducing his income).[24] At over £100, the total income of the Norwich incumbents in 1535 exceeded the sum for Newcastle; but as Norwich was divided into numerous parishes, no incumbent received as much as Newcastle's vicar. According to the *Valor*, the most profitable parish in Norwich for its occupant was St Michael in Coslany, at £13 6s. 8d. (although St Peter Mancroft was farmed at £16 18s. 11d., and was therefore in reality the wealthiest parish, with St Andrew, also farmed, at £11, perhaps also surpassing St Michael in real value). The range of recorded incomes among Norwich's other parishes was considerable, from St Botulph at 47s. 8d. and St Bartholomew at 53s. 4d. up to St Clement ad pontem at £7 9s. 1d. and St John Maddermarket at a shilling more. Most Norwich churches were rectories; only one vicarage appears in the *Valor* – St Stephen, which returned a clear income of £9.[25]

The variation in the incomes of Norwich's parishes must have reflected both their area,[26] and their relative wealth (itself affected by population distribution and industrial or trading activity as much as anything else). Not every parish had its own incumbent; the cathedral priory owned many of the town's rectories, and farmed them out. The declared receipts from these parishes presumably reflect income beyond the charges for priests, and in the *Valor* again covered a wide range, from St Gregory at £4 to St Giles at 5s., with another seven from which the priory declared nil receipts for several years past, for default and poverty of the inhabitants.[27] Norwich's parishes presumably had differing experiences of changes in urban fortunes in the preceding century or so, partly reflected in the variations in parish receipts in 1535.

Such fluctuations might affect a town's parochial geography. Despite the general stability of English parochial arrangements after 1300, some rearrangement of parochial boundaries continued, as individual churches ceased to serve a useful function. The alterations in the post-Black Death years tend to confirm the dire effect of the changing economic equations in that period, perhaps particularly within towns. It can be no accident that one of the first effects of the Reformation in York was a drastic cut in the number of parishes within the city, many of which had fallen into poverty in the preceding century or so.[28] Changes in the parochial map elsewhere also reflected changing economic circumstances. At Warwick, for instance, the collegiate church of St Mary was effectively the town's sole parish church by 1400: a century earlier there had been several rectories, but demographic changes had led to their decline and eventual extinction. Equally dramatic were the changes at Winchester, where what had been some 54 churches c.1300 had been reduced to around 25 by 1500.[29] There were also attempts to increase the number of parishes, as settlements outgrew the main church and sought juridical independence. The chapelry of St Nicholas at Bishop's Lynn made several attempts to break away from the mother church of St Margaret between 1379 and the 1430s, all unsuccessful. The town's other chapelry, St James, seems to have joined in one attempt in the 1420s, with equal lack of success.[30] Urban churches were perhaps less successful in the search for jurisdictional autonomy than rural chapelries: where they did break away, other motives might also have to be reckoned with.

Cash and kind

For towns included in a larger parochial entity, differentiation between the urban and rural receipts is often almost impossible. This would be the sort of parish held by Chaucer's parson in the *Canterbury Tales*: wide, with dispersed settlements, but centred on a *toun*.[31] Where there are parish records, the town is usually lost in the wider entity. Some analysis is occasionally possible, but the picture is always partial. The *Valor Ecclesiasticus* thus shows the position at Tewkesbury, where the town made a reasonable contribution to the total parish revenues.[32] Even here, the best that can be done is to deduct the amount for agricultural tithes from the overall sum, to give a figure for 'non-agricultural' receipts. Scarborough provides more detail of urban revenues: the accounts itemize receipts from individuals for personal tithes, detail income from fishing tithes, and list the receipts from celebrations at the main church and its subsidiary chapels.[33] While there is a clear distinction between town and country, the nature and extent of the agricultural income (and receipts in kind) remains obscure: the only available figures are those of 1535, which are not a valid base for comparison. A third town within a greater entity which provides some indications is Selby, where the rectory was appropriated to the abbey, and a stipendiary priest undertook pastoral duties in the town. In this case (which is probably repeated in many other places) the abbey took all the urban spiritual revenues, and an impression of their nature can be recovered. The receipts were shared between several of the abbey obedientiaries, so it is impossible to give an accurate picture of any one year, or to analyse trends. The abbey's presence – like the presence of any major church anywhere – added its own confusions to the picture.[34] The main benefit of the inclusion of the Selby revenues in the obedientiary accounts is that they include receipts in kind, which will require more attention later.

Although a town might be part of a wider parochial entity, it retained its own unity, and perhaps its own distinctiveness from the encompassing countryside. This might be emphasized by different payment arrangements for town and country components. This applied at Beverley, where the urban inhabitants of the parish of St John did not pay mortuary to their church, whereas the inhabitants of the outlying townships did.[35]

The surviving detailed accounts for urban parishes usually record only the cash income. It is probable that many of them omit income received in kind. Hints of this are provided by the general identification of receipts from mortuaries: they almost invariably refer to items sold, not the total received. If, as at Yarmouth, a mortuary might be an animal or a piece of plate, the chances of retention were undoubtedly rather better than if it was merely old clothes (a robe seems to have been the customary urban mortuary) – although even some of these might be kept by an incumbent.[36]

Beyond mortuaries, another rather obscure source of income in kind was wax offerings. England's medieval wax trade is under-studied, yet wax was used in great quantities for religious purposes.[37] Particularly important, although quite unquantifiable, would be wax from devotional offerings at shrines and images, or candles for altars.[38] Parish accounts often refer to sales of wax (as at Yarmouth and Lynn) but record purchases less commonly.[39] There is clear evidence for gifts of wax in parish receipts, which had a twofold destination: the wax might be resold to parishioners or other visitors; or the donations might be used within the church, so relieving the incumbent of the burden of provision and saving him money.[40]

The most significant source of revenues in kind was probably tithes (but not personal tithes, which were paid in cash). Here, obviously, much depended on the nature of the parish and how far it was integrated into a rural hinterland. A city-centre parish of a few acres would clearly receive fewer tithes in kind than a large agrarian parish with a small town at its centre – like Tewkesbury, for example.⁴¹ (The possibility of a town-centre parish having larger detached rural segments would qualify this statement. Several of York's parishes had such enclaves.)⁴² The industrial profile, and local commutation practices, would also be important: a coastal parish which maintained a sizeable fishing fleet could well pay a considerable tithe of fish which would not be recorded as cash receipts; salt might similarly be received in kind.⁴³ This affects analyses of the evidence for several coastal places, like Yarmouth, Lynn, Scarborough, and Whitby, where fish tithes appear among the receipts.⁴⁴ The available statements only give the cash receipts for fishing tithes, but at Yarmouth there are occasional references to donations of fish to images, and quite possibly some tithes went straight to the priory kitchen.⁴⁵

Opportunities to exploit fisheries were geographically limited. The possibilities of receiving tithes in kind in an urban context nevertheless require further consideration. Yarmouth here provides the most explicit evidence, with references to tithes of piglets, of pigeons, and of other poultry.⁴⁶ They might be an urban commonplace, but by the nature of most of the sources are almost never recorded. Indeed, the contribution of tithes in kind may have grown in several urban parishes after 1350; as settlement retreated many towns and built-up areas contracted to the main streets and the chief trading foci, so the possibility of exploiting the vacated ground for agricultural and industrial use increased, and with it the potential yield of tithes in kind.⁴⁷ Of course, if arrangements for tithe commutation had been made before the contraction, then the overall impact on receipts would be limited, but the possibility cannot be overlooked.

A good indication of the potential for a contribution in kind towards parochial revenues from urban inhabitants or resources appears in the Selby Abbey kitcheners' accounts. In 1416–17 the town's Lenten tithes came to £11 9s. 11d., with another £7 12s. 5d. 'profits' for its church, and 4s. 4d. for blessed bread. The kitchener also accounted for 20s. from tithe flax and hemp, 22 piglets, 3 lambs, 2 geese, and 520 eggs. Moreover, the granger received some tithe grain from lands around the town, amounting in value in 1404–05 to 120s. 6d., or in bulk to 1 quarter 4lb. 'corn', 8 quarters rye, 13 quarters barley, and 36 quarters oats. The kitchener's receipts are only noted from the stock account (apart from the sales of hemp and flax).⁴⁸ If these accounts do typify receipts in kind for parishes which were both urban and rural (or even for predominantly urban parishes), then they would have permitted an impressive standard of living.⁴⁹

The parish of St Margaret, Bishop's Lynn

The parish and the records

With all the caveats and possible variations, no one town can exemplify everything: differences in population, trading patterns, industrial structure, and other factors would all have an impact. Nevertheless, in trying to trace the financial development of urban benefices (and again stressing the distinction between the finance of the benefice, and the finances of the lay representatives with their own type of administration) reliance on a few runs of accounts is unavoidable. As Bishop's Lynn seems to offer the best urban series, its fiscal history (even though it may not be typical) provides the heart of what follows.

Bishop's Lynn owed its origins as a distinct parish to Herbert Losinga, a twelfth-century bishop of Norwich. The parish served only the town. It had no explicit rural connections. Nevertheless, it was divided into three, the main church of St Margaret having two subordinate (at times rebellious) chapels of St Nicholas and St James. The chapels acquired burial rights, but St Margaret retained the monopoly of baptisms, purifications and marriages, and receipts from payments for holy bread.[50] The late medieval town also housed Franciscan, Dominican, and Augustinian friaries, and a number of hospitals. The Carmelite friars had a house in the adjacent parish of South Lynn, and thereby also influenced religious life within Bishop's Lynn. There were also two major shrine chapels: St Mary on the bridge, and St Mary on the Mount (the latter erected in the late fifteenth century). The parish's most notable feature, which explains the survival of the run of rectorial accounts, was that its church was appropriated to the priory established within the parish, itself in turn a cell of Norwich cathedral priory.[51] The Lynn accounts now repose among the records of that priory's successor, the dean and chapter of Norwich Cathedral.

The parish accounts are conjointly those of the priory; disentangling the specifically parochial material and that for the priory is problematic, but less so for the income than for the expenditure. The surviving record is gratifyingly full, even if incomplete, giving information from the 1370s through to the 1530s.[52] Unlike many appropriated rural rectories and some urban ones (like fifteenth-century Westminster),[53] the rectory was never farmed, so the accounts do not degenerate into bland records of the annual rent due for the revenues. The official rectors were, throughout, the priory of Lynn, so the records have not shared the fate of those of unappropriated rectories which, belonging to individual transient incumbents, were mere ephemera, and are therefore generally lost. While the accounts survive, it is hard to define their proper context. The parish was under the Bishop of Norwich's direct jurisdiction, so the normal ecclesiastical administrative records do not exist to provide a background.[54] The economic and social context is similarly incomplete: despite the amount of evidence available, the economic development of late medieval Lynn has been rather neglected by recent historians.[55] Nevertheless, enough has been done to allow the parish accounts to be assessed as measures of the town's general economic history.

Although the run of accounts for Bishop's Lynn is impressive, they cannot simply be taken at face value. The difficulties they present must be recognized, even if they cannot be circumvented. Being exclusively cash accounts, they may well understate the rectory's true value. Tithe receipts in kind, for example, are never mentioned; yet such receipts at Yarmouth, the sister cell also established in an urban rectory, suggest that they might have been received.[56] Although Lynn's urban authorities (admittedly somewhat later) frequently sought to ban pigs, chickens, cows, sheep, and horses from the town – creatures which presumably generated offspring – there are no such tithes mentioned in the extant accounts.[57] Such receipts would almost certainly exclude grain tithes, precluded by the lack of a rural element to the parish. Some mortuaries and wax offerings may also have been kept.[58]

It can be argued that Lynn did receive some of its revenues in kind. With wax, for instance, although there is a heading for sales in many of the early accounts, purchases are rarely mentioned (although a waxmaker was employed). Purchases do appear in the late fifteenth century: this might indicate changes in the church receipts, with what was once received freely now being bought. The same may apply to tallow: purchases of tallow candles first appear in 1437–38, and are almost annual thereafter, perhaps reflecting a fall in tithe receipts from the butchers. The most significant evidence concerns the Lynn fisheries. Notices of tithes relating to fishing are rare in the Lynn cash accounts, in part because of their highly summary nature. References to receipts from 'Christ's part' (a portion of the catch allocated to the parish church) and ships (presumably fishing vessels) occur only in a few years of Henry VII's reign when the income of St Margaret's is broken down into its constituent parts.[59] From 1508 the accounts show what may have been a significant change, recording details of purchases of fish. While such purchases may have been previously hidden under another heading, it may be that hitherto the priory had usually received its fish tithes in kind, perhaps moving to commutation as the fishing industry declined.[60] With the collapse of the Lynn fishery, the priory had to look to the market for its supplies. If this did actually happen, then the impact on overall rectorial income would again be double-edged: a formerly concealed element of income which would have made the rectory wealthier than it appears now became a charge which had to be deducted from the cash receipts.

The income of any parish was a complex mix of voluntary and compulsory elements, whose differentiation in the totality of a parish's accounts is not always easy. The Lynn statements often combine the two categories to produce summary totals. The key compulsory levy would be tithes, in this case the personal tithes levied in cash on disposable income and trading profits.[61] Until 1429–30 they are amalgamated with 'testaments', presumably the voluntary legacies which in later years have an independent heading. Their inclusion with the tithes distorts any assessment of the totals, but it may be safe to assume that they did not seriously disrupt the trends which the accounts reveal.[62]

With the summary totals for oblations, initially a combined figure for all three churches, but later distinguishing between them, there is greater complexity. The receipts at St James and St Nicholas were probably mainly voluntary (perhaps except for offerings at the principal feasts, although it is unlikely that there was a formal rather than 'traditional' rate). The receipts at St Margaret included compulsory payments, which are itemized in a few years.[63] Even if there was no set rate for marriages, burials and purifications, the customary payments might well be effectively compulsory minima; some payment would be expected in any event.[64] Equally obligatory was the payment for holy bread, to provide the blessed but unconsecrated bread which provided a kind of communion. Although the arrangements for payment were decreed by the town authorities rather than the church,[65] this remained a compulsory charge. Offerings at principal feasts could also be considered obligatory, even if not at an established rate.[66]

Most other headings in the accounts reflect voluntary donations: legacies, purchases of wax, and payments for private masses (additional to the masses for the deed and guild ceremonies which are mentioned in the sums received from the individual churches).[67] The one unavoidable payment was for mortuaries, although the extent of the liability is never stated.[68]

Tithes and oblations

In using these accounts to assess Lynn's late medieval economic status, the details of receipts from personal tithes are perhaps the most informative element. Until 1407 these are combined with the revenues from testaments; for two years in the 1420s mortuaries are also included (but were probably not significant). The history of the tithe income is complex, obviously starting on a downward curve in the

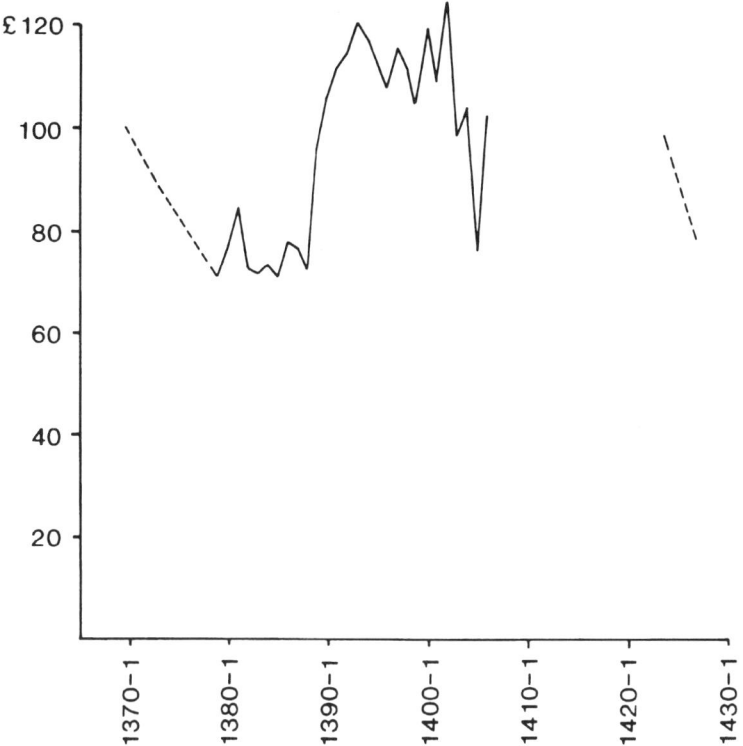

6.1 Tithes of Bishop's Lynn, 1370–1428. Until 1407, the totals are for tithes and testaments combined; for the 1420s for tithes, testaments, and mortuaries

1370s (see Figure 6.1). From just under £100 in 1370–71, the totals stayed between £70 and £80 in the 1380s, rising significantly (and so far inexplicably) in the last year of that decade. Until the end of this first run of figures in 1406–07, receipts from tithes and wills were almost always over £100, often over £110, and indeed reached £121 0s. 9d. in 1393–94 and £125 1s. 10d. in 1402–03. These sums must reflect the normal flow of cash and liability for payments; but payment was not always willing: in 1400–01 an extra £20 reflected unpaid tithes from one individual stretching back several years, while a similar payment of £15 5s. 6d. in 1406–07 was made only after the death of the person concerned. As personal tithes were levied on trading profits, among other things, they presumably also reflect Lynn's trading history at this time, based on a burgeoning cloth trade with the Baltic (in the hands of Lynn merchants rather than under Hanseatic control), and healthy contacts with Gascony and Calais. Certainly the town can be

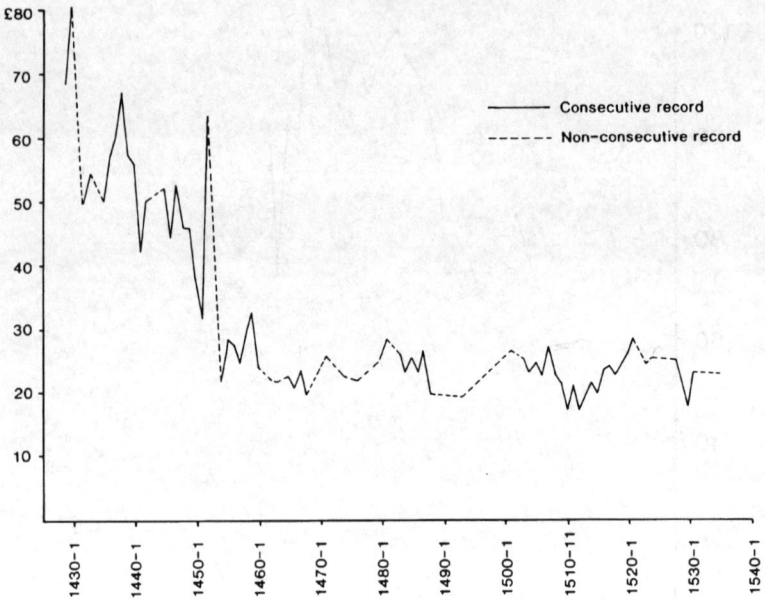

6.2 Tithes of Bishop's Lynn, 1429–1536

counted among the beneficiaries of what has been called an 'urban boom around 1400'.[69]

From 1429–30 (ignoring the two years for which tithes, testaments and mortuary receipts are lumped together) the income from personal tithes is treated on its own (see Figure 6.2). By then, the town had clearly entered a slump: the recorded sum was a mere £68 11s. 7d. In the following years the annual figures lack firm consistency, but a downward trend is discernible. Average annual receipts in the 1430s hovered at just under £60; in the 1440s at just under £50; in the 1450s at under £40. Whether contemporaries fully appreciated the trend is unclear: fluctuations in annual totals may have obscured the reality – particularly when in 1452–53 tithe income was £63 7s., more than twice the sum for the year before and almost three times the next recorded figure.

The 1452–53 receipts were an aberration, detectable as such from hindsight. Later tithe income only once exceeded £30, in 1459–60 (£32 19s. 3d.). With the 1460s, the doldrums really set in, later receipts hovering in the £20s almost continuously, sometimes falling below £20. The lowest recorded sum is £17 4s. 1d., in 1512–13. The best to be said of Lynn's tithe income is that it was stagnant. This must reflect on the town's economy, but whether it indicates an overall decline in trade, or merely that trading profits were not being retained by natives of Lynn, is not clear. There is a broad correlation between the history of these receipts and the general record of the transformations of the cloth trade through Lynn; but the fluctuation in tithe receipts cannot be accounted for by such changes alone.[70]

The trends apparent in these tithe figures are also detectable in the receipts at the main church of St Margaret, although the composite nature of the sums recorded precludes detailed analysis. The figures, moreover, can be analysed only from 1429–30: previous accounts combined the oblations of all three town churches into one sum. Even so, those earlier figures merit some preliminary consideration (see Figure 6.3). The first sum recorded, for 1370–71, is £101 12s. 5d. In later years there is no obvious correlation between the oblations and tithe income, although the trends appear similar. There was a steady decline through to the early 1390s, with receipts generally £85–95. From 1392–93 the figures are again consistently over £100, falling below that sum in 1401–02 but then recovering strongly to £118 in 1406–07. The forces determining these changes cannot be stated with any conviction; the only named influence is plague, which dramatically boosted receipts. In 1381–82 the summer mortality pushed oblations up to £113 17s., over £20 above the years immediately before and after. Even more striking was the reaction to plague in 1399–1400, which almost doubled the receipts in comparison with the years on either side, to a staggering £198 12s. 6d. Only in these two cases was the impact of plague acknowledged, but its recurrence may lie behind some later fluctuations in the figures.

The last two accounts which give the combined oblations of all the churches, 1424–25 and 1427–28, respectively note sums of £72 4s. and £80 8s. 1d. (to which might be added the £5 6s. 8d. entered on the first mention of *missis de certo*, which may be hidden in the oblations figure for earlier years). In 1429–30, when receipts from the churches are first separated, the total for oblations is just over £67, of which St Margaret's portion was £42 7s. 2d. This figure provides the baseline for comparisons over the next century (see Figure 6.4).

In fact, the St Margaret's receipts were fairly stable until the early 1450s, generally ranging between £39 and £49, but clustering at £42–45. Decline may be detected from 1454–55, when the sum was £33 10s. 2d., but the rest of the decade shows considerable variations. After 1459, St Margaret's only once contributed more than £30 to the sum of receipts (£32 18s. in 1498–99). Until the mid-1470s the average was about £23 a year, with a nadir in the 1480s when recorded totals were around £15–16, and a mere £13 12s. in 1486–87. Thereafter, fortunes revived. Under Henry VII, receipts usually exceeded £20, but under his

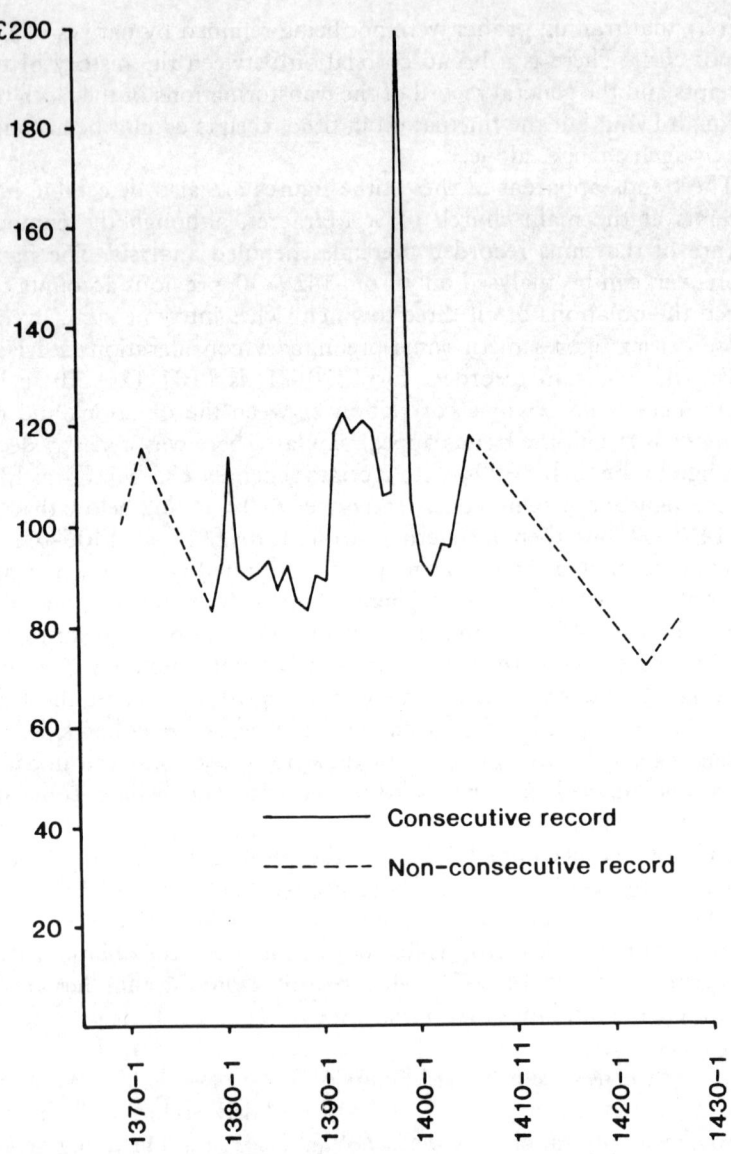

6.3 Oblations of Bishop's Lynn, 1370–1428

son there was another drop. After 1510, totals over £20 occurred only thrice, the range being from £13 11s. 9d. (in 1521–22) up to £22 10s. (in 1524–25), but the annual variations elude consistency.

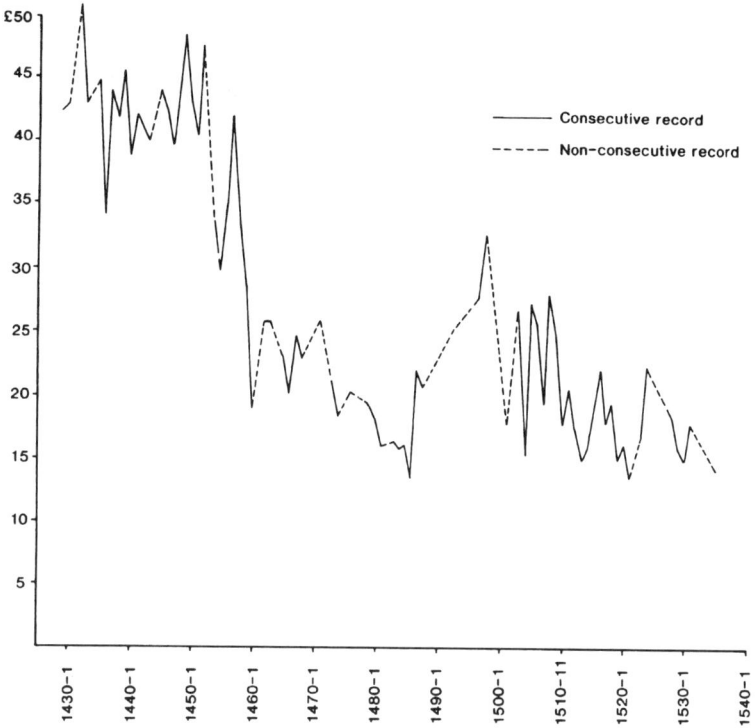

6.4 Receipts of St Margaret's Church, Bishop's Lynn, 1429–1536

Pilgrims

While the compulsory element was always significant in urban revenues, the voluntary receipts perhaps demand most attention. These might be provided 'internally' – from the parishioners themselves – or 'externally' – from non-parishioners. The key factor in boosting the latter would be possession of a shrine and encouragement of pilgrimage.

The distribution of urban shrines in late medieval England still requires detailed attention, although they were clearly widespread. This in part reflects the expansion of Marian cults in the period: in addition to the outstanding case of Walsingham, Marian shrines existed throughout the country, with several in London. Others of note were at Ipswich, Doncaster, Wakefield, Worcester and Woolpit.[71] Given the lack of work on such English shrines, their apparent urban concentration may be merely an accident of the sources.

Beyond the great shrines, there were many smaller centres which rose and fell over time. Almost every parish probably had its boxes and images before which donations would be made, totalling a few shillings a year. Their division between incumbent and churchwardens varied: at Salisbury, the churchwardens received the revenues from biannual displays of relics which included the hand and ring of St Edmund, linked to an indulgence for maintenance of the church fabric.[72] Generally, the incumbents (or, perhaps, their lessees) seem to have received these donations.[73] Certainly, Yarmouth accounts contain odd shillings for such receipts from boxes and images,[74] and the same applies to Lynn, where offerings in the general heading also included donations to the image of St Mary in the bridge chapel. They first appear in 1437–38, at £3 2s. 0½d. Thereafter, however, they fell: a decade later they were below £2, and in following years often lower (a mere 9d. in 1460–61). After 1480–81, they never exceeded £1, with the startling (and so far unexplained) exception of £3 5s. 0d. in 1500–01. Later receipts were usually under 10s., but this may not fully mirror the scale of devotion. When St Margaret's skull was displayed in the Trinity chapel in 1514, the town council minutes record a division of the receipts, with half of the proceeds going to the prior and convent.[75] Some of the money derived from bequests, like the 3s. 4d. left to Our Lady at the bridge by Roger Petman in 1499.[76] Some came from pilgrims. In 1448, for example, Alice Winter of Norwich wished a pilgrim acting on her behalf to visit St Margaret at Lynn, Holy Trinity (presumably the guild chapel) and All Saints (the dedication of South Lynn church).[77]

Voluntary receipts from devotion to saints were the most volatile type of income, as is evident in the Yarmouth accounts. The sudden rise of the cult of Henry VI is shown in a staggering increase in receipts after the building of a chapel containing his image. However, devotion waned almost as rapidly as it had arisen.[78] The seeming absence of Henrician devotion at Lynn is perhaps surprising, given the nation-wide extent of his cult.[79] Yet Lynn's accounts do show something similar. In 1507–08 they mention a new devotion: offerings to a 'good cross' in the cemetery of St Margaret's Church. In that year, receipts totalled £6 15s. 7d., but such heights were illusory. Decline was immediate: £4 2s. 0d. the following year, down to a mere 10s. 3d. in 1513–14. Although fortunes recovered intermittently thereafter, later receipts were almost always under £1, and from 1523–24 always under 10s.

If donations from pilgrims were to be tapped effectively, ideally a devotional focus was needed which existed independently of the parish. That might be provided by an indulgence. Lynn seemingly had one for only one year: in 1454–55, when ordinary receipts from the church boxes were £1 8s. 6d., another £5 7s. 0d. was received at the time of the indulgence. More effective would be a permanent cult. Here Marian and Christocentric devotions possibly had most impact. The scale of such 'passing trade' is shown by offerings at the chapel of St Mary of Arneburgh at Great Yarmouth: they were always a healthy boost for parish balances.[80] Lynn initially had nothing like that; but from the 1480s, until the 1530s, substantial sums were received from precisely such an arrangement. In the 1480s a new chapel was constructed in Lynn: that of St Mary on the Mount (why, and for what clientele, is not clear).[81] It still survives, described as 'one of the strangest Gothic churches in England'.[82] It first appears in the accounts in 1481–82, when receipts were an unimpressive £1 13s. 10¾d. This gave no foretaste of the future: when next mentioned the sum recorded is £20 17s. 5½d. – possibly for only six months from 24 February to 29 September 1485. Sums over £20 appear regularly until the end of Henry VII's reign, the all-time high being £34 13s. 4d. in 1497–98. Under Henry VIII, decline set in, a slow drop which in 1528–29 and 1529–30 actually took receipts below £10. The final mention of the chapel, in 1531–32, records offerings at £11 exactly.

Why there was such a chapel, and such devotion, is unclear. St Mary on the bridge elicited nothing like this response. Presumably the mount held a miracle-working image, but none is mentioned. The two accounts which split the chapel's receipts into half-yearly totals in 1489–90 suggest that devotion was concentrated in the spring and summer: between Michaelmas and the Annunciation, receipts were £4 18s. 8d., but between Annunciation and Michaelmas they were £16 9s. 3d.

The wide distribution of shrines in England, and the uncertainty of their contribution to parish incomes, make assessment of their significance hazardous. The *Valor Ecclesiasticus* it seems clear, under-records the distribution and receipts. Possibly there was some element in incumbents' accounting which allowed this: is it coincidence that the last account in the Lynn series, for 1535–36, makes absolutely no mention of any devotional receipts? It is not that headings appear for the boxes, the good cross, and the chapel of St Mary, with no totals recorded – there are no headings. The accounting system had been rearranged to exclude a major contribution to parochial revenues from the record.

The chapels

A particularly illuminating aspect of the Lynn accounts is the distinction between Lynn's church and its chapelries, which illustrates the problem of diversity within towns. Lynn can almost be treated as a town containing several parishes. The model is not exact: the chapel receipts are only for voluntary oblations, those of St Margaret include money for services only receivable from a mother church and the dues payable specifically to one. In only four years (1487–88, 1497–98, 1498–99,

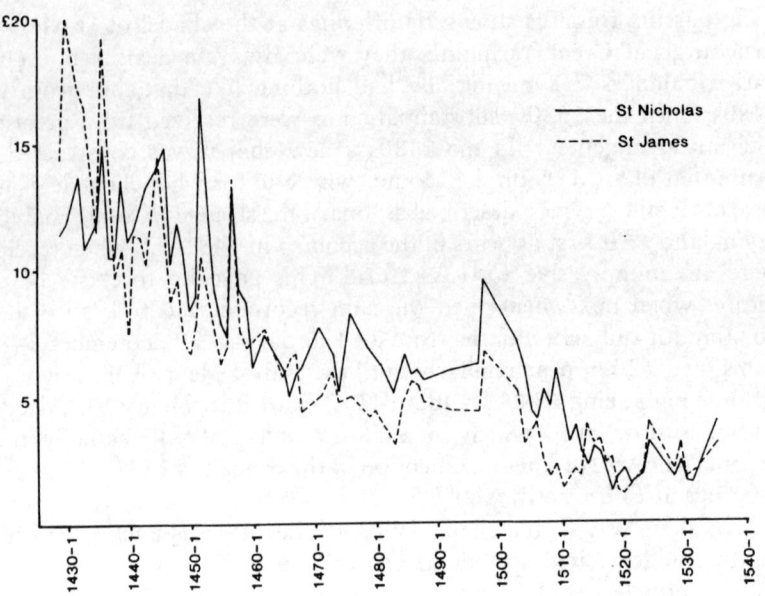

6.5 Receipts of the chapels of St Nicholas and St James, Bishop's Lynn, 1429–1536

1501–02) can the chapel sums be compared with equivalent figures for St Margaret's, an insufficient basis for any extrapolation. As the tithes are all combined, without distinction between areas of the town, they do not add to the picture.[83] Nevertheless, at least for the two chapelries, the figures show changes in voluntarily disposable income used for devotional purposes. They might illustrate either changing levels of wealth and population,[84] or changing levels of spirituality. When set against the pattern of overall tithe receipts and the records of receipts for oblations at St Margaret, it seems valid to consider them here primarily as evidence for the first of these options.

Until 1429–30, the amalgamation of the three churches' oblations prevents a comparison of developments in the separate sectors of the town. However, in that year, the three churches were recorded separately, St Margaret's providing £42 7s. 2d.; while receipts from St Nicholas and St James were respectively £11 10s. 4d. and £13 9s. 9d. The relative status of the two dependent chapelries at that point is noteworthy, suggesting a reversal of fortunes since St Nicholas first sought independence.

Predictably, at both chapels the receipts fluctuated (see Figure 6.5). The initial sums were sometimes surpassed later, but after 1450 such higher figures were rare at St Nicholas, and unknown at St James. The totals for St Nicholas were generally fairly stable (with a hint of improvement in the early 1440s) until 1450, when they first fell below £10. There was a slight downward drift to the mid-1460s, with receipts to the end of the century at £5–7. Another drop followed, so that after 1510 receipts rarely exceeded £3, except for the last year in the run (1535–36) when they were exactly £4.

St James has a similar tale of decline, Receipts were generally good during the 1430s (twice being over £19), usually exceeding those for St Nicholas by 25–50 per cent. However, in 1438–39 the paths crossed: later oblations at St James were generally less than at St Nicholas until the 1510s. As with St Nicholas, there is a rough stability from the mid-1450s until the end of the century, masking an obvious and insidious decline. After 1473–74 income generally wavered between £4 and £6, and was often under £2 in the early 1500s. From 1514–15 the pattern again changed: receipts from St James now often surpassed those from St Nicholas. The difference was usually only a few shillings, which, given the small sums involved, is trifling. In the final year the relationship again reversed: against the £4 from St Nicholas, St James produced £3 4s. 0d., but this again is not significant.

The pattern seems to be one of fairly relentless decline throughout the town. There were different patterns of change in the two chapelries, but in terms of oblations both had declined to relative insignificance by 1500. Their contributions to parochial revenues had been eclipsed by the chapel of St Mary on the mount. On these figures, their continued existence might be questioned; but as they were not separate cures there was probably little real incentive to suppress them. Even so, St James did go out of use after the Reformation.[85]

Miscellaneous income

The main figures in the Lynn accounts can be analysed, albeit tentatively, and can be linked with changes in the town's economic history. Other heads defy interpretation, or show no immediate correlation, especially if they incompletely reflect income. Mortuaries are noted as being sales rather than total receipts, and reveal little. There is no sign of what they were, or their number. (The only exception occurs in 1487–88, when it is stated that one mortuary had been sold for 1s. 6d.) As in other towns, mortuaries were probably a robe or other article of clothing,[86] but almost anything could be hidden here. Cash receipts varied considerably from year to year, from a high of 63s. 5d. in 1446–47 down to nothing in some years (as in 1497–98 and 1513–14). The lowest entry was a mere 6d. in 1459–60.

Legacies are equally obscure, with similar uncertainties about their number, frequency, and content. Presumably the sums in the accounts are only the cash receipts, perhaps under the rather formulaic arrangement 'for forgotten tithes' frequently encountered in late medieval English wills.[87] Bequests of goods would be included only if later sold. (These sums would be solely for bequests explicitly to the high altar; as elsewhere, legacies generally intended for the parish church, especially its fabric, probably went to the churchwardens.)[88] The Lynn accounts show wide fluctuations in the income from bequests, once they appear as a separate entry (in 1437–38). The highest figures appear in the earlier years, sometimes reaching double figures. After the mid-1440s they were rarely above £4, not infrequently below £1 (the lowest sum entered is 3s. in 1514–15). The interpretative problems are shown by the figures for two years: 1489–90 and 1510–11. In the former, legacies totalled 19s. 4d. Of this, 6s. 8d. came from Nicholas Bateman, ostensibly as the only bequest received between Michaelmas 1489 and Annunciation 1490. How many distinct legacies contributed to the 12s. 8d. entered for the second half of the year cannot be guessed. A similar situation arose in 1510–11. The total for legacies, at £7 16s. 4d., was the fourth highest in all the years which offer figures, and a marked contrast with the £1 10s. of the year before and the 5s. of 1511–12. However, £6 13s. 4d. of this was left by one man, Thomes Thursby. The total of the other bequests for that year falls to 23s., rather changing the picture.

Two final elements in this miscellany of lesser sources of revenue merit some comment. A heading for *missis de certo* first appears in 1427–28, providing £6 6s. 8d. Thereafter it is a regular feature, generally running at £3–5 between 1429–30 and 1463–64 (although with annual fluctuations), and between £2 10s. and £4 thereafter until 1504–05. From 1505–06 the recorded sum is always £2 a year, suggesting a change in the accounting system which lasted until the last surviving account for 1535–36, when the figure is £1 4s. As the heading usually says it includes the payment for the mass of the Trinity guild, regularly entered first at 20s. a year, and later at 40s., it seems clear that by the end, this mass is in fact the sole entry. What had happened to the other private masses is not stated – presumably they were included under the individual churches. (The Trinity guild mass was not the only guild mass celebrated: masses for other guilds were accounted for under the separate churches, although the guilds themselves were not itemized.)

Rather more striking, but harder to set in context, is the evidence of payments from the friars, based on the amounts from burial receipts due under the papal bull, *Super cathedram*.[89] The need to regularize relations with the mendicants on this is shown by the formal agreements about payment made with the warden of the Austin friars in 1361, and with the Carmelites in 1376.[90] The priory accounts include a heading for payments between 1431 and 1477, possibly a unique record of such dues. Given the usual assumption of the friars' popularity then, the small sums in the Lynn accounts are surprising. For many years, no receipts are entered at all. Those that are, range from 10s. 6½d. in 1450–51, to 1d. in 1468–69. Sums over 2s. appear only nine times; the second highest figure is 6s. 8d. in 1440–41. Most identified payments were from the Augustinians: the Dominicans are mentioned only in 1436–37 (contributing to a total of 1s. 1d.), while the Carmelites paid 1½d. (out of 4d.) in 1473–74, and the same amount (the sum of receipts from the friars) in the next year. The Franciscans are never mentioned, but may have contributed sometimes.

Conclusion

Although the spirituality receipts of Lynn parish fluctuated annually, each section responding to distinctive forces in the town's economy and society; and although new headings appeared intermittently as new devotions produced new income, for the priory (as for any rector) the crucial figure, and the crucial trend, was that for overall church receipts. Lynn priory did not include its rents from town properties among the 'church' revenues, and they are ignored here (although if they were seen as the urban equivalent of rural glebe, some analysis would be required).[91] To summarize the rental history briefly: the overall trend – downwards – is further confirmation of the apparent fall in Lynn's prosperity attested by the parochial receipts. However, producing valid overall totals for parish income is made hazardous by all the complexities indicated earlier. Moreover, the crucial indicator for the priory would be profitability, which cannot be treated here. Simply taking the figures derived from the accounts for the total church receipts, a decline seems undeniable.

The stress on income makes this a rather one-sided analysis of Lynn's revenues. It ignores expenditure, and the impact of the changes on pastoral care. Yet money was spent: on buildings, to priests, clergy and preachers, on the necessities for services, and lawsuits against rebellious chapelries and the friars. Any rector might face such outgoings and crises. Costs had to be considered when assessing a benefice's overall profitability. That would be affected by its status as rectory or vicarage, by whether it was farmed or not, and other factors. If incomes were falling and costs rising (or, at best, static), urban rectory-holders would be in a worsening financial position. Changes might cause tensions between clergy and laity, but there is little sign of that in Lynn's accounts. Organized under churchwardens, the laity's assumption of greater oversight of churches and chapels was also important, but cannot be treated here. Not all English towns had mendicant convents (although friars might be common visitors); not all had pilgrimage centres, certainly not on the scale of Lynn. To that extent, the Lynn records do not fairly reflect the income of 'normal' urban parochial benefices. If a town had both friaries and pilgrimage centres, and also several parishes, their contributions to parochial income would vary greatly. The range of revenues in any 'urban' parish, and the variety in their distribution, preclude generalization. Yet Lynn can offer a yardstick to assess other parishes; it also suggests that the records of parochial revenues provide a mirror of the scale of urban economic activity deserving more attention than they have so far received.

Appendix: List of Accounts of Lynn Priory

All the accounts are deposited at the Norfolk Record Office, Norwich, under the prefix DCN 2/1/. This list cross-refers from the date to the number in the series. Many accounts are duplicated: for these both numbers are given.

Year	Call no.	Year	Call no.
1370–71	1	1398–99	21
1372–73	2	1399–1400	21
1379–80[92]	3, 4	1400–01	21
1380–81	5	1401–02	21
1381–82	6, 7	1402–03	21
1382–83	8	1403–04	21
1383–84	9	1404–05	21
1384–85	10	1405–06	21
1385–86	11	1406–07[95]	21
1386–87	12	1407–08[96]	21
1387–88	13, 14	1424–25	22
1388–89	15, 16	1427–28	23, 24
1389–90	17	1429–30	25
1390–91	18	1430–31	26
1391–92	19	1432–33	27
1392–93[93]	20	1433–34	28, 29
1393–94	20	1435–36	30
1394–95	20	1436–37	31
1395–96	20	1437–38	32
1396–97	20	1438–39	33
1397–98[94]	21	1439–40	34

Year	Call no.	Year	Call no.
1440–41	35	1485–86	70
1441–42	36	1486–87	70, 71
1442–43	37	1487–88	70, 72
1443–44[97]	38	1488–89[99]	70, 73, 74
1445–46	39	1493–94	75
1446–47	40	1497–98[100]	76
1447–48	41	1498–99	77
1448–49	42, 43	1501–02	78
1449–50	44, 45	1503–04[101]	79
1450–51	46, 47	1504–05	80
1451–52	48	1505–06	81, 82
1452–53	49	1506–07	82, 83
1454–55	50, 51	1507–08	82
1455–56[98]	51	1508–09	82
1456–57	52, 53	1509–10[102]	82, 84
1457–58	54	1510–11	82
1458–59	55	1511–12	82
1459–60	56	1512–13	82
1460–61	57	1513–14	82
1462–63	58	1514–15	82, 85
1463–64	59	1515–16	82
1465–66	60	1516–17	82, 86
1466–67	61	1517–18	82, 87
1467–68	62	1518–19	82
1468–69	63	1519–20	82
1471–72	64, 65	1520–21	82
1473–74	66	1521–22	82
1474–75	67	1523–24	82
1476–77	68	1524–25	82, 88
1479–80	69, 70	1528–29	82
1480–81	70	1529–30	82
1481–82	70	1530–31	82, 89
1483–84	70	1531–32	90
1484–85	70	1535–36[103]	91

Acknowledgements

The University of Birmingham gave financial help for the research; the archivists of the Norfolk Record Office at Norwich provided a microfilm of the Bishop's Lynn accounts and helpful responses to repeated queries. A version of this paper was given at the meeting of the Commission international d'histoire ecclésiastique comparée, at Madrid in August, 1990

Notes

1. For a summary of the debate, and details of the bibliography, A.D. Dyer, *Decline and Growth in English Towns, 1400–1640* (1991).
2. A.R. Bridbury, 'English provincial towns in the later Middle Ages', *Economic History Review* (hereafter *Econ.H.R.*), 2nd series, 34 (1981), 14; R.B. Dobson, 'Urban decline in late medieval England', *Transactions of the Royal Historical Society*, 5th series, 27 (1977), 8–10; J.N. Bartlett, 'The expansion and decline of York in the later middle ages', *Econ.H.R.*, 2nd series, 12 (1959–60), 24–6, 28–32; D. Keene (with A.R. Rumble), *Survey of Medieval Winchester*, Winchester studies, 2, 2 vols (1985), vol. 1, 196–216.
3. *Victoria County History of the Counties of England* (hereafter *VCH*) *Warwick*, vol. 3 (1945), 247; *VCH York, East Riding*, vol. 6 (1989), 11–16; M.D. Lobel, *The Borough of Bury St Edmunds: a Study in the Government and Development of a Monastic Town* (1935); N.F. Trenholme, *The English Monastic Boroughs: a Study in Medieval History*, The University of Missouri Studies, a Quarterly of Research, II/iii (1927); M.D. Knowles, *The Religious Orders in England*, 3 vols (1948–61), vol. 1, 263–9.
4. Besides the examples cited below, see also A. Everitt, *New Avenues in English Local History* (1970), 12–14.
5. The parish's rural character is stressed in the *Inquisitiones nonarum* of 1342 (*Nonarum inquisitiones in cura scaccarii temp. regis Edwardi III* (1807), 176); see also D.L. Farmer, 'Two Wiltshire manors and their markets', *Agricultural History Review*, 37 (1989), 1–11. Some urban activity is suggested by tithe payments in the early extant cash accounts: Longleat archives, MSS 9599–9602, 9604–6, 9868, 10610, 10699.
6. R.N. Swanson, 'Standards of livings: parochial revenues in pre-Reformation England', in C. Harper-Bill (ed.), *The Church in Late Medieval England: Proceedings of the Strawberry Hill Conference* (1991), n. 21; see also p. 105.
7. Norwich: N.P. Tanner, *The Church in Late Medieval Norwich. 1370–1532*, Pontifical Institute of Mediaeval Studies: Studies and Texts, 66 (1984), 2–4, 173–8; York: D.M. Palliser, *The Reformation in York, 1534–1553*, Borthwick Papers, 40 (1971), 3; Cambridge: C.N.L. Brooke, 'The churches of medieval Cambridge', in D. Beales and G. Best (eds), *History, Society and the Churches: Essays in Honour of Owen Chadwick* (1985), 69–72; Worcester: map in N. Baker, 'Churches, parishes, and early medieval topography', in M.O.H. Carver (ed.), *Medieval Worcester. An Archaeological Framework*, Transactions of the Worcestershire Archaeological Society, 3rd series, 7 (1980), 30. London: see map of parishes *c*.1520 in M.D. Lobel (ed.), *The British Atlas of Historic Towns. Volume III: The City of London from Prehistoric Times to c.1520* (1989).
8. K.H. Rogers, 'Salisbury', in M.D. Lobel (ed.), *[Atlas of] Historic Towns*, vol. 1 (1969), 4 and map 6; also *VCH Wiltshire*, vol. 6 (1962), 79, 81,

83. These may understate the rural element of at least one parish. In 1269, the suburban church of Stratford-sub-Castle was given to St Thomas (W.D. Macray (ed.), *Charters and Monuments Illustrating the History of the Cathedral, City and Close of Salisbury* (1891), 348); it later appears either as an independent rectory or as part of St Martin's parish (*VCH Wiltshire*, vol. 6, 209–10; R.M. Haines, *Ecclesia Anglicana: Studies in the English Church in the Late Middle Ages* (Toronto, Buffalo and London, 1989), 56, 266–7).

9. *VCH Yorkshire. City of York* (1961), 311. On 'urban' parish boundaries, A. Rogers, 'Parish boundaries and urban history: two case studies', *Journal of the British Archaeological Association*, 3rd series, 35 (1972), 46–64. London's intramural parishes averaged only 3.6 acres each, those outside the walls were larger: C. Brooke, 'The central Middle Ages, 800–1270', in Lobel, *Historic Towns, London*, 36.

10. G. Rosser, *Medieval Westminster, 1200–1540* (1989), 251, 253.

11. Everitt, *New Avenues*, 8 (but the multiple intramural parishes are not his concern), 10; A. Everitt, 'The marketing of agricultural produce', in J. Thirsk (ed.), *The Agrarian History of England and Wales. Volume IV: 1500–1640* (1967), 467. The blunt linkage of market activity and urbanism is rather a hostage to fortune; for possible qualifications see R.H. Hilton, 'Towns in societies – medieval England', *Urban History Yearbook* (1982), 9 (compare Everitt, 'Marketing', 478); see also R.H. Hilton, 'Medieval market towns and simple commodity production', *Past and Present*, **109** (November, 1985), 9–10. For the number of parishes, R.N. Swanson, *Church and Society in Late Medieval England* (1989), 4.

12. Swanson, *Church and Society*, 44, 214.

13. C. Cross claims that 'monasteries had appropriated a disproportionate number of urban rectories in the Middle Ages' (C. Cross, 'The incomes of provincial urban clergy, 1520–1645', in R. O'Day and F. Heal (eds), *Princes and Paupers in the English Church, 1500–1800* (1981), 69). This may demand too rigid a polarization of 'urban' and 'rural' parishes, ignoring the variations between types of parishes containing, or contained within, towns.

14. J.C. Cox, *Churchwardens' Accounts from the Fourteenth Century to the Close of the Seventeenth Century* (1913).

15. A.T. Bannister (ed.), *Registrum Thome Spofford, episcopi Herefordensis, A.D. MCCCCXXII–MCCCCXLVIII*, Canterbury and York Society, 23 (1919), 150–52.

16. K. Wood-Legh, *Perpetual Chantries in Britain* (1965), 155–71, 178–81; Swanson, *Church and Society*, 257; E. Gillett and K.A. MacMahon, *A History of Hull* (1980), 90–91.

17. Swanson, 'Standards of livings', 154–5; *Taxatio ecclesiastica Angliae et Walliae auctoritate Nicholai IV, circa A.D. 1291* (1802); W.E. Lunt, *The Valuation of Norwich* (1926), 139–66, 573–83, 590–614; R. Graham, *English Ecclesiastical Studies* (1929), 281–300; J. Caley and I. Hunter (eds), *Valor Ecclesiasticus*, 6 vols (1810–34) (hereafter *VE*).

18. Swanson, 'Standards of livings', 159–60; *Nonarum inquisitiones*; Graham, *English Ecclesiastical Studies*, 283–5; Lunt, *Valuation of Norwich*, 143–6.

19. Swanson, 'Standards of livings', 155–9.

20. J.H. Tillotson (ed.), *Monastery and Society in the Late Middle Ages: Selected Account Rolls from Selby Abbey, Yorkshire, 1398–1537* (1988), 165.
21. D. Styles (ed.), *Ministers' Accounts of the Collegiate Church of St Mary, Warwick*, Dugdale Society Publications, 26 (1969), 2–3, 16–18, 42–3, 78–85, 87–9, 123–30, 132, 157–61; D. Styles, 'A financial account of St Mary's, Warwick, Michaelmas 1410–Michaelmas 1411', in R. Bearman (ed.), *Miscellanea I*, Dugdale Society Publications, 31 (1977), 137–58.
22. Keene, *Winchester*, vol. 1, 143–7, see also the figures of property boundaries in c.1300, 1417, and c.1550, in vol. 2.
23. W.G. Hoskins, *Local History in England*, 3rd edn (1984), 278. Newcastle's place is allotted on the basis of its apparent population, rather than taxation evidence (W.G. Hoskins, 'English provincial towns in the early sixteenth century', *Transactions of the Royal Historical Society*, 5th series, 6 (1956), 3–4).
24. *VE*, vol. 2, 327.
25. *VE*, vol. 3, 289, 293–4, 365, 369. The values for unfarmed benefices in Tanner, *Church in . . . Norwich*, are before deduction of allowances.
26. For the parochial history and parish boundaries, see J. Campbell, 'Norwich', in M.D. Lobel (ed.), *The Atlas of Historic Towns*, vol. 2 (1975), 23–4 and maps 2 and 7.
27. *VE*, vol. 3, 284.
28. D.M. Palliser, 'The unions of parishes at York, 1541–1586', *Yorkshire Archaeological Journal*, 46 (1974), 87–102.
29. *VCH Warwick*, vol. 8 (1969), 522; Styles, *Ministers' Accounts*, xv–xix; Keene, *Winchester*, vol. 1, 116–18, 134–6, and figs 153–5. See also *VCH Leicester, IV: the City of Leicester*, (1958), 388–9; Tanner, *Church in . . . Norwich*, 3–4.
30. D.M. Owen (ed.), *The Making of King's Lynn: a Documentary Survey*, Records of Social and Economic History, new series, 9 (1985), 29–30 and nos 126–31; E.M. Beloe, *Our Borough, Our Churches (King's Lynn, Norfolk)* (1899), 140–48, 199–201. See also J.A. Twemlow (ed.), *Calendar of Entries in the Papal Registers Relating to Great Britain and Ireland. Papal Letters, vol.VII: A.D. 1417–1431* (1906), 441–2; *Historical Manuscripts Commission. Eleventh Report, Appendix, Part III: the Manuscripts of the Corporations of Southampton and Kings Lynn* (1887), 162. Traces of these disputes appear in the priory accounts of 1379–80 to 1381–82, and 1427–28; possibly also in 1402–03 and 1436–37.
31. L.D. Benson (ed.), *The Riverside Chaucer* (1988), 31, l. 478. See also R.N. Swanson, 'Chaucer's parson and other priests', *Studies in the Age of Chaucer*, 13 (1991), 64–9.
32. *VE*, vol. 2, 481–2.
33. London, Public Record Office, E101/514/31-2; P. Heath, 'North Sea fishing in the fifteenth century: the Scarborough fleet', *Northern History*, 3 (1968), 53–69.
34. The sacrist accounted for altarage within the abbey: Tillotson, *Monastery and Society*, 217–19.
35. A.F. Leach (ed.), *Memorials of Beverley Minster: the Chapter Act Book of the Collegiate Church of St John of Beverley, A.D. 1286–1347*, with

Illustrative Documents, 2 vols, Surtees Society Publications, **98**, **108** (1898–1903), vol. 2, 331.
36. Norwich, Norfolk Record Office (hereafter NRO), DCN.2/4/9.
37. Swanson, *Church and Society*, 233–4, 247.
38. R.C. Finucane, *Miracles and Pilgrims: Popular Beliefs in Medieval England* (1977), 95–9.
39. Swanson, 'Standards of livings', 166, 188–9 (where sales of wax are generally included among the 'others' of column VI).
40. E.g. NRO, DCN. 2/4/19–20.
41. *VE*, vol. 2, 479.
42. *VCH City of York*, 312 (see also 311–13).
43. For salt, e.g. Windsor, St George's chapel archives, XV.55.75.
44. J.C. Atkinson (ed.), *Cartularium abbathiae de Whiteby, ordinis S. Benedicti, fundatae anno MLXXVIII*, 2 vols, Surtees Society Publications, **69**, **72** (1879–81), vol. 2, 567, 576–7, individual ships listed at 584 (these entries presumably reflect cash receipts; at 565–6 and 582–3, 'sales' of fish – some fictitious exchanges with obedientiaries – may indicate receipts in kind); Swanson, 'Standards of livings', 167, 188–9; Heath, 'North Sea fishing', 67–8.
45. Swanson, 'Standards of livings', 188–9; also NRO, DCN.2/4/16–17.
46. Swanson, 'Standards of livings', 165; NRO, DCN.2/4/16–17.
47. Keene, *Winchester*, vol. 1, 151–5.
48. Tillotson, *Monastery and Society*, 133, 156, 182–3, 185, 187.
49. For dietary standards, C. Dyer, 'English diet in the later middle ages', in T.H. Aston. P.R. Coss. C. Dyer, and J. Thirsk (eds), *Social Relations and Ideas: Essays in Honour of R.H. Hilton* (1983), 191–216. Even if the hypothetical incumbent had to provide for a household, his total receipts would be more than enough. For regulation of offerings in kind in a 'borough' context, M. Bateson (ed.), *Borough Customs*, vol. 2, Selden Society Publications, **21** (1906), 213.
50. Owen, *Lynn*, 28–9 and no. 128. See also n. 59.
51. M.D. Knowles and R.N. Hadcock, *Medieval Religious Houses: England and Wales* (2nd edn (1971), 55, 68, 214, 217, 222, 225, 233, 235, 240–41, 247–8, 324, 369; Owen, *Lynn*, 27–32.
52. Norwich, NRO, DCN. 2/1/1–91: see Appendix. Future references will usually be by year, the call number being obtainable from the list in the Appendix.
53. Rosser, *Medieval Westminster*, 334–41. Changes in the farm in the fifteenth century seem to mirror Westminster's economic fortunes as demonstrated elsewhere in the book.
54. Owen, *Lynn*, 30.
55. Below, n. 70.
56. Swanson, 'Standards of livings', 165, also above pp. 107–10.
57. V. Parker, *The Making of King's Lynn: Secular Buildings from the 11th to the 17th Century*, King's Lynn Archaeological Survey, **1** (1971), 160.
58. For mortuaries, see below, p. 119. Several Lynn accounts note that no wax had been sold as it had all been used in the church: they may reflect offerings, but this is not actually stated (see also above, n. 40).
59. The St Margaret's total is broken into its constituent elements in 1487–88, 1488–89 (Michaelmas–Annunciation), 1497–98, 1498–99, 1501–02, and 1503–04.

60. E. Carus-Wilson, 'The medieval trade of the ports of the Wash', *Medieval Archaeology*, 6–7 (1962–63), 199–200.
61. A.G. Little, 'Personal tithes', *English Historical Review*, 60 (1945), 67–88. On the 'economically-active' population of Lynn in 1377, see P.J.P. Goldberg, 'Urban identity and the poll taxes of 1377, 1379, and 1381', *Econ.H.R.*, 2nd series, 43 (1990), 209–11. For borough regulation of personal tithes, Bateson, *Borough Customs*, vol. 2, 213 (and cf. 207–8).
62. For bequests, see pp. 119–20.
63. Above, n. 59.
64. Swanson, *Church and Society*, 215–16; Swanson, 'Standards of livings', 168. Local authorities sought to regulate such payments: see Torksey prescriptions in Bateson, *Borough Customs*, vol. 2, 210–11.
65. Owen, *Lynn*, no. 146; *Historical Manuscripts Commission: King's Lynn*, 161. Compare Bateson, *Borough Customs*, vol. 2, 212.
66. Compare Bateson, *Borough Customs*, vol. 2, 212.
67. See p. 120.
68. See p. 119.
69. S.A.C. Penn and C. Dyer, 'Wages and earnings in late medieval England: evidence from the enforcement of labour laws', *Econ.H.R.*, 2nd series, 43 (1990), 363; T.H. Lloyd, *England and the German Hanse, 1157–1611: a Study of their Trade and Commercial Diplomacy* (1991), 91–4, 137–8, 166–8.
70. For exports through Lynn, Lloyd, *England and the German Hanse*, 166–8, 221, 227–9, 277, 285–6, 383. For Lynn's late medieval economy, Carus Wilson, 'Ports of the Wash', 195–201. Parker, *Making of King's Lynn*, 4–5, sees a 'steady level of prosperity' from the fifteenth to the seventeenth centuries (but cf. ibid., 11). The material in G.V. Scammell, 'English merchant shipping at the end of the Middle Ages: some East Coast evidence', *Econ.H.R.*, 2nd series, 13 (1960–61), 329–30 (esp. 330, n. 2) would counter notions of stagnation – but there is clearly a major drop from the baseline of the early fifteenth century. However, the figures are for trade going *through* Lynn without necessarily showing the wealth which stayed *within* the town. The most commonly used indicators of urban economic standing, population and taxation levels, seem inconclusive. Population rankings comparing 1377 and the 1520s suggest a fall from 6 400 to c.4 500 (D.M. Palliser, 'Urban decay revisited', in J.A.F. Thomson (ed.), *Towns and Townspeople in the Fifteenth Century* (1988), 9); the tabulated ranking for 1523–27 reflects taxpayers, not total population. Taxation rankings show a rise from eleventh to ninth place from 1334 to 1523–7 (ibid., 14); perhaps not very significant. The combination suggests some relative stability. Bridbury's proposition of tax ratios based on the assessments of 1334 and the 1520s gives Lynn a figure of 1:3, which in his terms suggests something more dynamic than 'sluggishness', but well below notable growth (A.R. Bridbury, *Economic Growth: England in the Later Middle Ages* (1962), 81, 112).
71. For circuits of Marian shrines, Tanner, *Church in . . . Norwich*, 85 (Our Lady of 'Armburghe' = Yarmouth); N.H. Nicolas (ed.), *Privy Purse Expenses of Elizabeth of York: Wardrobe Accounts of Edward the Fourth* (1830), 3–4.
72. H.J.F. Swayne (ed.),*Churchwardens' Accounts of S. Edmund and S. Thomas, Sarum, 1443–1702, with Other Documents*, Wiltshire Record

Society, 1 (1896), xv–xvi, 16–19, 25–6, 31, 33, 35, 37, 39, 42, 50, 53, 361–2, 365–6, 369–70.
73. For leasing, R. Whiting, 'Abominable idols: images and image-breaking under Henry VIII', *Journal of Ecclesiastical History*, 33 (1982), 41.
74. Swanson, 'Standards of livings', 169, 188–9.
75. Beloe, *Our Borough, Our Churches*, 91, n. 5.
76. Owen, *Lynn*, no. 292.
77. Tanner, *Church in . . . Norwich*, 85–6.
78. Swanson, 'Standards of livings', 169, 188–9.
79. P. Grosjean (ed.), *Henrici VI Angliae regis miracula postuma, ex codice Musei Britannici Regio 13.C.VIII*, Subsidia Hagiographica, 22 (Brussels, 1935), geographical distribution of recorded miracles tabulated at 76*–95*; B. Spencer, 'King Henry of Windsor and the London pilgrim', in J. Bird, H. Chapman, and J. Clark (eds), *Collectanea Londiniensia: Studies in London Archaeology and History Presented to Ralph Merrifield*, London and Middlesex Archaeological Society, Special Papers, 2 (1978), 237–48; J.W. McKenna, 'Piety and propaganda: the cult of King Henry VII', in B. Rowland (ed.), *Chaucer and Middle English Studies in Honor of Rossell Hope Robbins* (1971), 72–88; B. Wolffe, *Henry VI* (1981), 351–8.
80. Swanson, 'Standards of livings', 166, 169, 188–9.
81. It is usually identified as a way-station *en route* to Walsingham, but this seems to me a post-facto justification. For the area Parker, *Making of King's Lynn*, 30. For one pilgrim to the chapel, Tanner, *Church in . . . Norwich*, 85.
82. N. Pevsner. *The Buildings of England: North-West and South Norfolk* (1962), 229; E.M. Beloe, 'Our Lady's Hill, Lynn (the Red Mount), and the chapels thereon', *Norfolk Antiquarian Miscellany*, II/ii (1883), 630–50, does not use the priory accounts.
83. In its tithe receipts St Nicholas may sometimes have outranked St Margaret; certainly its area became the major trading centre: Parker, *Making of King's Lynn*, 36–7, 42, 143.
84. On population history, H. Clarke and A. Carter, *Excavations in King's Lynn, 1963–70*, Society for Medieval Archaeology, Monograph Series, 7 (1977), 428–32.
85. Parker, *Making of King's Lynn*, 149; Beloe, *Our Borough, Our Churches*, 167.
86. For urban mortuaries which were not clothing, NRO, DCN.2/4/9; W.P. Baildon (ed.), *Notes on the Religious and Secular Houses of Yorkshire*, Yorkshire Archaeological Society Record Series, 17, 81 (1895–1931), vol. 2, 66–7. Compare Bateson, *Borough Customs*, vol. 2, 211–12.
87. See Lynn wills in *Historical Manuscripts Commission: King's Lynn*, 331–4; Owen, *Lynn*, no. 292. See also Tanner, *Church in . . . Norwich*, 5, 127,
88. Tanner, *Church in . . . Norwich*, 127–9, fails to appreciate this distinction.
89. Clem. 3.7.2: E.L. Richter and E. Friedberg (eds), *Corpus iuris canonici*, 2 vols (Leipzig, 1879–81), vol. 2, cols 1462–4.
90. Owen, *Lynn*, no. 87; NRO, DCN. 87/1 (see also Owen, *Lynn*, no. 162).
91. Swanson, 'Standards of livings', 166, 187.
92. Printed in Owen, *Lynn*, no. 106 (misdated in the heading to 1375–76).

93. This year has two accounts, breaking at 25 January.
94. Two accounts, the year dividing as in the preceding note.
95. Two accounts, one from 29 September 1406 to 1 August 1407, the other from then to 29 September.
96. The account only covers 29 September 1407 to 25 January 1408.
97. Translated in F. Blomefield, *An Essay towards a Topographical History of the County of Norfolk*, 2nd edn, 11 vols (1805–10), vol. 8, 496–7.
98. A modified copy of the 1454–55 account, with new totals alongside that year's figures. The amended sums are undated, but the changed account must fit here in the series.
99. Two accounts, the year breaking at 25 March. The first wrongly gives the starting date as Michaelmas 1489. That is in Owen, *Lynn*, no. 111, which follows the faulty dating.
100. Damaged, some details of spirituality revenue are irrecoverable.
101. Damaged, some details of spirituality revenue are irrecoverable.
102. The figures for spirituality receipts translated in Blomefield, *Norfolk*, vol. 8, 497.
103. Translated in Blomefield, *Norfolk*, vol. 8, 497–8.

CHAPTER SEVEN

The Town and the Monastery: Early Medieval Urbanization in Ireland, AD 800–1150

B.J. Graham

The aim of this chapter is to explore several of the paradoxes which have emerged from contemporary attempts to develop a theory of early medieval urbanization in Ireland. In particular, the discussion addresses several of the ambiguities emanating from the relationship between town and monastery, and revisionist ideas concerning the role, structure and nature of the early Irish church. Traditional opinion held that the genesis of Irish towns derived from the Viking incursions of the tenth and eleventh centuries and the Anglo-Norman colonization in the years after 1169. Although archaeology has confirmed and clarified the importance of Dublin and a few other Hiberno-Norse towns, the contemporary consensus on early medieval urban origins assigns a key causative role to indigenous societal change after AD 800, a period typified by the transformation of a social organization defined by reciprocity and kinship, and dependent on pivotal people, into a redistributive rank structure based on clientship and requiring both central people and central places.[1] Such changes are indicative of the gestation of a feudal mode of social and economic organization, one in which surplus production was transferred from a subordinated majority to a social élite, both secular and ecclesiastical.

Consequently, Ó Corráin, for example, sees the concept of dynastic overlordship, already apparent by 800, evolving into the characteristic eleventh- and twelfth-century Irish lordships, polities which bore 'striking resemblance to the feudal kingdoms of Europe'.[2] Doherty also depicts an early evolution of feudal characteristics, pointing to evidence of vassalage and serfdom occurring as early as the eighth century.[3] By the ninth century, the documentary evidence indicates the emergence of a mass of peasant rentpayers. He, too, agrees that the politico-geographic expression of this societal transformation was the eleventh- and twelfth-century consolidation of lordships, controlled from central points. This assemblage of polities arose out of the *tuatha*, the 150 or so tribal kingdoms which were the basis of the kinship structure. In that system, every free man belonged to a kindred group or joint family, the *fine*, each of which owed loyalty to the small rural community of the *tuath*. Byrne sees this unit as having been incapable of evolving 'into even the embryo of a state'. It was too limited in area, the king had insufficient power and, above all, no army.[4] The emergence of the feudal polity in the eleventh and twelfth centuries demanded a new model of monarchy and system of administration to supersede the old, intensely local, tribal kingships. To a considerable extent, this seems to have occurred because *tuatha* became linked in federations and, implicit within that system, were the origins of hierarchical clientship from which lordship evolved. The corollary was the centralization of power and that had profound implications for settlement, not least for the origins of urbanization. It can be argued that the causative structural forces creating urbanization and other related institutions of social change were related to this emergence and centralization of secular power.

Such an interpretation, which depends upon the emergence of a feudal society as the primary progenitor of early Irish urbanization, underscores the unsatisfactory nature of the terminology used in one theory advanced to explain the indigenous origins of Irish urbanization, that of the 'monastic town'.[5] Indisputably, Ireland did differ from Roman Britain and Europe in that it possessed no towns, ruined or otherwise, which might have provided nuclei for early bishoprics or abbacies – the so-called *civitates*.[6] Nor did those same centres exist to attract kings in the way that Ethelbert of Kent had a house in sub-Roman Canterbury, or the West Saxon kings moved in on Winchester in the ninth century. Nevertheless, speculation on potential urban cores is entwined with the debate on the nature of the early medieval Irish church. In north-west Europe, monasticism – inspired particularly by Benedict's Rules – coexisted with an episcopal system, the geography of which was based upon *civitates*, the urban remnants of the Roman Empire. In contrast, the traditional model of the Irish church depicted a diocesan system of tribal bishoprics, each of which corresponded to the *tuath* of a petty king. During the sixth and seventh centuries, it was argued, this system was succeeded by an alternative, predominantly monastic, structure which by the eighth century, had evolved into a system of monastic federations or *paruchiae*, jurisdictional authority resting in the hands of abbots who were not necessarily bishops. Geographically, there was no territorial contiguity involved in the federations, the monastic *paruchiae* consisting of scattered houses. Thus, it was envisaged that a system of episcopal sees and their associated cathedrals was re-established only in the twelfth century after the Synods of Rathbreasail and Kells in 1111 and 1152 respectively.[7] In the most sustained critique of this interpretation, Sharpe argues that there is no direct evidence for the early existence of dioceses, nor is there any more reason to suppose that these were replaced by monastic federations.[8] Bishops existed beside abbots throughout the early medieval period, partly because many abbots were not even clerics. A common arrangement was for one branch of a ruling family to hold the kingship, while another controlled the abbacy of the most important local monastery.[9]

Therefore, by no means all early medieval churches were monastic; many were proprietary foundations and a wide range of church sites fulfilled different functions. Some were monastic, others were founded by bishops, while a number were local centres for clergy administering to a lay population. Consequently, it can be argued that a separation of clerical and lay society cannot be justified, the most powerful monastic houses evolving as the crucial centres of secular power as early as the seventh century. The two strands of society had become so intermeshed as early as the eighth century that any attempt to 'distinguish the traditional categories of church and state does some violence to the evidence'.[10] Thus, the monasteries were essentially profane, an eighth-century *monasterium* containing far more laymen than monks. Abbots, often secular figures, controlled lands and revenue and thus the Church in early medieval Ireland cannot be interpreted in purely ecclesiastical terms. Indeed, it has been argued that the real particularity of the Irish church between the seventh and eleventh centuries, lay in the extent of its secular nature, a characteristic developed to a degree not found elsewhere in western Europe.[11]

It is in this context that Doherty's terminology of the monastic town becomes both misleading and unduly limiting. Further, it detracts from his own argument that the origins of Irish urbanization are to be found in the increasing secularization of some of the more important monasteries in the period after AD 800.[12] In particular, this involved the centralization of administration and economic activity at certain sites as the political restructuring of early medieval Irish society evolved. As early as the ninth century, some major ecclesiastical sites such as Kildare were evolving into dynastic capitals for what were still peripatetic kingships. Doherty believes that the most significant economic process was the location of the annual tribal óenach or fair at some major churches, this giving way to a fixed market between the tenth and early twelfth centuries. Thus, Sharpe sees Kildare, for example, as a pastoral rather than monastic settlement, its governmental role preceding the sacramental. 'It was fully hybrid, with episcopal, secular and religious orders all represented within the town'; in the context of the present discussion, the debatable word which he does not consider is 'town'.[13]

The difficulty remains that none of the ostensibly monastic urban cores – even Kildare – demonstrate all the requisite social, economic and morphological features of urbanism.¹⁴ In particular, the theory of an indigenous Irish urbanization is markedly compromised by an absence of evidence relating to three crucial interconnected medieval urban attributes. These are, first, a plot pattern showing the existence of property laws, secondly, a system of municipal administration and, finally, urban defences and strongholds. There appears little likelihood that the documents will produce anything meaningful about either property laws or administration. Nor is the existing archaeological record particularly helpful in these regards. However, morphological analysis, in so far as it might illuminate the enigmatic documentary sources which, inevitably, are capable of sustaining several alternative interpretations, does appear to offer some possibility of resolving the issue of defences and strongholds.

There is a considerable paradox in a theory of medieval urbanization which does not include the function of defence, given its fundamental importance in the urbanization of early medieval western Europe, and the endemic warfare that was typical of pre-Anglo-Norman Ireland. The earliest medieval towns in western Europe were generally fortified in some form. This could be achieved through the presence of a stronghold as for example in Flanders and Brabant.¹⁵ Indeed, the fortress was by far the most common medieval urban core or *burg*, to use Pirenne's term. Additionally or alternatively, as at Carcassonne and Le Mans, imperial walls were modified and reused by the Visigothic and Merovingian successors to Rome. Often, the Roman town, the episcopal *civitas* and the early medieval fortified *cité* were coincident spatially although – as at Rheims for instance – the fortified ecclesiastical core did not necessarily display a continuity of site with its imperial predecessor. This latter evolved into a separately walled *bourg* or suburb. Mural defences became much more common as a result of the collapse of the Carolingian empire and the Norman invasions in the tenth century.¹⁶ Outer fortifications, enclosing all the separately walled component enclaves of the medieval town, could be as late as the thirteenth century. Of course numerous individual medieval towns were undefended by walls, but these tended to emerge from the rapid increase in town founding during the eleventh and twelfth centuries when population was expanding, and the feudal élite was increasingly preoccupied with devising means of enlarging manorial profit.¹⁷ One common solution centred on the establishment of small towns, a process which occurred everywhere in Europe including Ireland. Very many of these were protected only by seigneurial castles. Earlier towns, however, associated as they were with a more powerful and restricted élite – tended to be fortified by *enceintes* as well.

Given that there was considerable similarity in the structuring of society, the case for an indigenous origin of urbanization in Ireland would be much enhanced if secular alternatives could be identified to offset the ostensibly complete and unique dominance of the monastic nucleus which, as the theory presently stands, was undefended. In particular, it is difficult to reconcile this model with the evidence that by *circa* AD 1000, the handful of walled Hiberno-Norse towns in Ireland provided a telling illustration to Irish kings of the practical and conceptual importance of the defended urban capital. Influenced perhaps – at least in terms of defence and urban administration by the coeval Anglo-Saxon *burhs* of England – the growth of walled towns such as Dublin and Limerick accompanied the evolution of centralized authority within territories throughout Europe.[18] Thus, in turn it is difficult to believe that Irish kings were not unaware of the advantages of stimulating secular urban development, at least around their principal seats of power. In terms of the criticism voiced above concerning the usage of 'monastic town' to describe such settlements, the confusion may have arisen because often those seats were located next to monasteries, or at sites where the monastery now appears as the more readily identifiable artefact. Arguably, however, many extant ecclesiastical monuments of this period reflect the exercise of royal patronage rather than the centrality within early medieval Irish society of religious ceremonial centres.

Therefore, despite the undoubted particularity of its origins, European analogy and local example suggests that the early medieval indigenous urbanization of Ireland might well have been characterized by both secular and ecclesiastical cores, representative of the duality of the feudal élite. Indeed, we might expect to find individual places which possessed dual cores. Elsewhere, I have discussed the evidence for a multiplicity of urban cores in early medieval Ireland, an argument which underscores the terminological difficulties incurred in the continuing use of the phrase, 'monastic town'.[19] The point of this particular discussion is to advance an interpretation – based primarily on urban theory and morphological evidence – which might help resolve the paradox of the apparently undefended early medieval town in Ireland. The inevitably hypothetical conclusions are intended to provide no more than a basis for a future interpretation of both primary documentary and archaeological evidence.

The morphology of monastic sites

One ubiquitous feature of early medieval monastic sites in Ireland is the circular or elliptical enclosure, known as the *vallum*, *cashel* or *ráth*. Commonly, sites were defined by both an inner enclosure – still often relatively well defined – and an outer one which may well be apparent only from air photographs.[20] The dating of these features relative to each other is unclear. Both inner and outer enclosures may be incorporated within contemporary urban forms, particularly into street plans such as those of Kells and Duleek (Co. Meath) (see Figures 7.1 and 7.2).[21] The most logical explanation for this morphological continuity is that property boundaries and roads have remained aligned to the enclosures through time, thereby ensuring the survival of approximations of their geometrical configurations. A majority of surviving outer enclosures have diameters between 300 and 500 metres while most inner enclosures – surrounding the church or churches – are between 100 and 200 metres in diameter.[22] Many extant but deserted enclosures are characterized by earthworks – often apparently random in pattern – which subdivide their interiors for reasons not readily explicable.[23] The functions of enclosures have always appeared essentially self-evident. They apparently confined the thoughts and movements of the religious community and delimited the area of sanctuary around the monastic church. The enclosure, defined by whatever material means, functioned as the spiritual and legal boundary between the monastic establishment and the world beyond.[24] Thus in its listing of minor sanctions, the Penitential of St Columbanus states that if anyone 'has left the enclosure open during the night, let him do penance with a special fast'.[25] Consequently, this layout was intimately connected with the notion of spiritual sanctuary, a form of defence characterized by moral deterrence which held that persons or property within the church, or its ritual boundary, were immune from attack.[26] But excavation and documentary evidence, interpreted or reinterpreted within the constraints of the context discussed above, points to a markedly enigmatic structural feature that requires a considerably more discerning system of classification.

In its original form, the *vallum* was probably a relatively insignificant feature, a circular wall or bank of stone or earth, even a wooden fence or thorny hedge.[27] The concept of monastic enclosure was not specific to Ireland. Ryan suggests that the monasteries of the Merovingian world, powerful economic institutions with large estates and many lay dependants, provide the best analogies for the developed Irish examples. Merovingian – and Anglo-Saxon – monasteries were always sited within a ward or enclosure, which was not defensive but rather a definition of the sacred bounds of the monastery before the development of the cloister. This enclosure was 'the architectural embodiment of the monastic renunciation of the world'.[28] In an eighth-century life of St Philibert, the stone-built enclosure was the first feature mentioned in a description of the great monastery of Jumièges in Normandy.[29] However, the degree of

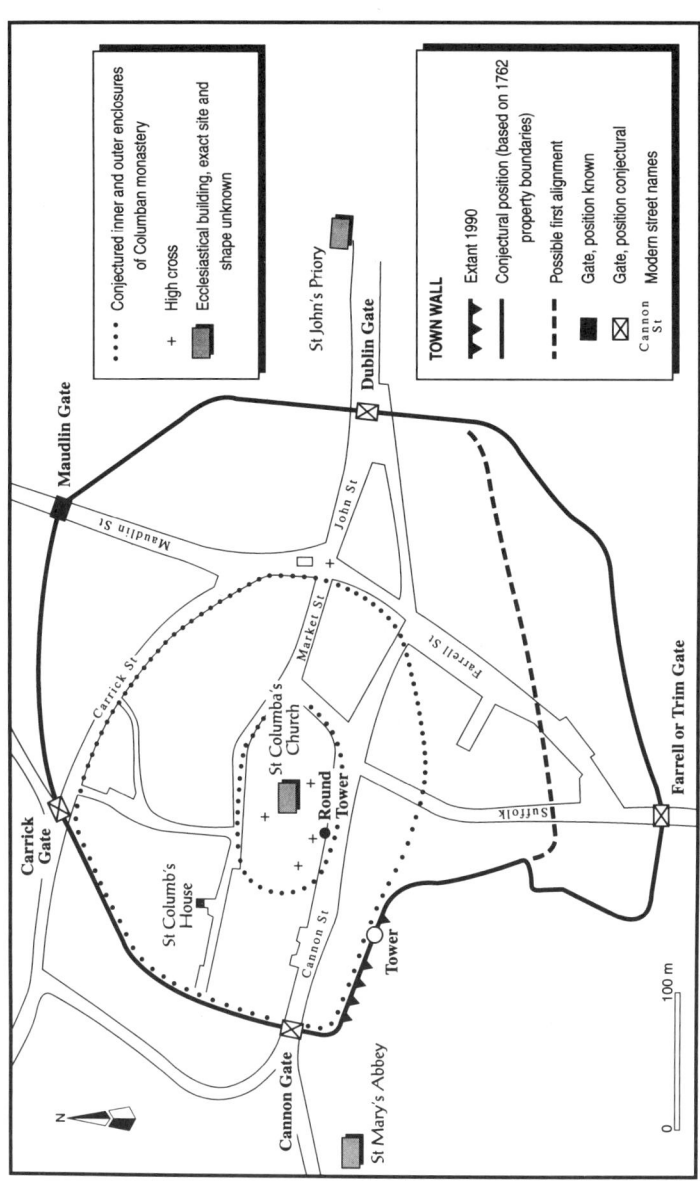

7.1 The morphology of Kells (Co. Meath) showing the projected lines of the enclosures and their relationship to the later medieval wall. Note the location of the market-place in relation to the inner enclosure. After A. Simms, 'Kells', *Irish Historic Towns Atlas*, 4 (Dublin, 1990), 3

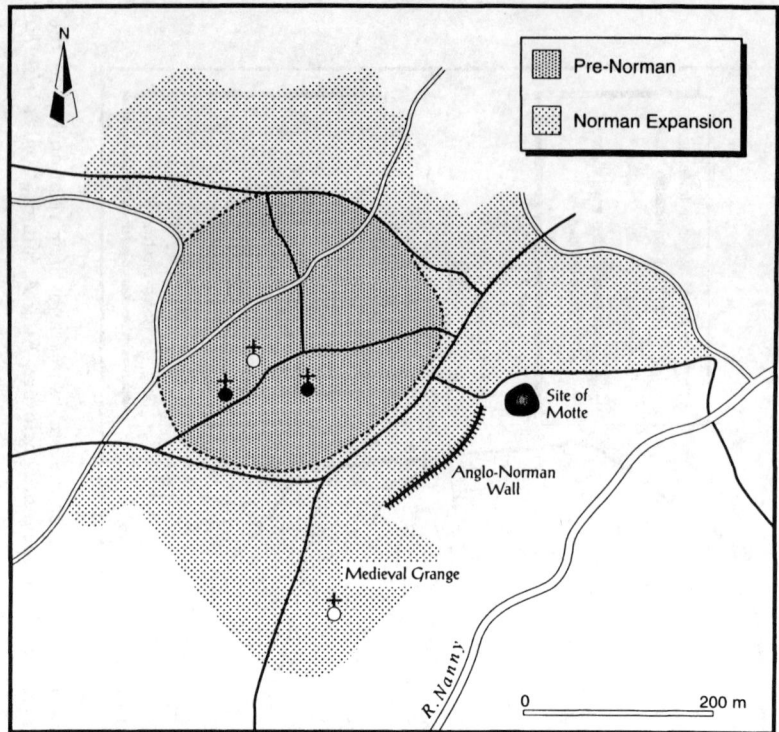

7.2 The medieval morphology of Duleek (Co. Meath). After A. Simms, 'Settlement patterns and medieval colonisation in Ireland: the example of Duleek in County Meath', in P. Flatres (ed.), *Paysages Ruraux Europeens* (Rennes, 1989), 159–77

separation should not be exaggerated for in urban monasteries, spiritual solitude *within* society was stressed rather than physical detachment from it, McKitterick making the very important point that it was the interdependent relationship between town and monastery which had developed by the ninth century.[30]

Enclosures were characteristic of the earliest early medieval Irish monasteries. In *Adomnan's Life of Columba*, written towards the end of the seventh century, the abbot and monks of Clonmacnoise (Co. Offaly) are described passing 'outside the boundary wall [*vallum*] of the monastery' to meet St Columba.[31] There are many references, too, in Plummer's collection of hagiographies, the *Vitae Sanctorum Hiberniae*, although these are later than the events they describe.[32] Both Bitel and Herity agree that as the monasteries grew, lay people were excluded from the sacred space and that their huts were to be found beyond the enclosure or *vallum*.³³ In its earliest manifestations, this feature may have been little more than symbolic. One of the earliest detailed descriptions of a monastery – that of Kildare by Cogitosus in the seventh-century *Vita Brigitae* – is quite specific that the site was unenclosed. Although the 'suburbs' had been marked out by St Brigit 'with a clear boundary', which presumably demarcated the limits of sanctuary for Kildare is described as 'the safest refuge for all fugitives in the whole land of the Irish', Cogitosus questions that it can 'rightly [be] called a city when it is surrounded by no circuit of walls'.³⁴ Presumably, the allusion is to the continental episcopal *civitas*, a term applied occasionally to monastic sites by writers of the early hagiographies. While it is sometimes translated as 'city', the appellation has much more ambiguous connotations in Europe where the extent of the urban nature of *civitates* has remained a topic of dispute. It has also been argued that high crosses might have been used as boundary markers to delimit the *termon* – the area of spiritual sanctuary – which would date these relatively common monuments from c. AD 800 or even earlier.³⁵ This interpretation depends on the diagram in the supposedly seventh-century Book of Mulling which appears to show the *termon* at St Mullins (Co. Carlow) delimited by high crosses.³⁶ But Nees dates this source to rather later – c.845 – and suspects that the diagram is in fact a copy of a Touronian illustrated manuscript, perhaps representing an evocation rather than the actual plan of an Irish monastery.³⁷ Therefore, in summary, we have a model of monastic sites divided into areas of sanctuary, the most holy space and artefacts at the core of the *platea*, separated by a *vallum* from the lay *suburbana* which lay beyond. It is this morphological complex which, it has been argued, evolved into the characteristic early medieval Irish town.

However, the issue of enclosures cannot be dealt with so simply. To acknowledge that enclosures date from the establishment of monasteries is not to argue that all extant examples are of such antiquity. Relatively few extant relict features at monastic sites – even great ones such as Clonmacnoise and Kildare – pre-date the extensive ecclesiastical reforms of the period after 1100. The earliest evidence takes the form of high crosses, grave slabs and round towers; very many of the churches, by contrast, were built, rebuilt or remodelled in the twelfth century. Indeed, their associations are often with imported continental religious observances, the most successful of which proved to be that of the Augustinians. The achievements of these orders, which were often sponsored by political leaders, is one of the most obvious symbols of Irish ecclesiastical reform and demonstrates in part the growth in royal power and patronage which characterized the pre-Anglo-Norman twelfth century. It is the contention here that the same process of rebuilding and remodelling might have been characteristic of the enclosure and, in turn, that this constitutes a most significant indicator of the evolution of urbanization.

Most writers – if they develop the point at all – have assumed that enclosures were contemporary with the monasteries and that their functions were primarily spiritual.[38] Thomas notes specifically that the monastic enclosure at Iona was not a defence against attack for it would have been useless against marauders from the sea.[39] Hamlin does allude to a general need for security but the point is not developed.[40] Conversely, Norman and St Joseph suggest that the *vallum* was used to keep cattle in, or as a defence during the Viking period.[41] In fact, monasteries were equally at risk from the Irish and the dismal history of burnings and massacres – particularly in the ninth and tenth centuries – points to a need for defences more substantial physically than the moral concept of sanctuary.[42] Nevertheless, although the various monastic Annals remain mute on examples of monasteries being successfully defended, there is some evidence to suggest that certain enclosures had defensive roles. At Glendalough (Co. Wicklow), for example, one of the most important monasteries, there still stands a stone gatehouse which may date to the tenth or eleventh century.[43] This was part of a stone, wattle and earth outer rampart, the function of which must have been to some extent defensive. Excavations at Tullylish (Co. Down) uncovered part of two massive defensive ditches; unfortunately, the dating evidence was ambiguous and the ditches may or may not relate to the minor monastic settlement.[44] Thus, while the delimitation of spiritual sanctuary is conventionally held to have been the primary function of enclosures, there are intimations that, unsurprisingly, these features fulfilled less ethereal and more prosaic roles as defences. It must also be remembered that in the wider European context of medieval monastic and cathedral precinct walls, the enclosure was a form of defence dependent on moral deterrence, seconded by a measure of physical strength, a response to everyday threat rather than open warfare.[45] Again, many sites possessed double enclosures. If inner enclosures served to demarcate sacred space, this cannot be true of the outer *enceintes* which suggests that there may have been a differentiation of function among such features. It is these points which will be developed below.

Archaeological evidence concerning enclosures is ambiguous, limited and often interpreted within the conventional assumptions which stress the role of sanctuary and ignore the possibility of chronological changes in function. Nevertheless, there is a distinct implausibility inherent within suppositions that all enclosures were necessarily characterized by coevality with the original monastic sites and by functional ubiquity. Indeed, it is probable that some enclosures were not monastic at all.

Fanning argues that the example at Reask (Co. Kerry) was not built to defend, but rather to define, the limits of the sanctified settlement and its cemetery; the cashel wall – around 1.5 metres high – enclosed the initial settlement of the sixth or seventh century. However, the excavator expresses a definite degree of caution in applying the word, 'monastic' to this site at all, suggesting that it might represent a secular, yet Christian, settlement, rather than the abode of Christian monks.[46] This is not dissimilar to another argument concerning what are unfortunately called 'ecclesiastical enclosures', a clear example of the assumption that the church was *the* – as distinct from *an* – élitist institution in early medieval Ireland. It is stressed that these sites were not monastic, but they are still described as 'ecclesiastical' for no better reason than they included churches.[47] These particular enclosures must have functioned as an elementary form of protection – against animals rather more than men – and as status symbols for small secular settlements;[48] they were in fact enlarged versions of ringforts. One excavated example at Kilpatrick (Co. Westmeath), which was not a monastery, produced evidence of Early Christian occupation as did another similar site at Doras (Co. Tyrone).[49] But this label – no more than a synonym for 'early medieval' – provides no justification for describing such features as 'ecclesiastical enclosures'.

Turning to excavations at monastic sites, several have demonstrated the danger of combining chronological assumptions with morphological evidence. Prominent earthworks within enclosures, themselves often lacking precise or even approximate dating evidence, have proved to be later in date than the encircling banks. One excavation investigated what appeared to be a deserted high-medieval settlement located within an Early Christian monastic site at Liathmore (Co. Tipperary). The enclosure here – which produced no dating evidence at all – was subdivided by a complex of earthworks. However, the site was apparently abandoned by c. AD 1050 and – excepting the fifteenth-century church – was not resettled until the seventeenth century.[50] Thus the earthworks dated either to this reoccupation or to the early medieval period although the latter attribution had to be assumed. Again, the as yet unpublished excavations by de Paor at Inishcaltra (Co. Clare) showed that prominent earthworks on the surface within the enclosure were late in date, while Sweetman concluded that banks and ditches at Clonard (Co. Meath) were of medieval provenance and unlikely to have anything directly to do with the early monastic site.[51] Nevertheless, Norman and St Joseph, depending upon landscape evidence alone, equated these latter earthworks with the fabled 'monastic city' of St Finian.[52] Such evidence calls into question the suggestion that interior earthworks axiomatically relate to areas of differing sanctity within enclosures.

The excavation evidence, therefore, demonstrates the limitations of plan analysis. Instead of coevality we find earthworks, many of which cannot be dated at all, originating over a wide time range; in turn, ubiquity of function cannot be assumed. But it is these very complexities which suggest a solution to the primary problem addressed in this chapter, the apparent absence of urban defences in early medieval Ireland. It could be hypothesized on both theoretical and morphological grounds that defence constituted one function of some enclosures, arguably of towns which had evolved around monastic cores – most probably after AD 1000 – as these became secular settlements under the control of the emergent feudal élite, both royal and abbatial. It must be emphasized that there is no convincing evidence that many of the enclosures still identifiable in the landscape are early. They may or may not be, but a number must have been built or rebuilt in the eleventh and twelfth centuries when monastic sites were remodelled in so many other ways. It remains to be seen if the documentary sources might provide some support for these contentions.

In attempting to develop an analogous context for these sites, it is apparent that the Irish monastic plan with its obvious inner and less clearly demarcated outer enclosures was very similar to that of the continental *burg* or *cité*, an inner core – by no means solely religious – to which urban functions gravitated, surrounded by *suburbana* which, in turn, sometimes possessed their own flimsy defences. In Ireland, there is no evidence at all that inner and outer enclosures were of the same date. In some cases the outer *vallum* might represent the later defences, erected to enclose all the various enclaves of the expanding town. In continental Europe, markets were commonly held outside the *enceinte* of the inner core.[53] In Ireland, a parallel is suggested – as at Kells (Co. Meath) – by twelfth-century evidence of high crosses denoting the sites of markets lying outside monastic enclosures (see Figure 7.1).[54] In European terms, such a nucleus for marketing could have been an abbey, palace, church, monastery and, most commonplace, a castle. But in Ireland, the monastery alone has hitherto been considered. Turning briefly to this related issue of the apparent monogenetic origin of indigenous towns, there remains a substantial possibility that secular urban cores – strongholds – also existed in pre-Anglo-Norman Ireland.[55] A number of places, including Athlone (Co. Westmeath), Galway and Dunmore (Co. Galway), Killaloe (Co. Clare) and Downpatrick (Co. Down), possessed clearly defined secular roles. Athlone and Galway for example were Ua Conchobair castles built in the early twelfth century while Killaloe (Cenn-Coradh) developed from the fort built by Brian Bóruma in AD 1012.[56] Interestingly, at Athlone, there are odd traces of an enclosure but ecclesiastical evidence is restricted to some eighth- and ninth-century grave slabs. The early history of the settlement remains firmly secular.⁵⁷

Arguably, therefore, royal fortresses were attracting settlement – possibly urban – prior to the Anglo-Norman invasion. These sites fulfil several of the same criteria of urbanization already applied to settlements at monastic sites.⁵⁸ But further, there is limited evidence to support the existence of dual cores consisting of juxtaposed strongholds and churches, so common elsewhere among the medieval towns of western Europe. Examples include Clonmacnoise, Durrow, both in Co. Offaly and Lorrha (Co. Tipperary).⁵⁹ But one site – Duleek (Co. Meath) (see Figure 7.2) – is worth examining here in more detail because it is illustrative of the almost perceptual nature of the problem which might be termed the assumption of monasticism. Simms has observed that the monastic morphology – by which is meant the *vallum* – remains discernible in the street plan of the contemporary village and indeed Duleek, the church of St Cianan, was a monastery of some significance.⁶⁰ It almost became the centre of a see after the Synod of Rathbreasail but was eclipsed in local importance by Clonard. Its documentary record is neither detailed nor particularly distinguished excepting that in 1123, the Gailenga stormed a 'house' at Duleek which was occupied by the King of Midhe, Mael Sechnaill mac Domnaill. The building was burnt together with 70 or 80 other houses around it and 'a multitude of the king's people were killed although he himself escaped'.⁶¹ Taking the morphological detail into account, one interpretation of this evidence is that Duleek was a royal settlement of some size with a core element of church and king's dwelling, surrounded by a defensive wall. Thus the feature incorporated in turn into the Anglo-Norman borough could have represented the *enceinte* of an early medieval secular town rather than a monastic *vallum*. In this settlement, the church was *one* but not *the* defining function. Duleek certainly demonstrates such urban criteria as institutional complexity, size and economic activity, an interpretation which would be more convincing if there was some material evidence of the king's *ghabail* – merely temporary abode or a more robust stronghold.

Thus, it might be argued that after AD 900, and more particularly in the eleventh and twelfth centuries, some monasteries developed as towns because they became loci of royal power, central places in the consolidation of *tuatha* into lordships. This may have been expressed morphologically by the construction of castles and palace strongholds and by the possible rebuilding of the enclosures. Thus the paradox raised elsewhere can be addressed. Apart from the walled Hiberno-Norse towns – which must have provided an example – the medieval urbanizing catalyst of marketing, administration and defence to which Carter alludes was present in Ireland.[62] It could be argued that a part of the supposed uniqueness ascribed to Irish urban origins in a western European context, is one consequence of a perceptual model that places undue emphasis on the role of the Church as the fundamental source of social change. In contrast, when thinking of eleventh- and twelfth-century Armagh and Kildare, for example, we ought not to be overly preoccupied with the ecclesiastical resonances in those names. The morphological evidence supports another interpretation. Arguably, enclosures were of varying age and function. As at Reask, the flimsier examples were no more than status symbols or enclosing walls delimiting the area of sanctuary. Many so-called ecclesiastical enclosures may not have been monastic or even ecclesiastical at all. Instead, they could have acted as defences to early medieval secular rural settlements. Is it possible that some of the later and much more massive and robust variants were *enceintes*, defending secular towns at monasteries or even the fortress towns into which some monastic sites had evolved? At these places, inner enclosures conceivably demarcated the *burg* or *cité* while the outer enclosures – not necessarily of the same date – may have been constructed as the circumjacent urban defences. Thus the inner *vallum* was not necessarily defining sanctuary – although it would if the core was a church – but instead the citadel. If these propositions possess any validity, we cannot talk about the 'monastic town', a terminology which clearly implies a causative linkage between the monastic model of the church and incipient urbanization. Rather, the fortified monastery was no more than one common urban core – as occurred elsewhere in Europe. Arguably, the crucial processes in urban genesis emanated from structural transformation – the evolution of feudalism – and the subsequent development of essentially secular towns. The remainder of the chapter examines a little of the evidence which might be used to support these contentions.

The evidence of defended towns in early medieval Ireland

The central concern here is to point to the physical, analogical and – in a very limited fashion – documentary material which might support the hypothesis of *vallum* as *enceinte*. The most famous of the early medieval ecclesiastical sites was, of course, Armagh where the Christian settlement appears to have succeeded a Celtic enclosure which it may be inferred was coincident with the *ráth* or inner *vallum* referred to in annalistic citations dating from the tenth century onwards.[63] To quote but one instance, in AD 1112 'the *raith* of Ard-Macha with its church was burned ... and two stretches of the *Trian Masan* and a third

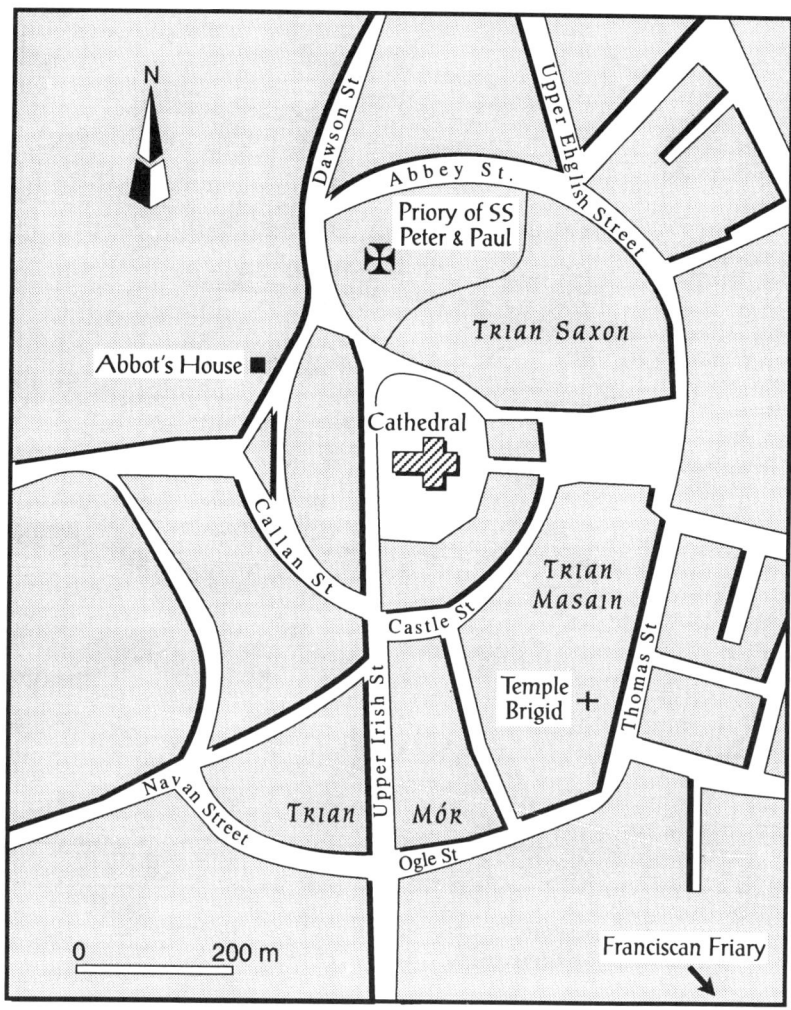

7.3 A simplified contemporary street plan of Armagh showing the survival of the lines of the enclosures. After J. Bradley, 'Recent archaeological research on the Irish town', in H. Jäger (ed.), *Stadtkernforschung* (Koln, 1987), 321–70; see 327

stretch of *Trian-Mor*.[64] From such references, it is evident that Armagh had an inner core with three outer *suburbana* or thirds (*trians*) which themselves were contained within a 'massive' outer enclosure, also still discernible in the contemporary street pattern (see Figure 7.3).[65] Armagh has always been interpreted unquestioningly as a specifically ecclesiastical city but what we have here is a pattern, repeated manifold

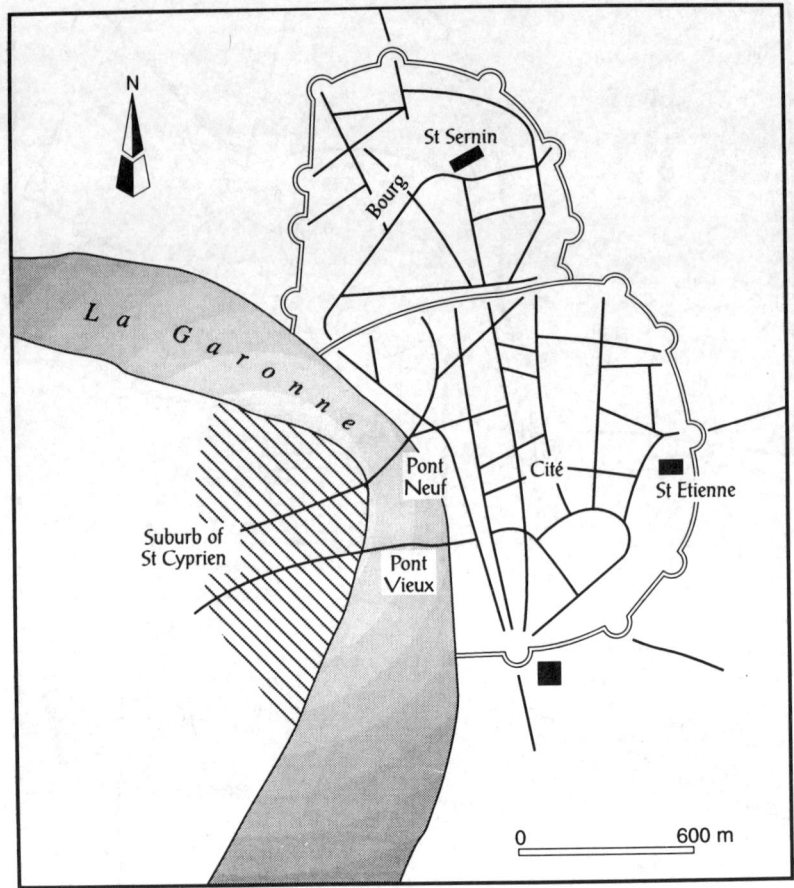

7.4 The comparative context: Toulouse in the early thirteenth century. After J. Sumption, *The Albigensian Crusade* (1978), 194

in continental Europe, of fortified core or citadel (which often contained a church) with its surrounding, separately walled suburbs. In this case the church was the dominant morphological feature, but again there is nothing unusual about fortified cathedral or abbey enclaves in medieval European towns. The higher echelons of the clergy were also great secular lords with vast estates, indistinguishable from those of the lay nobility. The archbishops of Armagh were no exception. Therefore, if Armagh is compared with but one example among many, the city of Toulouse during the Albigensian Crusade at the beginning of the thirteenth century (see Figure 7.4), it is the morphological similarities that are most striking. In one instance, there was the *ráth* containing its stone church, in the other the separately walled *cité* around the cathedral of St Étienne. Indeed one thirteenth-century reference to Armagh describes the *ráth* as the *civitas* within its wall (*murus*).[66] Again, the separately walled *trians* with their subsidiary churches such as SS Peter and Paul are matched by the *bourg* or suburb around the great Romanesque basilica of St Sernin with its own *enceinte* and, across the Garonne, the flimsily protected suburbs of St Cyprien. The abbots' house – possibly fortified – can be equated to the Chateau Narbonnais, the stronghold of the Counts of Toulouse and capable of independent defence, as was shown in Simon de Montfort's defence of the city in 1218. However, our ignorance of the structures of urban administration in Irish towns like Armagh is underlined only too clearly by Moore's detailed discussion of the social fabric of Toulouse at this time, demonstrating once again the Irish scholar's undue dependence on morphological detail.[67] Nevertheless, the analogical process suggests that if the nomenclature of the 'monastic town' is ignored, Armagh can be interpreted as a clearly recognizable medieval European town, no more than descriptively a town at a fortified ecclesiastical nucleus. It had morphological parallels in Ireland too in the walled Hiberno-Norse towns of Dublin and Limerick, the latter emerging as the political capital of the Ua Briain kings of Thomond. Therefore, despite differences in origins, it can be argued that the medieval analogues of Armagh (irrespective of the continental Romanic tradition) were cities like Toulouse, Rheims and Trier.[68] In this interpretation, eleventh- and twelfth-century Armagh was not a monastic but an archiepiscopal town, the religious leader effectively a secular feudal lord.

The enclosures of Armagh may have become urban defences – indeed the outer *vallum* might even have been constructed specifically as the town *enceinte* – and while this might not appear to be a surprising conclusion, it is a relatively novel interpretation within an Irish context. Morphological evidence of enclosures fulfilling similar functions can be found at several other sites. There is, for example, the fortified gateway and *enceinte* at Glendalough referred to earlier. In general terms, it may well be that an impressive *vallum* – inner or outer – relates to such activity in the eleventh and twelfth centuries. One example would be the massive high-banked enclosure at Seirkieran (Co. Offaly), which surrounds a site of about 10 hectares. Again, there is considerable landscape evidence at Clonmacnoise of what might well be ramparts. A substantial bank and ditch which appear to have been constructed in straight sections connected by obvious angles (which perhaps represent primitive bastions) enclose a considerable area around the monastery. The angles are rather more acute than Thomas's sketch diagram might indicate (see Figure 7.5).[69] That all outer enclosures were not necessarily

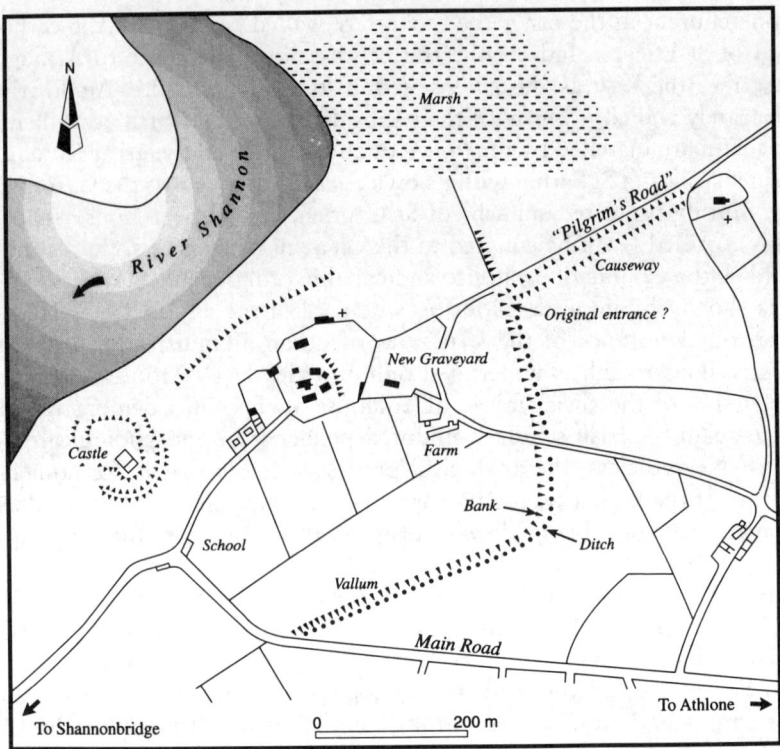

7.5 Clonmacnoise (Co. Offaly) showing the line of the rectilinear enclosure. After C. Thomas, *The Early Christian Archaeology of North Britain* (1971), 29

elliptical is demonstrated, too, by Kildare.[70] These features are generally incomplete and their geometry has to be inferred from property and street lines. Thus while an enclosure may approximate to an ellipse, so too could straight stretches of walls between bastions or towers (as at Toulouse). Thus, there may be grounds for arguing that all enclosures were not elliptical.[71] However, there are other possible explanations than the one offered here. For example, non-elliptical geometries might be attributable to later Anglo-Norman modifications, associated with the construction of earthwork castles – as at Clonmacnoise. Also, if some enclosures were actually urban *enceintes*, it could be asked why there do not appear to be any clearly rectangular plans such as those characteristic of ninth- and tenth-century *burh*s in England. Again, more substantial monuments might be expected although, presumably, earthen ramparts such as those at Clonmacnoise would have been surmounted by wooden palisades. Evidence of gateways is very limited although elaborate entrances can be seen on some of the air photographs of these sites – as at Fenagh (Co. Leitrim).[72] It could be, however, that the paucity of archaeological investigation of actual enclosures, combined with our preconceived interpretations, has obscured some of the morphological evidence.

Returning briefly to the written evidence, there are several very important twelfth-century documentary references which point to the possible existence of fortified citadels containing churches. Two examples, Tuam (Co. Galway) and Derry, have been discussed elsewhere.[73] Both were apparently remodelled in the twelfth century, and one interpretation of the inevitably ambiguous annalistic citations might point to the reconstruction of their respective enclosures as urban *enceintes*. At Derry, in particular, the *Annals of Ulster* for 1162 record a 'total separation of the houses from the churches of Derry was made by the successor of Colum-Cille (the abbot – Flaith-bertach) and by the King of Ireland' (Muirchertach Mac Lochlainn); 'eighty houses or something more' were demolished. In addition 'the stone way' of the centre was built and 'malediction [pronounced] upon him who should come over it for ever'.[74] Ostensibly this appears to be a definition of sanctuary but equally, it may indicate spiritual authority being used to legitimize the construction of a fortified core representing an alliance of essentially secular powers. During the process, the inevitable clearance of tenements took place. The structure created is again akin – without any corroborating archaeological or morphological evidence – to the European norm of a clearly demarcated fortified core with *suburbana* beyond, in other words a *cité* and *bourg*. The *vallum* is thus delimiting a citadel as well as an area of nominal spiritual sanctuary. The subsequent documentary history of Derry, recorded in the *Annals of Ulster* and *Loch Cé*, points to the secular nature of the settlement which is referred to as a *baile* or even a *portus*. Such evidence might be interpreted as indicating the emergence of the walled secular town of Derry in the twelfth century, the resultant settlement displaying unequivocal evidence of urban criteria. Of course it is flimsy corroboration – and late too – but that is the nature of the Irish documentation.

Conclusions

The discussion presented here proposes a possible resolution to the paradox of the undefended town in pre-Anglo-Norman Ireland. To summarize that argument, some early medieval towns may have possessed moral and physical defences, either walls or castles or both. So-called monastic enclosures may not have been ubiquitous in function nor were they necessarily contemporary with other relict features at ostensibly religious sites. Indeed, a number were not irrevocably ecclesiastical at all. Some defended towns originated around either secular or ecclesiastical cores or a combination of both. Hence, it can be argued that the processes explaining the gestation of early medieval Irish towns bear some similarity to those characteristic of other regions of western Europe, particularly by the eleventh and twelfth centuries. Fortified pre-Anglo-Norman urban settlements in Ireland can be seen as constituting one material outcome in the landscape of the evolution of an indigenous feudal social structure. Another was the construction of fortresses which began *c*. AD 1000. The evidence, slight though it often is, points essentially to an eleventh- and twelfth-century indigenous development of towns, a dating which fits in well with contemporary events in western Europe. These towns were relatively few for they were the settlements of only the highest and most powerful echelons of a noble élite. The elaboration of the urban network – as occurred similarly in England and north-west France for example – was a product of the twelfth and thirteenth centuries. But to propose similarities with cognate regions is not to deny the specific and local differences of the Irish examples. The Church was much more common as the core but the settlements should not be thought of as monastic: in its spiritual sense the Church was but only one function. As Sharpe argues, the fatal flaw in the traditional model of the early medieval Irish church lies in its failure to distinguish between pastoral and temporal jurisdiction.[75] It is in this context that 'monastic town' is an unhelpful label. Further, in reality, a number of these settlements may well have been 'castle towns' and several places possessed dual cores. The forces transforming enclosures and building castles were those of incipient feudalism with its twin – indeed indistinguishable – religious and noble élite. By proposing one possible resolution to the paradox of ostensibly undefended towns in a patently war-riven society, the concept of an indigenous early medieval Irish urbanization which possesses clear and logical linkages with that of the adjacent regions of western Europe, is theoretically enhanced. An assessment of the validity of the case argued here awaits further analysis – and even reinterpretation – of both archaeological and documentary evidence.

Notes

1. D. Ó Corráin, *Ireland Before the Normans* (Dublin, 1972): C. Doherty, 'Monastic towns in Ireland', in H.B. Clarke and A. Simms (eds), *The Comparative History of Urban Origins in Non-Roman Europe*, BAR

International Series **255** (1985), 45–76: B.J. Graham, 'Urbanisation in medieval Ireland, c. AD 900 to c. AD 1300', *Journal of Urban History*, **13** (1987), 169–96: J. Bradley, 'The interpretation of Scandinavian settlement in Ireland', in J. Bradley (ed.), *Settlement and Society in Early Medieval Ireland: Studies Presented to F.X. Martin o.s.a.* (Kilkenny, 1988), 49–78.
2. Ó Corráin, *Ireland Before Normans*, 32.
3. C. Doherty, 'Exchange and trade in early medieval Ireland', *Journal of the Royal Society of Antiquaries of Ireland*, **110** (1980), 67–89: C. Doherty, 'Some aspects of hagiography as a source for Irish economic history', *Peritia*, **1** (1982), 300–328.
4. F.J. Byrne, *Irish Kings and High Kings* (1973), 31.
5. Doherty, 'Monastic towns'.
6. H.B. Clarke and A. Simms, 'Towards a comparative history of urban origins', in Clarke and Simms (eds.), *Comparative Urban Origins*, 619–714.
7. K. Hughes, *The Church in Early Irish Society* (1966).
8. R. Sharpe, 'Some problems concerning the organisation of the church in early medieval Ireland', *Peritia*, **3** (1984), 230–70.
9. V. Hurley, 'The early church in the south-west of Ireland: settlement and organisation', in S. M. Pearce (ed.), *The Early Church in Britain and Ireland*, BAR British Series, **102** (1982), 297–332.
10. D. Ó Corráin, 'The early Irish churches: some aspects of organisation', in D. Ó Corráin (ed.), *Irish Antiquity: Essays and Studies Presented to Professor M.J. O'Kelly* (Cork, 1981), 327–41. See also A.P. Smyth, *Celtic Leinster: Towards an Historical Geography of Early Irish Civilisation, AD 500–1600* (Blackrock, 1982), 27–35.
11. Sharpe, 'Organisation of church', 268.
12. Doherty, 'Monastic towns', 66–7; Doherty, 'Hagiography', 302–3.
13. Sharpe, 'Organisation of church', 262.
14. Doherty, 'Monastic towns'; B.J. Graham, 'Urban genesis in early medieval Ireland', *Journal of Historical Geography*, **13** (1987), 3–16: B.J. Graham, 'Early medieval Ireland: settlement as an indicator of economic and social transformation, c.500–1100', in B.J. Graham and L.J. Proudfoot (eds), *An Historical Geography of Ireland* (1993), 19–57.
15. H. Carter, *An Introduction to Urban Historical Geography* (1983), p. 130.
16. A. Chédeville, J. Le Goff and J. Rossiaud, *Histoire de la France Urbaine 2: La Ville Médiévale* (Paris, 1980).
17. R.H. Hilton, *English and French Towns in Feudal Society: a Comparative Study* (1992).
18. P.F Wallace, 'Archaeology and the emergence of Dublin as the principal town of Ireland', in Bradley (ed.), *Settlement and Society*, 123–60.
19. B.J. Graham, 'Secular urban origins in early medieval Ireland', *Irish Economic and Social History*, **16** (1989), 5–22: Graham, 'Early medieval Ireland', 37–41.
20. L. Swan, 'Enclosed ecclesiastical sites and their relevance to settlement patterns of the first millennium AD', in T. Reeves-Smyth and F. Hamond (eds), *Landscape Archaeology in Ireland*, BAR British Series, **116** (1983), 269–94: L. Swan, 'Monastic proto-towns in early medieval Ireland', in Clarke and Simms (eds), *Comparative Urban Origins*, 70–102: H. Mytum, *The Origins of Early Christian Ireland* (1992), 80–84.

21. A. Simms, 'Settlement patterns and medieval colonisation in Ireland: the example of Duleek in County Meath', in P. Flatres (ed.), *Paysages Ruraux Europeens*, (Rennes, 1989), 159-77: A. Simms, 'Frühformen der mittelalterlichen stadt in Irland', *Würzburger Geographischer Arbeiten*, 60 (1983), 27-39: A. Simms, 'Kells', *Irish Historic Towns Atlas*, 4 (Dublin, 1990).
22. Swan, 'Monastic proto-towns', 97.
23. E.R. Norman and J.K.S. St Joseph, *The Early Development of Irish Society* (1969), 102-16.
24. C. Thomas, *The Early Christian Archaeology of North Britain* (1971), 29.
25. L. Bieler, *The Irish Penitentials* (Dublin, 1963), 106-7.
26. A.T. Lucas, 'The plundering and burning of churches in Ireland, 7th to 16th century', in E. Rynne (ed.), *North Munster Studies* (Limerick, 1967), 172-229.
27. A. Hamlin, 'The archaeology of early Irish churches in the eighth century', *Peritia*, 4 (1985), 279-99, see 282.
28. M. Ryan, 'Fine metal-working and early Irish monasteries: the archaeological evidence', in Bradley (ed.), *Settlement and Society*, 33-48.
29. E. James, 'Archaeology and the Merovingian monastery', in H.B. Clarke and M. Brennan (eds), *Columbanus and Merovingian Monasticism*, BAR International Series, 113 (1981), 33-55.
30. R. McKitterick, 'Town and monastery in the Carolingian period', in D. Baker (ed.), *Studies in Church History 16: the Church in Town and Countryside* (1979), 93-102.
31. A.O. and M.O. Anderson (eds and trans), *Adomnan's Life of Columba* (1961), 215.
32. C. Plummer (ed.), *Vitae Sanctorum Hiberniae*, 2 vols (1910).
33. L. M. Bitel, *Isle of the Saints: Monastic Settlement and Christian Community in Early Ireland* (Ithaca, 1990), 17: M. Herity, 'The buildings and layout of early Irish monasteries before the year 1000', *Monastic Studies*, 14 (1983), 247-84: M. Herity, 'The layout of Irish Early Christian monasteries', in P. Ni Chathain and M. Richter (eds), *Ireland and Europe* (Stuttgart, 1984), 105-16.
34. C.A.R. Radford, 'The earliest Irish churches', *Ulster Journal of Archaeology*, 3rd series, 40 (1977), 1-11, see pages 5-7.
35. Herity, 'Buildings and layout', 270-77.
36. Norman and St Joseph, *Early Development*, 100-102 and plate 56.
37. L. Nees, 'The colophon drawing in the Book of Mulling: a supposed Irish monastery plan and the tradition of terminal illustration in early medieval manuscripts', *Cambridge Medieval Celtic Studies*, 5 (1983), 67-91.
38. For example K. Hughes and A. Hamlin, *The Modern Traveller to the Early Christian Church* (1977); Herity, 'Buildings and layout'; Swan, 'Monastic proto-towns'.
39. Thomas, *Early Christian Archaeology*, 29.
40. Hamlin, 'Archaeology of early Irish church'.
41. Norman and St Joseph, *Early Development*, 96.
42. Lucas, 'Plundering and burning'.
43. F. Henry, *Irish Art During the Viking Invasions, 800-1020 AD* (1967), 45.
44. R.J. Ivens, 'The Early Christian monastic enclosure at Tullylish, Co. Down', *Ulster Journal of Archaeology*, 3rd series, 50 (1987), 55-121.

45. C. Coulson, 'Hierarchism in conventual crenellation: an essay in the sociology and metaphysics of medieval fortification', *Medieval Archaeology*, 26(1982), 69–100, see 75.
46. T. Fanning, 'Excavations of an Early Christian cemetery and settlement at Reask, Co. Kerry', *Proceedings of the Royal Irish Academy*, 81C (1981), 67–172.
47. Swan, 'Enclosed ecclesiastical sites'; for comments on this terminology, see Graham, 'Early medieval Ireland', 48–9; N. Edwards, *The Archaeology of Early Medieval Ireland* (1990), 114–21: C. Manning, 'The excavation of the Early Christian enclosure of Killederdadrum in Lackenavorna, Co. Tipperary', *Proceedings of the Royal Irish Academy*, 84C (1984), 237–68.
48. J.P. Mallory and T.E. McNeill, *The Archaeology of Ulster From Colonisation to Plantation*, (1991), 220–21.
49. L. Swan, 'Excavations at Kilpatrick churchyard, Killucan, Co., Westmeath', *Riocht na Midhe*, 6 (1976), 89–96: J.A. McDowell, Excavations in an ecclesiastical enclosure at Doras, County Tyrone', *Ulster Journal of Archaeology*, 3rd series, 50 (1987), 137–56.
50. R.E Glasscock, 'Liathmore-Mochaemog', *Medieval Archaeology*, 15 (1971), 136.
51. P.D. Sweetman, 'Excavations of medieval field boundaries at Clonard, Co. Meath', *Journal of the Royal Society of Antiquaries of Ireland*, 108 (1978), 10–22.
52. Norman and St Joseph, *Early Development*, 113–14.
53. Numerous examples are included in Chédeville, Le Goff and Rossiaud, *Histoire de la France Urbaine*.
54. Simms, 'Kells'.
55. D. Ó Corráin, 'Aspects of early Irish history', in B.G. Scott (ed.), *Perspectives in Irish Archaeology*, (Belfast, 1974), 64–75; B.J. Graham, 'Secular urban origins in early medieval Ireland', *Irish Economic and Social History*, 16 (1989), 5–22; Graham, 'Early medieval Ireland', 37–41.
56. These and other examples are discussed in B.J. Graham, 'Medieval timber and earthwork fortifications in medieval Ireland', *Medieval Archaeology*, 32 (1988), 110–29: B.J. Graham, 'Medieval settlement in County Roscommon', *Proceedings of the Royal Irish Academy*, 88C (1988), 19–38.
57. H. Murtagh, 'Athlone', *Irish Historic Towns Atlas*, 6 (Dublin, 1994).
58. Graham, 'Urban genesis'.
59. Henry, *Irish Art During the Viking Ages*, 39–47; Graham, 'Secular urban origins', 12–19.
60. Simms, 'Duleek'.
61. W.M Hennessy (ed.), *Annals of Loch Cé*, 2 vols (Dublin, 1871), vol. 1, 115–17; S. Mac Airt and G. Mac Niocaill (eds), *Annals of Ulster (to AD 1131)* (Dublin, 1983), 566–9.
62. Carter, *Urban Historical Geography*, 7; Graham, 'Urban genesis'.
63. Edwards, *Early Medieval Ireland*, 112–13.
64. Mac Airt and Mac Niocaill (eds), *Annals of Ulster*, 552–3.
65. Swan, 'Monastic proto-towns', 82, 84.
66. W.M. Hennessy and B. MacCarthy (eds), *Annals of Ulster*, 2 vols (Dublin, 1887–1901), vol. 2, see entry for 1266.
67. R.I. Moore, *The Origins of European Dissent*, 2nd edn (1985).
68. Chédeville, Le Goff and Rossiaud, *Histoire de la France Urbaine*; Carter, *Urban Historical Geography*, 1–15.

69. Thomas, *Early Christian Archaeology*, 29.
70. J.H. Andrews, 'Kildare', *Irish Historic Towns Atlas*, 1 (Dublin, 1986).
71. Edwards, *Early Medieval Ireland*, 107–8.
72. Norman and St Joseph, *Early Development*, 108–9.
73. Graham, 'Secular urban origins', 19–21.
74. Hennessy and MacCarthy (eds), *Annals of Ulster*, vol. 2, 141.
75. Sharpe, 'Organisation of church', 266.

CHAPTER EIGHT

Benedictine Town Planning in Medieval England: Evidence from St Albans

T.R. Slater

The monastic town was recognized as a distinctive type of town very early in the historiography of English medieval urbanism. This was primarily because of its distinctive socio-political characteristics and the conflict that periodically ensued between townspeople and monastic community over the degree of freedom the former possessed to manage their own affairs. The evidence from monastic towns was therefore vital in the debate concerning the legal status of boroughs which dominated late nineteenth-century scholarship.[1] It was of some significance, too, when historical debate moved on to consider the economy of medieval towns[2] since the wealth of many of the monasteries which held towns was substantial. Topographical historians have also utilized the category in their discussions of urban development,[3] though without any clear definitions of what constitutes the particularities of a monastic town, other than the mere presence of a monastery, but there have been few detailed investigations of this group of places or even of the topographical development of individual monastic towns.[4] Yet, from the sixth to the sixteenth centuries Christian monastic religious communities were an important dimension in the development of English medieval towns. Many of the earliest urban places were gathered around monasteries, and still more was this so in Ireland where research in the past decade has demonstrated the significance and the distinctive sub-circular forms of these proto-urban settlements,[5] forms which are now being recognized in England too.[6] In the high-medieval period, as towns began to grow rapidly, many towns were dominated topographically by the walled enclosures of monastic precincts of various kinds, some larger towns having six or more institutions by the fourteenth century. As well as the precinct itself, these monasteries, convents and friaries were major landholders; urban properties and agricultural lands, together with appropriated churches, being managed to support the life of the community.

The only comprehensive study of the urban foundations of any monastic order is that of the Cistercians,[7] paradoxically the order which eschewed town locations more than any other. The best known medieval monastic towns stand adjacent to abbeys of the Benedictine order of monks. Almost all have distinctively planned townscapes which show that they had been deliberately promoted by the monastic community as a means of increasing their revenue in the same manner as other lords. It is clear that the Benedictines were the most urban of the monastic orders and it was certainly the larger Benedictine houses which were most involved in the major legal and political disputes with the burghers of adjacent towns in the fourteenth and fifteenth centuries.[8] This chapter begins, therefore, by trying to establish the distribution and chronology of Benedictine planned towns and then develops a single case study to investigate the processes of urban topographical development in more detail. It uses the methodology of town-plan analysis[9] based on the large-scale Ordnance Survey plans of the late nineteenth century, which previous research projects have repeatedly shown to reflect the medieval town plan in terms of their street layout and plot patterns,[10] though not, of course, in the building fabric. The interpretation of town plans is necessarily an interdisciplinary procedure if any kind of chronology is to be attached to the pattern of plan units and the integration of historical and archaeological data as a means of providing that chronology is essential.[11]

Geography and chronology

The tenth-century monastic revival stimulated by Dunstan, Aethelwold and Oswald is usually regarded as the beginning of reformed Benedictine monasteries in England. It was their monasteries of, respectively, Glastonbury and Canterbury, Abingdon and Winchester, and Worcester and Ramsey which stimulated this revival, together with the general encouragement of King Edgar (959–73), who saw the creation of a network of such monasteries under royal protection as a means of unifying his kingdom and providing a powerful base of support against nobles.[12] It occasions little surprise that the distribution of these 40 or so reformed Benedictine monasteries and nunneries shows a concentration in the south and east of England (all were south of the Trent), both because of these political realities and because this was the arable and more economically prosperous zone of the country. It was that economy which allowed economic development to be undertaken by lords of all kinds and which provided the economic base for the new institutions. More surprising is that almost all of them were urban; that is to say they had adjacent towns of one kind or another by the later medieval period. What is less clear is which of these elements, town or monastery, came first.

There are notable concentrations of abbeys with adjacent towns in the central parts of Wessex, in the West Midlands; in East Anglia, in the Thames valley and in Kent.[13] The relationship with the pairs of reformed monasteries of the saint abbots noted above is obvious. An examination of the Wessex group of abbey towns suggests that although these were almost all reformed monastic foundations, the towns are notable as late-Saxon Alfredian *burhs*. The development of urban functions, and the planned urban layout, is therefore a function of royal control and direction, not of monastic instigation. In these places the Benedictine monastery may have been deliberately established to enhance the central-place functions of the *burh* and to enhance royal political control within it, but the planned townscape was determined by the Crown, not by the monastery. Examples include the convents at Shaftesbury, Wilton, and Nunnaminster at Winchester and the monasteries at Malmesbury, Bath, and the Old and New Minsters at Winchester. However, we must be careful in visualizing these *burhs* as entirely new central places since many of these reformed monasteries were developed from earlier secular minsters which recent work has suggested had significant central-place functions in the eighth and ninth centuries.[14] Thus, Cricklade, Wareham and Oxford, for example, though amongst the towns with very regular plans, were places which had existing secular minster churches.[15] There are other smaller places within this same region where monasteries of regular monks were created from earlier minster churches with secular canons, or even from Celtic monastic churches. Bruton (Somerset) might have been an example of the former, and Buckfast and Tavistock (Devon) possible examples of the latter. Such towns require detailed interdisciplinary studies to determine the degree of monastic initiative in the laying out of new urban areas.

There are, of course, also Benedictine-owned towns which did not have an adjacent monastery. These had been founded on detached parts of monastic estates. If these are added to the map, it is the concentration of towns in the West Midlands which becomes particularly notable. It seems that the West Midland Benedictine abbeys were especially active in founding towns on the outlying parts of their estates in the twelfth and thirteenth centuries when lords of all kinds were establishing new towns, but that abbeys elsewhere were less likely to engage in the development of their estates in this way.

All the larger towns of the West Midlands have a reformed Benedictine house beside, or at the heart of, the Aethelflaedan *burh* but, as in Wessex, most of these have earlier antecedents as secular minsters or cathedrals. Chester, Shrewsbury, Hereford, Worcester and Gloucester all come into this category and the recent studies of Worcester and Gloucester[16] well demonstrate the complexity of the development sequence of these larger English county towns. The study of Coventry, which follows in Chapter 9, provides a case study of another of these large towns, in this instance complicated further by divided lordship between monastery and secular lord and, again, there is shadowy evidence of an earlier secular minster preceding the reformed monastery established by Leofric and Godgifu in the eleventh century.[17]

Evidence for town planning

The most interesting towns for the early stages of this investigation into the nature of Benedictine planning practices, are those towns which were seemingly not associated with urban developments by the crown or a secular lord and which are unambiguously monastic in their development. This group might include the two places which feature prominently in most studies of monastic towns: St Albans and Bury St Edmunds, but also towns such as Sherborne, Battle, Rye, Evesham, Pershore, Burton-on-Trent, Peterborough, Ely and Reading. Even in these places, however, the chronology of urban development is often far from simple, especially in places such as Sherborne, Peterborough and Ely with known minster antecedents. The chronology of development in some of these towns is frequently defined documentarily with some clarity in monastic chronicles, though this evidence is rarely contemporary with the events being described. Thus, a companion chapter to this has recently explored the foundation and development of two moderate-sized Benedictine towns in the Midlands.[18] At both Evesham and Burton-on-Trent the town adjacent to the abbey was founded and developed entirely by the reformed monastery in a series of small-scale developments over a period of a century or more after 1050. Each of these developments was 'planned' in that it consisted of a regular street with a uniform plot series on both sides of that street. Each plot was about a quarter acre in size and was held in burgage tenure at the standard high-medieval rent of 12 pence per year. As a consequence, each of these towns seem regular in their overall plan characteristics but this impression belies the complexity of their topographical development, which is only revealed when the historical and topographical information is integrated. Both towns also display higher-order planning characteristics, too; notably in the way new streets were aligned on the monastic gateway so as to provide dignified processional routes into the abbey, a feature also found in Coventry.[19]

Perhaps the earliest documented planned monastic town is St Albans, where the abbey *Chronicle* attributes the founding of the town to Abbot Wulsin in *c*.950.[20] The assumption has always been that the new town took the form that dominated the plan in the high-medieval years: with the great triangular market-place stretching north from the abbey precinct and with the parish church terminating the apex of this market space. Such a plan gave scope for architectural display if the abbey gate filled the base of the triangle.[21] At St Albans this was not the case since the gate was already estabished to the west, fronting onto the probable royal *burh* of Kingsbury. At the Conqueror's new-founded abbey in the Wealden wastes of Sussex, however, given in thanks for the victory over the English at Battle, the abbey gateway was to dominate the triangular market-place of the new borough founded beside the abbey. Here we have another closely dated example of a town foundation (the early twelfth century) together with details of the nature of the early planning process (there were 115 tenements around the market-place and along the High Street by *c*.1180).[22] Despite what has been said earlier there are, in fact, comparatively few documented pre-Conquest monastic planned towns. The Longport borough of Canterbury,[23] the earliest phase of Bury St Edmunds,[24] Glastonbury[25] and Peterborough[26] are possible examples of tenth- or early-eleventh-century development, but most places were being actively developed only from the mid and late eleventh century. The extension of Sandwich, after it came into the hands of Canterbury Cathedral priory, dates from the mid-eleventh century;[27] Coventry Abbey was founded in 1043, by Leofric and Godgifu, and the monastic borough followed soon after;[28] the laying out of Rye by Fécamp Abbey dates from the 1070s or 1080s, since it is noted as *novus burgus* in Domesday;[29] the spectacular planned grid of Bury St Edmunds was probably laid out in the 1080s;[30] Evesham became a *port* in the 1050s and began its rapid rise to urban status thereafter;[31] as did neighbouring Pershore, a double abbey town after part of the estates of Pershore Abbey were gifted to the new monastery at Westminster, again in the mid-eleventh century.[32] The development of new Benedictine monastic towns therefore coincides with the rapid expansion of towns generally in England in the eleventh and early twelfth centuries.

The cathedral priories also began to involve themselves in new urban speculative developments in this period, mostly in suburbs: New Elvet is an unspectacular extension of Durham, with the legal status of a separate borough but with the physical form of a single street suburb to the older city. It was founded by the cathedral priory in the 1190s;[33] the cathedral priory at Worcester was responsible for the long street suburb developed to the north of the defended late Saxon city in the late eleventh or early twelfth century;[34] Bath Abbey was probably responsible for the development of the suburbs of Bath in the twelfth century as its precinct expanded to occupy a larger area of the city centre;[35] and the Bootham estate of St Mary's Abbey, York, had developed sufficiently to be promoted as a separate borough in 1275.[36]

The thirteenth century is characterized by the foundation of planned medieval new towns on estates of all kinds, as Beresford's studies made clear 30 years ago.[37] The Benedictine abbeys were as assiduous at developing their estates in this way as other lords, secular and ecclesiastical. Ramsey Abbey developed the river port of St Ives as a new market from 1110 and the Easter-week fair became one of the four great fairs of medieval England;[38] Burton Abbey acquired market and borough charters for Abbots Bromley in 1222 and laid out a new street of tenements for its urban tenants;[39] Evesham Abbey did likewise for its Cotswold estate centre at Stow-on-the-Wold in 1107–08;[40] Gloucester Abbey founded a new one-street borough with triangular market-place on its Cotswold estate at Northleach in c.1235;[41] and Worcester Priory developed Shipston on Stour between 1268 and 1275 as a small borough with a 'T'-shaped plan.[42]

The chronology of planned Benedictine urban developments comes to an end in the late medieval period as some abbeys tried to stimulate their rent rolls and their small boroughs by developing new suburbs in the late thirteenth or fourteenth centuries. These suburbs had large tenements of 2 acres or more as a way of attracting new tenants into the town but most, though succeeding for a short period were often largely abandoned in the economic decline after the Black Death. Examples include the Newland suburb developed by Pershore Abbey in its adjacent town from the late thirteenth century,[43] and Southam Newland, developed by Coventry priory as late as 1410–11.[44] Perhaps the most spectacular suburban development of this kind, though of an earlier period, was Reading Abbey's attempt to stimulate the growth of Leominster after it was gifted the ancient secular minster estate at its foundation in 1121. Each of the main roads approaching the settlement centre is lined by well-planned tenement series, with back access lanes, for a considerable distance from the town centre.[45]

The development of St Albans

Having provided a general context for the chronology and geography of Benedictine towns, the remainder of this chapter will be concerned to examine in more detail a single example of urban planning by a Benedictine abbey. The example is the classic monastic town of St Albans. The evidence of archaeological excavations and documentation will be integrated with the evidence of the town plan, to specify more closely the nature of the first planning exercise by the abbot of this key Benedictine community in the mid-tenth century. In fact, by the fourteenth century, St Albans contained not only the enormously wealthy abbey standing on the site of Alban's tomb, but two other Benedictine foundations: Sopwell Priory, which was founded in 1140,[46] to the south-east of the town, for the accomodation of the nuns that had previously lived in what had been, at least in pre-reform times, a double minster for men and women, serving Alban's shrine. By the twelfth century, however, the women seemingly lived in the almonry of the abbey, tending the poor, before being removed altogether to the site beside the Ver, beyond the borough boundary. The second priory was that of St Mary de Pre, beside Watling Street, well to the west of the town, which began life in 1194 as a leper hospital founded by the abbey for 13 women, 13 men, a warden, chaplain and clerk. But in 1328x36 it was converted into a priory for Benedictine nuns.[47]

Recent research is unanimous in describing St Albans as the place where the evidence for continuity of Christian commemoration from Roman times to post-Roman is most secure.[48] Given this long history of continuous occupation it should occasion no surprise that the plan of the town is of considerable complexity and that its interpretation needs particular care. Further, despite the interest of scholars of various persuasions from architectural historians to archaeologists, there has been no integrated study of the town since the publication of the *Victoria County History* at the beginning of the century. Page, the author of that history, provided a summary topographical review of St Albans which has formed the basis for almost all subsequent accounts of the town.[49]

Levison first developed the argument that the Roman Albanus's *martyrium* was to be found in a late Roman cemetery outside Verulamium and that the later abbey was constructed over the site[50] leading, eventually, to the emergence of the medieval town in this suburban location, rather than within the walls of its Roman predecessor. He looked to continental parallels for such a development, including the well-known case of Xanten in the northern Rhineland. This theory received archaeological support with the excavations by the Biddles in the 1980s, which proved that a Roman cemetery did, indeed, underlie the abbey.[51] Other excavations revealed a possible Roman cemetery church outside the south-east gate of Verulamium,[52] whilst the little church of St Germans close by, was rebuilt in the 930s by Abbot Eadfrith and commemorated the documented visit by Germanus in 429 (see Figure 8.1).[53]

The foundation of the medieval abbey is traditionally ascribed to Offa, King of Mercia, in AD 793, and Biddle has suggested that Offa probably translated Alban's body to a new shrine, rebuilt or renovated the church and founded a guarding monastic community of men and women under Benedictine rule[54] which was, of course, initially probably little different from secular minsters elsewhere. Offa's new foundation should not be seen as a rediscovery of the site since Bede, writing

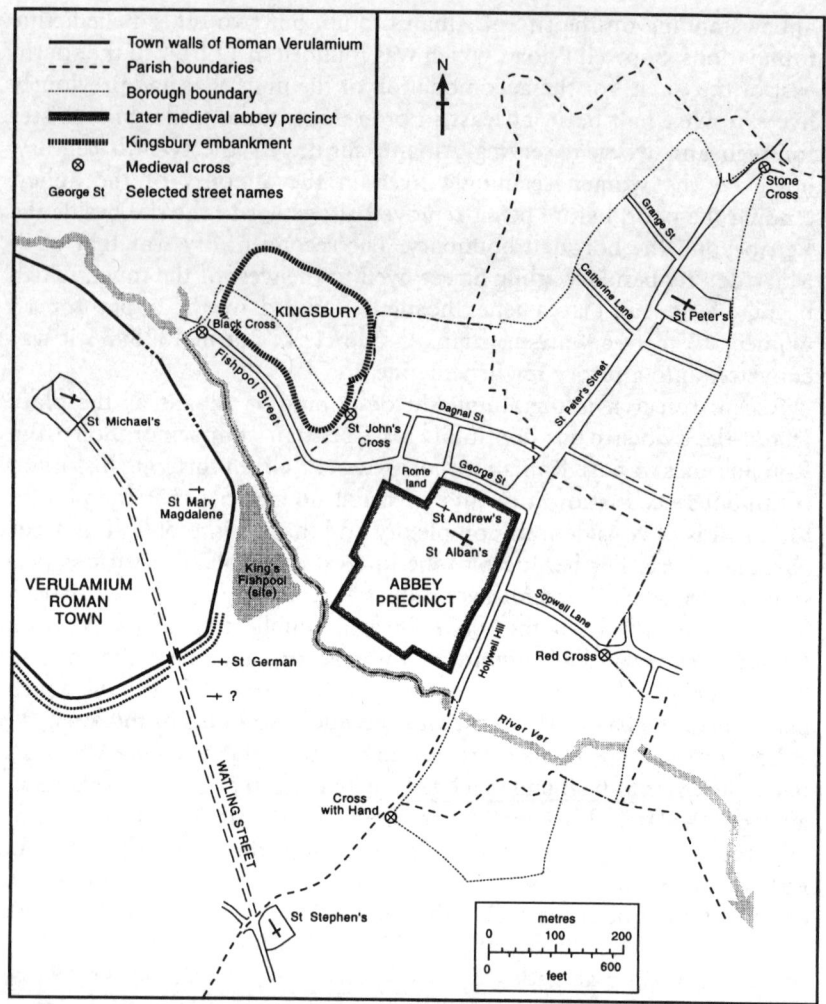

8.1   Borough and parish boundaries in St Albans

some 60 years earlier, speaks of the 'church of wonderful workmanship' where 'to this day sick people are healed in this place and the working of frequent miracles continues to bring it renown'[55] and all the evidence suggests that the martyr's church had been a site of veneration and pilgrimage from late Roman times onwards. Offa, himself, had a residence at St Albans in the south-eastern corner of his Mercian realm. Currently, there is no evidence to suggest whether this residence had been recently established or whether Verulamium had been a site of interest to the Mercian royal house for a much longer period as might be expected. What is clear is that the site of the royal palace followed the church out of Verulamium to the site of Alban's tomb. The palace, if that is what it was, was located to the north-west of the new abbey and to the north-east of Roman Verulamium, at Kingsbury. Kingsbury is first referred to in the tenth century as a *municipium* inhabited by the king's ministers and the fishermen who worked the great fishpool (see Figure 8.1).[56] It was defended by a substantial embankment but, seemingly, there was no ditch. Excavations have proved it to be post-Roman but have provided little evidence of interior structures or close dating.[57] Recent work has shown that this coincidence of a 'Kingsbury' site with a minster church community is quite common and possibly reflects the fixing of previously peripatetic royal households from the late ninth century onwards.[58]

Knowledge of the subsequent development of St Albans relies on the retrospective evidence of the abbey chronicle. This claims that Abbot Wulsin had founded a market in 948 but that it was oppressed by the inhabitants of Kingsbury. Wulsin's successor, Alfric (who was said to be king Ethelred's 'chancellor') purchased the fishpool from the king and drained it so that the fishermen could no longer earn their living and, towards the end of the tenth century, purchased Kingsbury itself and levelled most of the defences.[59] Wulsin's 'market' was clearly more than just a periodic trading place since the chronicle also notes that the abbey provided timber and other materials for the building of houses to anyone coming to settle in the new market.[60] This reads like the founding of a new town in much the same way as was to happen more widely in the twelfth and thirteenth centuries. Consequently, this is normally taken as the founding date of the new town laid out around its triangular market to the north of the abbey precinct.[61] The chronicle, repeated by successive generations of historians, also suggests that abbot Wulsin diverted Watling Street from Verulamium, around the north side of the monastic precinct through the market, and then southwards back to its original course. At the points of diversion St Michael's and St Stephen's churches were founded, whilst a third church, St Peter's, marked the northern extremity of the new market street (see Figure 8.1).[62]

By Domesday there was certainly a town here since, in addition to an agricultural populace, 46 burgesses and 4 Frenchmen are recorded, and the market tolls produced £11 14s. 0d. The abbey church was almost immediately rebuilt by Abbot Paul, of Caen (1077–93), nephew of Lanfranc, Archbishop of Canterbury, using a stock of building materials largely quarried from the ruins of Verulamium by his predecessors and, seemingly, with the encouragement and financial help of his uncle.[63] The later medieval precinct may also date from this time (see

Figure 8.1). The new abbey church was consecrated in 1115. From Stephen's reign at latest, the town was surrounded by substantial earthwork defences of embankment and ditches[64] and, during the later medieval period, the town became one of the principal staging posts on the road from London to the midlands, and a major market centre for produce destined for the London food market.[65]

Historical evidence takes us this far. However, we must be careful to remember that the abbey chronicle was itself a work of history and did not necessarily reflect the events of the late tenth and eleventh centuries as they occurred. Again, the town plan which can be observed on the earliest map of the town (which dates from the seventeenth century[66]) probably bears a close resemblance to the town as it was when the chronicle was compiled, but not necessarily to the place developing in the late tenth and eleventh centuries, which was not necessarily fully urban. Both of these assumptions need to be tested before they can be accepted. What, then, does the evidence of the town plan (and it is the first edition of the 1:2500 Ordnance Survey which is the basis of this analysis[67]) add to this framework, especially in concert with recent archaeological and historical research? The first point to note is that the plan evidence, especially of plot patterns, does not immediately affirm that the triangular market-place and the street northwards to St Peter's were laid out as a single planned entity. The plots on the western side of the street fall into four distinct blocks (plot series) of different width, depth and orientation (see Figure 8.2). The plots on the east side of St Peter's Street, as far south as the market-place, are notably irregular in breadth and depth but there is a firm back fence line on the borough boundary (see Figure 8.1). From the northern tip of the triangular market-place (modern Victoria Street) the plot pattern on the eastern side, and on southwards down Holywell Hill, is of an extraordinary depth within a continuation of that same firm back fence and with a regularity of plot widths. Sopwell Lane interrupts this plot series and acted as the medieval and early-modern link to the London road.

The abbey precinct wall was constructed some way in from the west side of Holywell Hill, and from the south side of the market-place, allowing shallow depth properties to be developed subsequently around the precinct in these areas, perhaps at the time that other properties were being established on the market-place itself. Such 'market accretions' are common features all over northern Europe. They are normally explained as deriving from market stalls becoming fixed properties, but there is more and more evidence accruing that most were deliberate developments by the ground landlord to increase rents. The three-storey, early fifteenth-century, timber-framed building at No. 2 Market Place is typical of the sort of structures that characterize market accre-

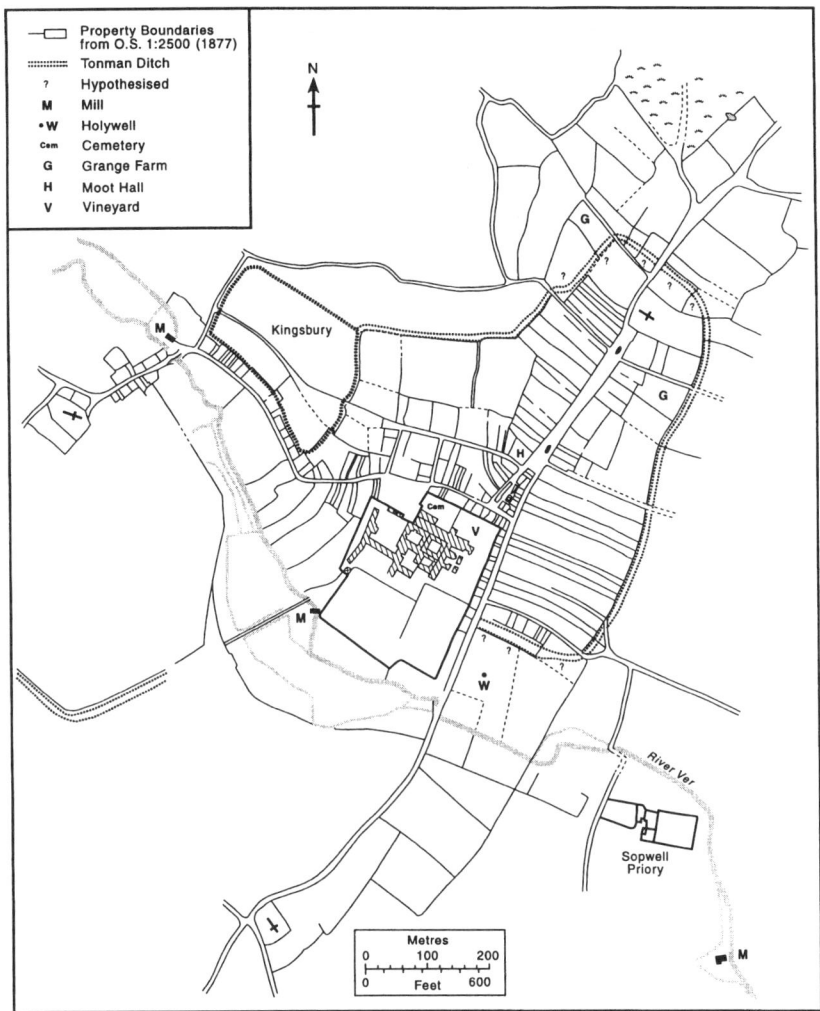

8.2 Plot patterns and defences in St Albans

tions[68] and Smith has noted a significant change in terminology from 'stall' to 'shop' occuring in the late thirteenth century in St Albans, which might suggest when the change from movable to permanent structures took place.[69] Official buildings are also to be found on the market-place and St Albans' famous clock tower, dating from 1403–12, is an example. It is notable that the market-place is more than the triangle in front of the abbey precinct since the regularity and breadth of St Peter's Street, and its deliberate termination by the churchyard of

St Peter's, show that this whole street was intended for marketing. This plan has much in common with the High Street at Evesham.[70]

The street plan to the north of George Street has a certain regularity about it, but the plot pattern at the junction with French Row (perhaps the place where the four Frenchmen of Domesday Book had their properties) is curvilinear and irregular. The square of Romeland was the public space in front of the great abbey gate in post-Conquest times, and the site of the town's fair. This is a distinctively different layout from most other Benedictine towns. No doubt the gate, leading into the Great Court at the west end of the abbey church, was an impressive spectacle architecturally but it did not impinge on the market-place. It would have been possible to have passed through the town and market-place from north to south and to have only seen the abbey above the foreground of houses and stalls. Romeland looks less to the commercial centre of the town than to the early location of royal patronage and power at Kingsbury. If Lower and Upper Dagnal Streets led to the main eastward-facing entrance of the Kingsbury enclosure (and there is no certainty as to where the entrance was), it is possible that the street block between Spicer Street and Wellclose Street may have formed a larger open space linking the entrances to Kingsbury and the abbey. Fishpool Street runs under the Kingsbury embankment and is characterized by two plot series, both notably irregular in all dimensions. Only two areas of the town, therefore, immediately suggest that they might have been planned: the George Street and Dagnal Street area and the eastern side of the town from Holywell Hill to St Peter's Church.

To take this latter first, the eastern side of the borough has all the characteristics of any of the scores of one-street planned market towns founded in thirteenth-century England. The tenements are almost geometrically rectangular and there is a continuous rear boundary from St Peter's Church in the north, almost to St Stephen's in the south. The one exceptional characteristic is their length; some 340 yards (311 metres) at its greatest, or nearly three times as long as the exceptional plots at Burton-on-Trent which are recorded as being 24 perches in length (132 yards).[71] Three narrow lanes divide the plot series into almost equal blocks and provide access from the street through to the town fields. It is quite clear that the southernmost, Sopwell Lane, derives from such a function and was not developed to act as the main access road to London; this function came later. Such an interpretation would certainly support the abbey chronicle references to the diversion by Abbot Wulsin of Watling Street through his new town, the intention being that visitors to or from London would arrive or leave via Holywell Hill and St Stephen's. The route of Watling Street has been lost between Verulamium and St Stephen's, though it is attested archaeologically (see

Figure 8.1), and both St Stephen's and St Michael's have upstanding later Saxon fabric,[72] so that all the available topographical evidence supports the story told in the chronicle.

A number of recent archaeological/historical studies have provided dating evidence for the plot series on the east side of the north–south routeway. First, there is the evidence of the Tonman Ditch. This is shown on the map of the town drawn by Benjamin Hare in 1634. It runs between St Peter's churchyard and Sopwell Lane along the rear of the plot series. It is followed by the borough boundary and, in part, by the parish boundary beween St Peter's and St Alban's/St Andrew's (the church attached to the north-west corner of the abbey which served its secular congregation).[73] South of Sopwell Lane, borough and parish boundaries cease to follow the rear boundary of the plot series (see Figure 8.1). The earliest documentation of the ditch is in a description of the borough boundary of 1327. It is notable that the borough boundary is described as running along Tonman Ditch only as far as Sopwell Lane. Excavations reported by Saunders and Havercroft show the inner embankment of this 'ditch' to have been at least 13 metres wide.[74] That the ditch was intended to be defensive is clear from the *Historia Anglorum*'s description of Stephen's attack on the town in 1142, which describes the town as 'surrounded by ditches'.[75] The matter is complicated further by Saunders and Havercroft's careful analysis of the evidence for a 'Monk Ditch' in the same area as Tonman Ditch, which they locate some one-third of the way back from the street frontage of St Peter's Street.[76] Unfortunately, they leave several unanswered questions, the answers to which are resolved by the evidence of the town plan. First, what happened to Tonman Ditch south of Sopwell Lane? Two hypotheses can be suggested: either it followed the rear property boundary that continues the plot series southwards to the River Ver and beyond, to either the line where the borough boundary cuts through to the main road at 'Cross with Hand' (see Figure 8.1) or, less likely, to St Stephen's churchyard. The second suggestion is that it turned westward to the south of Sopwell Lane to join the abbey precinct wall half way up Holywell Hill. This latter seems the more likely in providing a defensible circuit and is shown in Figure 8.2.

The second unanswered question was which of the two recorded ditches is the older earthwork? The answer, almost certainly, is Tonman Ditch. Monk Ditch and its access path, 'Hundespath', is frequently referred to in property abuttals in the fourteenth and fifteenth century and the abbey chronicle suggests that the abbey was still concerned to keep this clear of obstruction in the fifteenth century.[77] Knowledge of urban property development processes elsewhere suggests that exceptionally long tenements are a feature of the period before the mid-thirteenth century at latest. They imply a concern with gardening and orchards as well as urban crafts and trade. By the thirteenth century, urban tenements were being developed in new planned towns which rarely had an initial length to depth ratio greater than 3:1. There is no evidence elsewhere to show complete plot series being lengthened in the twelfth or thirteenth century; by contrast there is much evidence to show urban plot series being sub-divided along their length, often at their mid-point, to allow the subsequent development of a second street of properties on the rear of the original plots.[78] All of this suggests that the deep burgage series which makes up the eastern half of the town was laid out as a single act of planning; that the Tonman Ditch and bank was constructed as a defensible outer boundary in conjunction with bars at each end of the street (by 1142),[79] defensive necessities excluding the area beyond the River Ver towards St Stephens; and that at some later stage (by 1260x90) a second ditch, the Monk Ditch, was dug across the tenements about one-third of the way along their length where it could more easily be watched and defended from the houses on the street frontage in times of trouble. It survived longest in the area of St Peter's Street where the land of the Almoner and the town's archery butts led to the permanent shortening of the plots and the removal of all the boundaries at the rear (see Figure 8.2).[80]

The summary report of excavations within the series of long plots at Chequer Street, fronting the triangular market-place, suggests that the archaeological evidence shows that this area was laid out in the later twelfth century with plots 6–7 metres wide and some 28 metres long divided one from another by shallow ditches.[81] However, this is the market-place frontage and it seems more probable that these ditched plots represent the layout of new shorter, narrower plots within the framework of an older plot pattern of much broader, longer plots. We have still not arrived at a date for the longer plot series but, if the shorter plots represent a replanning of the town by the Norman abbots in the twelfth century, the implication is that the longer plot pattern takes us back to the pre-Norman period and, perhaps, back to Abbot Wulsin in AD 948, though that is certainly a speculative leap for which at present there is no archaeological evidence.

The increasing significance of Sopwell Lane within this plot series presumably post-dates the founding of the Priory at Sopwell in 1140, and led to the development of a short plot series at right angles to the original plots on either side of the lane. Thereafter, Holywell Hill, and the area beyond the bridge over the River Ver, declined in importance, though Holywell Hill was still lined with properties in the early seventeenth century.

If the plan evidence for the rest of the town is now examined, the plot pattern on the western side of St Peter's Street and the north side of

George Street is altogether more complex. However, it is worth making the point straight away that the borough boundary runs at a similar distance from the west frontage of St Peters Street as it does from the east, and that it is also similarly distanced from Dagnal Street as far as Kingsbury (see Figure 8.1). The Tonman Ditch is recorded as following the boundary from Kingsbury to Catherine Lane. This lane divides the St Peters Street western plot series and provides access to the fields in the same way as Hatfield Road on the eastern side. It would be possible to suggest that a similar series of very long plots once matched those that survive on the east side of the town (see Figure 8.2). However, if this were so, a much greater degree of subsequent disruption to the pattern needs to be explained for the western half of the town.

Explanation can commence to the north of Catherine Lane; the plots here are somewhat foreshortened from the borough boundary and the Tonman Ditch is recorded in 1327 as following the back fence line of these plots, not the borough boundary. Between the two, the grange of St Peter was recorded and a substantial farmhouse is still shown on Grange Street on Hare's map in 1634. This farm, and the fields beyond within the parish of St Peter's, was the glebe granted for the support of St Peter's Church, and therefore probably dates from at least the time of Abbot Wulsin in the tenth century. Tenements in this part of St Peter's Street were consequently necessarily foreshortened from the beginning because of the presence of the grange farm, but the farm was included within the borough.

South of Catherine Lane three large, long plots, similar to those on the east side, stretch back to the Tonman Ditch and the borough boundary but, southwards again, the plot series gets progressively shorter towards Dagnal Street, though there is a firm back fence line. Moving to the Dagnal Street plots; the pattern here is disrupted by the construction of Verulam Street in the nineteenth century. However, Hare's map, and that drawn by Dury and Andrews in 1766,[82] allow the pre-nineteenth century pattern to be reconstructed in reasonable detail. In this area the plots are of shallow depth and the primary boundaries suggest a series of squarish plots along the north side with a firm rear fence line and a number of field enclosures beyond, taking up the space as far as the borough boundary and the Tonman Ditch which here turns east to the corner of the Kingsbury enclosure. A narrow footpath, which survives on the Ordnance Survey first edition and is in part followed by the parish boundary between St Andrew's and St Peter's, provided an access to these fields and beyond from Dagnal Street, while the narrow Cross Street continues the angled line of the back fence of the St Peter's Street tenements. It is possible that the block of field land within the Tonman Ditch here represents another holding similar to St Peter's grange, but whether it was already in existence in Abbot Wulsin's time, or was created later, it is not possible to infer. The Andrew's and Dury map shows a 'college' on Dagnal Street which may be the eighteenth-century successor to this holding in the same way as the Duchess of Marlborough's almshouses succeeded the 'grange of John Baldewyne' to the rear of the eastern tenements on St Peter's Street (see Figure 8.2). However, equally, this field block may have resulted simply from the ditch taking the most direct route to the corner of the Kingsbury enclosure. If the entrance to the Kingsbury enclosure was on its eastern side, as seems likely, Dagnal Street would have initially linked Kingsbury to the abbot's new market-place but, once the abbey had gained control of the Kingsbury site, the significance of this road would have been superseded by Fishpool Street which linked the new town with St Michael's and the old road through Verulamium.

The key area for the interpretation of this complex plot pattern is where the St Peter's Street and Dagnal Street plots meet. The plan seam between the two plot series is distinctive and consists of a small block of very narrow plots which curve from the north side of Dagnal Street, across to the south side and then wrap round the St Peter's street plots to face the new market-place. The pattern has been badly disrupted by the nineteenth-century construction of Spencer Street and Verulam Street but is still sufficiently clear on the first edition plan to suggest that this area was one in which two major development phases in the town plan, represented by two very different plot series, came together. The key historical fact in the early history of the town is the two separate landholdings of the king and the abbey and the contest between the two groups of tenants for commercial supremacy. It was only the purchase of Kingsbury by Abbot Alfric in the later tenth century that united the two. I would suggest that the distinctive plan seam of curved plots represents the landownership division between king and abbey. To the north east, the St Peter's Street plots were part of the Abbot Wulsin's new market; to the west, the Dagnal Street plots lined the approach to the Kingsbury enclosure and were part of the royal estate.

Such an hypothesis provides an explanation for another of the unusual features of the St Alban's plan when it is compared with other Benedictine foundations, namely the way in which the triangular market-place is not focused on the abbey precinct gateway. If the land immediately to the north of the abbey was in the king's hands, then it would not have been possible for Abbot Wulsin to focus his new market-place in this way. However, what he did do was to locate the market-place in such a way that it was easy for the king's tenants to make use of it, the plots of their east–west oriented settlement gaining access to the west side of the market-place, and his own tenant's plots in the north–

south oriented new town taking up the east side of the market-place and the length of St Peter's Street. The careful location of a new market-place to bring together an older community and the community of a new-founded town has been observed elsewhere, in the Midland's episcopal centre of Lichfield,[83] though some 200 years later. It may also not be accidental that the moot hall of the fraternity of All Saints, the town's guild, was located on the corner of Dagnal Street and the market-place[84] as another symbol of the bringing together of two communities.

Conclusions

It is now possible to bring these threads together to suggest a coherent, and much richer, story of the topographical development of St Albans than that usually presented and it is one that affirms the essential truth of the abbey chronicle. The earliest phase of settlement was in the area to the east of Kingsbury, possibly centred around a large open space (of which Romeland was the later relict successor) used for religious festivals and processions at the west end of the church built over Alban's tomb. The settlement was sufficiently flourishing to be accorded the status of *municipium* in tenth-century documentation and, with a fortified palace of the increasingly settled Mercian royal house, the consequent presence of the king's ministers, the monastic church and its community of monks and nuns, the seasonal flow of pilgrims visiting the tomb of England's proto-martyr, the quarry of good building stone which the ruins of Verulamium provided, and the king's great fishpool, it should occasion no surprise that this place was contemporaneously regarded as urban. However, a cautious modern analysis would suggest that the settlement was perhaps proto-urban (though with a large number of central-place functions), at least until archaeological excavations can provide evidence of a larger community of residents earning their living from trade and craft production.

The monastic revival and reform of the later tenth century was accompanied at St Albans, as elsewhere, by urban development, almost certainly because the reformed monasteries needed to be rebuilt and extended, and towns were a source of money. This is most clear at Worcester because of the famous charter between abbot and king relating to the building of the *burh* there[85] but, as we have seen, almost all of the tenth-century Benedictine monasteries have towns at their gates. At St Albans, Abbot Wulsin laid out a new town to the east and north of the abbey church, along a single street, with very long plots which would have provided generously for orchards and vegetable gardens. The core of this town was a new planned market-place taking up the whole northern half of the new street but focusing on a triangular space where the older Kingsbury settlement and the new town came together. Settlement was encouraged through the provision of building materials. At the same time, churches were rebuilt or new-founded to mark the terminations of the town and the diversion of the road up the hill to the new market-place. In 1086, St Albans was a flourishing small town with 50 households recorded as holding through burgage tenure. By the mid-twelfth century it was enclosed within a ditch of significant proportions and, consequently, the town began to concentrate into the area around the market-place. Destruction during the civil war between Stephen and Matilda perhaps provided the stimulus for the abbey to replan the area on the western side of the market-place with narrower plots but, more likely, is that these narrower plots, attested by archaeology, derive from sub-division by individual burghers.

It is reasonably clear that St Albans is of considerable significance in the history of urban development in England. Its topography is very different from that of the more or less contemporary *burhs* of Wessex and midland England and, whereas in the *burhs* it was royal decision-making that was to the fore and Benedictine institutions were generally fringe features of the towns, in St Albans it was the abbot who took the initiative and the king's palace that was to become a fringe, and ultimately a derelict, feature. St Albans has none of the rectangular grid of streets that have come to be regarded as typical of the most developed of the *burh* towns and characteristic of their planned nature. It is, however, just as much a planned town as Winchester or Wallingford: but the plan of St Albans points the way to the hundreds of new single-street market towns that were to laid out by secular and ecclesiastical lords in the twelfth and thirteenth centuries to enhance the economic development of their estates in all parts of the kingdom.

Acknowledgements

I am grateful to Nicholas Brooks and Nigel Baker for sources of information and to Ann Ancorn for drawing the maps for publication.

Notes

1. A. Ballard, *The Domesday Boroughs* (1904); F.W. Maitland, *Township and Borough* (1898); J. Tait, *The Medieval English Borough* (1936).
2. H. Pirrene, *Medieval Cities, their Origin and the Revival of Trade* (Princeton, 1925); C. Stephenson, *Borough and Town* (Cambridge, Mass.,

1933); M.D. Lobel, *The Borough of Bury St Edmunds: a Study in the Government and Development of a Medieval Town* (1935); R.S. Gottfried, *Bury St Edmunds and the Urban Crisis: 1290–1539* (Princeton, 1982).
3. M. Aston and J. Bond, *The Landscape of Towns* (1976); T. Rowley, *The Norman Heritage 1066–1200* (1983).
4. M. Bonney, *Lordship and the Urban Community. Durham and its Overlords, 1250–1540* (1990) is a recent example which pays scant regard to topographical development.
5. L. Swan, 'Monastic proto-towns in early medieval Ireland: the evidence from aerial photography, plan analysis and survey', in H.B. Clarke and A. Simms (eds), *The Comparative History of Urban Origins in non-Roman Europe*, BAR International Series, 255 (1985); C. Doherty, 'Monastic towns in Ireland', in ibid., 45–76.
6. J. Blair, 'Minster churches in the landscape', in D. Hooke (ed.), *Anglo-Saxon Settlements* (1988), 35–58.
7. R.A. Donkin, 'The urban property of the Cistercians in medieval England', *Analecta Sacri Ordinis Cisterciensis*, 15 (1959), 104–31; R.A. Donkin, *The Cistercians: Studies in the Geography of Medieval England and Wales* (Toronto, 1978) ch. 5.
8. N.M. Trenholme, *The English Monastic Boroughs, A Study in Medieval History*, The University of Missouri Studies. A Quarterly of Research. 2.3 (1927), 1–115; M.D. Lobel, 'A detailed account of the 1327 rising at Bury St Edmunds and the subsequent trial', *Proceedings of the Suffolk Institute of Archaeology*, 21 (1933), 215–31; C.C. Dyer, 'Small town conflict in the later Middle Ages', *Urban History*, 19.2 (1992), 183–210.
9. M.R.G. Conzen, *Alnwick, Northumberland, a Study in Town-Plan Analysis*, Publications of the Institute of British Geographers, 27 (1960).
10. T.R. Slater, 'Medieval new town and port: a plan-analysis of Hedon, East Yorkshire', *Yorkshire Archaeological Journal*, 57 (1985), 23–41; idem. The topography and planning of medieval Lichfield: a critique', *Transactions of the South Staffordshire Archaeological and Historical Society*, 26 (1986), 11–35; idem. 'Ideal and reality in English episcopal medieval town planning', *Transactions, Institute of British Geographers*, new series, 12 (1987), 191–203.
11. N.J. Baker and T.R. Slater, 'Morphological regions in English medieval towns', in J.W.R. Whitehand and P.J. Larkham (eds), *The Urban Landscape: International Perspectives* (1992), 45–68.
12. J. Burton, *Monastic and Religious Orders in Britain* (1994), 1–21.
13. D. Knowles and R.N. Hadcock, *Medieval Religious Houses in England and Wales* (1953).
14. P. Sims-Williams, *Religion and Literature in Western England, 600–800* (1990); J. Blair, *Anglo-Saxon Oxfordshire* (1994) 56–69.
15. J. Blair, 'St Frideswide's monastery: problems and possibilities', *Oxoniensia*, 53 (1988), 3–20.
16. N. Baker and R. Holt, *Medieval Towns and the Church: Worcester and Gloucester* (1998 forthcoming).
17. K.D. Lilley, 'Coventry's topographical development: the impact of the Priory', in G. Demidowicz (ed.), *Coventry's first Cathedral* (1994), 72–97.
18. T.R. Slater, 'Medieval town-founding on the estates of the Benedictine Order in England', in F.-E. Eliassen and G.A. Ersland (eds), *Power, Profit*

        and Urban Land. Landownership in Medieval and Early-Modern Northern European Towns (1996), 70–93.
19. K.D. Lilley, 'Coventry's topographical development'.
20. —,*Gesta Abbatum Monasterii Sancti Albani I–III*, Rolls Series (1867–69). The author of the *Chronicle* was Matthew Paris writing in the thirteenth century.
21. The West Midland towns of Evesham, Coventry and Burton-on-Trent all provide examples of this type, see Slater, 'Medieval town-founding'.
22. E. Searle, *Battle Abbey and its Banlieu* (Toronto, 1980).
23. See Chapter 11, this volume.
24. See Lobel, *The Borough of Bury St Edmunds*; Rowley, *The Norman Heritage*, 74–78.
25. M. Aston and R. Leech, *Historic Towns in Somerset, Archaeology and Planning* (1977) 147–54.
26. E. King, 'The town of Peterborough in the early Middle Ages', *Northamptonshire Past and Present*, 6 (1980–81), 187–95.
27. N.P. Brooks, *The Early History of the Church of Canterbury. Christ Church from 597 to 1066* (1984) 292–4; T. Tatton-Brown, 'The towns of Kent', in J. Haslam (ed.), *Anglo-Saxon Towns in Southern England* (1984), 16–22.
28. Lilley, 'Coventry's topographical development'.
29. M.W. Beresford, *New Towns of the Middle Ages. Town Plantation in England, Wales and Gascony* (1967) 495–6.
30. Lobel, *The Borough of Bury St Edmunds*.
31. Slater, 'Medieval town-founding'.
32. C.J. Bond and A.M. Hunt, 'Recent archaeological work in Pershore', *Vale of Evesham Historical Society Research Papers*, 6 (1977), 1–76.
33. Bonney, *Lordship and the Urban Community*, 41–3.
34. Baker and Slater, 'Morphological regions'.
35. B. Cunliffe, *The City of Bath* (1986), 44–71.
36. A. Stacpoole (ed.), *The Noble City of York* (1972), 261.
37. Beresford, *New Towns*.
38. M.W. Beresford and J.K.S. St Joseph, *Medieval England, an Aerial Survey* (1979), 182–3.
39. Slater, 'Medieval town-founding'.
40. M.W. Beresford and H.P.R. Finberg, *English Medieval Boroughs: a Handlist* (1973), 115.
41. Slater, 'Medieval town-founding'.
42. T.R. Slater, 'The analysis of burgages: three case studies from the West Midlands', *West Midlands Archaeology*, 23 (1980), 57–9; C.C. Dyer, 'Small-town conflict in the later Middle Ages: events at Shipston-on-Stour', *Urban History*, 19 (1992), 183–210.
43. Bond and Hunt, 'Archaeological work in Pershore'.
44. T.R. Slater, 'Urban genesis and medieval town plans in Warwickshire and Worcestershire', in T.R. Slater and P.J. Jarvis (eds), *Field and Forest, an Historical Geography of Warwickshire and Worcestershire* (1982), 173–202.
45. Slater, 'Medieval town-founding'.
46. D. Knowles and R.N. Hadcock, *Medieval Religious Houses, England and Wales* (1953), 218; W. Page (ed.), *Victoria County History, Hertfordshire IV*, (1914), 422–6.

47. Knowles and Hadcock, *Medieval Religious Houses*, 218, 303; Page, *VCH IV*, 428–31.
48. C. Thomas, *Christianity in Roman Britain to AD 500* (1981), 180; R. Morris, *Churches in the Landscape* (1989), 35–9; M. Biddle, 'Archaeology, architecture and the cult of saints in Anglo-Saxon England', in L.A.S. Butler and R.K. Morris (eds), *The Anglo-Saxon Church, Papers on History, Architecture and Archaeology in honour of Dr H.M. Taylor*, The Council for British Archaeology Research Report, 60 (1986), 1–31.
49. W. Page (ed.), *The Victoria County History of Hertfordshire II*, (1908), 469–82; Page, *VCH IV*, 367–416.
50. W. Levison, 'St Alban and St Albans', *Antiquity*, 15 (1941), 337–59.
51. Biddle, 'Cult of saints', 13–16.
52. I.E. Anthony, 'Excavations at Verulam Hills Field, St Albans, 1963–4', *Hertfordshire Archaeology*, 1 (1968), 9–50; Morris, *Churches in the Landscape*, 38–9.
53. Chronicle, 20 (see n. 20 above); Morris, Churches in the Landscape, 36.
54. M. Biddle, 'Alban and the Anglo-Saxon church', in R. Runcie (ed.), *Cathedral and City, St Albans Ancient and Modern* (1977), 23–42.
55. C. Saunders and A.B. Havercroft, 'Excavations in the city and district of St Albans 1974–76', *Hertfordshire Archaeology*, 6 (1978), 1–77. The evidence for the Anglo-Saxon phase of St Albans is summarized on p. 74; E. Toms, *The Story of St Albans* (1975); Page, *VCH II* 469–82.
56. Page, *VCHII*, 469–82.
57. Saunders and Havercroft, 'Excavations in ... St Albans', 1–15;
58. J. Haslam, 'The towns of Wiltshire', in Haslam, *Anglo-Saxon Towns*, 87–149.
59. *Chronicle*, 23; see S. Keynes, *The Diplomas of King Aethelred 'the Unready', 978–1016* (1980), 136 for a discussion on the nature of Anglo-Saxon chancellors.
60. *Chronicle*, 22.
61. Beresford, *New Towns*, 326.
62. *Chronicle*, 22; Morris, *Churches in the Landscape*, 39.
63. C. Brooke, 'St Albans: the great abbey', in Runcie, *Cathedral and City*, 43–70; Page, *VCH II*, 483–515.
64. Saunders and Havercroft, 'Excavations', 35–7.
65. B.M.S. Campbell, J.A. Galloway, D. Keene and M. Murphy, *A Medieval Capital and its Grain Supply: Agrarian Production and Distribution in the London Region c. 1300*, Historical Geography Research Series, 30 (1993), 169–70.
66. B. Hare, *The True and Perfect Delineation of the Town of St Albans*, (1634); the plan survives only as a copy made in 1789, see C. Wilton, 'A plan of the town of St Albans drawn by Benjamin Hare in 1634', *St Albans and Hertfordshire Architectural and Archaeological Society Transactions* (1924), 35–42; the plan is also reproduced in W. Page, 'The origins and forms of Hertfordshire towns and villages', *Archaeologia*, 69 (1917–18), 47–60; and in Page, *VCH II*, 470–71.
67. Ordnance Survey 1:2,500 County Series, Hertfordshire, sheets 24.7, 24.8, 24.11, 24.12, surveyed 1877–78, published 1880.
68. J. T. Smith, *English Houses 1200–1800, the Hertfordshire Evidence* (1992), 143–4. Slater, 'Medieval town-founding', 75–6.
69. Ibid.

70. Slater, 'Medieval town-founding', 80.
71. Slater, 'Medieval town-founding', 75–7.
72. H.M. and J. Taylor, *Anglo-Saxon Architecture* (1965), 528–31; L. Webster and J. Cherry, 'Medieval Britain in 1982', *Medieval Archaeology*, **27** (1983), 183.
73. Brooke, 'The great abbey', 47. Saunders and Havercroft, 'Excavations', 35–8; F. Madden (ed.), *Matthaei Pariensis Historia Anglorum*, Rolls Series (1866) 270.
74. Madden, *Historia Anglorum*; Saunders and Havercroft, 'Excavations', 35–8.
75. Saunders and Havercroft, 'Excavations', 37–8.
76. Ibid.
77. Saunders and Havercroft, 'Excavations', 35–8.
78. T.R. Slater, 'Doncaster's town plan: an analysis', in P.C. Buckland, J.R. Magilton and C.C. Hayfield (eds), *The Archaeology of Doncaster 2: the Medieval Town* (1989), 43–61; Slater, 'The analysis of burgages'.
79. Saunders and Havercroft, 'Excavations', 35–8.
80. Ibid.
81. Webster and Cherry, 'Medieval Britain', 181–3.
82. This plan is reproduced in Smith, *English Houses*, 137.
83. T.R. Slater, 'Topography and planning of medieval Lichfield'.
84. J.T. Smith, 'Nine hundred years of St Albans: architecture and social history', *Hertfordshire Archaeology*, **11** (1993), 1–22.
85. N. Baker, H. Dalwood, R. Holt, C. Mundy and G. Taylor, 'From Roman to medieval Worcester: development and planning in the Anglo-Saxon city', *Antiquity*, **66** (1992), 65–74; Baker and Slater, 'Morphological regions'.

CHAPTER NINE

Trading Places: Monastic Initiative and the Development of High-Medieval Coventry

Keith D. Lilley

The complexity of medieval urban development creates problems for those who try to reconstruct the evolution of English cities, even where a substantial supply of material exists. Where detailed and early documentary records are available, the high-medieval townscape can be carefully reconstructed and, as at Canterbury and Winchester, something of the initiative behind urban development can be learned.[1] In these studies and others, the medieval church in England is shown to have influenced the control and design of townscape for its own purposes of administration and trade.[2] Likewise, in Ireland and Wales, the activities of the early medieval church and its communities have left tangible and characteristic urban forms, visible in the topography of towns through aerial photographs and cartographic sources.[3] Examining monastic initiative in medieval urban development is therefore far from being a new line of enquiry, but recently the processes involved have increasingly become recognized as a complex interaction between different power élites, each contesting their access to urban space, and as a consequence shaping the evolution of urban landscapes. This conflict over tenure and authority can be seen in the topographical development of medieval Coventry and in particular in the changing role of the Benedictine monastery of St Mary in the affairs of its urban estate after its foundation in *c*.1043.

As one of the more important cities of medieval England, Coventry ought to have an early and detailed documentary record, but instead the city's origins are obscure. Much of the evidence for early Coventry is negative and seemingly inconclusive. The charters that concern the foundation of the Benedictine house in Coventry have been shown to be forgeries,[4] fabricated sometime during the reign of Stephen, perhaps to provide legal clout over arguments with the earl of Chester or as a means for the prior 'to secure freedom from episcopal control'.[5] Turning to the entry in Domesday Book,[6] early-Norman Coventry has been interpreted as a 'mainly agricultural community of about 350 serfs living in single-story hovels'.[7] These sources provide only a partial view of early Coventry, however. When the contemporary written evidence is considered critically, along with other historical sources, a more controversial history can be gleaned. Central to this controversy is the origin of the Benedictine foundation, the extent of its original endowment and the policies of individuals connected with ecclesiastical administration within the town. With regard to the Domesday entry for example, the derisory interpretation of late eleventh-century Coventry may not be warranted *if* the entry is taken to be incomplete and *if* the transferral of the episcopal see in *c.*1102 is taken as an indication that Coventry was, by then, urban.[8]

The meteoric rise of Coventry in the medieval urban hierarchy of England makes the origins of the city all the more enigmatic, and, despite a number of recent studies, the temptation has still been to see it as a latecomer to the medieval urban scene.[9] Nor does the archaeology of the city help contradict this view, as much of the material excavated in recent years post-dates the Norman Conquest.[10] But however much the origins of Coventry look late, the evidence of the town's topography tells a different story. Using an approach which combines information from maps and plans with documentary material and archaeological evidence, the development of medieval Coventry is made clearer.[11] It becomes apparent that at the heart of this urban growth was monastic initiative, as it was in so many other towns in medieval England both before and after the Norman Conquest.[12] Despite the paucity of early documentary material and the wholesale destruction of Coventry's medieval fabric during the twentieth century,[13] the enduring role of monastic initiative, and its impact on the town's medieval topography, can be explored using the technique of town-plan analysis.

The morphogenesis of medieval Coventry

The origins of the plan-analysis approach to reconstructing the morphogenesis of urban landscapes is attributable to Professor M.R.G. Conzen, whose work on Alnwick, Northumberland has provided inspiration to urban historical geographers.[14] Over the last two decades this approach has been refined for the purpose of reconstructing medieval urban topography and has become increasingly sophisticated, combining techniques derived from geography, history and archaeology.[15] The large-scale Ordnance Survey plans of the mid to late nineteenth century provide a detailed and accurate cartographic base for plan analysis. This first involves simplifying the town plan into three plan elements, the streets, the plot pattern, and the surviving medieval buildings (mostly townscape dominants such as churches and guild-halls). The second stage of analysis uses the supposition that much of the late nineteenth-century street system and plot pattern is of broadly medieval origin, and that this can form a preliminary basis for showing how the town plan may have developed.[16] If early manuscript maps and plans are used in conjunction with the base plan, then obvious post-medieval changes, such as turnpike roads and industrial redevelopment, can be removed. Coventry's town plan was thus treated, the process being helped by the availability of the 1851 Board of Health (BOH) plan, drawn at a scale of 1:528, and also by earlier but less accurate plans.[17]

Using the simplified Ordnance Survey plan as a base, it is possible to hypothesize the phases of urban growth by disaggregating the town plan into 'plan-units'. Each plan-unit is defined on the basis that the town plan is a mosaic of morphologically distinct areas and that each such area has its own unity. This process is by no means straightforward, especially for a town as large as Coventry, where 21 major plan-units can be discerned (see Figure 9.1), but it is particularly helpful as a way of hypothesizing the spread of urban development and also as a means of providing a framework for managing information derived from documentary sources and excavations.[18] Immediately apparent in Coventry's town plan is a distinct difference between plan-units in the north part of the town and those spread along an east–west axial street: morphologically speaking, two plan-regions can be identified.[19] One explanation for this topographical divide of the town plan becomes evident, though contentious, when it is compared to the tenurial division of the medieval town.

Unlike some other large high-medieval cities, such as London, York and Norwich, Coventry did not have a complicated pattern of small, multiple-parish units.[20] Instead, the parochial topography of the medieval town was relatively simple, being divided between the large parishes of Holy Trinity and St Michael. For the most part, the boundary between the two plan-regions follows the same course as the parish boundary. This originally wove its way through the lanes and buildings in the centre of Coventry and is described in detail in two perambulations, in 1675 and 1815.[21] When these boundary perambulations are compared with the line of the parish boundary shown on the 1851 Board of Health plan, the two can be seen to match, confirming the longevity of its course and, in detail, its relationship with the plot pattern and street system within each of the two plan-regions. Using earlier documentary sources, a more distant origin for the parish boundary can be proposed. In a forged letter, which was supposedly written by Earl Hugh II (d. 1181), the boundary of the earl's fee was outlined.[22] Although the document is now thought to be dated to the time when the prior's lands and rights were being challenged

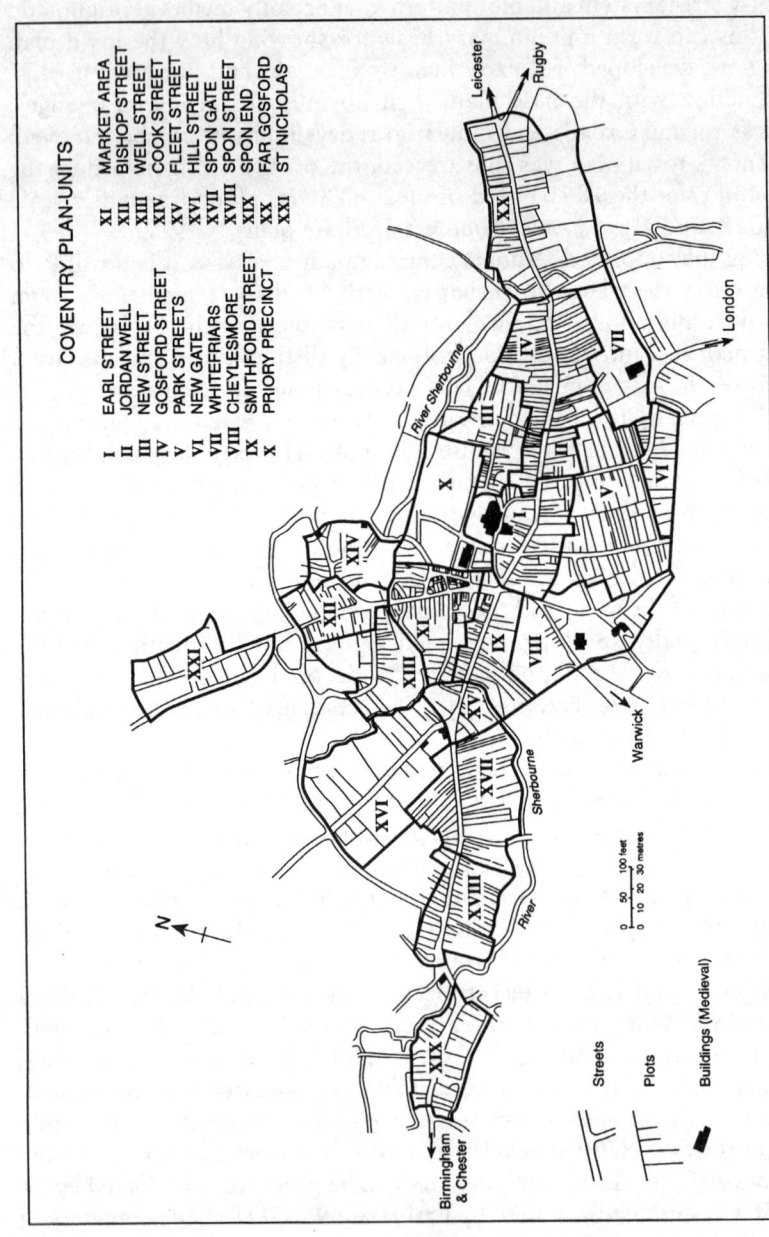

9.1 A plan analysis of Coventry

by Queen Isabella in the period 1337–48, it is also believed that the description of the boundary was based on 'an earlier statement of the bounds', perhaps of the late twelfth century.[23] Using this early description it is possible to see that the area of the prior's fee and earl's fee relates to the areas of Holy Trinity and St Michael's parishes.

The close correlation of the two boundaries, of the fee and the parish, is significant because it shows that the topographical division of Coventry dates to the period of its tenurial division. The date of the tenurial division therefore becomes a vital clue in understanding the morphogenesis of urban Coventry, in that Holy Trinity parish could represent the area first granted to the Benedictines by Earl Leofric of Mercia at the time when he founded the abbey in *c.*1043.[24] In other words, it may be that the charters relating to this monastic foundation, which have been shown to be forgeries,[25] were fabricated to reinforce what was actually already written into the townscape of high-medieval Coventry. Similarly, in the forged letter of Hugh II, the prior's jurisdiction over the market-place is asserted and it is also stated that the market is situated on the soil of the church's foundation (*in solo fund[ationis] ecclesie sue est . . .*).[26] Perhaps, then, the prior was right when he challenged tenants in the earl's fee for trading during his Friday market in 1309[27] and right, also, to claim that his fee in Coventry had initially been granted to the abbey by Earl Leofric.[28] Far from being a last ditch attempt to save his fee against Isabella in the 1330s,[29] the forging and reproduction of these charters and letters may have been an attempt legally to uphold the prior's claim at a time when his or his tenants' words alone were not enough to support his litigation.

Supposing this explanation for the origins of the prior's fee is accepted, there are, as a consequence, implications for understanding the origins of the area of St Michael's parish. If this, the earl's fee, represents the part of Coventry that was originally held by Earl Leofric after both he and Godiva had granted the Benedictines their fee on an area of adjacent land to the north, then the two fees together may be taken to reflect the original areal extent of Coventry as held under the Mercian earls. The land left in Leofric's hands after *c.*1043 ultimately passed to his wife Godgifu (Godiva), and then later came into the hands of the earls of Chester (by *c.*1088–92),[30] so fossilizing the earlier tenurial arrangement.[31] Such a long-standing tenurial division, dating back to the 1040s, would also explain why a topographical division came to be reflected in Coventry's town plan. If the tenurial division is of later origin, however, perhaps being evident only by the later-twelfth century[32] or contemporary with the foundation of Holy Trinity Church in *c.*1102,[33] then Coventry's topographical development, as shown by the plan analysis, must largely post-date the twelfth century. Either way, the role of monastic initiative is clearly central to understanding the origin and development of urban Coventry.

Monastic initiative in Coventry's urban development

To explore further each of these two suggested chronologies, a detailed appraisal of urban development within the prior's fee is necessary, using as a base the plan analysis of Coventry. There are four plan-units within Holy Trinity parish which seem to be relevant to this discussion, plan-units X, XI, XII and XIV (see Figure 9.1). They are clustered along the north–south axial route through the town and seem to represent phases of urban growth along this road, which linked two prominent places in later pre-Conquest Warwickshire, Tamworth and Warwick.[34] The two northern plan-units, Bishop Street and Cook Street (XII and XIV) are quite different in form from the precinct area and market area plan-units (X and XI), which lie to the south of the River Sherbourne. Even a superficial examination of the town plan reveals that these two plan-units are significant for understanding the role of monastic initiative in medieval Coventry.

The area of plan-unit X is on sloping ground and relatively devoid of streets and plots, even on late nineteenth century plans,[35] except on the southern side where the parish church of Holy Trinity is situated. Earlier plans of this area show it to be the site of the Benedictine cathedral priory and this suggests therefore that the plan-unit represents the priory precinct area, extending between the parish church of St Michael and the River Sherbourne.[36] Adjacent to plan-unit X, to the west, is the market area (plan unit XI). This is characterized by an altogether different physical form that has as its focus a triangular market-place containing two islands of encroachment. The north and west sides of the market-place are fronted by plots which are noticeably deeper and larger than a row of plots on the east side that represent, perhaps, a further, lateral encroachment onto the market-place. Separating these two plan-units (X and XI) is a distinct morphological boundary, a plan-seam, which would appear to form the line of the precinct's western boundary. These two plan-units, of approximately equal size and squeezed between the earl's fee to the south and the River Sherbourne to the north, may be the area of land granted to the Benedictines by Earl Leofric to found their abbey in c.1043. If this is the case, then some indication of monastic initiative should be evident in the organization and development of each plan-unit.

Part of the problem in unravelling the early ecclesiastical topography of Coventry arises from the destruction of many of the priory buildings in the later sixteenth century, following the dissolution of the monastery in 1538.[37] However, by plotting out on to the plan analysis the remains of the priory uncovered through past excavations,[38] as well as other historical evidence, it is possible to reconstruct the internal organization of the former precinct area (see Figure 9.2).[39] Three main areas of usage are revealed: one area to the west, consisting of the cathedral priory and its associated conventual buildings, together with Holy Trinity Church; an area of industrial activities to the north (along Priory Lane), and to the east, a more open area which contained the Priory Fields, the bishop's palace and, possibly, the prior's chamber. The precinct was, therefore, a carefully organized area of Coventry's townscape, with the cathedral overlooking the market area and being close to the commercial core of the town, rather than remote from it. The sloping site was not, however, a particularly suitable place for the building of a large monastery, especially when compared to the flat and relatively well-positioned riverside sites of other urban Benedictine houses, such as Burton-upon-Trent, Evesham and Peterborough, to give but three Midland examples.[40]

The awkward relief of the site at Coventry must have made it difficult to supply water to the monastery or to equip it with good drainage facilities, and this explanation has been used to account for the unusual reversed juxtaposition between the cathedral church and its associated conventual buildings.[41] Even so, such a difficult site must have been used not because it was preferred, but because it was an area of land that had been given as an endowment by Earl Leofric and because there was no alternative. A site further to the south was presumably unsuitable because this would have encroached upon the earl's fee and St Michael's Church (which would have been kept by Leofric after he founded the abbey), and also perhaps because the earl's fee was by then already built-up. Moreover, if, as legend has it, the monastery was raised to replace an earlier monastic foundation dedicated to St Osburga,[42] it would have been necessary to choose a site that could closely supersede it.[43] Unfortunately, however, any structural evidence of buildings belonging to the earliest pre-Conquest abbey (let alone the site of St Osburga's) was destroyed when the priory was rebuilt in the early twelfth century by using terraces dug into the sandstone hillside.[44] The ground plan of the priory, as far as it can be reconstructed, is therefore a later conjectural one.

Apart from the cathedral church and the conventual buildings, the plan-unit area also contains a range of outlying ecclesiastical buildings, some of which, like the bishop's palace and garden, are documented and shown on Speed's plan of 1610. The palace was enlarged in 1283 when it was in need of repair, a plot of ground having been first granted

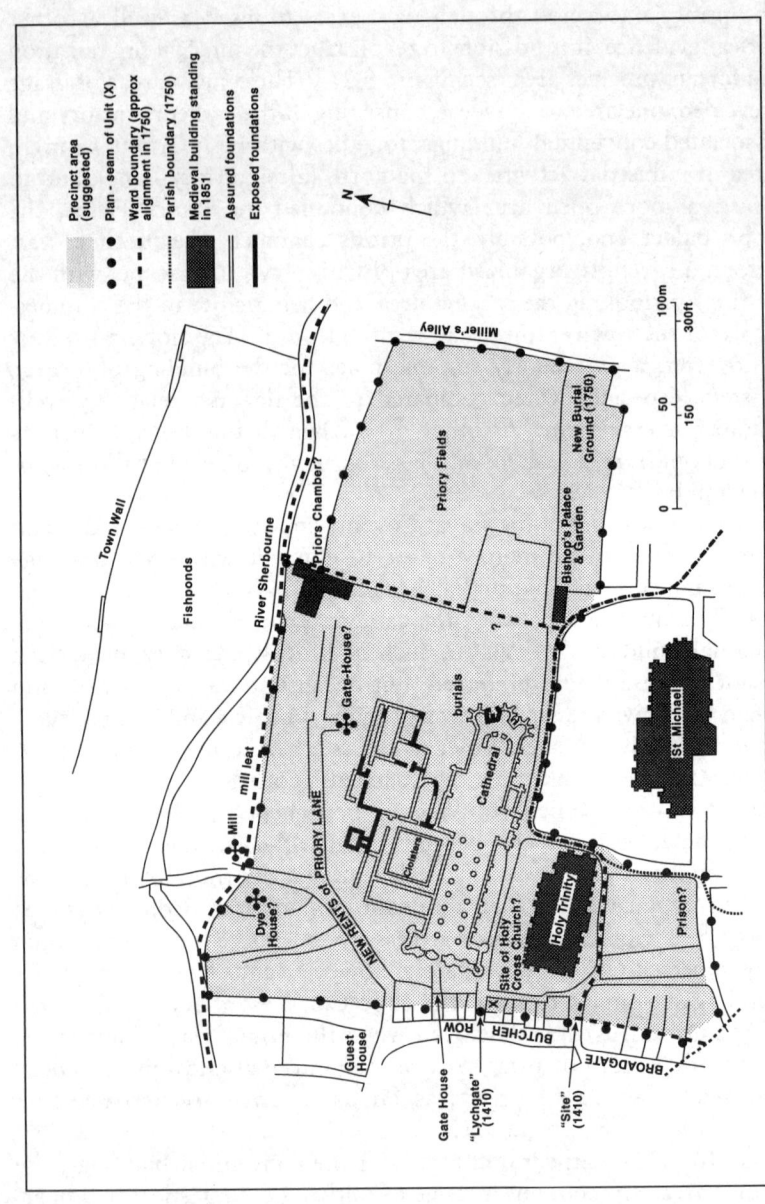

9.2 Plan-unit X: the priory precinct

to Bishop Alexander de Stavensby in 1224 by the prior.[45] It occupies a peripheral position in the precinct, next to the Priory Fields, and this may support the suggestion which has recently been made that the bishops of Lichfield and Coventry actually spent little of their time in the latter place.[46] Instead, the main focus of ecclesiastical activity in the precinct was to the west, nearer to the market-place. Here the priory mill was situated and perhaps also the dye-house, both requiring the diversion of the river along a leat, which subsequently formed one of the city's ward boundaries (see Figure 9.2).[47] In the south-east corner of plan-unit X lies Holy Trinity Church which seems to have been built when the bishop transferred the see from Chester to Coventry in c.1102, and in so doing converted the Anglo-Saxon abbey church of St Mary into a Norman cathedral priory.[48] As well as providing for the piety of the townspeople, by 1186–87 the prior also seems to have procured a prison for their punishment and, although there is some uncertainty over its location, a site close to that successively occupied by later prisons, in a corner of his fee, would seem to be most likely.[49]

The distribution of the buildings relating to the priory and the ecclesiastical affairs of medieval Coventry provides some indication of the large areal extent of the monastic precinct and its importance in the surrounding townscape. However, because no contemporary accounts exist describing the course of the precinct boundary, it is not possible to check with any certainty the relationship between it and the plan-seam of unit X. The boundary of Holy Trinity parish is probably a good indication of the precinct's southern limit and it presumably also included the Priory Fields and the mill and dye-house. The western boundary of the precinct has been shown to be fossilized by an intermittent, but straight, alignment of plot boundaries, shown by the 1851 Board of Health plan extending south from the River Sherbourne to Broadgate.[50] Along this plan-seam, entries in the *Pittancer's Rental* of 1410–11 can be used to confirm the position of two entrances into the precinct, a lychgate and stile. Also, Speed's plan of 1610 and unprovenanced archaeological finds help to locate the site of the priory gatehouse, opposite Little Butcher Row (see Figure 9.2).[51] Far from being cut off from the commercial activities of the market area, the juxtaposition of the priory buildings and the openings through the western precinct wall show that the precinct was very much at the heart of trading in medieval Coventry. This in itself suggests that monastic initiative was as responsible for the development of the market area as it was for the organization of the precinct area.

The plan analysis clearly reveals the former triangular-shaped market-place, developed over with island and lateral enroachments as with so many medieval market-places (see Figure 9.1).[52] The designed origin of

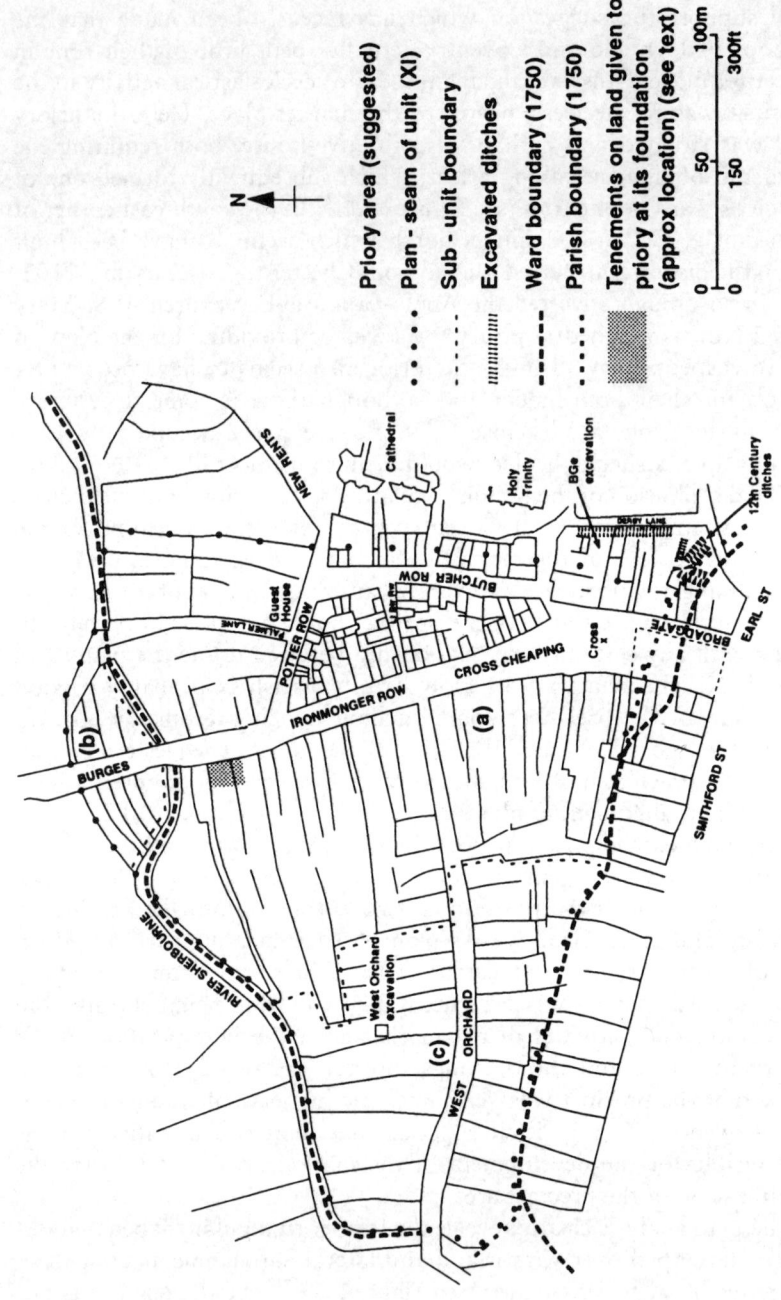

9.3 Plan-unit XI: the market area

this space is suggested by the way the triangular shape was used to broaden the north–south axial street on its approach, uphill, to join with the east–west axial street that ran through the earl's fee (Earl Street and Smithford Street) (see Figure 9.3). Assuming the priory precinct wall is represented by the plan-seam (as argued above), then the former width of the market-place would originally have been greater than that suggested by the street lines taken from the Board of Health plan of 1851. At the higher end of the market-place, at its southern neck, stood the medieval market cross, giving rise to the street name for this part of the market, Cross Cheaping.[53] This was located firmly within the prior's fee. The parish boundary can be seen to differentiate between two plot series fronting Smithford Street and Cross Cheaping, and so closely replicates the southern boundary of unit (XI). Again, therefore, at a detailed level, the morphological division between the two fees is reinforced.

If the market-place was designed, then some evidence for its planning should be apparent both in its form and in the historical record. Market infill and encroachment have often been thought to originate as informal developments undertaken by individual initiative,[54] but should this really be seen as the case when medieval markets were so well protected by custom and jurisdiction?[55] In Coventry, for example, the medieval street names in the market area show that a differentiated specialization of functions existed, which may be indicative of organization and control at one social level or another (see Figure 9.3). These street names are authentic and their topographical limits are recorded in street-by-street entries in the *Pittancer's Rental* of 1410–11.[56] The differentiation of specialist activities is also apparent, as the *Rental* notes the tenants' occupations, along with their property abuttals and, frequently, the names of earlier tenants too. Thus, along the west side of Butcher Row, William Balsale, John Lyrpole and John Northampton are recorded as butchers.[57] Earlier still, in the 1280s, Ironmonger Row can be identified as the 'place where iron is sold',[58] and in 1298, a messuage stood 'in the market place where corn is sold',[59] presumably at Cross Cheaping in the higher and drier part of the market-place. The early property deeds do not, unfortunately, reveal the process or date of infilling, unless a reference of the 1270s to 'the built-up land in the market place ... where fish is sold',[60] can be equated with a property called *Le Fyshbordes* which is recorded in 1565 on the east side of Broadgate;[61] and unless the properties situated *in foro* in *c.*1200 were literally standing 'in the market-place'.[62] It is of interest that during the demolition of properties in the area of market infill in the 1930s, an amateur archaeologist recorded what he considered to be timber-built farm buildings.[63] It does not seem too unlikely that what was really being seen were not farm

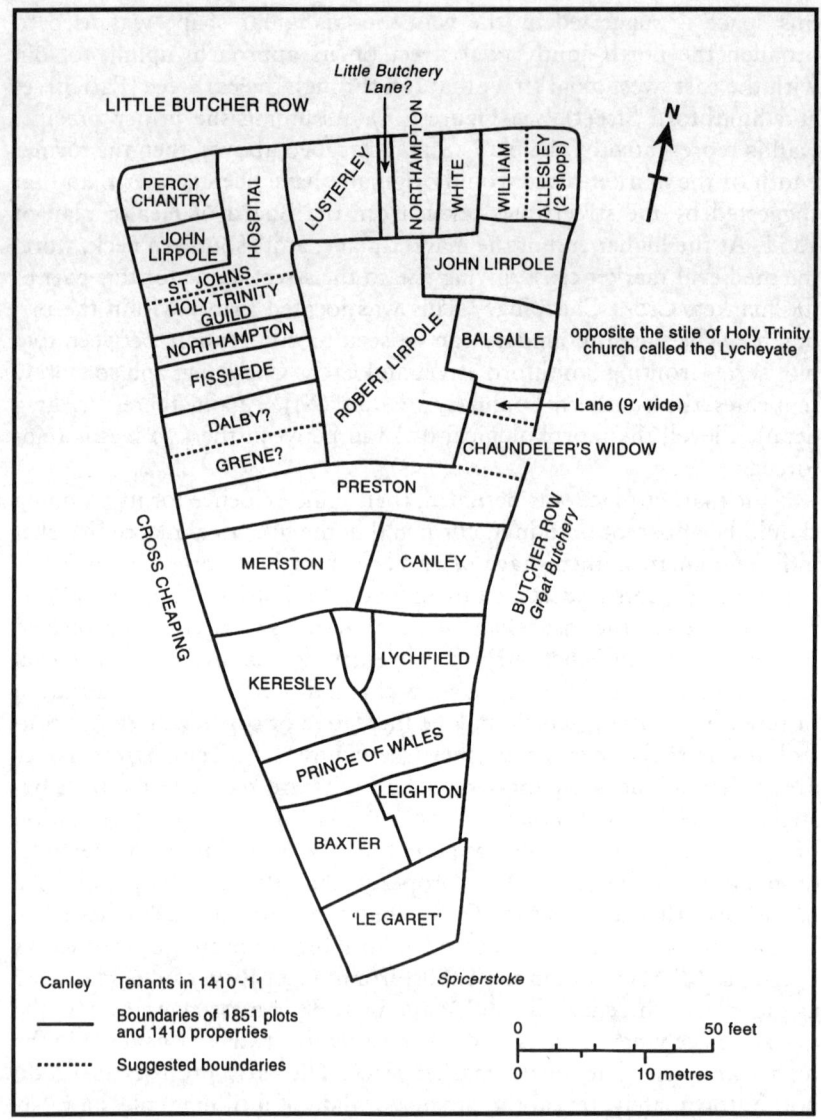

9.4 Market infill: suggested topography of Butcher Row, Little Butcher Row and Cross Cheaping in c.1410

buildings but the earliest timber structures built on the prior's market-place.

To understand further the origin of properties within the market-place it is necessary to have recourse back to the 1851 Board of Health plan and the *Pittancer's Rental*. Because the *Rental* entries are so complete for the Butcher Row area, and because the southern infill block has distinct topographical limits, it is possible to build up a picture of the property pattern for 1410–11 based on tenement abuttals.[64] The pattern is remarkably regular in its form, with properties extending back from Butcher Row through to Cross Cheaping, except at the wider, northern end where a covered entry gave access from Butcher Row to a piece of enclosed land belonging to Robert Lirpole – a butcher.[65] What is even more remarkable is that when the 1410–11 property pattern is compared with the 1851 plot pattern (taken from the Board of Health plan) a close relationship between the two is revealed (see Figure 9.4). This shows, first of all, an element of continuity in Coventry's townscape, even where commercial pressures for change would have been greatest, and secondly, that an element of control and planning existed in the laying out of the properties. Rather than the market-place developing on an *ad hoc* basis, the distribution of property holding was managed and inititiated, most probably, as the *Pittancer's Rental* suggests, by the prior himself.

Through infilling the market-place, and therefore imposing order by developing rigid property boundaries, an opportunity was created whereby the priory could maximize its rents and profits, as well as control trading. The planning of market infill was clearly to the prior's advantage, but to do it, he sacrificed both open space and ease of access in favour of more confined trading places. This would have created demand for further market provision within the prior's fee, perhaps away from the increasingly congested town centre, and also necessitated a new pattern of streets to provide access to the priory. The latter problem appears to have been solved by keeping a street space between the two infill blocks in front of the priory gate, and this, no doubt, is the origin of Little Butcher Row (see Figure 9.3). This in itself is indicative of a piece of planning on the prior's part, and it must be far from coincidental that Little Butcher Row and the priory gate also align with the street called West Orchard. West Orchard was seemingly opened up as a new means for gaining access to the priory from the west, avoiding Smithford Street, which runs parallel (see Figure 9.1). Such access would have been desirable, not least because it could allow those visiting the priory to use a route that ignored the earl's streets (and perhaps also his tolls)[66] and so bring them directly through the prior's market-place right up to the gates of the cathedral priory itself. So far, however, there is nothing to guarantee that the changes outlined above were anything but post-Conquest in date. Indeed, with the absence of early written sources, it is difficult to determine the chronology of changes to the market area morphology. Even so, there are clues which do point to an early origin for the market area plan-unit.

Although no systematic excavations have taken place within the area of the market-place itself, two sites have been excavated close by (see Figure 9.3). To the east of Broadgate, thirteenth-century building foundations were uncovered, probably the remains of properties which had developed by encroaching onto the market-place at the *Fyshbordes*.[67] Earlier evidence of occupation was found north of West Orchard, dating to the later twelfth century. It appears that the area behind the deep plots fronting on to Ironmonger Row was being used for small-scale industrial activities, such as metal-working and pottery manufacture (see sub-unit (c) on Figure 9.3).[68] This sequence may represent the early development of the West Orchard area, perhaps relating to curtilages which are first documented there in the 1250s, sited in *Wastogardino*.[69] Later, it seems, more substantial residential properties were built, as a 'stone-tiled house' is mentioned in a deed of 1270 and pits beneath a stone-flagged floor were found to contain fourteenth-century pottery.[70] These changes were taking place long after the first mention of properties at the east end of the street, next to Cross Cheaping and the market-place.[71] So, although West Orchard may have been first enclosed for gardens and occupied by workshops by the twelfth century, it was only much later, perhaps over a century later, that a more intense built-up fabric appeared. Such prolonged development suggests that the area did not appear attractive land when it was first opened up, perhaps because the market-place was being deliberately infilled by the prior.

Until the twelfth century, then, West Orchard was a relatively open space, a 'waste garden' (*Wasto Gardino*) as the name suggests, situated behind properties fronting on to the market-place. The area was probably a piece of land left over from when the market-place was originally laid out; an area of open garden land which occupied a corner of the prior's fee and became trapped between the development of Smithford Street properties in the earl's fee to the south, and to the north by the flood plain of the River Sherbourne. If this is so, then perhaps it was only when the area was opened up with a street (to provide an alternative means of access into the market-place) that it became a suitable place for urban development. The infilling of the market-place, the opening up of West Orchard with a street, and the earliest development of properties there, would therefore seem to be all contemporary with each other; in place by the late twelfth century at the latest. All of this would suggest that the market-place was actually laid out at an earlier date, capitalizing on the more profitable part of the fee that the Benedictines held, that is, the part through which traffic passed, between Tamworth and Warwick, outside the monastery gate.

That the properties fronting the market-place were developed on part of the land originally granted by Leofric is supported by a reference in the *Pittancer's Rental* of 1410–11. This states that three contiguous properties on the west side of Ironmonger Row were 'situated on the ground part of the original endowment of the ... Cathedral church' [*in solo fundacionis ecclesie Cathedralis* ...].[72] Of course, this does not necessarily mean that these properties had been laid out at the time of foundation, only that they subsequently lay on monastic ground. Buildings may soon have been developed on this land however, because in a letter of *c.*1072–85 from Lanfranc, Archbishop of Canterbury, to Peter, Bishop of Chester, the then Abbot of Coventry[73] was recorded as having complained that Peter had, 'pulled down their houses [*insuper domos eorum destruxisti*] and ordered the materials of which these were built to be taken to [his] own residences [*ad tuas villas*]'.[74] If these houses are taken to be those situated in the market area, then the possibility exists that the abbey's land was being developed well before the episcopal see was transferred to Coventry. One person who could have been responsible for such development is abbot Leofric, because as well as holding the abbacy at Coventry in 1053, he also held the Benedictine abbeys at Peterborough and Burton-on-Trent where towns were likewise planted outside the monastic gates.[75]

The influence of the bishops on Coventry's topographical development cannot be ignored. It has been argued, for example, that Bishop Street, to the north of the market-place, 'was a major development ... at a time when the bishops played a significant role in directing local affairs', and that it was perhaps initiated by 'Robert de Limesey and his successors, in the early twelfth century'.[76] However, there is also evidence that the area of Bishop Street was occupied earlier than 1102 and that its development was influenced by monastic rather than episcopal initiative.

From the plan analysis, Bishop Street can be seen to be one of three plan-units grouped together on the north side of the River Sherbourne in Holy Trinity parish (plan-units XII, XIII and XIV on Figure 9.1). Although each separate plan-unit has distinct morphological characteristics, they seem also to have similarities that suggests they are related (see Figure 9.5). Two of these three plan-units, XII and XIV, have particular features which make them significant in understanding the role of monastic initiative in Coventry. Bishop Street and Cook Street form a fork next to the hospital and chapel of St John the Baptist, on the north side of the Burges (otherwise called St John's Bridges).[77] This was a low-lying part of Coventry, where the River Sherbourne split into two channels to form an island which had become developed with properties by 1223 (see Figure 9.3).[78] The bridgehead location of the hospital and chapel, along with the bifurcating street-pattern, are all characteristic features of medieval suburbs.[79] Because their development

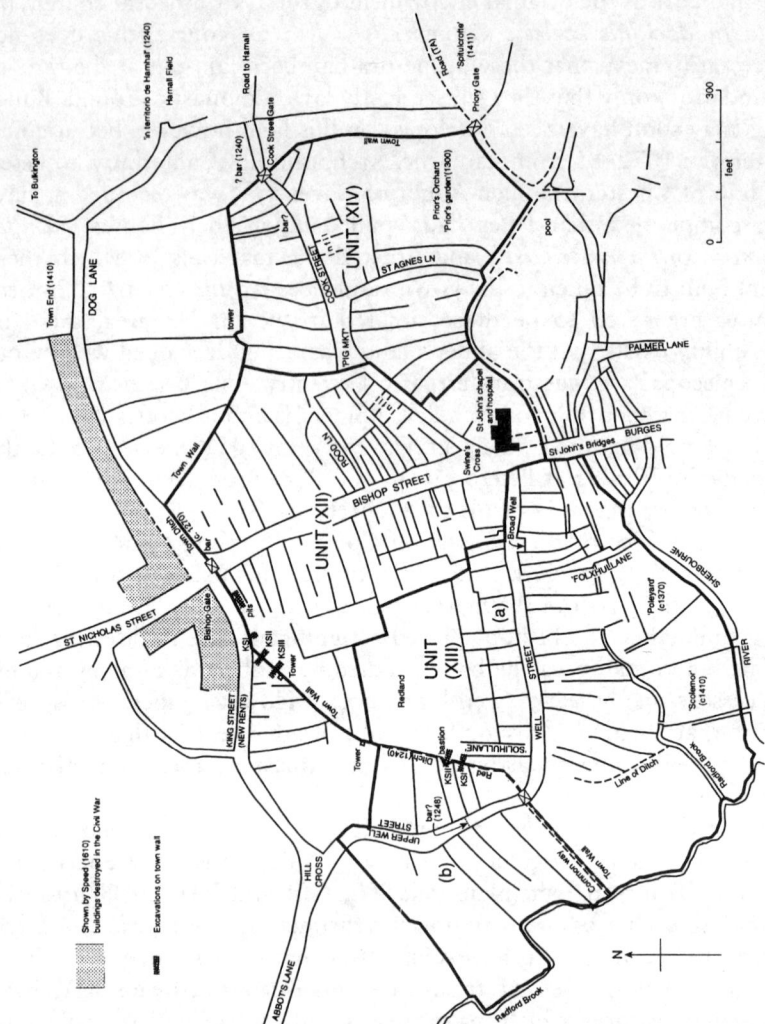

9.5 Plan–units XII and XIV: Bishop Street and Cook Street

is most likely to post-date the market area to the south, they can perhaps be used to provide further clues about the origins of urban development in the prior's fee.

The earliest reference to property in Bishop Street (*vico Episcopi*) is in *c.*1215,[80] but the chapel of St John the Baptist is mentioned earlier, in 1183–84, when Bishop Gerard Pucelle confirmed in a charter all the churches and chapels in Coventry belonging to the priory.[81] This may have been the time when Bishop Street became so-called, but equally the name could have arisen if it were the street used by the bishops to travel between Lichfield and Coventry. The priory's close relationship with St John's may have developed in the mid-twelfth century when the hospital was reputedly founded,[82] and certainly such a location would have been appropriate for providing accommodation for pilgrims visiting St Mary's. This connection may also have been preserved in the name of Palmer Lane, a street which connects the two institutions (see Figures 9.3 and 9.5). The chapel building overlooked the Swines Cross which Speed's plan shows to have stood at the junction of Bishop Street and Cook Street.[83] The origins of the cross are not known, but its location and name suggest it to be a market cross associated with livestock trading. In support of this, the plot pattern on the north side of Cook Street, between the cross and the Pig Market (named on the Board of Health plan), is characteristic of market infill. This can be seen in the way that a series of short plots extend up to a common back boundary that runs through from Bishop Street on the same line as the north side of the Pig Market (see Figure 9.5). To the east of the Pig Market, the south side of Cook Street also appears to have been infilled by encroachments in the same way. The original width of Cook Street was therefore much broader and, in view of this, it seems likely that the whole length was formerly used for livestock trading.

Markets for livestock were often situated outside the medieval urban core, because of the large space required for them. Although Bishop Street was itself unaffected by the market, presumably as a deliberate policy to avoid congestion, the origins of these two plan-units both seem to be related to trading activity. In 1355, when the prior was being forced to accept Isabella's demands over jurisdiction, he 'was allowed to retain his cattle and timber markets as of old on Fridays in Bishop Street and Cook Street'.[84] This places the development of the trade in the prior's hands and the most probable time when he would have needed such a large trading area is the period when he was infilling the triangular market-place. The more controlled organization of the specialized markets outside the priory precinct gate would have made it a less convenient place for dealing with large and bulky goods like timber and so by removing these actvities to an adjacent area, namely Cook

Street, he succeeded in further developing his fee. When the sheriff fined the prior three marks for moving his market in 1203, it is most likely to be a reflection of this outward expansion of marketing.[85] Perhaps, then, both the hospital and markets in Cook Street and Bishop Street were contemporary developments initiated by the prior, and followed the infilling of the triangular market-place.

By the mid-twelfth century, this whole area (the three plan-units of Bishop Street, Cook Street and Well Street) seems to have been important enough to be enclosed by its own defensive ditch (see Figure 9.5).[86] Some protection may have been needed during this period in the civil war of Stephen's reign, particularly since it is known that the Earl of Chester's enemy, Robert Marmion, fortified the priory to lay siege to the earl's castle.[87] Evidence for even earlier occupation of this area is also hinted at, particularly by a wooden vat, dendrochronologically dated to *c*.AD 1000, which was found during the redevelopment of Cook Street,[88] beneath the area of street infill, next to the site of Swines Cross (see Figure 9.5). Other early but unprovenanced finds, like a Saxon cross-head found in Palmer Lane and a *sceatta* dating to the 650s, are also indicative of pre-Conquest activity along the Sherbourne near the crossing-point later occupied by the Burges.[89] However, all of these finds may only be indicating changes that were taking place in late Saxon Coventry, rather than themselves representing the location of early habitation sites. Instead, it is the development of the central market area and the foundation of the abbey that are both likely to reflect a protracted process of settlement reorganization *initiated* by one or more of the new Benedictine abbots. Further evidence of monastic initiative can be found outside this main urban area, in the suburban development of Coventry.

Monastic initiative in the suburban growth of Coventry

The suburbs of medieval Coventry extended for nearly a mile and a half along an east–west axial street through the earl's fee, from Spon End (unit XIX) to Far Gosford (unit XX) (see Figure 9.2). This important route linked London and Chester and it is therefore not surprising that suburban growth occurred along it, perhaps being deliberately encouraged by the earls of Chester whose fee the road ran through. In the prior's fee the main area of suburban growth lay north of the Sherbourne, along the Bishop Street axis. The only suburb which lay on the east–west road within the prior's fee was Far Gosford, represented by plan-unit XX (see Figure 9.6). This suburb was physically separated from the earl's suburb of Gosford Street (unit IV), to the west, by the River

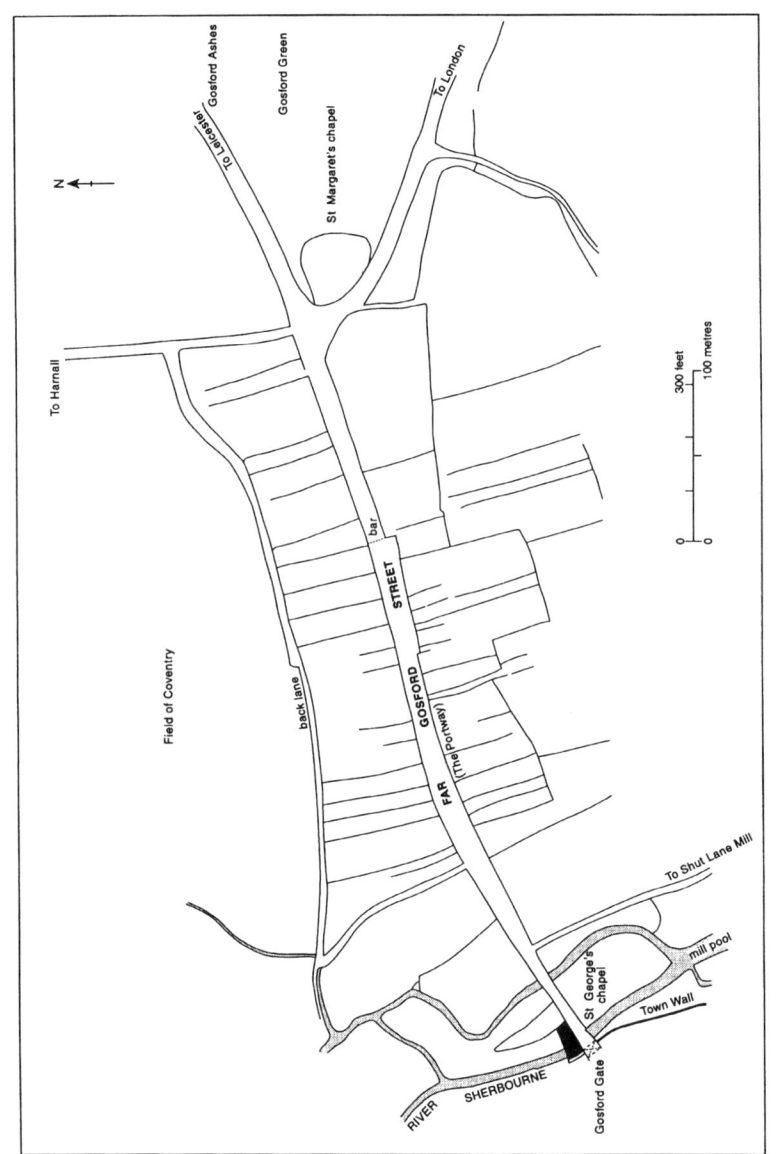

9.6 Plan-unit XX: Far Gosford Street

Sherbourne and the eastern part of the city walls. Although the defensive circuit was finally completed in the mid-sixteenth century, there is evidence of an earlier rampart defence along the same line.[90] The river also forms the tenurial boundary between the earl's and prior's fees. This boundary encompasses plan-unit XX by running along the southern back-fence of plots as far east as Gosford Green before turning northwards (see Figure 9.6).

Far Gosford is fronted by plots which are morphologically distinct from those along Gosford Street. The north side of Far Gosford Street had a back lane running parallel along its length and there was a footpath serving the same function behind plots on the south side of the street (see Figure 9.6). The width of Gosford Street is noticeably broadened between the bridge over the Sherbourne (the site of the goose ford) and the place where Speed's plan of 1610 shows the 'barres'.[91] Between the bars and the river, then, it seems likely that the street was intended to be used for exchange, perhaps livestock marketing. The regular plot pattern along both sides of the street, together with the two back lanes, is indicative that this was a planned development. Because this stretch of road entered the earl's fee it would have represented a lucrative site, especially for the prior since it was the only part of his fee that straddled this important road.

Before being developed with plots it seems likely that Far Gosford was a linear piece of waste that lay on the south side of the Prior's Field.[92] The presence of linear wastes along roads entering Coventry is quite apparent when former common lands are plotted from the first edition Ordnance Survey 1:10,560 scale maps and nineteenth-century enclosure maps (see Figure 9.7).[93] These linear wastes radiate out from Coventry and obviously reflect once more extensive areas of pasture which would have provided grazing for stock. The funnel shape of Gosford Green looks very much like the sort of field patterns identified in Lancashire and, more locally, at Brinklow, which are associated with pasturing livestock.[94] Perhaps, then, the main eastern approach into Coventry was originally used as a broad driftway that gave access to outlying pastures at neighbouring vills like Stoke.[95]

An indication of the early importance of this route into Coventry is provided in a property deed of the 1280s which refers to Far Gosford Street as *le portway*.[96] This name, meaning 'market-way' in Old English, suggests that the road was being used as a way to get to the markets at Coventry in the pre-Conquest period. Such long-standing use of this road for traffic entering Coventry would have made Far Gosford an ideal location for development, something which is unlikely to have escaped the notice of the prior. A further indication of the importance of this route is the chapel of St Margaret at the east end of

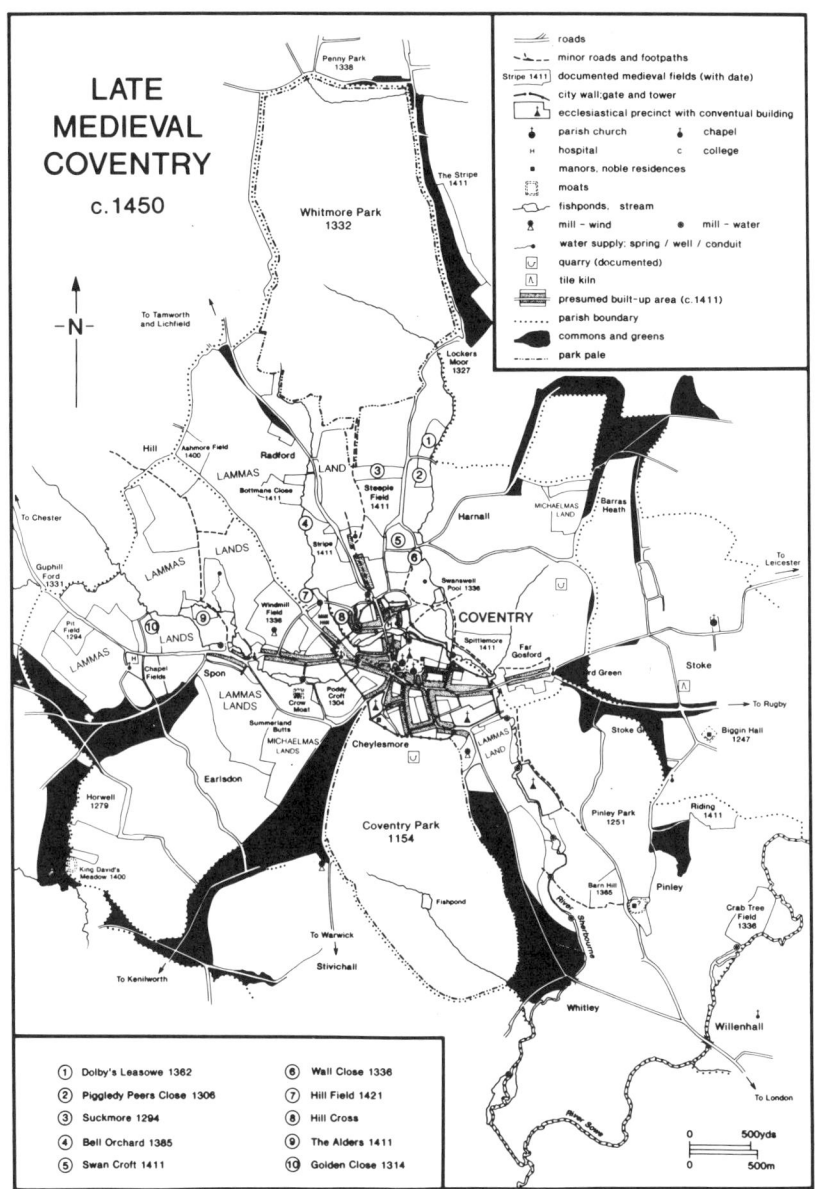

9.7 Coventry and its hinterland, c.1450

plan-unit XX in the corner of the Leicester and Rugby roads.[97] This was probably the site of the *hermitescroft* mentioned in the 1280s and it may have originated as a wayside chapel for travellers and traders.[98] With the evidence for such traffic it is easy to explain the broadened street space of Far Gosford Street and see the whole plan-unit as a deliberate attempt to accommodate livestock exchange. The planned layout of the suburb suggests that the suburb was established to this effect, most probably by the prior utilizing a piece of wasteland within his fee.

Trading places and monastic initiative in Coventry

The morphology of medieval Coventry reveals the importance attached by the Benedictine monks to the provision for trade and exchange within their fee. The development of streets and plots within the town and its suburbs all show signs of monastic initiative in their layout and design.[99] Using a plan analysis it is possible to read through the texts of the forged charters that had been fabricated to secure the rights given to the Benedictines at the foundation of St Mary's. By relating the documentary record to the discourse of history offered by Coventry's town plan, the claims made by the prior, that his forebears had been given half of Coventry by Earl Leofric, do not seem so unlikely. Although, in defending his claims, the prior was unable to draw on the town plan as evidence, the topographical imprint of monastic initiative in Coventry's urban development would have lent support to his case.

The importance of market space in the development of the prior's fee, in the parish of Holy Trinity, can be seen to have extended beyond the confines of the urban core. This reflects the growing importance of commercial motives in the estates of Benedictine houses in high medieval England; that the monastic town was more than a focus of ecclesiastical affairs, liturgy and pilgrimage. This is not to belittle the importance of these other aspects of monastic urbanism which can also be seen to have influenced the built form of the prior's fee in Coventry. The monastery was already a centre of pilgrimage in the late eleventh century as Earl Leofric and his wife Godiva had endowed their foundation with a collection of relics,[100] some of which may have been destroyed during the episcopate of Bishop Robert de Limesey (who had transferred the see to Coventry and whom the then prior complained had assaulted him and some of his brethren).[101] The commercial exploitation of this pilgrimage traffic to Coventry was, of course, an incentive behind the urban development of the prior's fee (there is archaeological evidence for the manufacture of pilgrim's tokens from the thirteenth century).[102] The role of Coventry as an episcopal seat, as a centre for ecclesiastical jurisdiction, and in the management of the priory's scattered lands, also had an influence on the high-medieval townscape.[103] Processions, visitations and religious festivals would all have contributed to the shaping of the townscape alongside its commercial functions. Open spaces like the market-place, and later streets like West Orchard, provided foci for these liturgical activities and futher illustrate how important church authority was in the production of urban spaces in Coventry.[104]

Coventry, then, was a long-standing religious centre and stood as a symbol of Benedictine wealth from the abbey's foundation right up until the dissolution of the priory and the destruction of the precinct buildings (most significantly the cathedral church, in the 1560s).[105] This status brought commerce and perpetuated the position of Coventry as a regional capital, particularly after the episcopal see had been transferred from Chester. Unless the abbey had already been developing its lands at Coventry in the mid-eleventh century it is hard to explain the motivation for this move. What other reason could there be, other than that the abbots were becoming more and more powerful and wealthy from the trade and traffic passing by the precinct gates? It would seem that the new Norman bishops had wanted a piece of the action that Coventry offered and with Lanfranc's decree of 1075[106] credence was given to their greed; as the archbishop's letter of complaint said, Peter, the Bishop of Chester, had removed lands from the abbot 'by force'.[107]

In examining the effects of monastic initiative in Coventry, it becomes obvious that the influence of Leofric and the earls of Chester was also crucial in the early development of the high medieval town. St Michael's parish, the earl's fee, is surely the part of Leofric's estate of Coventry that the Mercian earl kept after granting lands to found the abbey of St Mary. Likewise, at the abbey's foundation, Leofric had given land at Sowe which, unlike the Coventry land, appears in the folios of Domesday Book as land belonging to 'Coventry Abbey'. This idea assumes, then, that the earls of Mercia had already been developing their estate of Coventry and the most likely core for any nascent urban settlement would have been Earl Street.[108] Such a tenurial arrangement, so clearly reflected in the plan analysis, would have ultimately passed from Leofric to the earls of Chester who, eventually, certainly by the 1120s, had granted burgage rights in Coventry, presumably to those living in the earl's fee.[109] The bishops, then, were not the only element of the new Norman hegemony deriving from Chester at this time. Burgage tenure may have been granted as a response to balance the commercial success of the monastery's markets which seem by this time to have been burgeoning with prosperity. So, when the earl's tenants tried to trade on the same day as the prior's Friday market[110] perhaps they were following a long-standing tradition which pre-dated the abbey's foundation and hence the prior's market. It is of note that the earl's fee did not contain a market-place anywhere near the size and extent of the prior's markets and this in itself must have become a source of discontent, perhaps even jealousy, amongst the traders in Earl Street, despite having been endowed with burgage privileges and the customs and laws of Lincoln by Earl Ranulf I.[111]

The period after the laying out of the triangular market-place, next to the priory precinct, was one which witnessed the development of urban land in the prior's fee, with streets for trading and properties for rent all adding to the increased prosperity of the Benedictine priory. In this, the prior was imposing control over his tenantry and looking after his own commercial interests. The early Norman focus in Coventry was therefore shifted away from Earl Street and, instead, firmly located within the prior's fee. The new street through West Orchard, leading across the market-place and right up to the precinct gate and the west door of the cathedral, may be seen as part of this reorientation of power within high medieval Coventry. This imaginative piece of planning is part of a lasting testimony of the influence of monastic initiative in Coventry's medieval morphogenesis. It is this rich topographical legacy, fossilized by surveyors' plans centuries later, that is helpful in resolving some of the uncertainties surrounding the obscure origins of this important English medieval city.

Acknowledgements

This paper is based on doctoral research funded by the ESRC (award number RO0429024833) and undertaken at the School of Geography, University of Birmingham, supervised by Dr T.R. Slater. It has benefited from the comments and advice of members of the Urban Morphology Research Group, particularly Dr R.A. Holt and Dr N.J. Baker. My thanks to Mr K. Burkhill and the late Mrs J. Dowling for redrawing the maps.

Notes

1. W. Urry, *Canterbury Under the Angevin Kings* (1967); M. Biddle (ed.), *Winchester in the Early Middle Ages* (1976).
2. T.R. Slater, 'Ideal and reality in English episcopal medieval town planning', *Transactions of the Institute of British Geographers*, new series, 12 (1987), 191–203; T.R. Slater, 'Medieval town-founding on the estates of the Benedictine Order in England', in F.-E. Eliassen and G.A. Erland (eds), *Power, Profit and Urban Landownership in Medieval and*

Early Modern Northern European Towns (1996); N.J. Baker and R.A. Holt, *The Church and Urban Growth, Worcester and Gloucester* (1998 forthcoming).
3. D.L. Swan, 'Monastic proto-towns in early medieval Ireland: the evidence of aerial photography, plan-analysis and survey', in H.B. Clarke and A. Simms (eds),*The Comparative History of Urban Origins in Non-Roman Europe* (1985), 77–102; R.A. Butlin, 'The monastic city in Wales', *Bulletin of the Board of Celtic Studies*, 28 (1979), 458–67.
4. J.C. Lancaster, 'The Coventry forged charters: a reconsideration', *Bulletin of the Institute of Historical Research*, 27 (1954), 113–46.
5. P.R. Coss (ed.), *The Early Records of Medieval Coventry* (1986), xvii–iii.
6. J. Morris (ed.), *Domesday Book. Warwickshire* (1976), folio 239c.
7. W.B. Stephens (ed.), *The Victoria History of the County of Warwick* (1969), vol. 8, 256.
8. As suggested by R.H.C. Davis, *The Early History of Coventry* (1976).
9. Coss, *Early Records*; J.C. Lancaster, 'Coventry', in M.D. Lobel (ed.), *The Atlas of Historic Towns II* (1975).
10. M. Rylatt (ed.), *Coventry Archaeology and Redevelopment* (1981); M. Rylatt and M.A. Stokes (eds), *The Excavations in Broadgate East, Coventry* (forthcoming); see also *West Midlands Archaeology*, Annual Reports, Council for British Archaeology, Group Eight.
11. K.D. Lilley, 'Medieval Coventry: a study in town-plan analysis', (PhD thesis, University of Birmingham (1994).
12. See Chapter 8, this volume.
13. On the effect of the war on Coventry see Stephens, *Victoria History*, 12–18.
14. M.R.G. Conzen, *Alnwick, Northumberland. A Study in Town-plan Analysis*, Publications Institute of British Geographers, 21 (1960); T.R. Slater (ed.), *The Built Form of Western Cities, Essays for M.R.G. Conzen on the Occasion of his Eightieth Birthday* (1990).
15. N.J. Baker and T.R. Slater, 'Morphological regions in English medieval towns', in J.W.R. Whitehand and P.J. Larkham (eds), *Urban Landscapes: International Perspectives* (1992), 43–68; T.R. Slater, 'Doncaster's town plan: an analysis', in P.C. Buckland, J.R. Magilton and C. Hayfield (eds), *The Archaeology of Doncaster (2): the Medieval and Later Town* (1989), 42–61.
16. The methodology is outlined in detail in Lilley, 'Medieval Coventry', 56–120.
17. The Board Of Health plan is housed in the Coventry City Record Office, a photostat copy is kept at Warwick County Record Office (z734). Earlier plans of Coventry which proved most useful in the plan analysis are Bradford's plan of 1750 and Speed's of 1610.
18. Methodological details can be found in Lilley, 'Medieval Coventry'.
19. In the southern plan-region are plan-units I, II, III, IV, V, VI, VII, VIII, IX, XV, XVI, XVII, XVIII, XX, XIX; and in the northern region are plan-units X, XI, XII, XIII, XIV, XXI. See n. 21 below.
20. For the parish topography of York, Norwich, etc., see R. Morris, *Churches in the Landscape* (1989), 168–226.
21. The coincidence between the plan-region boundary and the parish boundary is only contradicted by plan-units III and XX. Unit III is divided in

two by the parish boundary, which ran along Earls Mill Lane. Plots on the east side of the lane (in St Michael's parish) are however different in form to those along New Street and it has been suggested that unit III is made up of two sub-units each with different origins (see Lilley, 'Medieval Coventry'). Plan-unit XX is actually situated on the east–west axial street despite being within the prior's fee (Holy Trinity parish) (see below). The two descriptions of the parish boundary perambulations are cited in full by B.J. Poole, *Coventry: its History and Antiquities* (1870), 175–8, 206–8.
22. Coss, *Early Records*, deed 7.
23. For this see ibid, 1–2; Davis, *Early History*; P.R. Coss, 'Coventry before incorporation: a re-interpretation', *Midland History*, 2 (1974), 137–51.
24. For the suggested foundation dates, see J. Hunt, 'Piety, prestige or politics? The House of Leofric and the foundation and patronage of Coventry priory', in G. Demidowicz (ed.), *Coventry's First Cathedral*, (1994), 97–117.
25. Lancaster, 'Forged charters', 135.
26. Coss, *Early Records*, deed 7.
27. Davis, *Early History*, 7.
28. For historical interpretations and debates on the forged charters, see Lancaster, 'Forged charters'; Coss, *Early Records*, 1–2, deed 7; R.H.C. Davis, 'An unknown Coventry charter', *English Historical Review*, 86, 539–45.
29. As suggested by A. Gooder and E. Gooder, 'Coventry before 1355: unity or division', *Midland History*, 6 (1981), 15.
30. Coss, *Early Records*; C.P. Lewis, 'The formation of the honor of Chester, 1066–1100', in A.T. Thacker (ed.), *The Earldom of Chester and its Charters* (1991), 37–68.
31. See Lilley, 'Medieval Coventry'.
32. As suggested by Davis, *Early History*.
33. Coss, *Early Records*, xvii.
34. On the Mercian seat at Tamworth, see *Anglo-Saxon Chronicle*, D. Whitelock (ed.), *English Historical Documents I, c. 500–1042* (1955); on Warwick, see T.R. Slater, 'The origins of Warwick', *Midland History*, 8 (1983), 1–13; also M. Gelling, *The West Midlands in the Early Middle Ages* (1992), 146–69.
35. The first edition Ordnance Survey 1/2500 plan of 1889 shows the site of the priory as an antiquity and the area was then being used for extensive light industries, such as timber merchants.
36. Both Speed's plan (1610) and Bradford's (1750) show this area with the ruined remains of monastic buildings and relatively few new developments apart from New Buildings which was a renaming of an earlier street called Priory Lane (compare Speed's plan with Bradford's).
37. J. Scarisbrick, 'The dissolution of St Mary's priory, Coventry', in G. Demidowicz (ed.), *Coventry's First Cathedral* (1994), 158–68; R.K. Morris, 'The lost cathedral priory church of St Mary, Coventry', in G. Demidowicz (ed.), *Coventry's First Cathedral* (1994), 17–66.
38. B. Hobley, 'Excavations at the cathedral and Benedictine priory of St Mary, Coventry', *Transactions of the Birmingham and Warwickshire Archaeological Society*, 84 (1967–71), 45–139.
39. For details, see K.D. Lilley, 'Coventry's topographical development: the

impact of the priory', in G. Demidowicz (ed.), *Coventry's First Cathedral* (1994), 72–96.
40. See Slater, 'Medieval town-founding', and this volume, Chapter 8.
41. Hobley, 'Excavations'.
42. On this legend see W. Dugdale, *The Antiquities of Warwickshire, Illustrated* (1656); W.G. Fretton, 'The Benedictine monastery and cathedral of Coventry', *Birmingham & Midland Institute Archaeology Section Transactions*, **8** (1880), 20.
43. For site-succession, see Morris, *Churches in the Landscape*.
44. A meagre piece of evidence which may support this view is a lead token found during excavations of the priory site, see Hobley, 'Excavations', 95. On one side of the token a spread eagle is shown and on the other a cross. These symbols may be associated with the house of Leofric.
45. Stephens, *Victoria History*, 316.
46. J. Röhrkasten, 'Conflict in a monastic borough: Coventry in the reign of Edward II, *Midland History*, **18** (1993), 1–18.
47. Remains of both the mill and the dye-house were revealed during the redevelopment of the former medieval market area in the 1930s. For the identification and interpretation of these remains, see W.G. Fretton, 'Benedictine monastery', 37; Lilley, 'Topographical development'; M. Rylatt and A.F. Adams, *A Harvest of History. The Life and Work of J.B. Shelton M.B.E.* (1983).
48. See Coss, *Early Records*, xvii; Lilley, 'Topographical development'.
49. Stephens, *Victoria History*, 296.
50. This is covered in detail in Lilley, 'Topographical development'.
51. *Ibid*. The relevant section in the *Pittancer's Rental* is folio 32-3 (A. Gooder, E. Gooder, J. Hunt, J. Shulman, C. Steele and C. Walker (eds), *The Pittancer's Rental; 1410–11* (1973), 25–9). The archaeological finds are those recorded by J.B. Shelton in the 1930s (see Rylatt and Adams, *Harvest of History*).
52. M.R.G. Conzen, *Alnwick*, considers the different forms of market-place encroachment in a detailed study and draws on the work by J. Leighly, 'The towns of Malardalen in Sweden: a study in urban morphology', *University of California Publications in Geography*, **3** (1928), 1–134. Leighly notes the development of 'booths' on the *torg* or market-place, 73.
53. The location of the market cross can be determined quite precisely because its foundations were noted during redevelopment in the early nineteenth century (see Poole, *Coventry*, 326, 328). The foundations were said to lie opposite the Castle Inn in Broadgate and, in support of this, the 1851 Board of Health plan shows the Castle Inn and marks the site of the former cross in front of it.
54. According to M. Aston and C.J. Bond, *The Landscape of Towns* (1976), 96; 'market stall holders tended, unless forced to do otherwise, to leave their stalls in position from one market day to the next, and in consequence many developed eventually into permanant inhabited structures'.
55. For jealously guarded market rights more generally see C.C. Dyer, 'The hidden trade of the Middle Ages: evidence from the West Midlands of England', *Journal of Historical Geography*, **18** (1992), 141–57. The *Coventry Leet Book* (M. Dormer Harris (ed.), Early English Text Society, old series, **134** (1907), 29) contains an ordinance that clearly states stall-

holders must take down their booths once trading has ceased on Saturday afternoon and then sweep clean the street. This may be a practice that had been going on for a long time before it was put into writing by the Corporation at the Michaelmas leet in 1421.

56. *Pittancer's Rental*, 23–33.
57. Ibid., 26–7.
58. Coss, *Early Records*, deed 670.
59. Ibid., deed 694.
60. Ibid., deed 683.
61. See *Coventry Leet Book*, 276; N.W. Alcock, in an unpublished documentary contribution to an excavation report, notes that the Fishboards lay along the east side of Broadgate (Coventry Museum Archaeological Unit archive material).
62. Coss, *Early Records*, deed 660.
63. This is J.B. Shelton, who had the foresight to use an engineers' plan of the Trinity Street development as a basis for plotting on his finds and observations whilst the medieval market place was being destroyed. This map is reproduced in Rylatt and Adams, *Harvest of History*, 36–7. It formed the basis for transferring the information on to the plan analysis (see Lilley, 'Medieval Coventry'). The farm structures are numbered 34, 35 and 36 on Shelton's map and are labelled 'cattleshed piles' and 'farmhouse foundations'.
64. The relevant section of the *Pittancer's Rental* is folio 31v–34 (Gooder et al., *Pittancer's Rental*, 23–33); the details of the tenement reconstruction can be found in Lilley, 'Topographical development', 88–91; and Lilley, 'Medieval Coventry'.
65. *Pittancer's Rental*, folio 32v (Gooder et al., *Pittancer's Rental*, 27).
66. A bar existed at the Smithford Bridge end of the street by the mid-thirteenth century (see Coss, *Early Records*, deeds 385, 454), but the exact location of the bar is not made clear in the deeds. It could have been sited next to the bridge (as mapped in Lobel, *Atlas of Historic Towns*), or slightly further west next to Bablake Hall, where Fleet Street forks into Hill Street and Spon Street (for details, see Lilley, 'Medieval Coventry').
67. See above, n. 60.
68. The excavations at West Orchard preceded the redevelopment of part of the 1950s shopping precinct and reports can be found in *West Midlands Archaeology*, 30 (1987), 66; 32 (1989), 97.
69. These curtilages, apparently quite large as one contained a fishpond, are mentioned in Coss, *Early Records*, deeds 648, 649, 650.
70. Ibid., deed 651; *West Midlands Archaeology*, 32 (1989), 97.
71. Coss, *Early Records*, deeds 657, 658.
72. *Pittancer's Rental*, folio 34 (Gooder et al., *Pittancer's Rental*, 31–2). The significance of this statement does not otherwise seem to have been noted. The three properties belonged to John Brightmer, Thomas Doude and Thomas Parker. These properties appear to lay on the west side of Ironmonger Row because the next entry, following on, is for a property which lay on the east side. This property belonged to John Sutton and, unlike the previous three entries, no mention is made of it having been sited on the ground of the 'original endowment' of the priory. This suggests that Sutton's property was part of the infill development on the

market-place and that it was later in origin than the properties along the west side of Ironmonger Row.
73. Perhaps Leofwine.
74. H. Clover and M. Gibson (eds),*The Letters of Archbishop Lanfranc*, (1979), letter 27.
75. Fretton, 'Benedictine monastery', 21, notes the plurality between Coventry, Peterborough and Burton-on-Trent under Abbot Leofric; for the topography of Burton, see Slater, 'Medieval town-founding'.
76. Coss, *Early Records*, xxx; the material taken from the abbot and monks of Coventry and used by the bishop for building his own residences (as noted in the letter from Lanfranc) could, of course, be a reference to the rebuilding of Bishop Street dwellings (see Clover and Gibson, *Letters*, 112). There is, however, no clear indication that the bishop actually held land in Coventry.
77. Parts of this building still survive today. For the history of the hospital, see W.G. Fretton, 'The hospital of St John the Baptist', *Birmingham and Midland Institute Archaeology Section Transactions*, 13 (1887), 32–50.
78. Coss, *Early Records*, deed 641; the plot pattern on the Board of Health plan clearly shows the former existence of two bridges; for similar plot patterns, see N.J. Baker, J.B. Lawson, R. Mawell and J.T. Smith, 'Further work on Pride Hill, Shrewsbury', *Transactions of the Shropshire Archaeological and Historical Society*, 68 (1993), 3–64.
79. On medieval suburbs generally, see D. Keene, 'Suburban growth', in M.W. Barley (ed.), *The Plans and Topography of Medieval Towns in England and Wales* (1976), 71–82. More detail can be found in Biddle, *Early Medieval Winchester*; Urry *Canterbury Under the Angevin Kings*. Two other bridge chapels in Coventry are St George's at Gosford and St James and St Christopher at Spon (see Lilley, 'Medieval Coventry').
80. Coss, *Early Records*, deed 582.
81. Ibid., deed 12.
82. Fretton, 'Hospital of St John', 32–3.
83. The cross had been removed by 1763 and was a 'smaller cross of a different character and humbler pretension' compared to the cross in Cross Cheaping (Poole, *Coventry*, 112).
84. Coss, *Early Records*, xxx; but see also, Davis, *Early History*, 25; Gooder and Gooder, 'Coventry before 1355'.
85. See Coss, *Early Records*, xxx, fn. 2; where he argues that the fine was because the prior had moved the market from Cook Street to Cross Cheaping.
86. Sections of a v-shaped ditch were found beneath the town wall north of Well Street during excavations in advance of redevelopment in the 1960s. This ditch appeared to have a fill of mid-twelfth century material and the same alignment was later used for a stretch of the town wall (E. Gooder, C. Woodfield and R.E. Chaplin, 'The walls of Coventry', *Transactions of the Birmingham and Warwickshire Archaeological Society*, 81 (1966), 99–138. In the 1970s, another section of a defensive ditch was excavated south of Earl Street (the so-called Red Ditch) and was found to have become silted up by the later twelfth century. This ditch had a 'stepped profile' but was recut to a v-shape by the early thirteenth century before being infilled and converted to a stone-lined culvert by the mid-fourteenth century (for details see *West Midlands Archaeology*,

24 (1981), 61. These two early ditches would seem to be evidence for a (re)fortification of Coventry during the mid-twelfth century and probably formed two circuits, one around the earl's part of Coventry (plan-unit I) and the other around Bishop Street (plan-units XII, XIII and XIV); for more details on this see Lilley, 'Medieval Coventry'.

87. William of Newburgh, *Chronicles of the Reigns of Stephen, Henry II and Richard I*, R. Howlett (ed.), Rolls Series, 4 vols (1884–89), vol. 1, 47.
88. W.M. Elliott, 'Two antiquities from Coventry', *Transactions of the Birmingham and Warwickshire Archaeological Society*, 87, 129–31.
89. For the *sceatta*, see Rylatt, *Archaeology and Redevelopment*. The cross fragment is discussed by Hobley, 'Excavations'; see also P.B. Chatwin, 'Stone carvings found at Coventry [1937]', *Transactions of the Birmingham Archaeological Society*, 61 (1940), 85. A date of the tenth century is suggested. It could be a market cross or, as Morris, 'Lost cathedral', prefers, a door pillar.
90. The construction of the town wall has been dated to various phases between the late fourteenth century and the mid-sixteenth, see E. Gooder, *Coventry's Town Wall* (1971). One reason why the Gosford Street section was the last to be completed may have been because a substantial rampart already existed there. An excavated section of the wall along the north side of Gosford Street revealed some evidence for an earlier rampart beneath the later stone-built wall, see J. Bateman and M. Redknap, *Coventry: Excavations on the Town Wall 1976–1978* (1986), 36; Gooder, *Coventry's Town Wall*, 48. An earlier bar may have been situated close to where Gosford Gate was later built, see Lilley, 'Medieval Coventry', 274.
91. Gosford may be derived from 'goose ford', see J.E.B. Gover, A. Mawer and F.M. Stenton, *The Place-Names of Warwickshire* (1936), 162; the 'barres' are numbered 57 on Speed's plan, just on the eastern border of the plan.
92. The field, including *Bromyforlong*, is mentioned in the 1260s as belonging to the prior (Coss, *Early Records*, deed 287). In a dispute of 1480 between the prior and people living in Far Gosford it is recorded that his pasture in Harnall Field was being grazed wrongly and that people were breaking down his hedges (M.D. Harris (ed.), *Coventry Leet Book*, (1909), 445). This suggests that the prior had turned over his arable land to pasture, perhaps to graze his own livestock (see Lilley, 'Medieval Coventry', 318–19).
93. The Enclosure Map is of 1860 (Warwick County Record Office: Qs75/37). The evidence behind the drawing of this map is given in Lilley, 'Medieval Coventry', 320–40.
94. For Lancashire, see M.A. Atkin, 'Some settlement patterns in Lancashire', in D. Hooke (ed.), *Medieval Villages* (1985), 171–86; for Brinklow, see K.D. Lilley, 'A Warwickshire medieval borough: Brinklow and the contribution of town-plan analysis', *Transactions of the Birmingham and Warwickshire Archaeological Society*, 98 (1994), 51–60.
95. The place-name is itself suggestive of pasture for stock, see Gover, Mawer and Stenton, *Place-Names of Warwickshire*, 179; and, although Stoke is not recorded until the twelfth century, the parish may once have

been part of a large outlying area of open grazing land, including Wyken and Caludon too (see Lilley, 'Medieval Coventry', 167–86).

96. Coss, *Early Records*, deed 306.
97. The site of the chapel is shown on the first edition 1:2500 scale Ordnance Survey plan as a circular enclosure. The chapel stood on Gosford Green and had been demolished after 1837 (Stephens, *Victoria History*, 330).
98. Coss, *Early Records*, deed 306; for medieval wayfaring chapels, see A. Everitt, *Continuity and Colonisation: the Evolution of Kentish Settlement* (1986).
99. Outside Coventry, in other parts of Warwickshire, some rural and urban settlements belonging to Coventry priory also show signs of monastic initiative in their morphological and commercial development. For example, at Walsgrave on Sowe the first edition 1:2500 scale Ordnance Survey plan shows a triangular open space, situated next to the church of St Mary, which may have been used for exchange. Coventry Abbey is recorded in 'Domesday Book' as having possession of land at Sowe (see Morris, *Domesday Book*, folio 239a), and indirect documentary evidence suggests that trading was taking place at Sowe in the thirteenth century (see Dyer, 'Hidden Trade'). Walsgrave on Sowe may, therefore, have functioned as an extra-urban market for the priory. At Priors Marston, too, there is an open space, to the south of the church, which may have been designed and used for exchange by the priory's tenants in much the same way (see the plan in B.K. Roberts, *The Making of the English Village* (1987), 83). Evidence for town planning on the priory's Warwickshire estates is evident at Southam in the 'Newlands' extension of the town; see T.R. Slater, 'Urban genesis and medieval town plans in Warwickshire and Worcestershire', in T.R. Slater and P.J. Jarvis (eds), *Field and Forest: an Historical Geography of Warwickshire and Worcestershire* (1982), 185, 192.
100. William of Malmesbury, *De Gesta Regum Anglorum*, W. Stubbs (ed.), (Rolls Series, 1887–89), vol. 2, 311; Fretton, 'Benedictine monastery', 20; Hobley, 'Excavations', 51.
101. Hobley, 'Excavations', 54.
102. In particular, stone moulds for bronze castings from the site in the corner of Bailey Lane and Earl Street, see *West Midlands Archaeology*, 31 (1988), 44.
103. On the status and roles of the bishopric and monastery in Coventry, see R.N. Swanson, 'The priory in the later middle ages', in Demidowicz, *Coventry's First Cathedral*, 139–57; as well as, Röhrkasten, 'Conflict in a monastic borough'.
104. The pageants, processions and festivities associated with ecclesiastical activities and royal visits are revealed in a number of entries in the *Coventry Leet Book*, particularly one of 1457 describing a processional route from the cathedral, see Dormer Harris, *Coventry Leet Book*, 299. The cross in Cross Cheaping was also, clearly, an important focus for meetings (ibid., 289, 392). See also, C. Phythian-Adams, 'Ceremony and citizen: the communal year at Coventry, 1450–1550', in P. Clark and P. Slack (eds), *Crisis and Order in English Towns, 1500–1700* (1972), 57–85.
105. See Scarisbrick, 'Dissolution of St Mary's priory'.

106. That is, to transfer all episcopal seats from villages to towns (the significance of which was first raised by Davis, *Early History*).
107. Clover and Gibson, *Letters*, letter 27.
108. Most probably an area close to that defined in the plan-analysis as unit I. The plan-seams delimit a defensive circuit which certainly existed by the mid-twelfth century and was perhaps based on an earlier circuit. For this and other thoughts on the early origins of Coventry under the Mercian hegemony, see Lilley, 'Medieval Coventry', 351–5; and K.D. Lilley, *Power and Process in an English Medieval City* (forthcoming).
109. There has been much debate over whether the earl's charter referred to all his men of Coventry (i.e. the whole town), or just the area within his jurisdiction (i.e. St Michael's parish, the earl's fee); see Coss, 'Coventry before incorporation'; Gooder and Gooder, 'Coventry before 1355'; Davis, *Early History*.
110. See above.
111. For the charter, see A.A. Dibben (ed.), *Coventry City Charters* (1969), 7. For a discussion of its importance, see Coss, 'Coventry before incorporation', 144; Coss, *Early Records*, 7–8.

CHAPTER TEN

The Origins of Urban Parish Boundaries

Nigel Baker and Richard Holt

There is now broad agreement as to the process by which rural parishes and their boundaries developed. In summary, between the tenth and the twelfth centuries there was a rapid proliferation of local, 'private' churches, each with a resident priest. At a local level, these came to supersede the functions of the smaller number of senior churches – the 'old minsters' and 'lesser minsters' – staffed by communities of priests serving large dependent territories which historians have often referred to as *parochiae*, but now more usually as minster parishes. Within its *parochia* or minster parish – according to established practice and law codes of Aethelstan (926–930) and Edgar (960–962) – each minster had had the right to collect a series of dues, including tithe, soul-scot or burial fees, church-scot, and plough-alms.[1] As lords founded their own local churches, these rights were either delegated by agreement, or were appropriated: new churches established their right to extract some or all of these dues from their own much smaller dependent territories – parishes – that were frequently coterminous with their founders' property. The result was a rural parochial system that had been completed within fossilized boundaries by the thirteenth century.[2]

These processes may be observed across most of rural England. But investigators of urban parishes, by contrast, have no such common ground to work from. No consensus has emerged concerning the development of urban parishes and their boundaries; the experience of each town that has been studied appears to have been different.

One of the most influential studies of town parishes has been Alan Rogers' 'Parish boundaries and urban history'.[3] Rogers was in no doubt as to the origin of urban parishes. Having discussed the origin of rural parishes he noted:

> the private origin of churches was the same in the towns (where many parish churches began life as private chapels) and in the country. Urban parishes thus reflect property divisions, although perhaps not such early ones as in rural areas, for urban properties probably changed relatively more frequently than did rural property.

After discussing evidence for the long-term stability of parish boundaries, Rogers then turned to a pair of case studies to demonstrate his main theses, that

> Parishes which include large areas of the town's lands would seem to be early; those which are purely urban in character came later and were cut out of existing parishes. Again, early parish boundaries would seem to lie along natural features and pre-existing landmarks like roads; later ones relied upon property divisions and frequently run, not along roads, but along the backs of tenements.

The link between an early parish and the possession of rural or extramural territory, and the contrast with two later, purely intramural, parishes was demonstrated very clearly by the example of Nottingham. The relationship was less uniformly convincing in Stamford, his second case study. There, amongst a much larger number of urban churches, all the 'early' churches with a stake in the town fields lay on the periphery of the pre-Conquest fortified area[4] – a pattern repeated at Worcester, as we shall see.

The relationship of urban parishes to early private properties was pursued further, in London, by Brooke and Keir. They distinguished two types of parish: first, those that originated in the property – the soke – of a church founder, his tenants worshipping in the church and contributing to its maintenance, and the priest being his chaplain; and second, parishes that originated in neighbourhood communities of 'pious craftsmen', such parishes being distinguished by their geography. 'In every case a major thoroughfare runs through their midst; sometimes an important cross roads forms their centre. They are thus natural units, not formed by artificial frontiers'. The territorial definition of parishes, the authors suggested, was largely a question of the allocation of tithes: 'London citizens had the privilege to be buried where they liked; burial privileges were therefore not of the essence of London's parochial rights'. Some intramural parishes were still being defined in the early twelfth century, but the pattern was fully formed by 1200.[5]

More recently, Derek Keene has proposed that a different and very precise mechanism for the determination of parish boundaries was used in Winchester and London and, implicitly, much more widely. The lesser churches of Winchester lacked rights of baptism and burial – amongst the normal characteristics of a parish church – until the very end of the Middle Ages, these being reserved to the cathedral. They did, nevertheless, acquire other attributes of parochial status and appear to have had territorially defined parishes by the middle of the twelfth century. Working from the boundaries recorded on maps of the eighteenth and nineteenth centuries and from surviving fifteenth-century property records, Keene deduced that the principle that had been used to determine parochial limits was simply that of the nearest church to any given property:

> what mattered in the definition of the parish boundary was the relationship of the church to a particular house or household from which payments were made rather than to an area of land. The distance between the front door of the house and the door of the church was the critical factor in determining to which parish a house belonged and physical obstacles to movement, such as the city or precinct walls, had a marked effect on the pattern.

The operation of this 'nearest-church-door' principle was deduced solely from the boundaries themselves in Winchester, but it also appears to have operated in London, for a lease of 1566 stipulated that the position of a tenement's front door, nearest the church of St Pancras, be maintained, and with it the parochial loyalty of the property's inhabitants. Even notable eccentricities in Winchester's parochial geography were explicable in terms of the operation of this principle; only in a single instance was there 'a direct correlation between the parish boundaries and a unit of land ownership, in this case the bishop's demesne land administered as the manor of Wolvesey'.[6]

Nevertheless, connections between early units of land tenure and urban parochial geography have been observed or proposed elsewhere: in Chichester, for example, where the parish of All Saints' in the Pallant appears to perpetuate a pre-Conquest soke belonging to the archbishops of Canterbury;[7] and also in London, where the parishes of St Mary Staining and St Michael Bassishaw have been identified with the pre-Conquest *Staeningahaga* and *Basingahaga* respectively.[8]

It has been suggested that some towns saw the deliberate creation of planned parochial units and hierarchies. In Hereford, a planned reorganization of parishes in the mid-twelfth century, with the churches centrally placed within their parishes, has been tentatively proposed.[9] Richard Morris has suggested that there may have been 'an element of formal parochial apportionment' in the arrangement of the three churches and their parishes at the central crossroads in Bristol.[10] And in London, Jeremy Haslam has suggested that the restoration at the end of the ninth century was accompanied by the creation of wards in the eastern part of the city, each centred on a gate, and each provided with a new minster whose *parochia* or parish was coterminous with the ward.[11]

Together these individual studies have presented evidence for very diverse origins for urban parishes: in the fragmentation of large tenurial units, the earliest of which can be recognized by their maintained rural territory, lesser tenurial units (sokes); collectives of pious craftsmen; the rational apportionment of clerical catchment areas; and in acts of ecclesiastical planning. The only unifying factor amongst these disparate views is the universal acknowledgement that urban parochial systems had fossilized, or at least reached completion, by c.1200.

It is quite clear, therefore, that to make sense of the complexities of the urban parish we need more close studies of individual towns: of their historical development, their churches, and their parish boundaries. Recent intensive study of the early medieval topography of the cities of Gloucester and Worcester provides just such an opportunity to test existing theories of parish formation. Both towns had a multiplicity of early churches, and indeed in both cases it can be shown that the period of church foundation was substantially finished by 1100. Gloucester had ten churches by that date,[12] and Worcester probably as many.[13] But to what extent did all or some of these churches have full parochial rights in 1100, and how early can distinct parishes, or districts within which those rights were exercised, be identified? In both Worcester and Gloucester there are references to parishes in documents purportedly from the 1090s, though in each case probably dating from the mid-twelfth century.[14]

Central to any discussion of the origins of the parochial topography must be a consideration of the role played in each of these towns by the ancient mother church:[15] in Gloucester by St Peter's Abbey, the Old Minster, and in Worcester by the cathedral. Both were seventh-century foundations, and pre-dated the urban identity of the communities which in time grew up around them; both had important rights which were respected when their towns were extended or otherwise remodelled as *burhs* during the late ninth century. But as each of these towns contained additional churches even before that period of urban reorganization, it follows that the minsters had no local monopoly of pastoral care; the view that before 1000 the urban minsters were largely unchallenged in their role by local churches built mostly between that date and 1150[16] may need modification in the light of the certainty that Worcester already possessed several lesser churches in the tenth century, and that Gloucester probably did so too.[17] Of crucial importance is the question of how far these churches enjoyed parochial rights: of baptism, burial, and the collection of tithes. Nothing is known of tithe payments in either town during the early Middle Ages; baptism, certainly, was performed at the lesser churches of Worcester by the middle of the eleventh century, whilst the Old Minster's claim to a monopoly of burial within the walls of the *burh* of Gloucester could not be sustained after the early twelfth century.[18] Not that the local churches of either town had entirely supplanted the mother churches during the eleventh century: Worcester cathedral maintained an effective monopoly of burial in the city until the Reformation.[19] The parish churches of Worcester and Gloucester were for the most part located upon prominent sites, whether on the main streets or at the gates; and they had not been founded by private citizens, as has been suggested happened elsewhere, but instead were nearly all foundations by the crown or by the ecclesiastical authorities – by the minsters themselves. There is little doubt that the churches of Worcester and Gloucester were built for public devotion, to provide the people of these growing towns with an alternative to the minsters.[20]

The evidence from Worcester

Turning now to the evidence for the physical presence of parishes in these towns: what is to be deduced concerning the period of parish formation, and the constraints upon that process? Beginning with Worcester: before attempting to interpret the parochial geography and the processes behind its formation, it is necessary to compare the pattern of parish boundaries with what other sources have to say about the development of the secular and ecclesiastical landscape. But Keene's model – attractive in its simplicity, apparently with the power to explain the parochial geography of Winchester, and supported by documentary evidence elsewhere – suggests that parish boundaries were determined quite independently of tenurial boundaries above the level of the individual plot. We also need, therefore, to test that 'nearest-church-door' principle, to assess whether its operation might have determined the layout of parishes in Worcester as well (see Figure 10.1).

At a few places, the line followed by a Worcester parish boundary has been dated; in each instance, the parish boundary has been found to reflect a late, post-twelfth century, feature. This is a limited sampling of a system that can be shown to have been subject to a degree of recurrent mobility, and does not imply that the parochial structure was of late medieval date throughout. The latest large-scale pre-nineteenth century adaptation of the parochial geography probably occurred during the Reformation: the preservation within St Helen's parish of the outline of the Greyfriars' precinct on the eastern edge of the city demonstrates that the parish boundaries were modified when formerly extra-parochial land served by the friars was taken into a city parish (see Figure 10.1).[21] This is not surprising and, as we shall see, it has echoes in Gloucester and in Winchester as well.[22] As part of Worcester's new city wall of the late twelfth century served as a parish boundary, it follows that the parochial geography was modified when it was built.

Rather more precision is possible in two instances where the line of a parish boundary has been excavated. The north–south boundary between St Andrew's and St Helen's ran on a staggered or dog-legged line

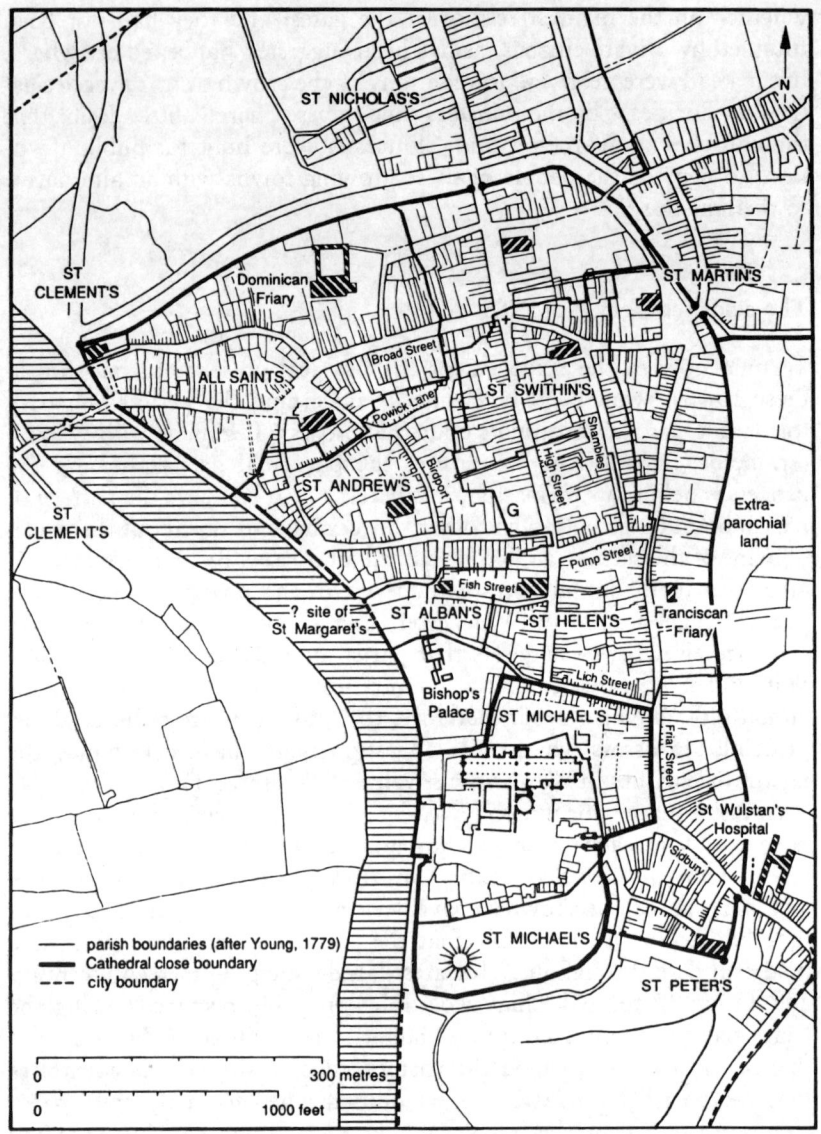

10.1 The historic parishes of Worcester (parish boundaries taken from Young's map of 1779)

to the west of the High Street reflecting, it seems, a former junction between the High Street plots and those facing westwards to Birdport. At the point where it was excavated, the property boundary followed by the parish boundary was shown to have been newly established in the late medieval period.²³ We have suggested elsewhere²⁴ that the staggered back fence line of the High Street west-side plots arose through a protracted process of extension and retraction of individual plots, as ground was exchanged with the plots at the rear facing Birdport according to the vagaries of the local property market. In that case, the parish boundary would represent no more than a tide-mark left by an essentially transitory situation. A closely comparable process was revealed in the second example, between Broad Street and Powick Lane. Here, the boundary between All Saints' and St Andrew's followed a property division between plots fronting on to Broad Street and the plots behind which fronted onto the lane. The excavated property boundary was found to have been inserted at the end of the medieval period, the undivided plot having formerly stretched from one street frontage to the other.²⁵ Before the plot's lateral sub-division, the parish boundary is likely to have followed Powick Lane with the whole of the undivided plot lying within All Saints' (see below); earlier than this, there are indications that the first boundary between the parishes was the standing Anglo-Saxon defences that ran across this area.²⁶

Examples of localized mobility in urban parish boundaries – unlike gross movements through parochial amalgamation – might appear to contradict the prevailing orthodoxy of their relative antiquity and post-twelfth-century stability.²⁷ But mobility in parish boundaries has been noticed before. In Norwich, Alan Carter observed that fluctuations in parish boundaries 'were a result not only of medieval and post-medieval parish amalgamations ... but also of eighteenth- and nineteenth-century adjustments to "fit" boundaries to newly-constructed buildings'.²⁸ A similar process is implicit in Keene's description of the parochial attribution of a vacant plot according to its attachment to a particular house.²⁹ On Pride Hill, in Shrewsbury, at the end of the Middle Ages, a section of ancient parish boundary was moved to a new alignment as a substantial property was subdivided following the demolition of its principal dwelling after a fire.³⁰ A case in Gloucester in which a boundary was moved – first in the early thirteenth century by agreement and again, later, by a less transparent process – is described below.

At first sight there is no strong correlation between Worcester's parochial geography and the structure of the town plan. The central section of the High Street, a planned development with a rectangular arrangement of streets on its east side³¹ is, for instance, bisected by a parish boundary. There is, however, an undeniable relationship at a general level between the parochial geography and what has been deduced of the layout of the late Saxon *burh* (see Figure 10.2). This is most strongly apparent at the margins, there being a clear distinction between the central block of parishes – St Helen's, St Alban's, St Andrew's and St

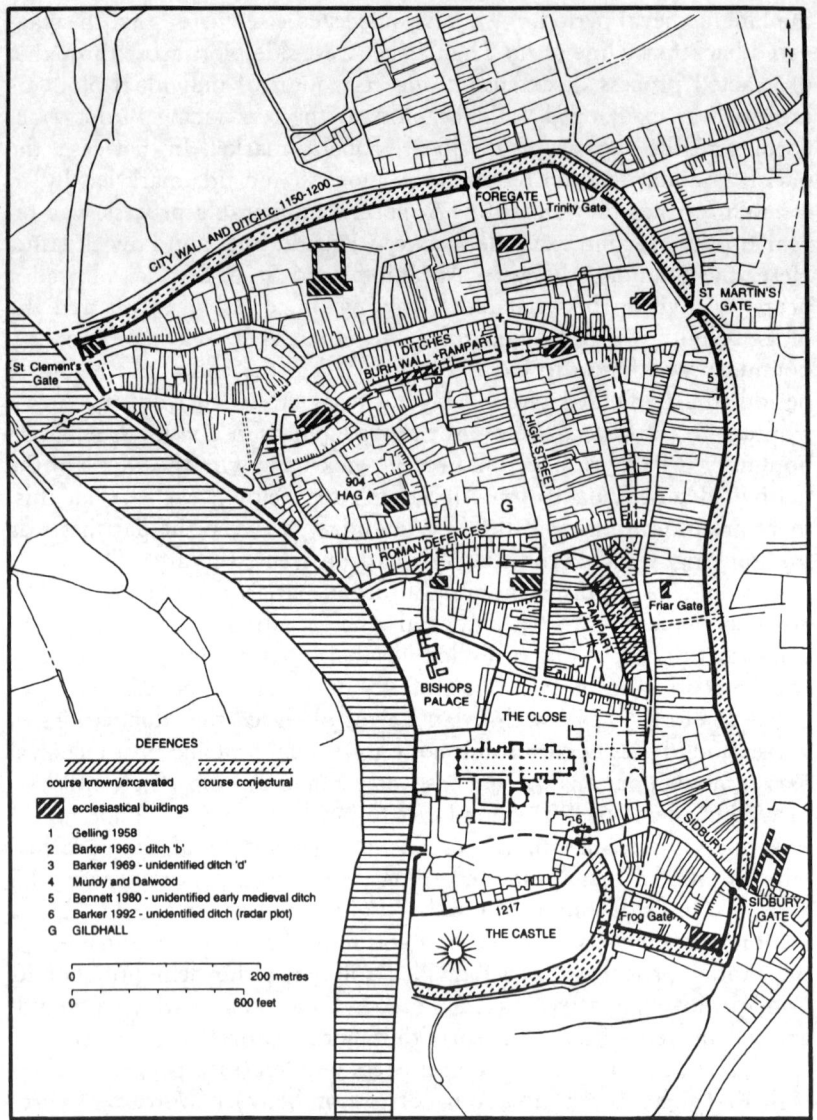

10.2 Worcester: a reconstruction of the Anglo-Saxon *burh*

Swithun's – that were entirely intramural in later medieval terms, and an outer ring of churches with sometimes very extensive extramural and rural parishes. The extent of this central block of parishes corresponds closely to the limits of the *burh*, as they are at present perceived from excavated, documentary, and topographical evidence (see Figures 10.2

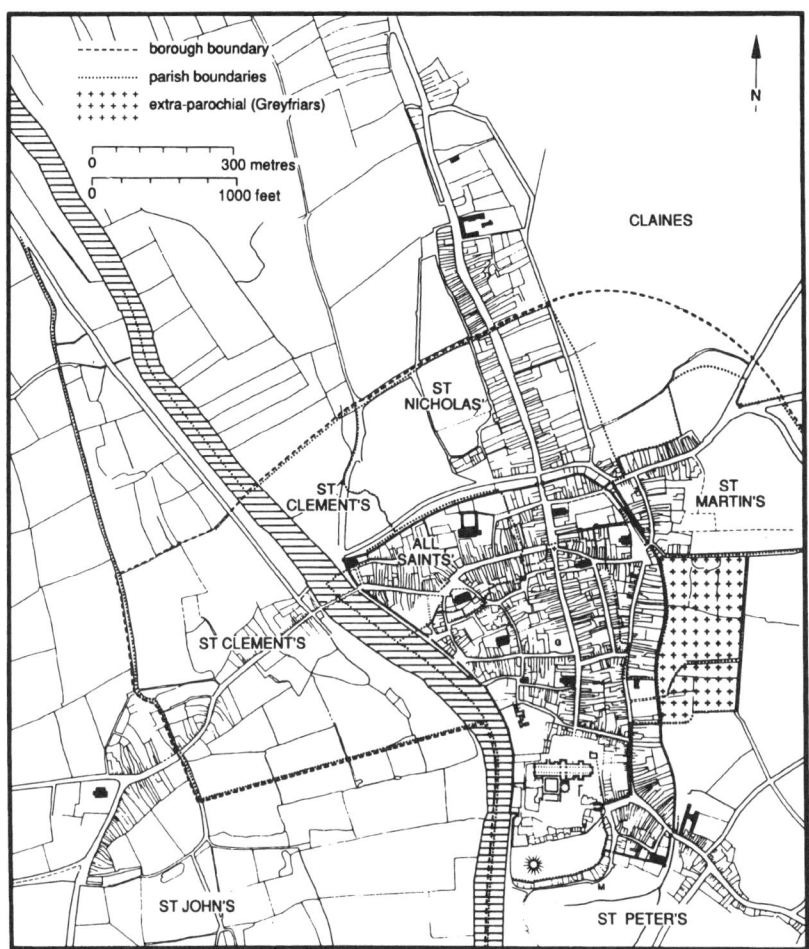

10.3 Worcester: historic city parishes with extramural territory

and 10.3). Around this block lay the churches and parishes of St Clement's, St Nicholas's, St Martin's, and St Peter the Great, of which St Nicholas's alone was a post-Conquest foundation. St Clement's originated as a chapelry dependent upon All Saints', itself a probable gate-church with a parish that was almost entirely extramural to the late Saxon *burh*, and it is possible that St Clement's parish on the west bank of the Severn was annexed from territory that had belonged to its parent church.[32] St Martin's and St Peter's both stood outside the Anglo-Saxon defences, although they were brought within the later medieval circuit, and both had extensive rural parishes; St Peter's, at any rate, was in use during the mid-tenth century, if not before, and certainly while the *burh* defences were still standing.

Two points arise from this. The first is that some elements of the parochial geography may have been determined within the lifetime of the Anglo-Saxon defensive circuit – acting as a landmark or an administrative barrier, if no longer a military one. This is not so helpful as it might be in establishing a chronology of parochial development, as the demise of the *burh* defences in Worcester cannot yet be dated; it does, however, indicate some form of parochial territorialization well before, say, the twelfth century. The second point that arises is that this pattern appears to duplicate that in Stamford, described by Rogers,[33] although there is also a strong suggestion that the equation between the 'earliest parishes' and the possession of rural land is far from universally valid, or at least needs qualification.

It is possible to argue for a further correspondence between the late Saxon secular geography and the parochial geography of the central block of parishes covering the former *burh* area. Tenth-century Worcester was divided between the old Roman earthwork enclosure containing the cathedral, and the defended extension to the north founded in the 890s. This was itself divided between a 'planned' eastern half based on the High Street and its series of large regular plots, and an 'unplanned' western half consisting largely of the land between Birdport and the river (see Figure 10.2). The boundaries of St Andrew's parish reflect, in a very general way, the location of the excavated *burh* defences to the north, the excavated Roman defences to the south, and the edge of the planned High Street to the east. The 'planned' sector of the *burh* was represented parochially by the extension of St Helen's northward beyond the Roman defences and its continuation by St Swithun's. The correspondence is rarely precise, although that is not surprising; an explanation for discrepancies could be the mobility of the precise line of parish boundaries in conformity with the expansion and contraction of individual properties.

Might other factors have determined Worcester's parochial geography? Derek Keene's 'nearest-church-door' hypothesis for Winchester and London is a strongly argued predictive model that can be tested against the parochial geography of this town as of any other. Figure 10.4 is a map of hypothetical parishes in Worcester determined solely by the 'nearest-church-door' principle. It contains some problems and imponderables, notably the lack of information regarding the position of the doors of churches demolished before they could be reliably illustrated. This, and doubt as to the medieval status of some paths or alleyways, leaves a degree of uncertainty as to the precise placing of some boundaries, although the churches were generally so widely and

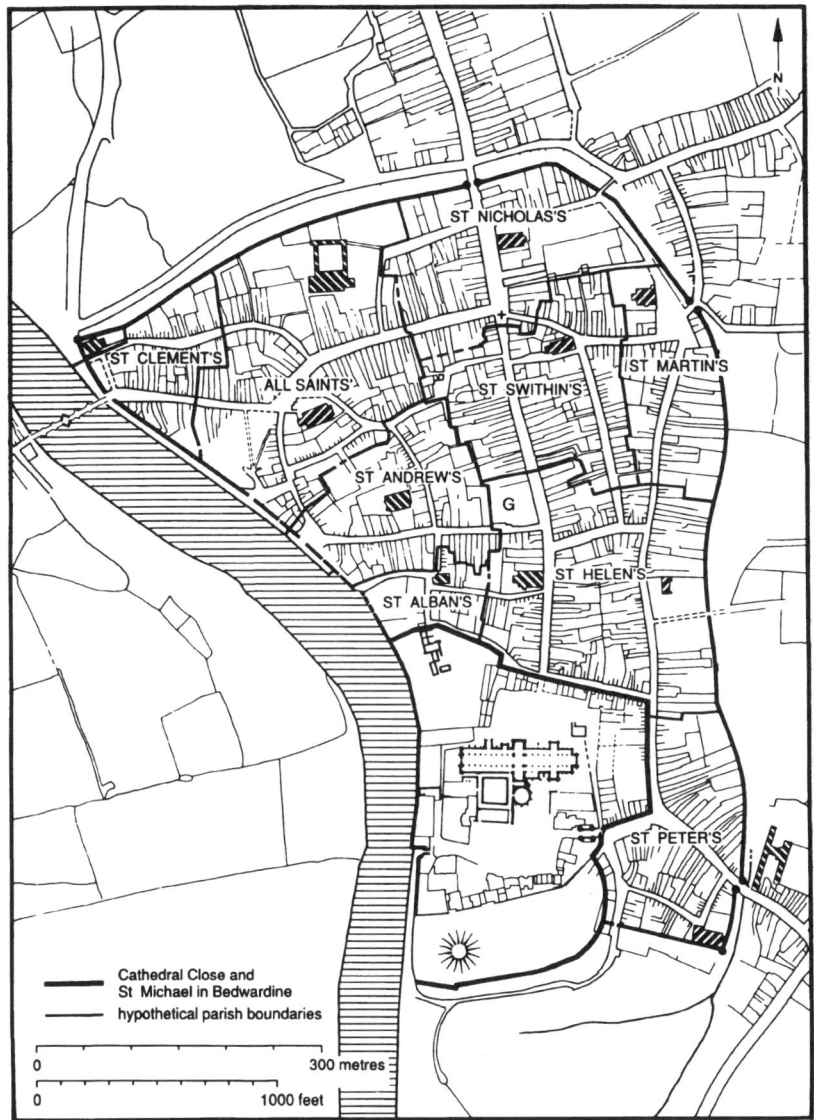

10.4 Worcester: hypothetical parish boundaries determined by the 'nearest-church-door' principle

evenly spaced that the error involved is unlikely to be critical – involving at most the incorrect attribution of one or two contiguous plots. With that reservation in mind, the correspondence between the theoretical and actual pattern of parish boundaries is often remarkably close. It is worth drawing attention to a few instances: the southward extension of St Swithun's parish along the Shambles (formerly Baxter Street), which offers a particularly close correlation; the division of the properties on Fish Street as closely half-way between St Helen's and St Alban's as possible; and the general degree of similarity between the latter's actual parish and its hypothetical counterpart. The correspondence between actual and theoretical boundaries in the St Alban's area casts doubt on an earlier suggestion[34] that the parish boundaries must have been determined directly by the course of the Roman defences.

Of course, there are obvious discrepancies, although some can be accounted for. St Clement's never acquired an intramural parish comparable with its hypothetical parish, which surely reflects its original status as a dependent chapel of All Saints'. Similarly, St Michael in Bedwardine should, in a 'free market', have taken control of the plots on the north side of Lich Street and on the northern part of Sidbury; it did not, because as a cemetery chapel its parish boundaries were predetermined by the extent of the cathedral close. The eastern boundary to St Swithun's, parallel to the Shambles, is anomalous in not following the backs of the plots – which formed a continuous parallel back fence line – but instead cut across them closer to the street along a line which, we have argued, may accurately reflect the course of the Anglo-Saxon defences.[35]

A particularly important departure from the theoretical boundary is to be found close by. According to the 'nearest-church-door' principle, St Helen's should have had a substantial block of its parish on the east side of Friar Street – sandwiched between St Martin's to the north and St Peter's to the south – by virtue of the easy communication between this area and St Helen's via the east–west Pump Street. In reality, it did not; the parish boundary followed Friar Street, at least before St Helen's took over the former Greyfriars precinct (which it may well have acquired on the basis of this principle). Friar Street formed the eastern limit of an area that was arguably laid out for planned settlement following the levelling and infilling of the Roman earthwork defences that had separated the cathedral area from the new *burh*.[36] St Helen's parish boundary may at first, therefore, have followed those defences, being adapted later to encompass the plots laid out over their levelled remains. Alternatively, the parish boundary may simply not have existed before the levelling and redevelopment had taken place. Julia Barrow has suggested that the replanning was part of a reorganization of the cathedral precincts by Oswald in 966;[37] Steven Bassett has suggested that the area covered by St Peter's parish represents an estate that became associated with St Peter's 'shortly after 969' perhaps having earlier been served by the church at Whittington, which was a dependency of St Helen's.[38] In short, the intramural parochial geography of this area does not appear to have been determined by the principle which Keene outlined; rather, it appears to preserve a memory of the Anglo-Saxon perimeter or of its subsequent redevelopment.

Other anomalies – the eastward projection of St Andrew's parish into the High Street, for example – remain unexplained, and there is a recurrent loose or inaccurate correlation between the theoretical and actual boundary positions that defies interpretation. Taking the division of the High Street between St Helen's and St Swithun's, for example: was the known boundary of the eighteenth century identical with that of the Middle Ages, or had the 'nearest-church-door' principle not been applied, or had it been applied inaccurately? In this instance, the positions of the church doors are not in doubt.

The evidence from Gloucester

Turning now to consider the case of Gloucester, where a similar comparison of the parochial geography with what is known of the developing secular landscape, and with changes in the ecclesiastical establishment, provides insights into how the town's parishes might have emerged. Again, the map of historic parishes (see Figure 10.5) can be compared with a hypothetical parish map drawn according to the nearest-church-door principle (see Figure 10.6); the convergences and divergences can be analysed, and the principle's likely contribution to the evolution of the parish boundary system can be assessed. The rental of the town made in 1455[39] provides further comparative information of the greatest value, revealing as it does some of the town's early and fundamental tenurial divisions through the distribution of the already ancient landgable payments.

The long-term stability of most of Gloucester's defensive perimeter simplifies the analysis of its parochial system. Just as in Worcester, a fundamental distinction can be drawn between the churches beyond the walls, or those having substantial extramural parishes, and those within. Outside the original circuit of walls there is now very little doubt that the most ancient ecclesiastical foundation was the church of St Mary de Lode: its antiquity has been established by excavation, and Steven Bassett has suggested that its early history was analogous with that of St Helen's at Worcester – that it pre-dated the Saxon ecclesiastical presence of $c.679$ when the Old Minster, or St Peter's Abbey, was founded.[40] Archaeological evidence shows that burials took place around it by the tenth century at the latest.[41] Inside the walls, it would have been the Old Minster that cared for the souls of the population, and exercised the right of burial.

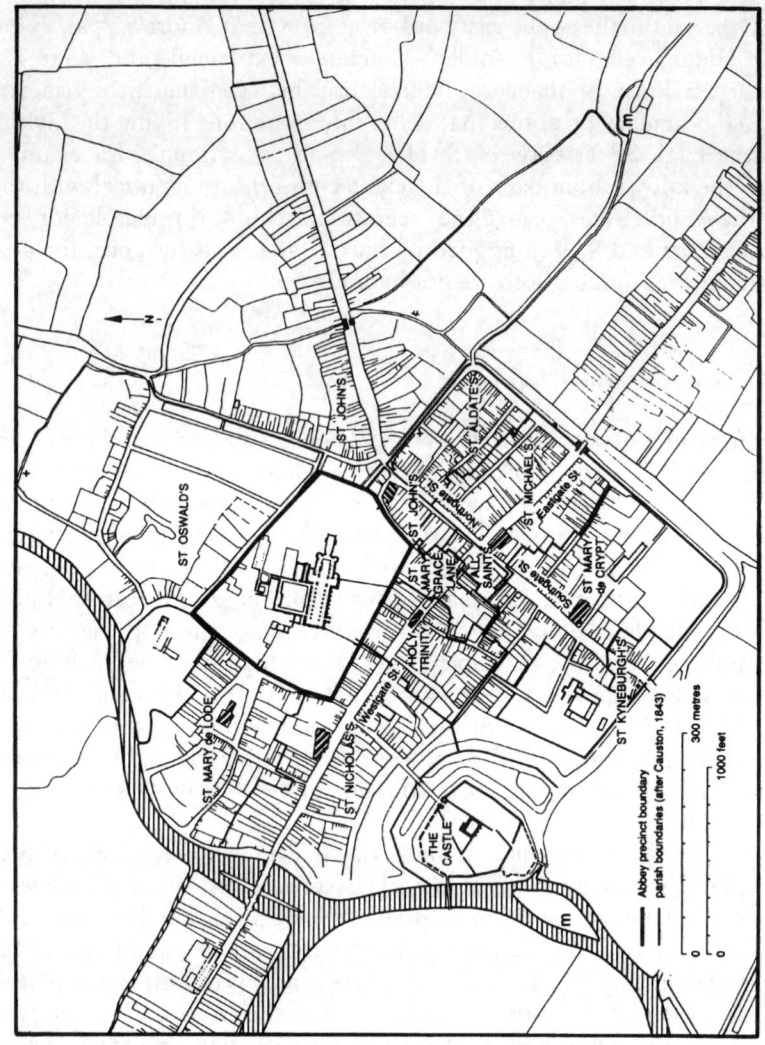

10.5 The historic parishes of Gloucester (parish boundaries taken from Causton's map of 1844)

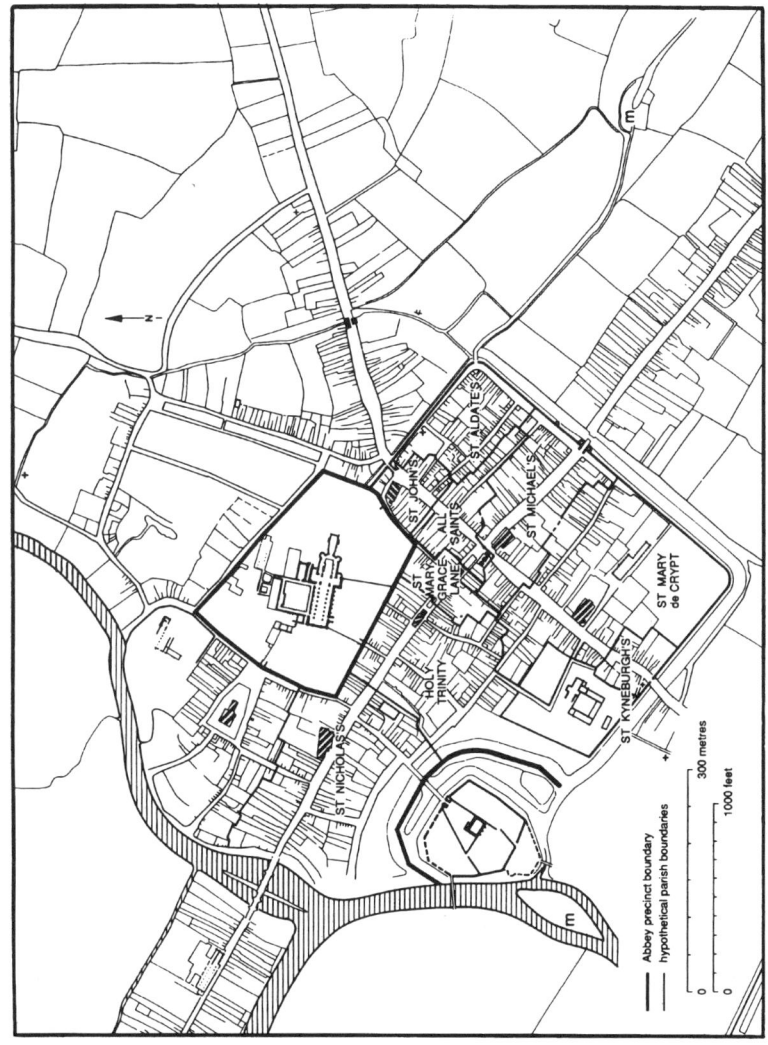

10.6 Gloucester: hypothetical parish boundaries determined by the 'nearest-church-door' principle

This appears to have been the earliest stratum of ecclesiastical provision in and around Gloucester. A second, later, stratum is represented by the fragmentation of St Mary de Lode's extramural *parochia*, a process that perhaps began with the foundation of the New Minster (later St Oswald's Priory) at the end of the ninth century.[42] St Kyneburgh's, too, sited within or next to the south gate, had some of the characteristics of a lesser minster, but its origins are unknown and the period during which it acquired its extensive *parochia* to the south of the city is obscure.[43] St Kyneburgh's had the right to bury its parishioners in the 1090s, and may possibly have done so from a much earlier date; similarly, the church of St John, a probable tenth-century foundation by the north gate, could bury its mainly extramural parishioners by 1197[44] but may, like St Kyneburgh's, have had this right long before. At Winchester, the development of cemeteries in the suburbs much earlier than within the walls has been noted.[45]

A third stratum of parish formation, which must have overlapped chronologically with the second, was represented by the fragmentation of the Old Minster's *parochia* and the gradual demise of its intramural monopoly of pastoral provision. How this process happened is more obscure than that outside the walls, but a few clues suggest that there were two principal stages, divided chronologically by the Norman Conquest and separated geographically between the western and eastern halves of the intramural area. From its location on a corner site on the central crossroads, St Michael's church is likely to have been an early foundation, quite possibly contemporary with the planned street grid occupying the eastern half of the *burh*. It is uncertain how, and when, it acquired a territorially defined parish, but there are grounds for thinking that it may have been an act of planned ecclesiastical provision. St Michael's parish – at least in the state in which it was eventually recorded – was closely related to the planned layout of the *burh*, and it does not appear to have been at all influenced by the 'nearest-church-door' system of boundary demarcation. Its western boundary was the main north–south street; this was also used to delimit the parishes to the north of St Michael's and, it will be argued, possibly to the south as well. The use of the street as St Michael's boundary with All Saints' suggests that the 'nearest-church-door' principle had not been applied, and that other factors determined the layout of the parish. The hypothetical configuration of parishes determined by the 'nearest-church-door' principle cannot be predicted with absolute certainty or accuracy in this area because of the proximity of the two churches to each other and uncertainties as to the position of their doors, but it is probable that All Saints' would have commanded properties on both sides of Northgate Street – which it seems never to have done – while St Michael's would have had rights over the properties to the south of All Saints' church that were almost opposite its own front door. St Michael's southern boundary also followed a street until deflected by the northward projection of St Mary de Crypt's parish: this was very probably a later diversion to encompass properties owned by Lanthony Priory, St Mary's patron.

St Michael's was the only intramural church other than the gate-churches to have included extramural land in its parish. This was land along Eastgate Street and may have been a relatively late accretion, coincident with the post-Conquest development of the Barton Street suburb, St Michael's being the nearest place of worship for the inhabitants.

St Aldate's parish, to the north, also had the appearance of a planned territorial unit, representing exactly half of the north-eastern quadrant. It was, furthermore, very closely coincident with an area of the town that did not pay landgable to the crown, evidently owing chief rent to another lord: the parish can be claimed with some confidence to have been coeval with a pre-Conquest estate belonging to Deerhurst Priory.[46] The bounds of the parish corresponded with the hypothetical parish predicted by the 'nearest-church-door' model only along Oxbode Lane, away from the frontage, where St Aldate's would have had little competition. The crucial area of the principal Northgate Street frontage was in St Aldate's parish, though it was directly opposite the east end of St John's: here, at least, proximity was of no account in determining boundaries.

The origins of St Mary de Crypt are obscure. Its parish was remarkable mainly for its size, though there are some indications that this was a relatively late feature and that the pre-twelfth century parish was confined to the area east of Southgate Street. Towards the end of the eleventh century, St Mary's may have acquired rights to the land on the opposite – west – side of Southgate Street from a lost church, whose existence is implied by the abbey's claim in 1164x79 to have formerly had a chaplain serving the inhabitants of the district of Gloucester cleared for the building of the old castle soon after the Conquest,[47] and from archaeological hints of an otherwise unexplained concentration of pre-Conquest burials in that area.[48]

It should be recognized that the phenomenon of undocumented, short-lived urban burial grounds and churches of middle and late Saxon date is likely to have been more widespread than the present, limited, evidence might suggest. It is necessary to be aware, therefore, that lost churches of this sort might have influenced the final shape of the parochial geography of any of the early major towns. An exact parallel to the possible situation in Gloucester has come from Norwich, where a previously unknown timber church of probable eleventh-century date, with font and associated burials, was uncovered in 1979. It had had only a brief existence – no more than 75 years – as it had been demolished after the Conquest to make way for the castle bailey. An earlier discovery of an unrelated series of burials from another site within the area of the bailey suggests that simultaneously a second unknown church of Anglo-Saxon date was similarly destroyed.[49] In an earlier period, the inhabitants of Hamwic used a number of small, short-lived cemeteries, of which at least nine have been identified, possibly most of them not associated with a church.[50] Perhaps that practice points to attitudes to death and burial distinctive to the eighth and ninth centuries, but not characteristic of the later Saxon urban population; nevertheless, we ought to be aware that pre-Conquest urban ecclesiastical geography, and the circumstances of religious observance, may have been irregular and fluid. Certainly, given both this example and that of Norwich, we must be careful of assuming that urban parish identities were necessarily evolving within the relatively stable pattern of ecclesiastical provision revealed by our documentation – almost all of it dating from after 1100.

Returning to the Gloucester parishes: on the opposite side of the axial north–south road, in that part of Gloucester apparently not subjected to major replanning when the *burh* was founded, the Old Minster's parish may have been maintained intact until much later. Holy Trinity and St Mary Grace Lane were almost certainly twelfth-century foundations, and it is surely no coincidence that the boundary between them, and with All Saints', appears to have been determined on the 'nearest-church-door' principle. Not so the boundary between Holy Trinity and St Nicholas's, however. Close to Westgate Street this reflects the line of the infilled western city ditch; further away from Westgate Street, it reflects the back fence line of properties built over the ditch. In other words, therefore, it was determined by the western defences and their successor features.[51] Before the twelfth century this boundary would have separated St Mary de Lode's extramural parish from the Old Minster's intramural parish. Possibly, therefore, the area covered by the combined parishes of Holy Trinity, St Mary Grace Lane and All Saints' represented the last vestige of the old intramural *parochia*, finally subdivided following the Winchester model in the course of the twelfth century.

St Nicholas's was founded in the early twelfth century.[52] As it lay outside the old intramural area, it probably met no opposition from the abbey in burying its late parishioners from the time of its foundation. Its boundary with St Mary de Lode – out of whose *parochia* it would have been formed – followed an evidently long-established property boundary dividing the Lower Westgate Street plots, which paid landgable to the crown, from the abbey's tenants around St Mary's Square.[53]

Finally, the gate-churches' intramural parishes remain to be considered. St Kyneburgh's, as recorded, may well bear little relation to its earlier form. The foundation charter of St Owen's shows St Kyneburgh's to have had an intramural parish by the end of the eleventh century.[54] But the mapped boundaries of the parish respect the friary precincts either side of Southgate Street and must have been redrawn after both were established early in the thirteenth century. The north side, at least in part, coincides exactly with a boundary determined by the Winchester model and may represent a rationalisation of an earlier boundary. St John's has already been briefly discussed. It was confined by the boundary drawn along the middle of Northgate Street and was unable to command the plots lying immediately opposite its east end. This parish is of particular interest, however, because an unusually detailed account has survived of a series of modifications to its southern boundary, an extended process in which plot-to-church proximity ostensibly played no part, until perhaps the final act.

An ordinance of Bishop W. of Worcester, attributed by its editor to 1186x90[55] but from the evidence of the Lanthony Priory cartularies dated to c.1218x32 – the time of Bishop William de Blois (1218–36)[56] – records that a dispute arose when two neighbouring houses on the west side of Northgate Street were made into one. They had formerly belonged to Ailwin the Mercer and to Osbert the Cellarer, and had lain in separate parishes, in St John's and All Saints': to which of these parishes, then, should the new house be assigned? Lanthony Priory and Gloucester Abbey, to whom the churches belonged, agreed that since the house's principal entrance lay in All Saints', and since that, furthermore, was the church that Richard Rufus, the new tenant, already attended, then it should lie in All Saints'. However, it was also agreed that one-third of the oblations should continue to be paid to St John's; and the abbey had evidently been able to insist that its rights in the matter should not be alienated in perpetuity, for it was stipulated that should the houses ever be divided again, then each would revert to its original parochial allegiance.

Richard Morris has observed that the terms of this agreement illustrate how necessary precision in parish boundaries had now become; but he also believed that the agreement indicated how the concept of the parish had originated in a system of personal allegiances.[57] That observation seems to press the evidence too far; what the agreement shows above all is how each parish and its parishioners were regarded as the property of their church, and how rigid, as a consequence, parish boundaries were. Adjustments might be made by agreement, and the bishop's solution to the dilemma implies that conventions for dealing with such disputes already existed; but the abbey's ability to insist on the continued payments to its church of St John confirms that parish rights were not easily to be set aside. Finally, the provision allowing for the eventual restoration of the parish boundary might be taken to indicate that the boundary was held to have an intrinsic identity, and that parochial rights were in effect immutable, for the arrangement was thus defined as a temporary one. What we do not know is how this case might have turned out had not the two parties been powerful religious houses, with the greater of the two in effect giving ground but able to insist that its rights be recognized. If St John's had belonged to a less influential patron, would its existing rights have been so tenaciously safeguarded?

As it turns out, not only can this property be identified, but its subsequent history can be traced. The Lanthony Priory records show that the amalgamation of the two houses took place under Prior John (c.1218–40): both Ailwin and Osbert had previously granted their respective houses to Lanthony, and it was from Prior John that Richard Rufus took a lifetime lease on the property, with its shops and other buildings, for the considerable rent of £2 10s.[58] The lease did not expire on Richard's death, and his successor as tenant, Ralph of Cornwall alias Vintner, added small parcels of land to the property in 1232 and 1240.[59] Ralph's son and heir – also Ralph – relinquished all this tenement to Lanthony, and in 1244 the priory granted it, together with some adjacent shops it had acquired, to Herbert the Mercer, to hold in fee.[60] In none of these transactions was any reference made to the parochial location of the property or to the obligations of its tenants. Having been held by a succession of tenants,[61] during the reign of Edward III the property came into the possession of Nicholas Bursy and Henry Drapere who, with Lanthony's permission, divided it: Nicholas, it was reported, received the part in the parish of All Saints, and Henry that within St John's.[62] So the terms of the agreement of more than a century before had been remembered, and were adhered to in preference to any other method of determining the parochial allegiance of the two new tenements.

But that was not the end of the story. In 1363 the abbot of Gloucester bought Henry's portion – John Pirie, Thomas Baverton and John Godwot having acted as intermediaries.[63] By the 1430s a great inn had been built here by John Twynnyng, the collector of the abbey's rents, who had similarly built the still-surviving New Inn on the opposite side of the street; in 1455 this inn was leased to the merchant and vintner Philip Monger.[64] According to the entry in Lanthony's rental, compiled in the 1440s, the tenement lay now not within St John's but within St

Michael's parish,[65] and although there is no sign of how the change had come about, it is surely not a coincidence that both St John's and St Michael's belonged to the abbey. That circumstance had sufficed to stifle any objection to the setting aside of St John's parochial rights; evidently it had suited the abbey to divert – or to allow to be diverted – this wealthy tenant's tithes from his historic parish church to another, and admittedly slightly nearer his front door. There is no other evidence for St Michael's parish ever having included houses on the west side of Northgate Street.

Conclusions

In conclusion then, what were the mechanisms by which the parish boundaries of these towns were defined, and when were their parochial systems established? The pattern of parish boundaries in Worcester was evidently a palimpsest, the result not of a single period of agreed boundary demarcation, and certainly not of a single act of ecclesiastical planning by a central authority. But neither does it wholly or accurately reflect tenurial patterns and the secular landscape of the tenth century. Instead, it appears to contain a number of chronological components and an overlay of continuous small-scale change. During the modern period, and at least the later Middle Ages, we may envisage a continuous process of very localized boundary movement, in response to changes in the secular landscape, that only becomes visible under exceptional conditions: a relationship with a known and datable feature (a friary precinct for example); the survival of unusually detailed documentation for particular properties; or evidence from excavation that allows us to date a physical boundary.

In Worcester, it seems that a fundamental distinction can be drawn between those parishes that lay wholly within the medieval city walls and those that extended beyond them. The churches with no extramural parochial land in the later Middle Ages (St Helen's, St Alban's, St Swithun's, St Andrew's) all lay within the Anglo-Saxon defences; the churches whose parishes extended beyond the medieval city walls all lay demonstrably outside the Anglo-Saxon defences (All Saints', St Martin's, St Peter's) or were founded after the defences had become redundant (St Nicholas's): thus the perimeter known to have been in use from at least the late ninth to the mid-tenth centuries left a permanent, if partially mobile, imprint on the parochial geography. The chronology of parish formation is little clearer outside the town than in, but it is possible that, for a while, the *burh* defences formed a boundary between a cathedral parish (or *parochia*) within, and St Helen's vast *parochia* without, the latter subject to a steady process of fragmentation as territory was annexed by the cathedral and as chapelries sought independence. Parish formation – or *parochia* fragmentation – may have taken place or been allowed to take place a good deal earlier outside the walls than within, where the process is likely to have been retarded under the stern gaze of the cathedral.

In part, this supports Rogers' hypothesis that the earliest parishes were those with a share of the town fields. But two vital qualifications are necessary. First, whilst this hypothesis may in some circumstances have applied to parish formation – or acquisition – it did not apply to the sequence of church-founding. Those churches with extramural parishes in the later medieval period were, like those at Stamford, peripheral to the *burh*, at least in part associated with suburban growth, and far from being the earliest stratum of foundations. Second, what is meant here by 'parish'? St Helen's parish was purely intramural in the late-medieval period but there is little doubt that its once extensive rural *parochia* was extremely ancient.[66]

The Worcester evidence, however full and detailed, fails the final test: it is insufficiently decisive to support a single line of argument, and indeed it can be used to lend equal support to two opposed views of the origin of the wholly intramural parishes. The first would stress the general correspondence between the broad divisions of the late Saxon town plan and the parochial geography, and would claim that parish formation, patently in progress by at least the mid-twelfth century, had in fact begun early enough in Worcester to reflect the defended perimeter and the internal tenurial landscape of the tenth century. Departures from this relationship could be explicable in terms of the mobility of property boundaries and thus of the parish boundaries that followed them. This is the more radical view – given the cathedral's powerful presence and undeniably jealous and monopolistic tendencies – and demands a higher level of proof than is currently possible.

Contrary to that interpretation of the evidence, it is possible to cite the close overall relationship between the historical parishes of Worcester and a parochial map determined by the 'nearest-church-door' hypothesis. Given its applicability in Winchester, could this organizational principle be characteristic of late – maybe twelfth-century – parochial organization under monopolistic conditions? There seems little doubt that some boundaries within the former *burh* at Worcester were determined using this method – the southward projection of St Swithun's parish into St Helen's provides a fine example of this principle in operation.

Of course, the truth may lie somewhere between these extremes. The correspondence between the late Saxon town plan and the parochial

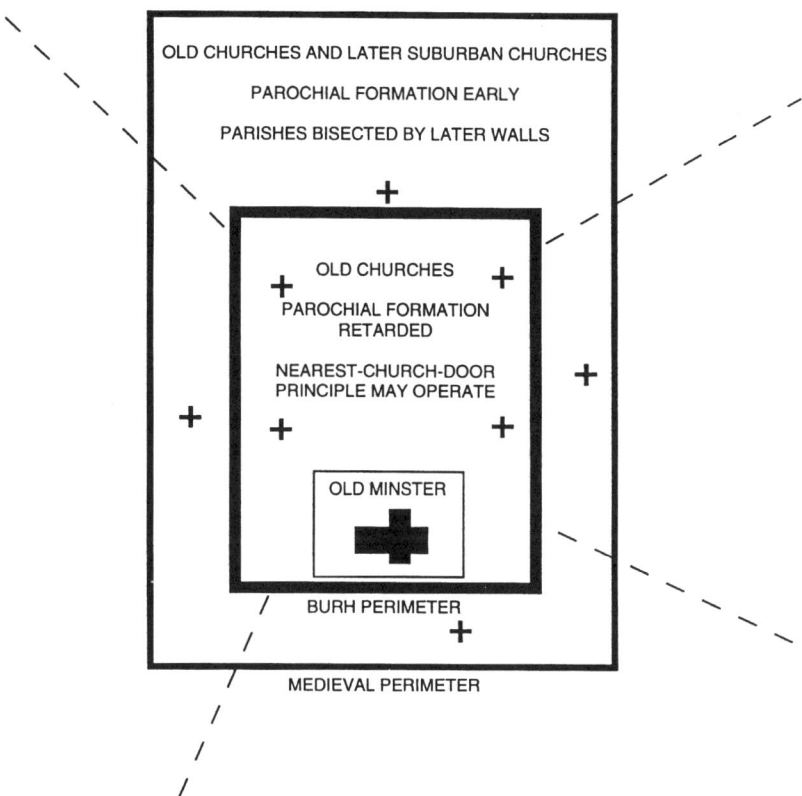

10.7 A model of parish formation in minster towns with numerous churches

geography may be explicable simply in terms of the distribution of churches around the street system and the gradual formation of natural constituencies amongst the inhabitants of the adjoining streets. The 'nearest-church-door' principle evidently played a part in the determination of parish boundaries, but so too did other factors: the influence of the pre-Conquest defences has been noted, as well as those instances where the extent of parishes was determined by known legal–ecclesiastical constraints. Inconsistencies with that model also give pause for thought, although it is restricted by the lack of precise information as to the accuracy of the prototype system in Winchester; possibly it was used more as a method for rationalizing existing boundaries and settling disputes than in creating parishes where none had existed before, or rather in determining the outcome of *parochia* fragmentation (see Figure 10.7).

By contrast, the parochial geography of Gloucester leads to rather different conclusions. The principal difference is that Gloucester provides more unambiguous evidence of planned parochial provision which reflected major secular boundaries. This appears to have been characteristic of the first stage of the fragmentation of the Old Minster's intramural *parochia*, and was confined to the eastern half of the city. There is evidence that Gloucester saw the simple proximity principle employed, both in the boundaries themselves and perhaps in the documented boundary adjustments we have seen; but it appears to have been less influential and more characteristic of a late phase of development, by which time much of the historic boundary pattern had already been established.

From these two towns some more general conclusions can be reached regarding the development of urban parishes and their boundaries. Urban parishes were like rural parishes, inasmuch as their formation required a process of *parochia* fragmentation, the lesser churches acquiring rights at the expense of an older minster church. Worcester and Gloucester may have been fairly typical of English minster or cathedral towns, where fragmentation was delayed or retarded by the proximity of the respective senior churches and doubtless also by their ownership of property. Beyond the town walls, however, fragmentation could advance and rights be acquired significantly earlier. Whereas rural parishes were often coterminous with large tenurial units or estates, such correlations occur much less frequently with urban parishes: being delayed, parish formation in towns was liable to post-date the subdivision of large early plots or *hagas* into a multitude of smaller burgage-type properties.

In Gloucester, nevertheless, evidence has been found for a parish based on a large tenurial unit – St Aldate's – and certainly there are signs of a phase of deliberate, planned, parochial provision. There is also extensive evidence for the use of the 'nearest-church-door' principle. But this was certainly not the only mechanism that determined boundary positions; rather, it appears to have been strongly characteristic of situations where rights were acquired late and needed definition in an already densely populated landscape. It was also particularly appropriate to the settlement of disputes between existing parishes and the rationalisation of earlier arrangements. Where a town was dominated by a number of ancient minsters of more or less equal status – as at Shrewsbury – and its parochial geography thus established at an early date, this principle could make no contribution to the way that parish boundaries evolved.[67]

The most intractable problem remains that of chronology. The documentary evidence from both Worcester and Gloucester appears to show the respective mother churches attempting to halt the fragmentation of their intramural *parochiae* in the middle of the twelfth century. Suspicions that the intramural parishes in Worcester had begun to have some kind of territorial definition as early as the tenth century remain unconfirmed due to the level of coincidence between the known parish boundaries and the predictive model based on the 'nearest-church-door' principle: the possibility that they were substantially freshly defined in the twelfth century cannot yet be completely ruled out. The more secure evidence for an earlier start in Gloucester – though hardly incontrovertible – rests on the preservation in parochial form of what appears to have been a pre-Conquest estate, and the evidence for 'planned' parishes closely associated with the planned eastern half of the Anglo-Saxon *burh*.

Notes

1. F. Liebermann, *Die Gesetze der Angelsachsen* (Halle, 1903–16), vol. 1, 146–9, 196–7.
2. J. Blair, 'From Minster to Parish Church' in J. Blair (ed.), *Minsters and Parish Churches: The Local Church in Transition 950–1200*, Oxford University Committee for Archaeology, Monograph 17 (1988), 1–19; R. Morris, *Churches in the Landscape* (1989).
3. A. Rogers, 'Parish boundaries and urban history: two case studies', *Journal of the British Archaeological Association*, 3rd series, 35 (1972), 46–64.
4. Ibid., 48, 51–6, 58–9, 63. For the exceptional case of St Peter's, Stamford, see C. Mahany and D. Roffe, 'Stamford: the development of an Anglo-Scandinavian borough', *Anglo-Norman Studies*, 5 (1982), 196–219.
5. C.N.L. Brooke and G. Keir, *London 800–1216: the Shaping of a City* (1975), 130–3.
6. D. Keene, *Survey of Medieval Winchester* (1985), 107, 116, 124–6.
7. W.D. Peckham, 'The parishes of the city of Chichester', *Sussex Archaeological Collections*, 74 (1933), 68; J. Munby 'Saxon Chichester and its predecessors' in J. Haslam (ed.), *Anglo-Saxon Towns in Southern England* (1984), 327–8.
8. A. Dyson and J. Schofield, 'Saxon London', in Haslam, *Anglo-Saxon Towns*, 306–7.
9. A.M. Pearn 'Origin and development of urban churches and parishes: a comparative study of Hereford, Shrewsbury and Chester', PhD thesis, University of Cambridge (1988).
10. Morris, *Churches in the Landscape*, 210.
11. J. Haslam, 'Parishes, churches, wards and gates in eastern London', in Blair, *Minsters and Parish Churches*, 35–43.
12. London, British Library, Cotton MS Vespasian B xxiv f. 57r; text edited by H.B. Clarke in J.S. Moore (ed.), *Domesday Book: Gloucestershire* (1982), Appendix, Evesham K.
13. N.J. Baker and R.A. Holt, *Medieval Towns and the Church: The Growth of Worcester and Gloucester* (1998, forthcoming), ch. 7.
14. R.R. Darlington (ed.), *The Cartulary of Worcester Cathedral Priory*, Pipe Roll Society, new series, 38 (1968), 31–2, n. 52; D. Walker (ed.), 'Char-

ters of the earldom of Hereford, 1095–1201', *Camden Miscellany XXII*, Camden Society, 4th series, 1 (1964), 37–8.
15. C.N.L. Brooke 'The church in the towns, 1000–1250', *Studies in Church History*, vi (1970), 76–7.
16. G. Rosser, 'The cure of souls in English towns before 1000', in J. Blair and R. Sharpe (eds), *Pastoral Care before the Parish* (1992), 274–5.
17. Baker and Holt, *Growth of Worcester and Gloucester*, ch. 4, ch. 7.
18. Baker and Holt, *Growth of Worcester and Gloucester*, ch. 15; J. Barrow, 'Urban cemetery location in the high Middle Ages', in S. Bassett (ed.), *Death in Towns* (1992), 84–6.
19. Baker and Holt, *Growth of Worcester and Gloucester*, ch. 15; Barrow, 'Urban cemetery location', 86.
20. Baker and Holt, *Growth of Worcester and Gloucester*, ch. 4, ch. 7.
21. Ibid.
22. Keene, *Medieval Winchester*, 125.
23. C.F. Mundy, *Deansway Archaeology Project Interim Excavation Report*, Hereford and Worcester County Council Archaeology Section (1989), 14; and personal communication.
24. Baker and Holt, *Growth of Worcester and Gloucester*, ch. 6.
25. C.F. Mundy, *Deansway Excavation Report*, 24.
26. N.J. Baker, H. Dalwood, R.A. Holt, C.F. Mundy, and G. Taylor, 'From Roman to medieval Worcester: development and planning in the Anglo-Saxon city', *Antiquity*, 66 (1992), 65–74.
27. Rogers, 'Parish boundaries and urban history', 49; Brooke and Keir, *London*, 129–31.
28. A. Carter, 'The Anglo-Saxon origins of Norwich', *Anglo-Saxon England*, 7 (1978), 175–204.
29. Keene, *Medieval Winchester*, 125.
30. N.J. Baker, J.B. Lawson, R. Maxwell, and J.T. Smith, 'Further work on Pride Hill, Shrewsbury', *Transactions of the Shropshire Archaeological and Historical Society*, 68 (1993), 27–8.
31. Baker et al., 'From Roman to medieval Worcester', 67.
32. Baker and Holt, *Growth of Worcester and Gloucester*, ch. 7.
33. Rogers, 'Parish boundaries and urban history', 56–63.
34. N.J. Baker, 'Churches, parishes, and early medieval topography', in M.O.H. Carver (ed.), *Medieval Worcester, an Archaeological Framework*, Transactions of the Worcestershire Archaeological Society, 3rd series, 7, (1980), 31–7.
35. Baker and Holt, *Growth of Worcester and Gloucester*, ch. 6; Baker et al., 'From Roman to medieval Worcester', 73.
36. Baker and Holt, *Growth of Worcester and Gloucester*, ch. 6; Baker et al., 'From Roman to medieval Worcester', 67, 73.
37. J. Barrow, 'The community of Worcester cathedral, 961–*c.*1100', in N.P. Brooks and C.R.E. Cubitt (eds), *St Oswald and his Times* (1996).
38. S.R. Bassett, 'Churches in Worcester before and after the conversion of the Anglo-Saxons', *Antiquaries Journal*, 69 (1989), 225–56.
39. W.H. Stevenson (ed.) *Rental of all the Houses in Gloucester, AD 1455* (1890).
40. S.R. Bassett, 'Church and diocese in the West Midlands: the transition from British to Anglo-Saxon control', in Blair and Sharpe (eds), *Pastoral Care*, 20–29.

41. R. Bryant, 'Excavations at St Mary de Lode, Gloucester, 1978–1979', *Glevensis*, **14** (1980), 4–12.
42. C. Heighway, 'Excavations at Gloucester: fifth interim report: St Oswald's Priory 1977–8', *Antiquaries Journal*, **60** (1980), 207–26.
43. Baker and Holt, *Growth of Worcester and Gloucester*, ch. 4; D. Walker (ed.), 'Charters of the earldom of Hereford, 1095–1201', *Camden Miscellany XXII, Camden Society*, 4th series, **1** (1964), 37–8.
44. Baker and Holt, *Growth of Worcester and Gloucester*, ch. 4; W.H. Hart (ed.), *Historia et Cartularium Monasterii Gloucestriae*, vol. 1 (1863), lxxvii–lxxviii, vol. 2 (1865), 8–9.
45. B. Kjølbye-Biddle, 'Dispersal or concentration: the disposal of the Winchester dead over 2000 years', in S. Bassett (ed.) *Death in Towns: Urban Responses to the Dying and the Dead, 100–1600* (1995), 224.
46. Baker and Holt, *Growth of Worcester and Gloucester*, ch. 4; C. Heighway, 'Anglo-Saxon Gloucester', in *Victoria County History, Gloucestershire, IV* (1988), 5–12.
47. Hart (ed.), *Historia et Cartularium*, vol. 1, lxxvi–vii; H. Hurst, 'The archaeology of Gloucester castle: an introduction', *Transactions of the Bristol and Glos. Archaeological Society*, **102** (1984), 73–128.
48. M. Atkin, 'Blackfriars assessment project: excavations on Ladybellegate Street Car Park', *Glevensis*, **26** (1992), 37.
49. B. Ayers, 'Excavations within the north-east bailey of Norwich castle, 1979', *East Anglian Archaeology* **28** (1985), 7–26, 63–5.
50. A. Morton, 'Burial in middle Saxon Southampton', in Bassett (ed.), *Death in Towns*, 68–77.
51. C. Heighway, 'Saxon Gloucester', in Haslam (ed.) *Anglo-Saxon Towns*, 366–7.
52. Baker and Holt, *Growth of Worcester and Gloucester*, ch. 4.
53. Stevenson (ed.), *Rental of the Houses in Gloucester*, 58a–70a, 52b–56b, and passim.
54. Walker, 'Charters of the earldom of Hereford', 37–8.
55. D. Walker (ed.), 'A register of the churches of the monastery of St Peter's, Gloucester', *An Ecclesiastical Miscellany, Bristol and Glos. Archaeological Society, Records Section*, **6** (1976), 15, no. 11.
56. London, Public Record Office (hereafter PRO), C115/K1/6678, fos 64v–66v; C115/L1/6687, fos 76r–83r.
57. Morris, *Churches in the Landscape*, 226.
58. PRO, C115/L1/6687, fos 78r–79r.
59. PRO, C115/L1/6687, fos 76r–77v; C115/K1/6678, fos 66r–66v.
60. PRO, C115/L1/6687, fos 80r–82r.
61. PRO, C115/K1/6678, fos 64v–67v.
62. PRO, C115/K1/6678, fos 64v, 65v. Nicholas' portion was the tenement which Thomas Byseley held in 1455: Stevenson (ed.), *Rental of the Houses in Gloucester*, 70b–2b.
63. PRO, C115/K1/6678, fos 65v, 68r; *Calendar of Patent Rolls, 1361–64* (1912), 401.
64. Stevenson (ed.), *Rental of the Houses in Gloucester*, 84b.
65. PRO, C115/K1/6678, fo. 65v.
66. Bassett, 'Churches in Worcester'.
67. S.R. Bassett, 'Anglo-Saxon Shrewsbury and its churches', *Midland History*, **16** (1991), 1–23.

CHAPTER ELEVEN

Medieval Parishes and Parish Churches in Canterbury

Tim Tatton-Brown

Over 25 years ago the late Dr William Urry pointed out that there were already 22 parishes and churches in Canterbury by the late twelfth century, and that, although large in number, they were small in size.[1] It is also very well known that one of these churches, St Martin's, has an exceptionally early fabric and documented history[2] which go back at least to the late sixth century. The later Anglo-Saxon history of the Church in Canterbury has been fully discussed by Brooks,[3] and it can be shown that two further churches, apart from the cathedral and St Augustine's Abbey, may have been constructed before the Norman Conquest.[4] These are St Dunstan's[5] and St Mildred's which were perhaps first built just before the Norman Conquest in the mid-eleventh century. This chapter builds on these studies and looks in more detail at the surviving above-ground fabric of the Canterbury parish churches. It incorporates, too, the results of recent excavations on several of the churches that are no longer extant (St Mary Bredin, All Saints, St Margaret's and St George's). It will also examine the history of the graveyards in the city and the topography of the parishes.

Of the 22 parish churches in the city one, St Helen's, has a very short life (late twelfth century to c.1220);[6] the others all lasted until the Black Death, and only subsequently, and particularly after the Reformation, did their numbers decrease. Today, 11 medieval churches survive, at least in part, above ground (though only five of them are still used ecclesiastically) and two further churches have been studied from their excavated remains only. These churches are:

1. St Martin
2. St George (tower only, but church excavated)
3. St Mary Northgate (nave, north wall and roof only)
4. St Mildred
5. St Dunstan
6. St Alphege (redundant)
7. St Mary Bredin (excavated)
8. St Peter

CANTERBURY PARISHES AND CHURCHES

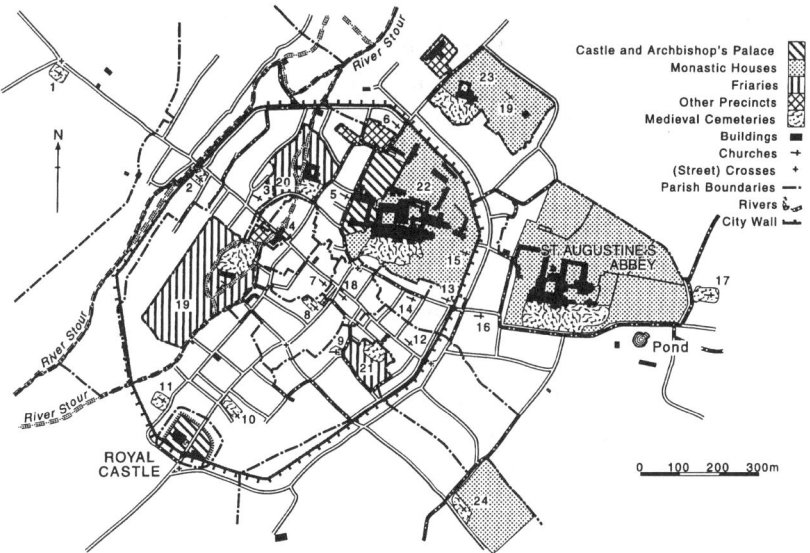

1.	St Dunstan's Church	13.	St Michael's Church
2.	Holy Cross Church	14.	St Mary Magdalen's Church
3.	St Peter's Church	15.	St Mary Queningate
4.	All Saints' Church	16.	St Paul's Church
5.	St Alphege's Church	17.	St Martin's Church
6.	St Mary Northgate	18.	St Andrew's Church
7.	St Mary Bredman	19.	Franciscan Friary (Greyfriars)
8.	St Margaret's Church	20.	Dominican Friary (Blackfriars)
9.	St Mary Bredin Church	21.	Augustine's Friary (Whitefriars)
10.	St Mary-de-Castro	22.	Christ Church Priory
11.	St Mildred's Church	23.	St Gregory's Priory
12.	St George's Church	24.	St Sepulchre's Nunnery

11.1 Town plan of Canterbury c.1500

9. All Saints (excavated)
10. St Margaret (redundant and excavated)
11. St Paul
12. St Mary Magdalen (tower only)
13. Holy Cross.

The church of St Mary Queningate might also be added to this list since a few foundations were uncovered in 1919 when the memorial garden in the cathedral precincts was made. A little evidence exists of a few other churches (for example, there are some useful eighteenth-century drawings of St Mary Bredman and St Andrew), while other early drawings throw more light on churches that have been either partially

238 THE CHURCH IN THE MEDIEVAL TOWN

destroyed or heavily restored in the last two centuries (St Margaret, Holy Cross, All Saints, St Mary Northgate, St Mary Magdalen, St Mary Bredin and St George). Of particular interest is a fine series of watercolours made by John Buckler in the early nineteenth century.[7] There are still, however, at least seven churches about which we know nothing as they all disappeared soon after the Reformation. The sites of all 22 churches are, however, known (see Figure 11.1).

Early history of the parish churches

From early times, Canterbury was dominated by the archbishop and his two great churches, the cathedral and St Augustine's Abbey, and even with the formation of the parochial system in the late eleventh and early twelfth centuries, these two great Benedictine churches with their large lay cemeteries continued to dominate the city. Two other major religious houses, St Gregory's Priory and the Benedictine nunnery of St Sepulchre's (the latter also having a parochial nave) were created in the late eleventh century; and between them, these four monasteries and the archbishop controlled all the parish churches as patrons. The two rival Benedictine houses of Christ Church and St Augustine's controlled the majority. The pattern of patronage divides the medieval churches into the following five groups:

The archbishop:	St Martin and St Alphege
St Gregory's Priory:	St Dunstan, Holy Cross and St Mary Northgate[8]
Christ Church Priory:	St Peter, St Michael Burgate, St George, St Mary Bredman, St Mary Queningate, St Sepulchre, St Helen
St Augustine's Abbey	St Mildred, All Saints, St Andrew, St Margaret,[9] St John, St Mary-de-Castro, St Paul and St Mary Magdalen
St Sepulchre's Priory:	St Edmund Ridingate and St Mary Bredin

The origin and early history of many of these parish churches have been traced by William Urry. He was able to show, for example, that St Sepulchre's Priory's two small churches had been founded in the very late eleventh century by a father and son: St Edmund Ridingate by Hamo, son of Vitalis and St Mary Bredin by his son William. St Sepulchre's itself, with its parochial nave, was founded at about the same time, and was, no doubt, a round church like others founded at the time of the first Crusade. By the later fourteenth century, all three parishes seem to have been joined together as one main parish of St Mary

Bredin.[10] Three other churches are already well documented as in existence before the death of William the Conqueror. These are St Andrew and St Mary-de-Castro, both given by him to St Augustine's Abbey in compensation for land taken for the castle; and St Mildred, which is mentioned as being near the castle in the story of a demonstration by monks from St Augustine's in c.1087.[11] St Mildred, as we have seen, may well have been built by St Augustine's Abbey in the 1030s, just after the abbey had brought the remains of St Mildred to Canterbury from Minster-in-Thanet.[12]

An interesting feature of certain of these early churches (i.e. those founded in the eleventh century) is that they appear to have started life above the Roman gates of the city. This was certainly the case for St Mary-upon-Northgate and Holy Cross Westgate (until rebuilt beside the new gate in 1379–80); and also probably for St Michael Burgate, and St Edmund Ridingate. It is also just possible that St Mary-de-Castro had been above the Worthgate until the new castle was built there in c.1080.

There has been much discussion of the date of the fabric of St Martin's Church since the pioneering work of the Reverend G.M. Livett and the Reverend C.F. Routledge nearly a century ago.[13] This is not the place to go over this ground again but, in summary, it may be suggested that the western part of the chancel had already been constructed by the time of the arrival of St Augustine in AD 597.[14] It is made almost entirely of roughly laid Roman bricks, but it is not, as yet, possible to determine whether the main walls were built in the late Roman period (possibly part of a Roman villa)[15] or in the later sixth century. Only further excavation work will provide the answer. Wrapped around the western part of the earlier structure is the present nave of St Martin's Church (see Figure 11.2). The original walls, constructed in a late Roman technique, which can perhaps be described as *opus quasi vitatum*, and having small pilaster buttresses, survive almost to their full height. The Roman brick string-courses and the roughly coursed Tertiary sandstone are set in a coarse-grained sandy mortar which is salmon-pink in colour due to the use of crushed Roman brick in the mix. The building technique is very much in the Italian early Byzantine style,[16] and it seems reasonable to suggest that the nave of St Martin's was built by some of the Italian monks who came with St Augustine to Canterbury in 597.[17] Throughout the later Anglo-Saxon period, and right up to the eve of the Norman Conquest, when it was used as the base for a succession of suffragan bishops (the *Chorepiscopus*), St Martin's was an important extramural church.[18] By the late twelfth century, however, it was just one of the parish churches of the city and its only enlargement was a lengthening of the chancel in the thirteenth century, and the building of a very small west tower (above a porch) at the end of the fourteenth century.

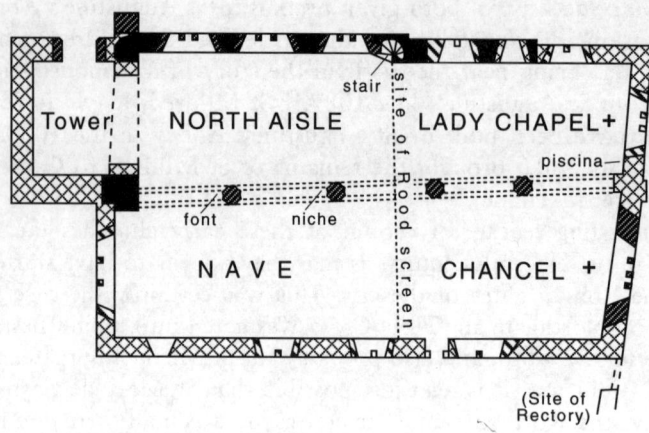

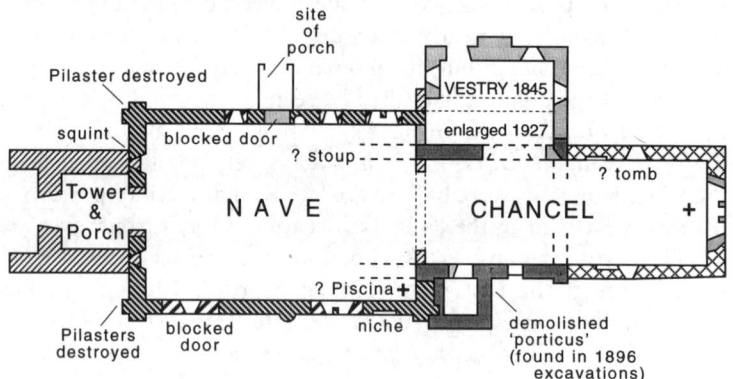

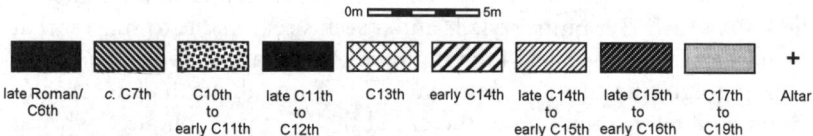

11.2 Structural analysis of St Alphege's and St Martin's churches

Recent research on the fabric of the nave of St Martin's has shown that the main quoins were made of a French limestone called *Calcaire Grossier*. This originates in the Paris basin, and is apparently only used elsewhere in late Roman contexts like Richborough Castle or in seventh-century churches like St Mary's or St Pancras in Canterbury.[19] Its seventh-century appearance must result from the reuse of material from Roman sites in the east Kent area, rather than from direct import from the Paris basin.

Below-ground archaeological remains of parish churches

Excavations have taken place in recent years at four parish churches in Canterbury. These were St Mary Bredin (1978 and 1980), St Margaret's (1986), All Saints (1986) and St George's (1991), and as a result of this much new light has been thrown on the post-Norman Conquest development of these churches.[20]

At the church of St George-the-Martyr, recent excavation work has uncovered the surviving foundations of the earliest phases of the church (see Figure 11.3). All of the first three phases must date to the late eleventh and early twelfth centuries, and they show that the church developed rapidly at the beginning. First, there was a simple rectangular nave (c.7.7 by 5 metres internally) with a small sanctuary to the east, which was surrounded by a slightly stilted apse. Soon after this a small north aisle was added to the church, and not long after that the whole of the eastern part of the church was demolished and rebuilt. The nave and north aisle were lengthened, and a new enlarged eastern apse was constructed, which was almost certainly in a tri-conch form, unique in England. On the north and east only the large rammed gravel foundation had survived, but, on the south (and incorporated into the later chancel wall), is the southern lobe of the lower part of the wall, made of large coursed flints. The curvature of the wall is too 'shallow' to allow it to continue around the whole apse, hence the reconstruction with three lobes.[21]

At all the other parish churches in Canterbury where the evidence has survived above ground, or where there has been an excavation, the original east end of the church encloses a small rectangular space, and this includes the three early chapels *en echelon* that were excavated at St Gregory's Priory in 1989–90.[22] In 1978 an excavation in the back garden of 16 Watling Street found part of the remains of the foundations of the two original phases of the church of St Mary Bredin (see Figure 11.4). The earliest church was of wood and this is confirmed by a rental of c.1180 that refers to an *ecclesia lignea*. A slightly later Christ Church rental, of c.1206, says that the church 'used to be made of wood', and the name of St Mary 'Bredin' perhaps refers to the use of boards for making the church. The second masonry phase comprised a

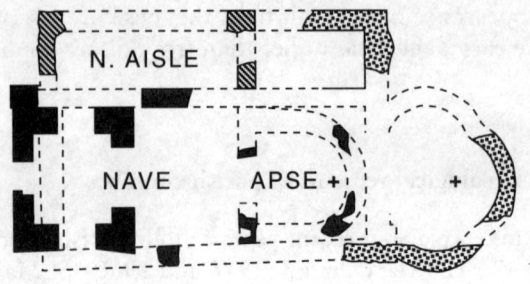

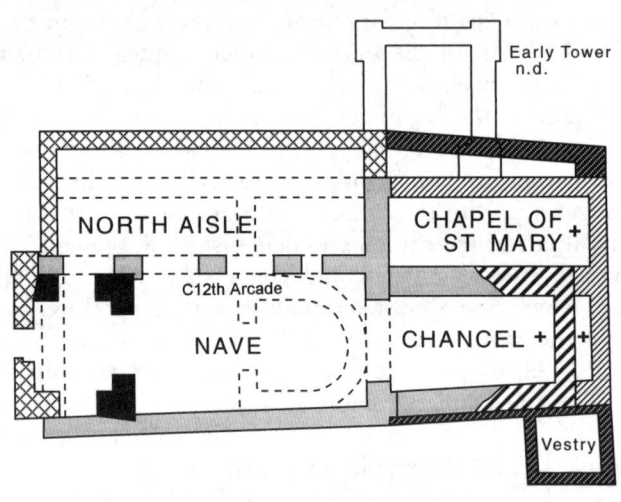

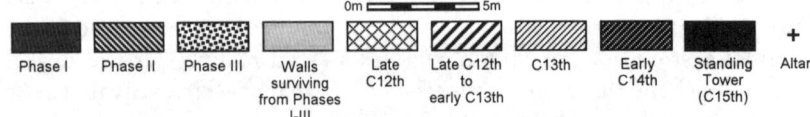

11.3 St George the Martyr: archaeological evidence and structural analysis, late eleventh to early fourteenth century

small rectangular chancel, and part of the north wall of a similar small rectangular chancel survives at the church of St Alphege.[23] Elsewhere in Canterbury later rebuilding of the chancel has destroyed the evidence above ground.

St Mary Bredin's Church

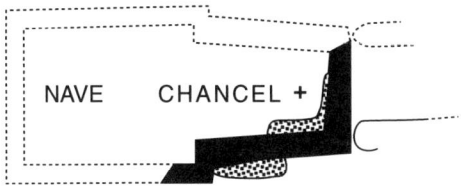

Site 1 (1978 excavation)

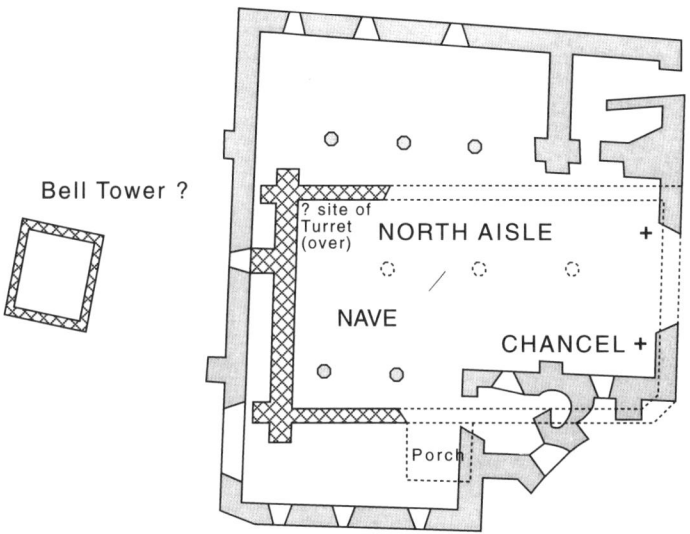

Site 2 (1980 excavation)

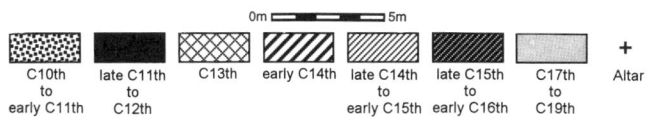

11.4 St Mary Bredin: archaeological evidence

At St Margaret's Church, the below-ground archaeology revealed a pair of narrow aisles on either side of the nave, that were probably added in the mid-twelfth century (see Figure 11.13). Also at St Margaret's,

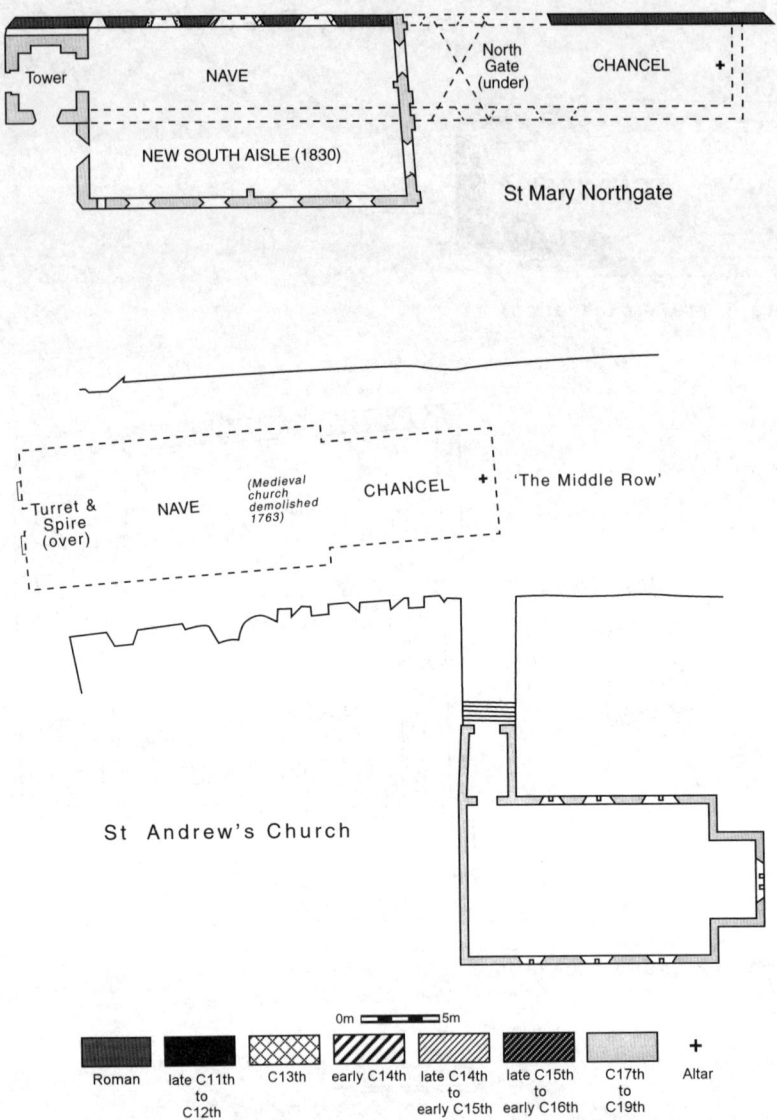

11.5 Structural analysis of St Mary Northgate and St Andrew's

a much-restored mid-twelfth-century west doorway survives, but the east end of the church was demolished and rebuilt in two stages (in 1771 and 1850), when the road was widened. The church of St Mary Magdalen (except for the tower) was pulled down in 1871, but early views of the interior show a later twelfth-century south arcade, indicat-

11.6 Early nineteenth-century view of the chancel of St Mary Northgate from the south (demolished, 1830)

ing that this church also received a south aisle at this time.[24] Finally, St Peter's Church has surviving fragments (including one complete arch) of the early twelfth-century north and south arcades.[25] It is also possible that All Saints Church received its north aisle in the twelfth century, but the excavation there was only on a small scale, and not able to prove this.[26] St Alphege may also have received a south aisle in the twelfth century, but there is no above-ground evidence for this.

Plainly, most of the churches in central Canterbury were being enlarged with aisles during the twelfth century as the population expanded. By contrast, however, the peripheral churches, like St Martin's, St Dunstan's, St Mildred's and probably St Paul's, did not acquire aisles at this time. One oddity is the church of St Mary Northgate (see Figure 11.5), where a new nave was built immediately north west of the old church alongside the inside of the city wall.[27] The original church, now totally destroyed, was above the gateway (see Figure 11.6) and must have become the chancel at this time with many steps down into the nave, making the plan of this church one of the longest, in relation to its width, in Britain. By the end of the twelfth century, as we have seen, all 22 of Canterbury's parish churches were in being, and no other new churches were to be built subsequently.

Thirteenth-century rebuilding and enlargement

As is often the case in English parish churches, the first major development of the thirteenth century was the enlargement, or total rebuilding, of the chancel. We certainly find this in Canterbury, and quite often it was soon followed by the erection of a side chapel (usually a Lady chapel, as later wills tell us), and sometimes by the addition of a small tower. At St Martin's the chancel was doubled in length eastwards but no chapel was added. An altar was, however, tucked into the south-east corner of the nave (from the evidence of the piscina). St Peter's Church has a greatly enlarged chancel (with a double piscina), and a Lady chapel on the north, which was rebuilt later (see Figure 11.7). At St George's (Figure 11.8) the excavations have shown that the chancel was extended eastwards in two stages in the thirteenth century, with the second stage being contemporary with the building of a northern Lady chapel (see Figure 11.3). Shortly afterwards, a small north tower seems to have been added to this chapel. At St Alphege's, on the other hand (for topographic reasons), a new much larger nave and chancel were built to the south, and the old chancel was lengthened and converted into the Lady chapel (see Figure 11.2). The old nave became the north aisle, and a small tower was added at its west end. At the same time as all this work was going on, the archbishop, who owned the church, was completing the building of a huge new great hall complex (the second largest in Britain) a few feet away from the east end of the church, on the other side of the street. Perhaps the same workmen were involved.[28]

At St Mildred's Church, a north chapel was built on to the chancel and, to the west of this, a small low tower was added which survived until its demolition in 1836 (see Figure 11.9). Drawings of the church before this date, show that the tower barely extended above the nave roof.[29] All Saints Church, in the High Street, also had a Lady chapel, on the north-east, but here the tower was added above a stone porch on the south side of the nave (see Figure 11.7). The tower porch was demolished for street widening in 1769–70 (see Fig. 11.10), and partially excavated in 1986.[30] The rest of the church was totally rebuilt by Rickman in 1828, closed in 1902, and demolished in 1937. Even where chancels were not enlarged, new windows, usually lancets, were inserted. A good surviving example of this is on the north-east side of St Dunstan's Church.

A much more remarkable discovery, during the 1978 and 1980 excavations on the 'Marlowe' car-park sites, was that the church of St Mary Bredin was moved about 160 feet to the north-east when it was rebuilt in the later thirteenth century.[31] The original church, built of wood, has already been referred to. It was rebuilt in stone in the late twelfth century,

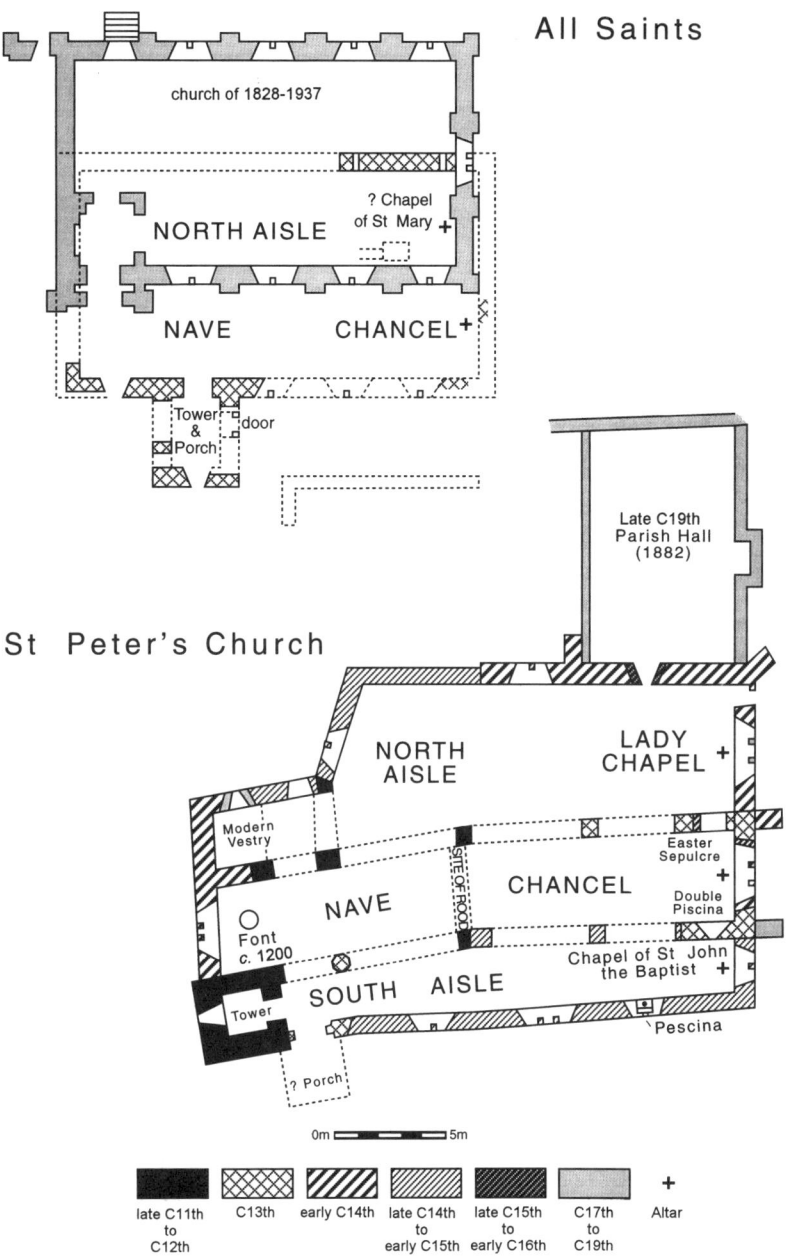

11.7 Structural analysis of All Saints' and St Peter's churches

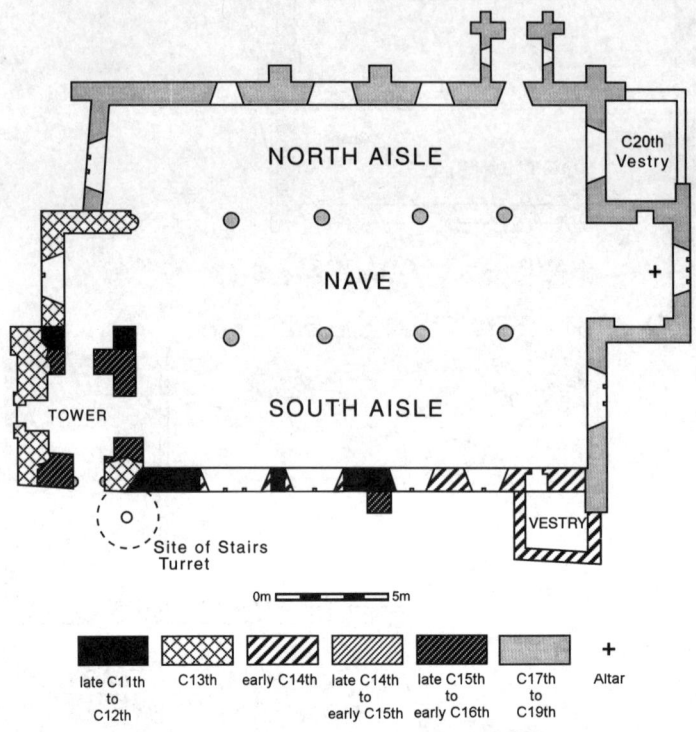

11.8 Structural analysis of St George the Martyr, fifteenth century to 1942

and then, in the early thirteenth century given an extended chancel (see Figure 11.4). Then sometime later in the thirteenth century, the move took place and a completely new church, with a contemporary north aisle was built on the Rose Lane frontage surrounded by a small graveyard. This church was also totally demolished in 1866, and in the following year a new large church was built around it, which was itself destroyed in the 1942 bombing of Canterbury. Due to the post-war widening of Rose Lane, only the west end of the church could be excavated in 1980, ahead of the redevelopment of the area. These excavations were, however, able to confirm that the buttressed west wall of the church was built in the thirteenth century (reusing, in the rubble work, a fragment of a late twelfth-century capital), though all the floor levels inside the church had been destroyed by later burial vaults. Pre-1866 views of the church also show a later thirteenth-century triple lancet in the east wall and a double lancet on the south side of the chancel.[32]

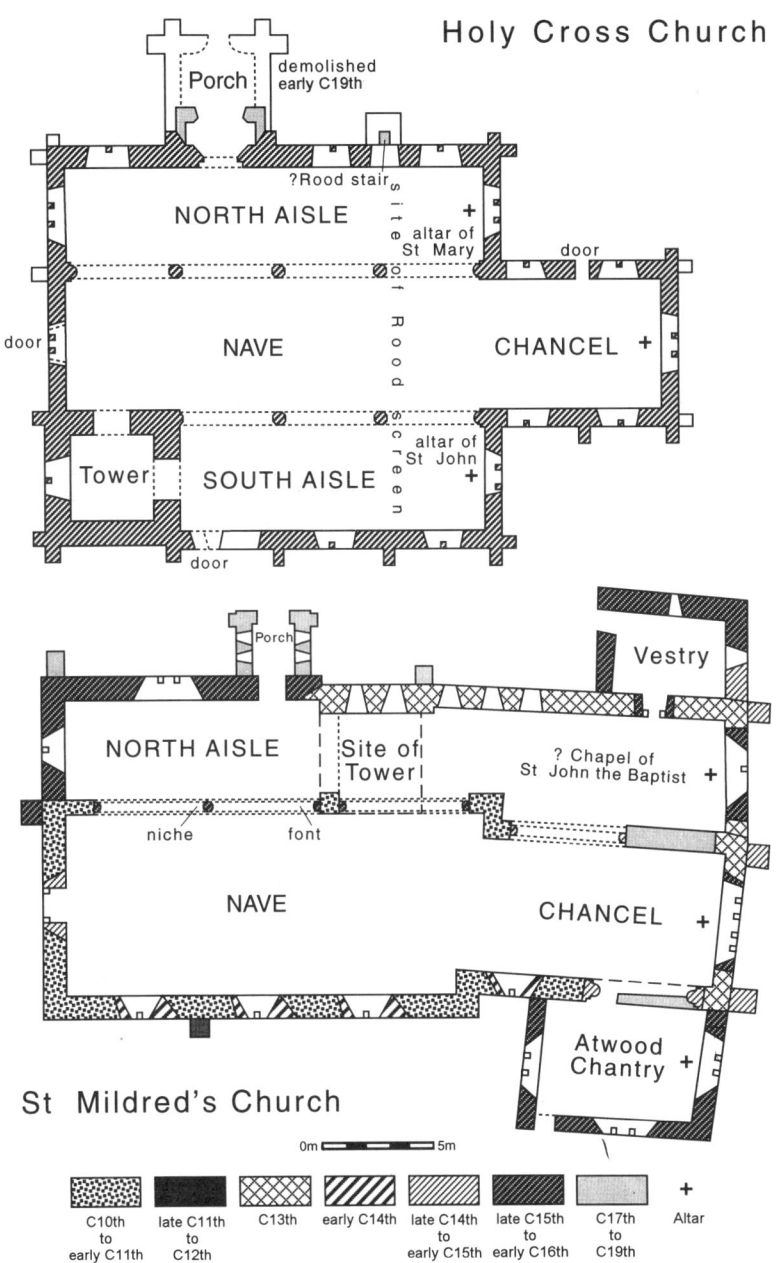

11.9 Structural analysis of Holy Cross and St Mildred's churches

11.10   Mid-eighteenth-century engraving of All Saints' Church from the south-east

Of added interest for this new church is the documentation by William Somner, in the early seventeenth century, of the 'name, effigy and coat [of arms], being Argent, lions rampant, azure' of Thomas Chiche in the west window of the church, 'as the coat also is of stone in one corner of the chancel of this church'.[33] Thomas Chiche, who owned the nearby manor of Dane John from the mid-thirteenth century, was one of the bailiffs of the city for much of the time between 1254 and 1280,[34] and it is highly likely that it was this man who paid for the church to be rebuilt in about the third quarter of the thirteenth century. The coat of arms may, however, be a later medieval addition, by a later member of the Chiche family.

Another church that was almost completely rebuilt in the late thirteenth century was St Paul's outside the Burgate (see Figure 11.11). This church, which was close to its patron, St Augustine's Abbey, was heavily restored in the mid-nineteenth century and given a new south aisle. Before this there was only a small nave, chancel and west tower, with a much larger south aisle and Lady chapel to the east of it. All show signs of later thirteenth-century rebuilding and we have unique documentary evidence for 60 feet of the north wall of the church being rebuilt $3\frac{1}{2}$

St Paul's Church

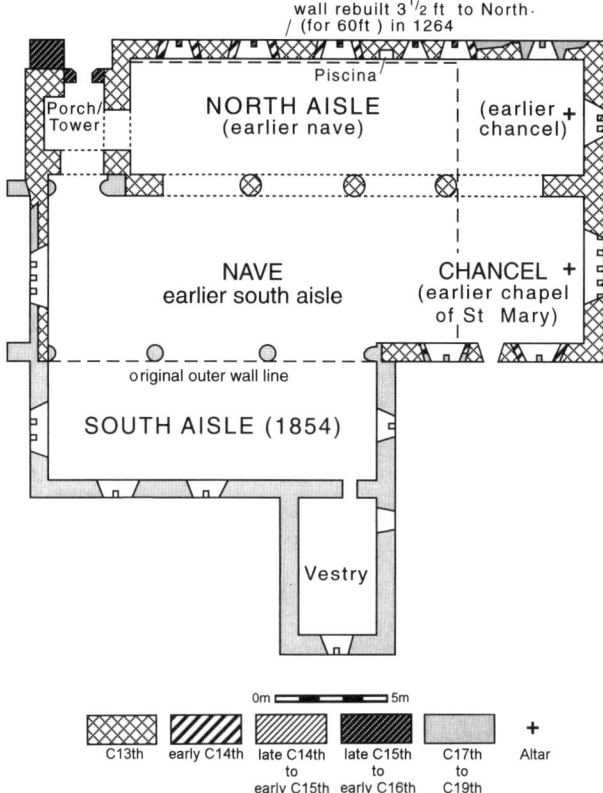

11.11 Structural analysis of St Paul's Church

feet further north (into the street) in 1264.[35] The east windows of the chancel and Lady chapel still contain fine geometric tracery of the late thirteenth century, and we can almost certainly attribute this rebuilding to another prominent Canterbury citizen and lawyer, Master Hamo Doge,[36] who was also rector of St Paul's from at least the 1260s.[37]

Hamo Doge was an almost exact contemporary of Thomas Chiche, and like Chiche he was involved in many local affairs. He was a friend of the abbot of St Augustine's, Roger of Chichester (who died in 1272), and when Doge himself died (sometime after 1280), he was buried beside the abbot in the abbey church. Much earlier than this (by 1252), Hamo Doge was able to found and endow a chantry at his own house in the eastern part of the city. The chantry chapel was also in the church of St Paul's (almost certainly in the new chapel, south of the chancel), and it seems clear that the major rebuilding of St Paul's Church after *c.*1264 was partly to incorporate the new chantry chapel. One unusual feature, which still survives, is the use of Purbeck marble for the whole of the pillar (moulded capital, column drum and base) between the chancel and chapel. The two similar pillars to the west are made only of Caen stone. The fine geometric tracery of the two east windows has already been mentioned, and we are again fortunate to have a record, made in the early seventeenth century, that 'in the chancelle-Windowes-foote is this remembrance of Mr Hamon Doge, in an ancient character or letter'.[38] William Somner's records of various inscribed and heraldic panels, as well as pictorial scenes, in the stained glass windows of several Canterbury churches constitute a unique record, as most of this glass was destroyed soon afterwards in the Commonwealth period.

Both St Paul's and St Mary Bredin churches are able to show us, therefore, that the owner of the most important house in a parish was still partly able to look on the parish church as his own in the late thirteenth century. This echoes the developments in many rural parishes, where a parish church that had been founded and built beside the manor house in the late eleventh or twelfth century was rebuilt with a fine new chancel and flanking chapels in the late thirteenth century. The finest example of this near Canterbury is at Chartham church, where the monks of Christ Church built a magnificent new chancel and flanking transept chapels at the very end of the thirteenth century.[39] This chancel still retains not only its magnificent 'split cusp' (Kentish) tracery in its many windows, but also much of its fine stained glass.

Fourteenth-century developments

In the early fourteenth century, many parish churches in Canterbury received fine new traceried windows, and no doubt most of them were filled with glass. Perhaps the best surviving example of large new windows of this date can be found on the south side of St Mildred's Church (three windows in the nave and one in the chancel), where the windows are unusual in having square heads above tracery lights. Other surviving examples can be seen in, for example, the churches of St Martin, St Alphege and St Peter, and along the north side of the recently rebuilt St Paul's church (see above). At other churches, the windows have been destroyed in the last 150 or so years, but earlier pictorial evidence records them. On the south side of St George's Church there were some new windows in the nave as well as a rebuilt south chancel wall that

11.12 Drawing of St Mary Bredman from the north-east in 1788, by Francis Grose

incorporated two new windows and a sedilia.[40] The 1991 excavation was able to show that on the south-east side of the chancel was a small contemporary vestry.

A drawing by Francis Grose, made in 1788 (see Figure 11.12), shows that the north side of the chancel of St Mary Bredman church contained a fine three-light window with a gable above.[41] This contains early fourteenth-century 'split cusp' tracery, while the window in the nave just to the west has early Perpendicular tracery.

St Dunstan's Church is unusual in having a completely new south aisle of the early fourteenth century (see Figure 11.13). This no doubt indicates population expansion at this time on the extreme west side of the city. St Dunstan's also acquired, in 1330, a small chantry chapel

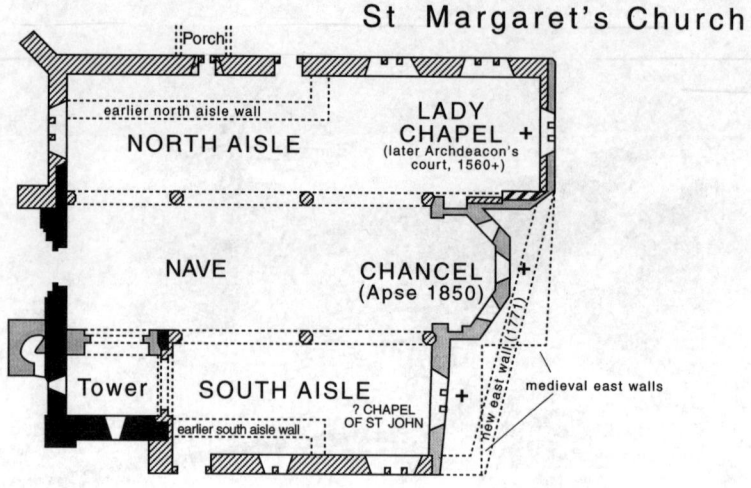

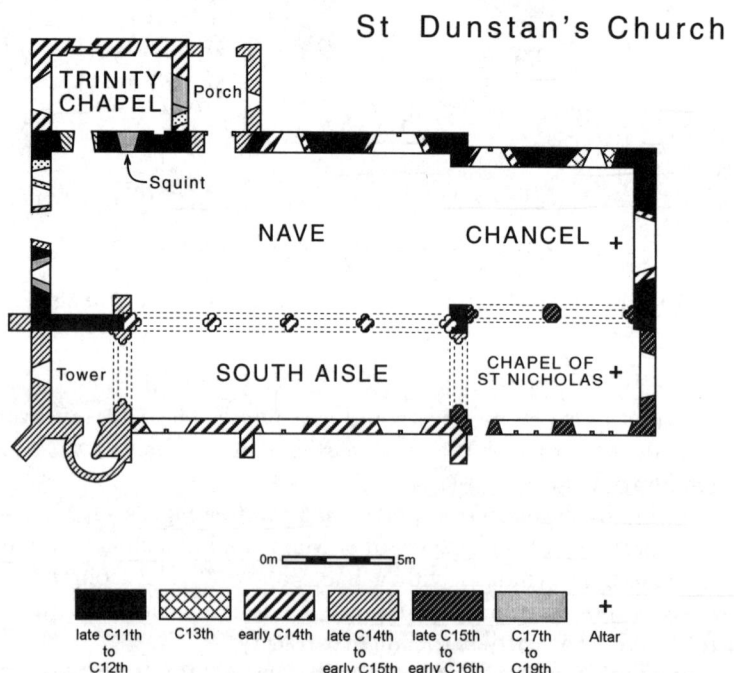

11.13 Structural analysis of St Margaret's and St Dunstan's churches

of the Holy Trinity, which was built on to the north-west side of the nave near the important street corner on the main road out of the city to London.

At St Peter's Church, the west end of the fabric was rebuilt and realigned in the early fourteenth century (to give more room to the street to the west) (see Figure 11.7), and three new three-light east and west windows were inserted. The upper part of the tower was also rebuilt at this time and, unusually, it still contains its two original fourteenth-century bells.[42] The north-east (Lady) chapel was also considerably enlarged and, shortly afterwards, the eastern part of the north aisle was greatly widened on the north. While this was being done, the two eastern piers were removed, and very wide arches were put in instead, making this into a large open space (perhaps for preaching).[43] The final stage of the rebuilding at St Peter's, which probably did not take place until near the middle of the fourteenth century, was the rebuilding of the whole of the south aisle east of the thirteenth-century south doorway (see Figure 11.7). The aisle still remained very narrow in width, but the eastern chapel of St John the Baptist was extended eastwards. As all this work was completed, new crown-post roofs were built to cover the various irregular spaces.

St Peter's Church is a good example of how a small church in a very restricted space was enlarged piecemeal in the thirteenth and fourteenth centuries to cope with the rising population and with the need for additional chapels. An even more tightly restricted church was St Andrew's, which stood in the centre of the High Street, in that section of it now called The Parade (see Figure 11.5). This church only had a nave and chancel, with the Middle Row (and Archbishop Abbots' conduit from 1620) beyond it, and the whole lot was demolished in 1763.[44] We do, however, have a small mid-eighteenth-century vignette of the church from the west showing its west doorway, flanked by blind arcading, all perhaps of the thirteenth century.[45] Above the west window (with a clock in it) is a crenellated parapet, behind which is an octagonal timber turret and spire. For the late medieval and immediately post-Reformation history of the church, we are lucky to have surviving churchwardens' accounts,[46] while a whole series of wills of just before the Reformation tells us much about the fittings.[47] Another church in the centre of Canterbury that was considerably rebuilt in the middle part of the fourteenth century was St Margaret's. New north and south arcades were built and the aisle walls were moved outwards.[48] A rebuilt Lady chapel flanked the chancel on the north,[49] while the chapel of St John the Baptist was to the south (see Figure 11.13). Its east end, along with that of the chancel, was cut off in 1771, to allow carriages to turn more easily into the Fountain Inn opposite.

In the middle years of the fourteenth century, the great plague struck the city, and no doubt a third to a half of the population died. The only clear evidence in the churches for depopulation, however, is on the south-eastern part of the city, where the church of St John the Baptist (also called St John the Poor) was abandoned, and the parish united with that of St Mary-de-Castro to the west. The nearby church of St Edmund Ridingate also disappeared at this time, and its parish was joined with St Mary Bredin to the north. Neither of these sites have been excavated, although St Edmund's Church may have been immediately above the Roman Ridingate, the foundations of which have been fully excavated.[50] The final traces of this church were, therefore, probably destroyed when the city walls were rebuilt here in the late fourteenth century.[51]

In 1363, a Royal Commission of inquiry had found that 'the walls of Canterbury are for the most part fallen because of age and the stones thereof carried away and the ditches under the walls obstructed'.[52] As a result of this, and because of a renewed threat of invasion by the French, work on rebuilding the walls and gates started in 1378. This commenced at Westgate, and helped by large donations from the archbishop, Simon of Sudbury (who was murdered in 1381), the gate was rebuilt on a grand scale. The old church of the Holy Cross, which had been built on top of the old Roman gateway, was rebuilt on a new site, just inside the city walls on the south, surrounded by its own graveyard (see Figures 11.9 and 11.14). This is a rare example in Kent of a completely new church of the later Middle Ages.[53] Unfortunately, the church was mutilated during the nineteenth century, both by restoration work and by the widening of the road around it on the north and east.[54] Despite this, there is still a fine uniform interior (now redundant, and used as a council chamber since 1978), with north and south aisles of four bays (the tower is built above the western bay of the latter), and a two-bay chancel beyond. At the east ends of the aisles were the usual altars of Our Lady (to the north) and of St John the Evangelist (south), and when the rood screen was built in the early sixteenth century, it ran across the whole building one bay west of these altars.[55]

The rebuilding of this church in c.1379–80,[56] shows that the population of the parish, along the western boundary of the city, was still in need of a fairly large church despite the depopulation of previous decades. Almost no other rebuilding work is, however, known to have taken place on the Canterbury churches after this until the later fifteenth century. The one very small-scale exception is the addition of a west tower, with a porch beneath, to the already very ancient church of St Martin in about 1397 (see Figure 11.2).[57]

11.14 Late eighteenth-century engraving of Holy Cross Church from the north-east. The west gate is to the right

The late Middle Ages and early Tudor period

As in many parts of England, the last half century or so before the Reformation saw renewed building work at many parish churches. None of this was on a very large scale in Canterbury, but it is, on the other hand, often well documented. In this time, almost all churches must have had rood screens and lofts inserted, and there is good documentary evidence for the 1519 screen at the Holy Cross Church. Evidence for now vanished screens and lofts (stairs and doorways) also survives at St Peter's, St Alphege's and, until the last century, at St Mildred's.[58] A contemporary drawing of the chancel arch in St Andrew's Church surrounded by the rood screen and loft, can be found inside the back cover of the churchwardens' account book.[59] It also shows the line of candles along the top of the rood loft, which are mentioned in a will of 1508.[60]

Among other additions of the period are some small bell-towers. Two of these now survive at churches where the rest of the building has been demolished. The tower at St George's, which was inserted into the west

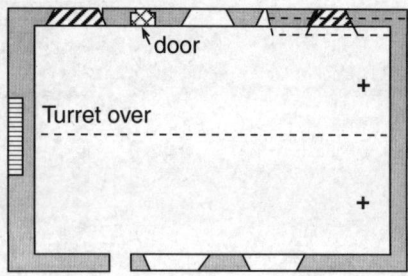

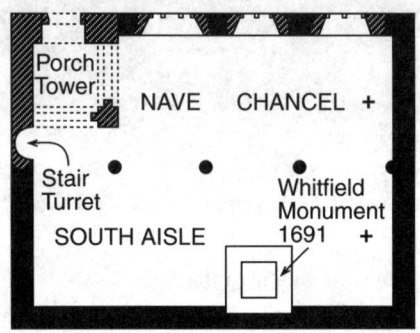

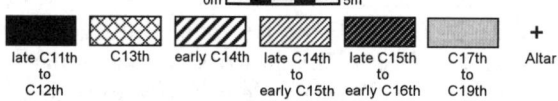

11.15 Structural analysis of St Mary Bredman and St Mary Magdalen churches

end of the nave, was very heavily restored in 1955 after wartime damage, and shows little of its original fabric. That at St Mary Magdalen, on the other hand, which was built in about 1501,[61] has a tower porch made with an ashlar facing of large Ragstone blocks on its northern (i.e. street-frontage) side (see Figure 11.15). Ashlar masonry is also used for the top part of the west side, above the roof line of the timber-framed buildings which flanked it on the west, but the effect has now been destroyed by the removal of these buildings after destruction in the Second World War. The windows into the tower are all cinquefoil-headed with square hood-moulds. Views of the church before its demolition in 1871 show that there were similar windows along the north side of the church and that this wall of the church (as well as the tower) was rebuilt around 1500. There are also two fine moulded arches which led into the west end of the nave, and one of the features of this period is the making of elaborately moulded new arcades.

At St Alphege's, the whole of the earlier arcade between the nave and chancel and the north aisle and Lady chapel was removed, and an elegant new five-bay arcade was put in instead (see Figure 11.2). It has octagonal piers with concave faces, and the arches have double hollow-chamfers. On the west face of one of the columns is an image niche below which is a memorial brass engraved with a heraldic shield inscribed '*Gaude Prude Thoma per quem fit ista columna*'. This exceptional survival ties in very well with Thomas Prowde's will of 1468 which gives 'to the building of a column in the church, as much money as necessary to build the same'.[62] The building of this new arcade is clearly contemporary with the rebuilding of the north wall of the north aisle with a moulded plinth and three new three-light Perpendicular windows with square hoods. Just to the east of them is a contemporary stair to the rood-loft which is entered via a doorway surmounted by an ogee canopy with a finial, crockets and head stops. The main four-light east window in the chancel was built inside the thirteenth century one at a slightly later date.[63] In addition to this, the church acquired a new font in the late fifteenth century, and all the roofs were rebuilt. There was also a new north doorway into the tower from the street.

At St Mildred's Church, a new north aisle was added to the nave, west of the thirteenth-century tower (see Figure 11.9). This has a moulded plinth and, above it, a three-light window with round-headed lights all under a square hood-mould. In the external spandrels to these lights are some unusual carved heads. To the east of it is a fine new doorway, which still contains its original pair of doors. The arcade between the nave and north aisle, including that into the tower, is very similar to that at St Alphege's, and the western pier also has an almost identical niche to that at St Alphege's. Again, we are lucky in having a will, of 1486, which refers to 'the work and reparation of the nave of the church, and a new vestry'.[64] This 'new vestry' also survives on the north side of the church, and it too has its original window and door into the north chapel. The east window in this chapel and the main five-light east window in the chancel, were also rebuilt in the fifteenth century, as were the roofs in the church and, as at St Alphege's, a new font was put in the church.

A fine early sixteenth century addition to St Mildred's Church was a new chantry chapel on the south-east side of the chancel (see Figure 11.9). This is built with an attractive chequer-work pattern on the outer walls, and an original consecration cross survives on a large block on the east wall. Once again, the side windows (in the south and west walls) are of three lights with rounded heads under square hood-moulds. The east window, however, contains Perpendicular tracery, and there is a wide four-centred arch between the chapel and the south-east side of the chancel. Once again it is William Somner who records that it was Thomas Atwood 'that lived in Hen.8 days' who 'built the South-side Chancell or Chapell, for a peculiar place of Sepulture for himself and his family, divers of whom lye here interred, under faire grave-stones, sometimes inlaid with brasee, all not worne but shamefully torne away, even founders and all'. Somner also recorded the inscriptions in the stained glass windows, which mention Thomas (At)Wood and Margaret, his wife, the daughter of John Moyle.[65] None of this glass, or any of the leger stones survive, but we know that Thomas Atwood lived nearby in the parish and was five times mayor of Canterbury between 1477 and 1495, while Thomas 'Wode' was mayor in 1504 and 1512. It was perhaps the latter who built the chantry chapel 'in Henry 8th days'.[66]

A much more famous chantry chapel is the Roper chantry on the south-east side of St Dunstan's Church. This was founded in 1402, but the chapel was rebuilt in brick in its present form about 1524 by John Roper (see Figure 11.13). This chapel of St Nicholas is now famous because the burial vault beneath it contains the head of Thomas More, which was brought here secretly, soon after the Reformation, along with the body of More's daughter, Margaret, who had married William Roper.[67]

In several other Canterbury churches work was also being undertaken on the fabric and fittings at this time, though the surviving evidence for this is not very complete. For example, an early sixteenth-century doorway in the north wall of the Lady chapel at St Peter's Church tells us that there must have been an early vestry here, the site of which is now covered by the 1882 parish hall. The best surviving evidence for late-medieval work in the now vanished churches comes, however, from the documentary material, especially wills and churchwardens' accounts.[68] To take just one example, money was left in 1496 towards making a new window at St Mary Bredin.[69] There is also some evidence for the state of a few of the churches in Archbishop Warham's visitation of September 1511. Thus, at St Dunstan's Church we are told that the windows and glass are 'sore in decay' by the default of St Gregory's Priory, while the Trinity chapel there (on the north-west corner of the nave) was also in 'sore decay', and the provision of a chantry priest was not being maintained to sing three masses a week. This was the responsibility of the Master of the Poor Priests' Hospital.[70] Despite this, there is much evidence that the churches were, on the whole, being maintained, and increasingly filled up with images, lights, organs and pews. There is also much evidence for the burial of the more prominent citizens within the church itself.

Graveyards

The earliest map of Canterbury to show the site of graveyards in and around the city is the W. and H. Doidge map of 1752. This shows graveyards beside ten churches: St Dunstan's, Holy Cross, St Peter's, All Saints, St Alphege's, St George's, St Margaret's, St Mary Bredin's, St Martin's and St Mildred's (see Figure 11.1). It also shows a large graveyard on the site of the demolished church of St Mary-de-Castro (and used by the churches of St Mary Bredman, St Andrew and St Mary Magdalen, which did not have their own graveyards). As well as this, there are detached graveyards for the churches of St Mary Northgate and St Paul, both of which are post-medieval.[71]

This rather muddled situation was caused by the Dissolution when the graveyards (lay cemeteries) at all the religious houses were closed. The two most important were to the south of the cathedral and of St Augustine's Abbey, but there were also large cemeteries at St Gregory's Priory,[72] St Sepulchre's Priory and the Greyfriars, Blackfriars and Austin friars. Burial in all these cemeteries is documented in many wills of the fifteenth and early sixteenth centuries.[73] These wills also tell us that people were being buried within virtually all the churches of Canterbury, including the churches of the religious houses and many of the hospital chapels. They also partially confirm the post-medieval evidence of which churches had graveyards and which did not, at least in the late medieval period.[74] As might be expected the seven churches in the densely populated centre of the city and above the gates did not have churchyards (St Mary Magdalen, St Michael Burgate, St Paul, St Andrew, St Mary Northgate, St Mary Bredman and St Mary Queningate), while the churches in the more open area of the city did have graveyards (St Dunstan, Holy Cross, St Martin, St Mildred, St Mary-de-Castro, and St Sepulchre). We also know that St Margaret's had a small graveyard on the west,[75] and a tiny graveyard surrounded St Mary Bredin.[76] Four of the central churches (St Alphege, St George, All Saints and St Peter) had graveyards alongside them by the seventeenth century, but it is not yet certain whether there were medieval graveyards there. This seems unlikely, however. We certainly hear, at St Alphege, for example, of parishioners requesting burial 'within the holy ground and precincts of Christchurch' (i.e. the lay cemetery of the cathedral) and at the nearby Blackfriars church and cemetery in the few decades before the Dissolution.

The even larger lay cemetery of St Augustine's Abbey was a favourite place of burial, and there are wills requesting burial there by parishioners from St Mary Bredman, St Andrew, St Alphege, St Michael (Burgate), St George, All Saints, St Mildred, St Paul, St Mary Magdalen and Holy Cross.[77] This shows that prominent citizens, at least, were able to get burial at St Augustine's, even if they lived in parishes with their own graveyard. Burials came not only from St Augustine's own churches, but also from those belonging to the archbishop, the cathedral priory, and St Gregory's Priory.

St Gregory's Priory, as might be expected, acted as the cemetery for the nearby St Mary Northgate, but requests for burial in the church or churchyard came from other parishes as well. In the same way, St George's parishioners often used the nearby cemetery of the Augustinian friary (White Friars), but so did other parishes. The same was also true for the Black and Grey friars and we even hear of one request for burial 'in the cloister of the House of the Friars Preachers [Black Friars], near the grave of my son' by a St Alphege parishioner in 1481.[78]

The evidence from wills alone should be treated with caution as they only tell us about the important people in the city. For the ordinary citizen, however, it seems likely that burial was in the graveyard most closely associated with his or her own parish if it did not have its own churchyard. So, for example, the lay cemetery at St Gregory's Priory was certainly the main place of burial for all the parishioners of St Mary Northgate.[79]

Sixteenth-century abandonments and parochial topography

After the Dissolution and Reformation, four parish churches were abandoned, and their parishes were joined to the neighbouring ones. These churches were St Sepulchre's, which from the late fourteenth century was already joined to St Mary Bredin; St Mary-de-Castro, which was joined to St Mildred's; St Michael's Burgate which was joined to St Mary Magdalen, and St Mary Queningate. The last named church had already, by 1492, lost most of its parochial area, when this land was taken into the precincts of Christ Church Priory. Despite this, wills tell us that this church was still in use as late as 1514, and it probably went on being used until the Reformation, though no date of its final abandonment is known.[80] St Michael's parish also lost much land to Christ Church Priory in the fifteenth century and, in 1516, the benefices of St Michael and St George (both of which belonged to the cathedral priory) were united. The church itself was perhaps rebuilt just inside the Burgate on the north side of the street in the fifteenth century.[81] It was probably demolished, except for its small west tower, in 1525, when the Burgate was completely rebuilt,[82] and by the late sixteenth century all the parochial land was taken into St Mary Magdalen parish.[83]

St Sepulchre's Priory, as a Benedictine nunnery, was dissolved in 1536[84] and demolished soon afterwards. This included the demolition of the parochial nave and the large extramural parish of St Sepulchre's was subsequently joined to the intramural one of St Mary Bredin.[85] Finally, St Mary-de-Castro, too, was abandoned after the Reformation, and its quite large parochial area was taken into St Mildred. The chancel was still standing in the early seventeenth century[86] and, as we have seen, its large graveyard was used after the Reformation for the parishes of St Mary Bredman, St Andrew, and St Mary Magdalen.

By the nineteenth century, when the first accurate maps of the parishes of Canterbury were made,[87] there is a mixture of small city centre parishes, those at All Saints, St Alphege, St Andrew, St George, St Margaret, St Peter and St Mary Bredman, and a series of larger areas like the parish of St Mildred, mentioned above, which contains the medieval parishes of St Mildred, St Mary-de-Castro and St John. There are also still a large number of extra-parochial areas such as the precincts of the castle, the hospitals and the cathedral. In addition, there are extra-parochial areas for the precincts of the religious houses and other areas such as the land belonging to the Black Prince's chantry and the archbishop's Staplegate borough. These also, remarkably, survived intact and extra-parochial until the later nineteenth century.

It seems likely that the urban parochial areas came into existence between the late eleventh and mid-twelfth century. Their boundaries are already being referred to in rentals from the later twelfth century.[88] Some of the earliest churches, as we have seen, were associated with the six main gates of the city, and it was around these gates that the ward system for the city was created. Urry did not believe that the date of the ward system was any earlier than the mid-twelfth century,[89] but their unique name, *bertha*, perhaps suggests that they are late Anglo-Saxon in origin, and that groups of parishes relate to them thus:

Northgate	St Mary, St Alphege
Burgate	St Michael, St Mary Queningate, St Mary Magdalen, St Paul
Newingate	St George, St Andrew
Ridingate	St Edmund, St Mary Bredin, St John, St Sepulchre
Worthgate	St Mary-de-Castro, St Mildred, St Margaret
Westgate	Holy Cross, St Peter, All Saints, St Mary Bredman, St Helen, (St Dunstan).

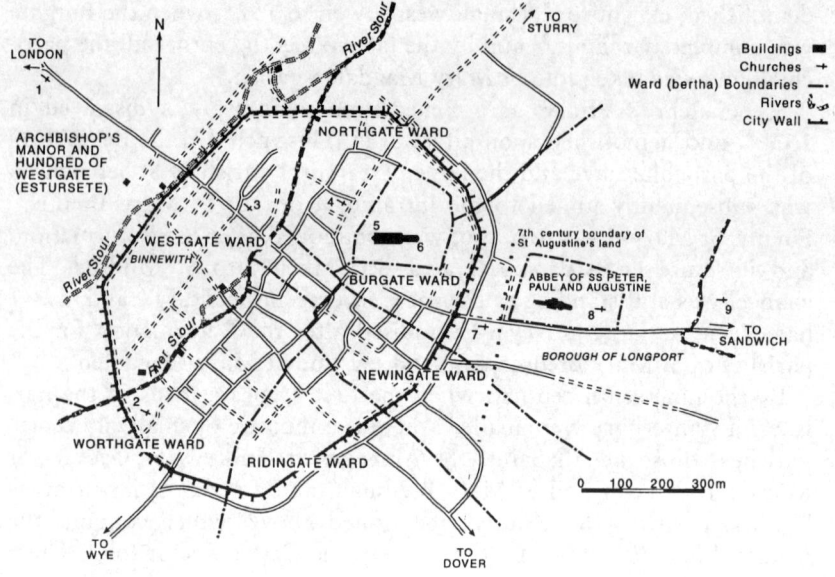

1. St Dunstan's Church
2. St Mildred's Church
3. St Peter's Church
4. St Alphege's Church
5. St Saviour (Christ Church)
6. Church of St John the Baptist
7. St Paul's (? Chapel)
8. St Pancras's Church
9. St Martin's Church

11.16   Town plan of Canterbury c.1050

The parish boundaries do not often follow the ward boundaries inside the city walls (they are also much confused by later medieval precincts), but this is perhaps due to a rationalisation of the parish boundaries in the twelfth century (see Figure 11.16).

Outside the city walls, in the large area of the County Borough to the south and east of the city, the plan is slightly more straightforward. We know that this area was attached to the city from the late Anglo-Saxon period at least,[90] and after the Norman Conquest it was divided up into three main wedge-shaped areas, roughly separated from each other by the main Roman roads to Sandwich and Dover. These three areas belonged to the archbishop (to the north east),[91] St Augustine's Abbey (to the east, and called the borough of Longport), and the king (to the south east). This latter area was clearly that attached to the castle (later the manor of Dungeon or 'Dane John') and it was soon divided up into small sub-manorial units called Dungeon, Staplegate, Stuppington and Merton. It became the parish of St Sepulchre's. St Augustine's large extramural manor of Longport became the parish of St Paul. The church, as we have seen, was always closely connected with the abbey, even when it was being rebuilt by Hamo Doge in the later thirteenth century.

Finally, the archbishop's area to the north east of the city has a more complicated history, and by soon after the Norman Conquest (if not before) it was divided into two main areas: the manor of Colton (or Barton) which ran northwards from the Northgate on either side of the main road to Sturry, and the larger manor of Caldecote to the east. Colton manor was given by Archbishop Lanfranc to his monks at Christ Church Priory, after he had cut precincts out of it for St John's Hospital and St Gregory's Priory. This became the parish of St Mary Northgate. The eastern area of Caldecote manor, with a smaller unit (a yoke) called 'Wic' beyond it,[92] was retained by the archbishop and attached to his large manor of Westgate. This area was then made the parish of St Martin. The archbishop's manor of Westgate, which was immediately to the west of the River Stour outside the city walls was, from the late eleventh century, outside the jurisdiction of the city (see Figure 11.16). It contained the parish of St Dunstan, as well as a section of Holy Cross parish 'without'.[93]

One final extramural area should also be mentioned. This is the area to the south-west of the city outside Worthgate. Most of this belonged to another section of the archbishop's manor of Westgate, and was in the parish of Thanington Without. A smaller area immediately outside the city walls, around the northern part of Wincheap was, however, part of St Mildred's parish.

In summary, we see the parochial system developing rapidly in the late eleventh and early twelfth centuries in relation to the manorial system outside the city walls, and perhaps in relation to the ward system within the walls. There are many parallels here with the City of London, and Brooke's conclusion that the ward boundaries are slightly older than the parishes seems to fit the rather tenuous evidence best. He also makes the point that: 'if the wards were entirely stable before the parish boundaries began to take their final shape, or vice versa, we should expect much closer coincidence between the two: the divergences are eloquent testimony that in some measure they grew up together'.[94] It is therefore clear that the urban parish churches and the parishes of Canterbury are a phenomenon of the immediate post-Conquest period, even though the more peripheral churches like St Martin's, St Dunstan's and St Mildred's were built earlier. The parish boundaries in the extramural area must also relate directly to the earlier manorial boundaries, as we have seen. Inside the Roman city walls, however, the parish boundaries must have been defined and worked out in the period of rapid church-building and population growth following the arrival of Lanfranc in 1070. By the early twelfth century, the process was complete.

From the sixteenth century to the present day, the story of Canterbury's churches and their parishes has been an equally complicated one of decline and destruction, which needs a paper in its own right. One can, however, add that the churches which have survived until the 1970s are now looked after better than ever before, and that the below-ground archaeological work of the Canterbury Archaeological Trust is uncovering more and more of the early history of these churches.

Acknowledgements

Detailed surveys of all the surviving churches have been made by the writer in recent years for the Canterbury Diocesan Advisory Committee, and these form the basis for the central part of this chapter. Copies may be obtained from Diocesan House. I am also extremely grateful to Dr Nigel Ramsay and Mrs Margaret Sparks for their many helpful comments on an earlier draft of this text.

My wife, Veronica, has laboured much, under difficult circumstances, to produce this word-processed text from a messy handwritten original. Without her help, this chapter would never have been written.

Notes

1. W. Urry, Canterbury under the Angevin Kings (1967), 208. For more detailed notes on each of the surviving churches, see T. Tatton-Brown, 'Churches in and around Canterbury', *Archaeologia Cantiana*, 114 (1994), 189–235.
2. L.S. Price (trans.), *Bede. A History of the English Church and People*, revised edn (1986), vol. 1, 26.
3. N.P. Brooks, *The Early History of the Church of Canterbury* (1984).
4. T. Tatton-Brown, 'The city and diocese of Canterbury in St Dunstan's time', in N. Ramsay, M. Sparks and T. Tatton-Brown (eds), *St Dunstan: his Life, Times and Cult* (1992), 75–87.
5. Strictly speaking St Dunstan's Church was outside the jurisdiction of the city (later the County Borough) on the west in the archbishop's manor and hundred of Westgate. It is, however, included in this study as it forms part of the extramural area along with St Martin's, St Paul's and St Sepulchre's churches. The seventh century church of St Pancras (within the precincts of St Augustine's Abbey) was, however, never a parochial church and is therefore excluded.
6. See Urry, *Canterbury*, 210 and C.E. Woodruff, 'The church of St Helen in Canterbury', *Archaeologia Cantiana*, 54 (1941), 5–9. There are also references in an early twelfth-century rental to property *in parochia Ste Elena, Canterbury Cathedral Archives* Register D, para.291.
7. Buckler made pencil sketches in 1804 and then worked up a pair of

watercolours for each church in c.1805 (usually views from the northeast and south-west), and those for St Dunstan's, Holy Cross and St Mildred's are in Canterbury Museums. The sketches, as well as the other drawings, are in the Dept. of Manuscripts at the British Library, Add. Mss. 3637-8. Other useful drawings of the Canterbury churches were made by Francis Grose in the later eighteenth century (All Saints, St Dunstan's, St Mary Bredman, St Mary Northgate and St Mildred's). These are in Canterbury Museums. There is also a drawing of each of the 15 churches extant in 1801 by H. Petrie (copies in scrapbook in the Kent Archaeological Society Library, Maidstone).
8. These three churches were all given to St Gregory's priory by Archbishop Lanfranc in the foundation charter of c.1087, see A.M. Woodcock (ed.), *Cartulary of the Priory of St Gregory, Canterbury*, Camden, 3rd series, 88 (1956), 1. Dr Martin Brett, however, points out that the 'foundation' charter was almost certainly made in the thirteenth century.
9. The church of St Margaret was given to the Poor Priests' Hospital in Canterbury in 1271. See the grant printed in W. Somner, *The Antiquities of Canterbury*, 2nd edn (1703), apps XXIV and XXV, 19–22.
10. Urry, *Canterbury*, 211.
11. Ibid., 208.
12. R.U. Potts, 'St Mildred's Church, Canterbury: further notes on the site', *Archaeologia Cantiana*, 56 (1943), 19–22; D.W. Rollason, *The Mildrith Legend* (1982); Brooks, *Early History*, 35.
13. The church was stripped of its internal plaster facing and several excavations were carried out in 1896. See C.F. Routledge, 'St Martin's Church, Canterbury', *Archaeologia Cantiana*, 22 (1897), 1–28. This was followed by much heated discussion, particularly in relation to the date of the fabric. For a contemporary summary see, *idem.*, *The Church of St Martin, Canterbury: an Illustrated Account of its History and Fabric* (1898), 94-8.
14. For a more recent summary of the history of the early fabric see T. Tatton-Brown, 'St Martin's Church in the 6th and 5th centuries', in M.J. Sparks (ed.), *The Parish of St Martin and St Paul, Canterbury* (1980), 12–18. For a recent history of St Martin's see M. Sparks and T. Tatton-Brown, 'The history of the ville of St Martin's, Canterbury', in J. Rady, 'Excavations at St Martin's Hill, Canterbury, 1984–5', *Archaeologia Cantiana*, 104 (1987), 200–212.
15. But not as a *cella memoria* as first suggested by the late Professor J.M Toynbee in her 'Christianity in Roman Britain', *Journal of the British Archaeological Association*, 16, 3rd series (1953), 1–24.
16. This masonry technique can be found in c. fourth- to sixth-century buildings in Italy, while in Britain the Anglo-Saxons were at this time only erecting timber buildings.
17. The second (nave) phase at St Martin's presumably relates to the period after Aethelbert allowed St Augustine and his monks to settle in Canterbury, *Bede, History of the English Church*, vol. 1, 26.
18. Sparks and Tatton-Brown, 'St Martin's Church', 205–6.
19. B.C. Worssam and T. Tatton-Brown, 'The stone of the Reculver Columns and the Reculver Cross', in D. Parsons (ed.), *Stone: Quarrying and Building in England AD43–1525* (1990), 57–61 and fig. 20.
20. Interim reports on these excavations are K. Blockley, P. Blockley and M.

Day, 'St Mary Bredin, Canterbury', *CBA Churches Bulletin*, **19**, Winter (1993), 1–4; P. Bennett, 'St Margaret's Church', *Archaeologia Cantiana*, **103** (1986), 100–202; *idem*, 'All Saints Church', *Archaeologia Cantiana*, **104** (1987), 308–11; and T. Tatton-Brown, 'The church of St George-the-Martyr, Canterbury', *Archaeologia Cantiana*, **109** (1991), 311–17, also note and plan in *Archaeologia Cantiana*, **110** (1992), 359–68.
21. This form of apse is, of course, unique in an English parish church, but extra lobes can be found at this time in the side chapels attached to the ambulatories at Norwich cathedral and the priory church of St Bartholomew-the-Great in Smithfield. Are these forms all offshoots of the new knowledge of the church of the Holy Sepulchre in Jerusalem?
22. See T. Tatton-Brown, 'The beginning of St Gregory's Priory and St John's Hospital in Canterbury', in R.G. Eales and R. Sharpe (eds), *Canterbury and the Norman Conquest* (1995).
23. The original chancels of both St Dunstan's and St Mildred's were also almost certainly rectangular.
24. Some of the architectural elements of this church were reused for the north arcade of the nearby St George's Church when it was enlarged in 1871.
25. See T.P. Smith (with S.E. Rigold), 'The church of St Peter, Canterbury', *Archaeologia Cantiana*, **86** (1971), 99–108.
26. See note and plan in *Archaeologia Cantiana*,**104** (1987), 308–11.
27. See survey drawings of this church in S.S. Frere, S. Stow and P. Bennet, 'Excavations on the Roman and medieval defences of Canterbury', *The Archaeology of Canterbury*, volume 2 (1982), 101–2 and figs 44–9.
28. See J. Rady, T. Tatton-Brown and J.A. Bowen, 'The archbishop's palace, Canterbury', *Journal of the British Archaeological Association*, **144** (1991), 1–60.
29. By Buckler, for example; see n. 7 above.
30. See n. 26 above.
31. For the full report on the excavations see K. Blockley, P. Blockley and M. Day, 'Excavations in the Marlowe Car Park and surrounding areas', *The Archaeology of Canterbury*, vol. 5 (1995), 375–8 and 385–93; see also the interim report, K. Blockley, P. Blockley and M. Day, 'St Mary Bredin, Canterbury', *CBA Churches Bulletin*, **19**, Winter (1983), 1–4.
32. Sir Stephen Glynne also visited and described the church in 1861. He mentions the lancets (with internal shafts), and an 'Early English sedilia with shafts' on the south side of the chancel; see S.R. Glynne, *Notes on the Churches of Kent* (1877).
33. W. Somner, *Antiquities of Canterbury*, 79, 169.
34. See W. Urry, *The Chief Citizens of Canterbury, a List of Portreeves, Bailiffs, etc.* (1978), 24–31. There may have been two Thomas Chiches at this time, father and son, as well as a Stephen and John Chich who were also bailiffs at this time. The Chich family were also hereditary aldermen of Burgate ward, see Urry, *Canterbury*, 176.
35. *Calendar of Patent Rolls* (hereafter *Cal.Pat.Rolls*) 1258–66, 380.
36. W. Urry, 'Master Hamo Doge, founder of the Chantry', in M. Sparks (ed.), *The Parish of St Martin and St Paul* (1980), 36–40.
37. Doge was able, with papal authorization, to institute a vicar. See A.H. Davis (ed.), *William Thorne's Chronicle of St Augustine's Abbey, Canterbury . . .* (1934), 525–6.

38. Somner, *Antiquities of Canterbury*, 337.
39. See note by S. Rigold in *Archaeological Journal*, **126** (1970), 265–6.
40. All finally destroyed in the 1950s, after the church was gutted by incendiary bombs in 1942.
41. Drawing by Francis Grose in Canterbury Museums, reproduced in *Archaeologia Cantiana*, **114** (1994), 190. St Mary Bredman was rebuilt in 1822, and then demolished in 1900.
42. These bells probably hang in the fourteenth-century frame, which was heightened and enlarged for three bells in the early seventeenth century. A fourth bell (from St Margaret's Church) was hung there after the 1968 restoration.
43. As suggested by Stuart Rigold in Smith (with Rigold) 'Church of St Peter', 108.
44. The church itself was rebuilt to the south of the street in 1755; this Georgian church was closed in 1882 and finally demolished in 1956.
45. This vignette is on the 1798 and 1825 editions of W. and H. Doidges 1752 map of Canterbury that was published in the later editions of William Gostling, *A Walk in and about the City of Canterbury* (1777).
46. Charles Cotton, 'Churchwardens' accounts of the parish of St Andrew, Canterbury from AD 1485 to AD 1685', *Archaeologia Cantiana*, **32** (1917), 181–246; ibid., **33** (1918), 1–61; ibid., **34** (1920), 1–46; ibid., **35** (1921), 41–108; ibid., **36** (1923), 81–122.
47. A. Hussey (ed.), *Testamenta Cantiana: East Kent* (1907), 44–5.
48. The whole of the interior of this church was excavated in 1986, and the earlier aisle wall foundations were uncovered, see *Archaeologia Cantiana*, **103** (1986), 199–202 with plan.
49. This became the Archdeacon of Canterbury's court after 1560.
50. P. Blockley. 'Excavations at Riding Gate, Canterbury, 1986–7', *Archaeologia Cantiana*, **107** (1989), 117–54.
51. The rebuilt gateway was in turn destroyed in 1782.
52. *Cal.Pat.Rolls 1361–64*, 373.
53. The parish church in Maidstone, rebuilt by Archbishop Courtenay a decade or so later, is another much grander example, however. There is also the church of Queenborough, in the Isle of Sheppey, built ten years earlier in Edward III's new borough.
54. The north porch was removed, as well as buttresses on the north and east, for this road-widening in the early nineteenth century. Then between 1868 and 1908 a whole series of restorations was carried out with all the window tracery being renewed in Bath stone, and most of the walls refaced in a heavy knapped flint.
55. Sadly the rood screen and loft have disappeared. However, a rare surviving contract for the making of the rood loft at St Stephen's, Hackington in 1519, says that it should be 'made Carven and wrought in every forme of woorkmanship or better as nowe is wrought & made after the newe Roodeloft nowe sett and being in the parishe Churche of the holie Crosse of Westgate.' This contract is transcribed in Aymer Vallance, 'The Rood Screen of St Stephen's, Hackington', *Archaeologia Cantiana*, **44** (1932), 264–8. The new rood loft is also mentioned in wills of 1517 and 1521.
56. See Somner, *Antiquities of Canterbury*, app. LXXIII, for the foundation charter of the new church, dated 3 Richard II.
57. The building of this tower is fortuitously referred to in the first will, that

of the Rector of St Martin's, John Vagge, in the earliest surviving register of the Canterbury consistory court, transcribed in F. Hull, *Guide to the Kent County Archives Office* (1958), 234.

58. Evidence for this was seen by Sir Stephen Glynne, *Notes on Churches*, 20.
59. Illustrated in *Archaeologia Cantiana*, **32** (1917), 196, where the accounts are also published.
60. 'Towards the making of the new bolls for the candlesticks of the Rood Loft' (1508), in Hussey, *Testamenta Cantiana: East Kent*, 57–9.
61. Wills of 1501 mention 'the making of the steeple' and 'the restoration of the bell-tower', in Hussey, *Testamenta Cantiana: East Kent*, 57–9.
62. Ibid., 44.
63. A will of 1504 mentions a window being made in the high chancel', see A. Hussey, 'Further notes from Kentish wills', *Archaeologia Cantiana*, **31** (1915), 26. This also mentions, in a will of 1503, 'that the steeple of the church be overcast with sand and lime, forwith a boterace'. The buttress still survives on the north-east side of the tower.
64. Hussey, *Testamenta Cantiana: East Kent*, 60.
65. Somner, *Antiquities of Canterbury*, 335.
66. Urry, *Chief Citizens of Canterbury*, 51–2 gives Thomas Atwode as Mayor in 1477, 1479–80, 1486 and 1495. A William Atwode was Mayor in 1500, and a Thomas Wode in 1504 and 1512. No documentary evidence for the Atwood chantry seems to survive.
67. A, Hussey (ed.), *Kent Chantries*, pt 1, Kent Records, **12** (1932), 56–9; also T. Tatton-Brown, 'The Roper chantry in St Dunstan's church, Canterbury', *Antiquaries Journal*, **60** (1980), 227–46.
68. Apart from the churchwardens' accounts of St Andrew's already mentioned, those of 1484–1580 for St Dunstan's church have also been fully transcribed and published by J.M. Cowper in *Archaeologia Cantiana*, **16** (1886), 289–321 and ibid., **17** (1887), 77–139.
69. Hussey, *Testamenta Cantiana: East Kent*, 60.
70. K.L. Wood-Leigh (ed.), *Kentish Visitations of Archbishop William Warham and his Deputies, 1511–1512*, Kent Records, **24** (1984), 56.
71. St Paul's churchyard in Longport dates from 1591, while the St Mary Northgate churchyard in Broad Street dates from about the same time. Some of the hospitals like St John's, Northgate, also acquired post-medieval graveyards.
72. Partial excavation of this cemetery found over 1 250 burials.
73. For a summary of the evidence in these wills see Hussey, 'Further notes from Kentish wills', 36–53; idem, *Testamenta Cantiana: East Kent*, 41–69.
74. St Mary, Northgate did not have its own graveyard, but excavation in 1977 found five burials, probably of a twelfth or thirteenth century date, immediately west of the church, cut into the rampart behind the city wall, see Frere, Stowe and Bennet, 'Excavations', 87–90.
75. Burial in the churchyard 'before the procession door' in 1477 is recorded, see Hussey, *Testamenta Cantiana: East Kent*, 53. This doorway must be the twelfth-century west doorway.
76. Many burials packed into the tiny space around the west end of the church were excavated in 1980, though it is not clear how many were put here before the Reformation. See n. 20, above.
77. See list in Hussey, 'Further notes from Kentish wills', 49–52.

78. Hussey, *Testamenta Cantiana: East Kent*, 66.
79. After the Dissolution, St Gregory's churchyard continued to be used by the parishioners of St Mary Northgate, until the tenant, Sir John Boys, was able to close it, and provide a new graveyard in Broad Street in the late sixteenth century. Earlier there were complaints (in the 1573 visitation) that the churchyard was 'not decently kept, neither can they bury in it unless they pay 2d. for an old body and 1d. for a child'. This is quoted in Somner, *Antiquities of Canterbury*, 49.
80. Ibid., 163-70 describes all these changes just a century after they had happened.
81. See D. Gardiner, 'St Michael, Canterbury', *Archaeologia Cantiana*, 47 (1935), 166-9.
82. See T. Tatton-Brown, 'Burgate: documentary evidence', *Archaeologia Cantiana*, 106 (1988), 164-8.
83. By this time, the church, which had belonged to St Augustine's Abbey, had passed to the dean and chapter. It was united with St George's in 1681.
84. *Victoria County History of Kent*, vol. 2 (1926), 142-3.
85. St Mary Bredin had belonged to St Sepulchre's priory before the Dissolution, and the two parishes, along with that of St Edmund Ridingate, were already joined by the late fourteenth century. After the Reformation it was given to the lords of the nearby manor of Dane John, whose place of burial it had been since the thirteenth century, as we have seen.
86. Somner, *Antiquities of Canterbury*, 165.
87. In the tithe maps and first edition of the Ordnance Survey (1873). There are, however, some earlier maps in the city archives, and also a 1784 map of the parish of St Alphege in the parish records.
88. Urry, *Canterbury*, 207-13.
89. In correspondance (1978) Urry wrote: 'I doubt if [they are] any earlier than the date of the Assize of Clarendon (1166).' There are, however, many similarities with the wards of the city of London and these are certainly earlier, see C.N.L. Brooke and G. Keir, *London 800-1216: the Shaping of a City* (1975), 162-70.
90. It is specifically mentioned in Domesday Book, and part of Edward the Confessor's *parvus burgus* at Fordwich is cut out of it, see T. Tatton-Brown, *Canterbury in Domesday Book* (1987) and *idem*, 'The Anglo-Saxon towns of Kent', in D. Hooke (ed.), *Anglo-Saxon Settlements* (1988), 213-22.
91. See Sparks and Tatton-Brown, 'St Martin's, Canterbury'.
92. The extreme north-east corner of the area was cut out of it to make a park for Odo, Bishop of Bayeux, and an original charter (of between 1071 and 1082) recording this still survives, though heavily charred in the Cotton library fire of 1731, see Tatton-Brown, 'Recent fieldwork around Canterbury: the deer parks', *Archaeologia Cantiana*, 99 (1983), 115-19. See also Sparks and Tatton-Brown in 'St Martin's Church'. Caldecote manor was also given to the monks of Christ Church priory, but not until the early fourteenth century.
93. Westgate manor, which covered a huge area (7 sulungs), also contained other rural parishes like Hackington and Harbledown on the edge of the forest of Blean.
94. Brooke and Keir, *London 800-1216*, 169.

CHAPTER TWELVE

Clerical Communities and Parochial Space: the Planning of Urban Mother Churches in the Twelfth and Thirteenth Centuries

John Blair

The organization of later medieval urban religion was powerfully influenced by two legacies from the past. One has recently been much discussed: the multitude of 'private' churches, usually small and informally planned, founded by eleventh-century landlords and groups of neighbours.[1] The other, still relatively neglected, is my theme here: the continuing role of ancient mother churches. This chapter will argue that the forms of clerical life developed in minsters during the pre- and proto-urban Anglo-Saxon centuries conditioned, both by survival and by example, the use of space in major urban churches from the twelfth century onwards.

Most research hitherto has been too fragmented, both chronologically and thematically, to emphasize the links between early institutional character and later architectural form. There is a hiatus between the work of Anglo-Saxonists on the survival of minster churches and their impact on urban regrowth between the eighth and twelfth centuries, and that of architectural historians on the abundant physical remains of town churches after the mid-twelfth century. Pre-Conquest religious communities perpetuated as houses of monks or regular canons have been treated as a class apart; those perpetuated in less formal guises have been ignored. Yet such inheritances from the past were fundamental to many late medieval towns. Often a minster enclosure was the nucleus around which a town first developed, and then invaded it cuckoo-like as the urban community grew and the monastic one dwindled. The essential character of a late Anglo-Saxon minster, combining communal or collegiate life with pastoral care, proved very resilient: a reformed minster rarely lost entirely its parochial attributes, nor an unreformed one its collegiate attributes.

Liturgical and social use of architectural space is the theme of this chapter. I shall focus on a range of large, mainly cruciform churches

CLERICAL COMMUNITIES AND PAROCHIAL SPACE 273

12.1 Crediton, Devon: the later medieval development of a cruciform collegiate church originally built c.1160

(see Figure 12.1) which were built or enlarged between the mid-twelfth and late thirteenth centuries and which were, in varying degrees, parochial. A very high proportion of these are identifiable as the sites of Anglo-Saxon religious communities; probably all of them are witness (if often silent witness) to the various forms of collegiate life practised in post-Conquest England, which in Oxford and Cambridge included academic collegiate life. Most are also 'urban' if the word is defined broadly enough to include small market towns, the organic local centres which Alan Everitt characterized as 'primary towns' and which have emerged from recent work as the most typical minster-generated settlements.²

Yet it would be unreasonable to expect a perfect correlation between form, status and function, and there are no fully consistent means of definition. On the one hand, the urbanization of minster sites was conditioned by local factors still largely unexplored: by the thirteenth century these places had reached stages of development ranging from big towns to market villages. And however urban the centre, most minsters also retained a larger than average 'mother parish' in the surrounding countryside: on the great feasts at least, much of the congregation would be rural. On the other hand, some large and elaborate churches built specifically for the needs of urban congregations in large towns were not ex-minsters, and their number increased rapidly after the end of the twelfth century. These owed their size and pretension to other causes: imitation as against continuity, the wealth of current patrons or parishioners as against inherited status. The evidence shows not a rule but an early and very widespread norm, underlying developments which tended, after about 1200, to go increasingly in new directions.

The hundreds of minster communities which still existed, albeit at a reduced level, in late Anglo-Saxon England experienced very diverse fates.³ A few were refounded in the late tenth century as Benedictine abbeys, or in the early twelfth as Augustinian priories; many show no sign after the eleventh century of being anything more than rich parish churches. An unknown number, though, acquired a distinct character which is no less real for being elusive of definition. They continued to house groups of clergy, following one of the various forms of clerical life which had developed in Europe since the eighth century. In practice these could range from the strictest (a monastic-type community with dormitory, refectory and all assets in common) to the laxest (married clergy with separate prebendal lands and living in separate houses), but it seems likely that most of them continued to provide pastoral care for their ancient mother parishes.

It is important to stress how many of these 'secular colleges' were later winnowed out, and how very little we know about them. Sources from between 1000 and 1150 provide numerous traces of communities which had vanished by 1250; the handful of collegiate churches which tend to be cited in general works were just the favoured minority which lasted in a formal guise into the late middle ages.⁴ This causes formidable problems with the evidence. Before bishops' registers begin in the early thirteenth century, we know much less about the English parish clergy than most historians have cared to recognize; from written sources we are really in no position to say how many churches in 1200 might still have been staffed by teams of priests. Once registers do become available, they reveal a surprising number of anomalies inherited from the past. Early thirteenth-century vicarage ordinances dealing with large or multi-chapel parishes sometimes establish two, three or even more *clerici* or *capellani* additional to the vicar.[5] Some of these may have been completely new arrangements in the interests of better pastoral care, but some clearly were not. When bishops such as Hugh de Welles encountered residual minster communities, they were liable to reorganize and redefine them in accordance with terms and concepts developed during the previous two decades, and formalized at the Fourth Lateran Council of 1215.[6] The reality underlying formal and legal arrangements can be very elusive.

Such a 'crypto-collegiate' church was the ex-minster in the Oxfordshire market town of Bampton, where a religious community existed in the 950s.[7] Sources spanning c.1160–1220 reveal a clerical establishment comprising a 'prebend-farmer' and two 'prebend-portioners', some of them career pluralists, and there are hints of lesser clergy under them.[8] We know nothing of their liturgical life, but around 1160 the church was enlarged into a spacious cruciform building of a type which will be discussed later. In 1220 the Bishop of Lincoln transformed these 'portions' into three perpetual vicarages served by resident vicars, an arrangement which survived until the 1840s.[9] The churchyard is flanked on its north, south and east sides by vicarage houses, and on its west side by the manor house of the corporate rector (see Figure 12.2); even today, the atmosphere is oddly reminiscent of a cathedral close. The late medieval vicars were clergy of status, richer than many ordinary rectors. The epitaph for vicar Holcot (d. 1500) is scarcely modest: 'Orate pro anima venerabilis ac scientifici viri Magistri Roberti Holcot, sacerdotis ac artium magistri, necnon huius insignis ecclesie vicarii' [Pray for the soul of the venerable and learned Master Robert Holcot, priest and Master of Arts, vicar of this illustrious church]. Both Holcot and his predecessor vicar Plimiswood (d. 1417) are shown on their brasses wearing the almuce, a vestment reserved for canons and higher dignitaries, which they were scarcely entitled to wear. Clearly this church was collegiate in all but name; but without the scraps of evidence scattered through some exceptionally rich sources, the only clue to the survival of a clerical community would have been a building which is abnormally complex by twelfth-century parochial standards.

As this example suggests, the strongest evidence for former collegiate status may often lie in the building itself. How the interiors of big

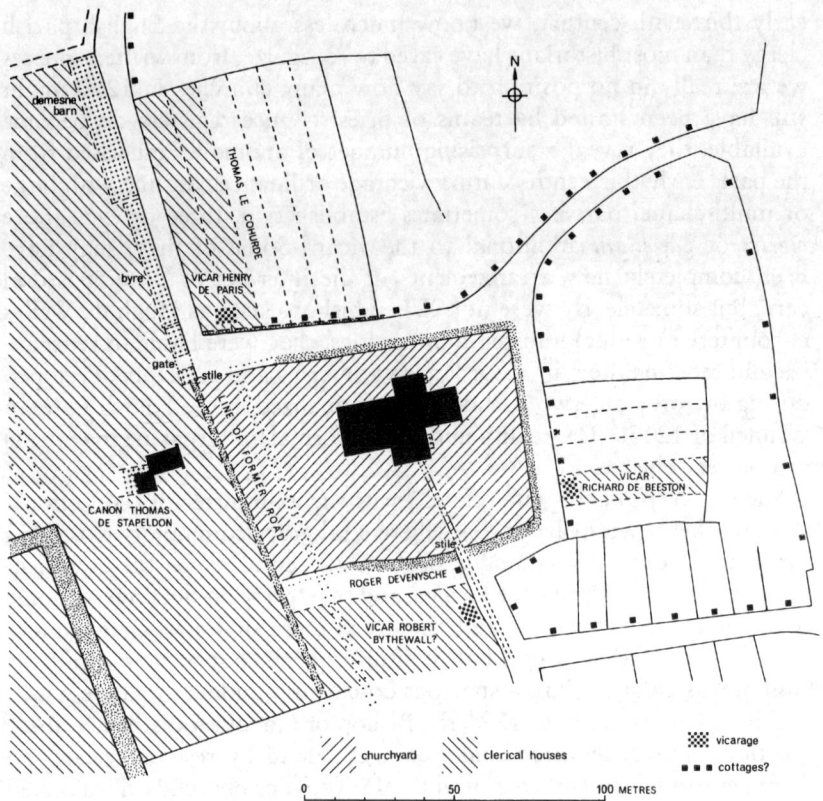

12.2 Bampton, Oxfordshire, in 1317: a crypto-collegiate church with a rectory to its west and vicarages on the other three sides. (Data from Exeter Cathedral, Dean and Chapter MS 2931; topographical reconstruction after Bampton Research Project)

churches were divided up between competing interests is an oddly neglected topic. Preoccupied with developments in the nave, work on parochial ritual has failed to see the implications of the long chancels, the crossing-towers and the transepts which so many mother churches acquired during the twelfth and thirteenth centuries. Admittedly, practice was to some extent conditioned by the downwards diffusion of models: a patron might adopt a grand Romanesque format because it was prestigious rather than because it was wholly necessary. But even allowing this, it is inconceivable that these large internal spaces had no practical purpose whatsoever: they imply liturgical arrangements of some complexity, and staffs larger than a single parish priest with his normal assistants.

A problem, especially acute in some urban contexts, is whether this deduction can be extended to post-Conquest cruciform churches which do *not* have a minster background. After 1200, large and elaborately staffed urban churches with humble or recent origins become more and more common. Obviously not all the great churches of fourteenth- and fifteenth-century towns were ex-minsters, and some were not even established parish churches. One of the grandest late medieval churches in England is Holy Trinity at Hull, which housed a body of clergy including 12 chantry priests and 10 parochial guilds; yet it remained a mere chapel of Hessle until 1661.[10] But when we go back into the twelfth century, when the parochial system was still undeveloped and so little is known about local clergy, it is very hard to know what to think. How should we interpret the pair of churches at Devizes built by Bishop Roger of Salisbury; or St Giles at Northampton, a twelfth-century cruciform parish church in a town which already had a minster; or St Mary-de-Haura at New Shoreham, a large cruciform church of *c.*1130 which acquired an extremely lavish aisled choir in the 1180s?[11]

Although the simple answer might seem to be that rich patrons and aspiring towns built grandly, it is also arguable that collegiate staffs are exactly what one might expect them to establish in their grand churches. In Norman England the Anglo-Saxon tradition of minsters fused with the French one of *collégiales*, and at their castles magnates founded new colleges which were doomed to extinction within decades.[12] If this principle had been extended to towns, the buildings themselves might in many cases be our only evidence for it. Roger of Salisbury, for instance, was a noted engrosser of former minsters, and at Devizes he could well have established clerical groups comparable to those which he controlled elsewhere.[13] Certainly the twelfth-century churches of this kind are comparable, in their scale and planning conventions, to the known ex-minsters which were rebuilt at the same time.

Is it possible, then, to identify a distinctive architecture for twelfth- and thirteenth-century collegiate churches? Certainly they were not leaders of fashion. On the contrary, their ambiguous and perhaps sometimes insecure position encouraged them to imitate the forms of greater churches, especially those housing established and well-defined religious communities. It would probably be true to say that they combined respect for tradition with an eagerness to be metropolitan and up to date. Thus, despite their generally modest scale, they relate to the planning conventions of cathedrals and monasteries much more than to the simple, straightforward idiom of ordinary Anglo-Norman village churches.

A proportion of collegiate and crypto-collegiate churches shade off into the two extremes of 'great' churches and of ordinary parochial

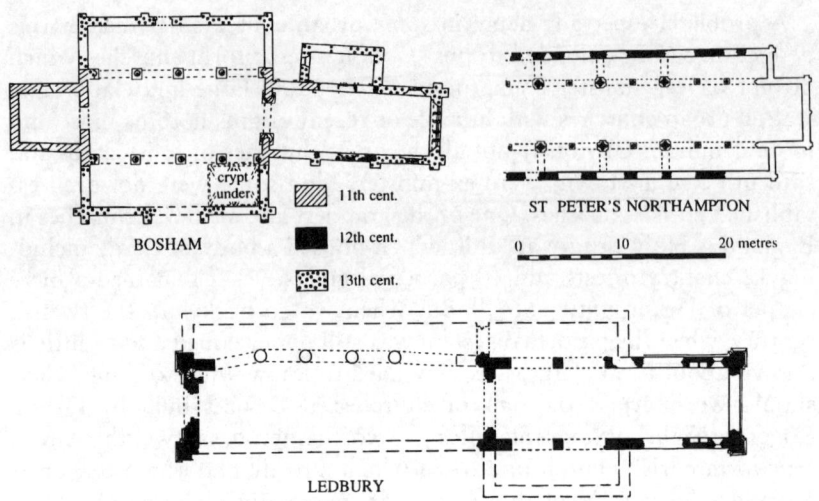

12.3 Non-cruciform collegiate churches (pre-1250 features only): Bosham, Sussex (after *VCH Sussex*, 4, 186); St Peter's, Northampton (see note 17); Ledbury, Herefordshire (see note 17)

planning. Examples of the former are St John's at Chester, Beverley and Ripon Minsters and Waltham Holy Cross, secular colleges of a local importance equalling that of great monasteries: they were equipped with churches of a commensurate scale, in the forefront of English architectural development.[14] By contrast, the straightforward non-cruciform plan (see Figure 12.3), with the chancel arch the only structural division between nave and chancel, was maintained when some pre-Conquest minsters such as Bosham[15] were updated for collegiate use in the twelfth and thirteenth centuries. Michael Franklin has pointed out that several Northamptonshire minsters were rebuilt or remodelled at this date to comprise nave, chancel and sometimes west tower;[16] cases such as Ledbury and St Peter's at Northampton show that this form was thought suitable even for churches of considerable pretension.[17] We only have the bare bones of these buildings, which may mislead us: screens or partitions could have been used to form spaces equivalent to the crossing and transepts of a cruciform church.

Between these two extremes lies a larger category of churches built to a simplified cruciform plan. This format had compelling advantages for churches with a complex liturgy and several priests, especially if they also housed lay congregations. The pattern of aisleless nave with north, south and east *porticus* was established early in the Christian Anglo-Saxon period (for instance the late seventh-century cathedral at Winchester), and persisted as perhaps the most widespread and characteristic plan for unreformed minsters until the Conquest and some years beyond.[18] By the eleventh century the crossing was being given, under Romanesque influence, a greater emphasis,[19] and many minster churches had an arch or other division on the west as well as the east side of the central space. Anglo-Norman churches with lateral adjuncts narrower than the crossing-space, in other words *porticus* rather than transepts, continued the earlier eleventh-century tradition, for instance the college of canons at Bramber (Sussex) and the proto-Augustinian church at Haughmond (Shropshire).[20] But during the later eleventh century the fully-fledged Romanesque cruciform church was quickly disseminated in England, and became the almost invariable form of great churches. It is therefore entirely predictable that it should prove the favoured model for minsters which retained any pretensions beyond the 1140s, and this fact has now been recognized in several local studies.[21]

One format that was to be notably popular among the rebuilders of collegiate ex-minsters was the so-called 'austere' monastic plan, as it had emerged by the middle years of the twelfth century. For present purposes the essential features are an aisleless nave, a crossing-tower, a rectangular square-ended chancel, and transepts with single or double square-ended eastern chapels.[22] The type is associated above all with the earliest Cistercian houses, but it was quickly taken up by the Augustinians[23] – a significant association given the historical links between regular and secular canons.

It is most instructive to compare some of these monks' and canons' churches with a selection of parochial ex-minsters and other large parish churches of the second half of the twelfth century (see Figure 12.4).[24] In the first place there is a continuum, with no clear break in terms of planning between the bottom end of the monastic range and the top end of the collegiate or parochial; the one real difference is that most of the non-regular churches have single rather than double transeptal chapels, and even here there are exceptions (Crediton and St Mary's Shrewsbury). Secondly, several of the churches are so similar in size and proportion as to suggest that a stereotyped plan – the 'right' way to rebuild an ex-minster if one had sufficient funds – had gained wide currency by the 1160s.

A crucial distinguishing feature of all these churches, whether cruciform or not, is that they have long (often double-square) rectangular chancels, capable of containing choir, presbytery and perhaps a screened off space behind the high altar. Chancels on this scale became so common in the thirteenth century[25] that it is easy to overlook their singularity in the twelfth, when the ordinary parish church had no more than a square cell with flat or apsidal east end. In England as in France, the developed chancel was adopted for monastic and collegiate churches in

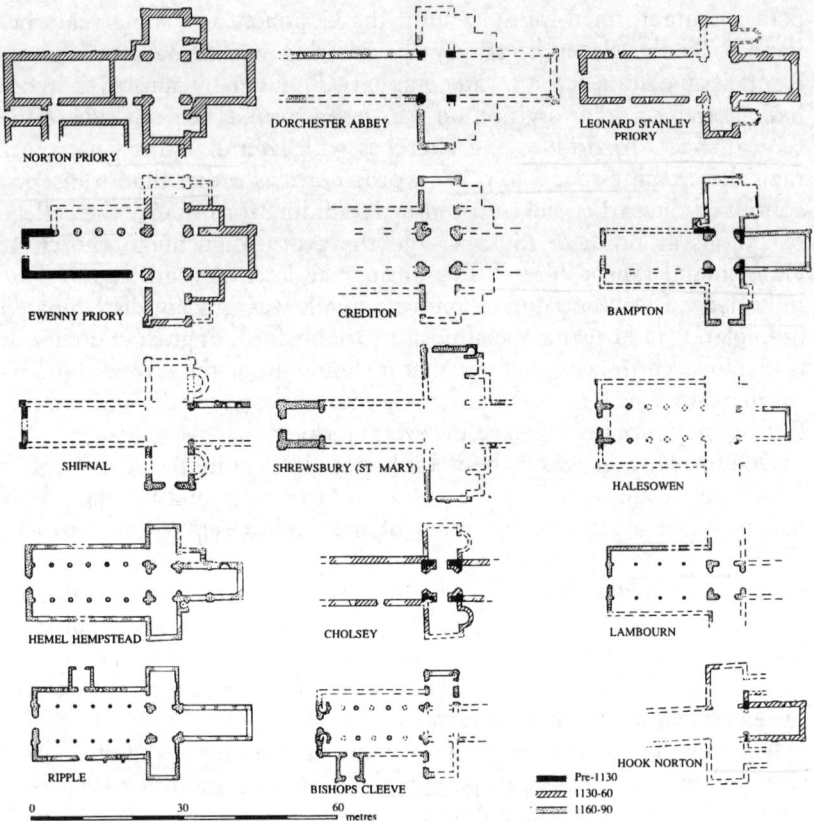

12.4 A selection of cruciform churches, monastic, collegiate and parochial, based on the 'austere' plan (pre-1200 features only). These plans are at exactly half the scale of Figures 12.3, 12.5, 12.6 and 12.7. For sources see note 24

the Romanesque period, but for ordinary parish churches only in the Gothic.[26] In twelfth-century ex-minsters even aisled choirs are not unknown, as Ledbury and St Peter's at Northampton (see Figure 12.3) illustrate.

This architectural contrast reflects a contrast in history and status which must be the starting-point for analysing functions. In England as elsewhere, the importance of an early medieval religious site was marked not by a single large church but by a multiplicity of churches with specialized functions; it was part of the 'Romanesque revolution' to gather these various functions under one vast roof.[27] Many of the ex-minsters shown in, for example, Figure 12.4 occupy sites which a few centuries earlier would have contained two or three small churches. The basic difference between ordinary parish churches and ex-minsters is that the former began as simple buildings serving one simple purpose, whereas the latter were in the tradition of 'portmanteau' Romanesque buildings into which groups of churches were subsumed. Thus it is not just a matter of collegiate churches copying monasteries and cathedrals: all these categories reflect a single course of development, evolving between the tenth and thirteenth centuries, in the use of liturgical space. Only at the very end of that period, by contrast, did the resultant architectural forms reach the little churches which had been proliferating in town and countryside.

A basic function of collegiate parish churches must have been to accommodate the dual claims of clergy and laity. Given their architectural sources, it is fair to assume that this accommodation would have been influenced by the practice of those 'great' churches which also served parishes. Scholars have recently shown a good deal of interest in the pastoral functions of cathedrals and monasteries.[28] Many, perhaps most, of the churches of monastic and other religious communities which had existed in some form before the Conquest were still being used by lay congregations up to c.1150. In the more tidy-minded ecclesiastical world of the later twelfth and thirteenth centuries, there were widespread efforts to restrict and regulate these functions. The two most effective expedients were to move the laity out into a new parish church or *capella ante portas*, or to build a completely new monastic church, relinquishing the old one to parochial use. But when resources were inadequate for such drastic measures the lay and religious congregations continued side by side, uneasy and sometimes hostile bedfellows. Such cases may offer analogies for how space was demarcated in the collegiate parish churches, which although virtually undocumented must have faced very similar problems.

The nave, west of the pulpitum, was most obviously the preserve of the laity, and the naves or nave aisles of monastic cathedrals, Benedictine monasteries and churches of Augustinian canons often housed parochial congregations. At Ely the 'church of St Mary' and the 'church of St Peter', two 'parishes' served by chaplains appointed by the monastic sacrist, had grown out of communities worshipping before the Holy Cross altar in the nave.[29] Even this could be difficult when, as at Rochester, the parishioners' need for ready access in emergency conflicted with that of the monks to lock up their church at night.[30] But by historical accident the parish 'church' might be sited in the eastern arm, usually one of the transepts, and this caused greater problems. The Augustinian priory of St Frideswide's, Oxford, contained a parochial congregation inherited from the ancient minster, served by a chaplain at the Holy Cross altar which in some way adjoined the north transept near St Fridewide's shrine. In 1298 the bishop suppressed this 'parish' because it disturbed the canons in their choir, the monastic and parochial offices being celebrated 'not under one roof but in completely adjoining places, with no space between them worth mentioning'.[31] At Hereford the 'parish church' of St John, a chapel in the north transept, was inconvenient for the same reason, the parishioners and the canons spoiling each other's singing.[32]

Not all monastic churches were so badly organized: careful planning seems sometimes to have achieved an acceptable *modus vivendi*. A splendid demonstration of this is Paul Binski's recent analysis of the use of space in St Alban's Abbey.[33] During c.1230–1310 a series of paintings (of parochial rather than high monastic quality) on the west faces of the north nave piers, marking altars which served lay groups, spread gradually eastwards from the entrance of a parochial chapel attached to the north nave aisle. The townsfolk also had access, via the north aisles of the nave and choir, to the north transept, where images for the 'edification and worldly consolation of lay people' – specifically of the Crucifixion and the Virgin Mary – were displayed in the 1220s. By the early fourteenth century, when the laity consolidated their hold on the nave by adding further devotional paintings, their relations with the abbey were poor, but it looks as though the original division of space had been planned to allow harmonious use of the church by both monks and townsfolk.

The admission of laity to parts of the east arm may have been especially common among the Augustinian canons, who of all the religious orders came closest, in their background and functions, to groups of minster-priests. Many Augustinian priories had been founded in the early twelfth century in former minsters, had been rebuilt and endowed by minor noble and gentry families, and enjoyed broad-based support among local freeholders.[34] They must have had some regard for the sensibilities of their patrons, whether greater families whose tombs lay near the monastic choir or lesser ones who formed the parochial congregation. At Norton (Cheshire) (see Figure 12.4), Lilleshall (Shropshire) and Kirkham (Yorkshire), a passage around the back of the north-west pier gave access, by-passing the crossing, from the nave to the north transept. It looks as though in these cases, as at St Alban's, the north transept had functions to which lay users of the nave were admitted, and at Norton at least these included the burial of distinguished benefactors.[35]

In collegiate and crypto-collegiate churches, the demarcation of space may have been equally precise. As Jean Hubert has written of the French *collégiales*, 'on disposait à l'intérieur de l'édifice sacré comme deux églises juxtaposées, celle des fidéles et celle des chanoines' [one finds the interior of the holy building was arranged like two juxtaposed churches, one for the laity and one for the canons].[36] The laity's prime space was of course the nave, dominated (on the model of great churches from a much earlier date) by the standing rood at its east end. The great secular canons' church of Waltham Holy Cross seems to have had a sanctuary space, presumably containing the parish altar, marked by the spiral columns in the easternmost bay of the nave.[37] Sometimes, as at Bosham, the collegiate clergy employed chaplains to discharge their parochial functions at nave altars.[38] In the later middle ages the focus of the main parish fraternities was often the rood and its altar: the Gild of Smiths of Chesterfield (Derbyshire), 'worshipping before the greater cross in the nave' of this large cruciform ex-minster, is one example among many.[39]

Strictly speaking a non-parochial collegiate church, like a private chapel, had no use for a nave. It is the absence of obligations to the laity which explains the simple form normally taken by late medieval domestic and collegiate chapels, a single-space choir with an antechapel. Three exceptions proving this rule are Michaelhouse and Peterhouse, Cambridge, and Merton College, Oxford, which took over existing parish churches as their chapels.[40] Only the first was finished; the churches attached to Merton (St John, begun by 1290) and Peterhouse (St Mary the Less, begun by 1340) survive to this day as the choirs and crossings of cruciform churches whose parochial naves were never built. The problem was solved at Peterhouse by dividing the choir in two and at Merton by the decay of St John's parish, but the original intentions are clear (see Figure 12.5). Walter de Merton's scholars were so much a part of the new world of universities and professions that it is easy to forget their links with an older world, in which colleges of clergy controlled parishes and served lay congregations. By a strange quirk the T-plan of their incomplete church, its parochial aims frustrated, became a model for most of the college chapels later built in Oxford.

In contrast to the nave, ambiguities surround the use of the crossing-space and transepts. A cruciform or axial-tower church forces us to confront a problem irrelevant in a simple two-cell one: do the rood and rood-screen coincide with the west or the east arch of the crossing? In full-scale Romanesque churches the area used by the clergy normally extended westwards under the crossing (where the liturgical choir was often located), or even beyond it into the nave.[41] Late medieval arrangements may perpetuate a similar division of smaller cruciform churches: it is a matter of observation that where these retain evidence for fifteenth-century rood-lofts, they were usually against the *west* arch of the crossing. The rood-screen could have controlled lay access to the crossing and transepts like the pulpitum of a monastic church, and at least in the late

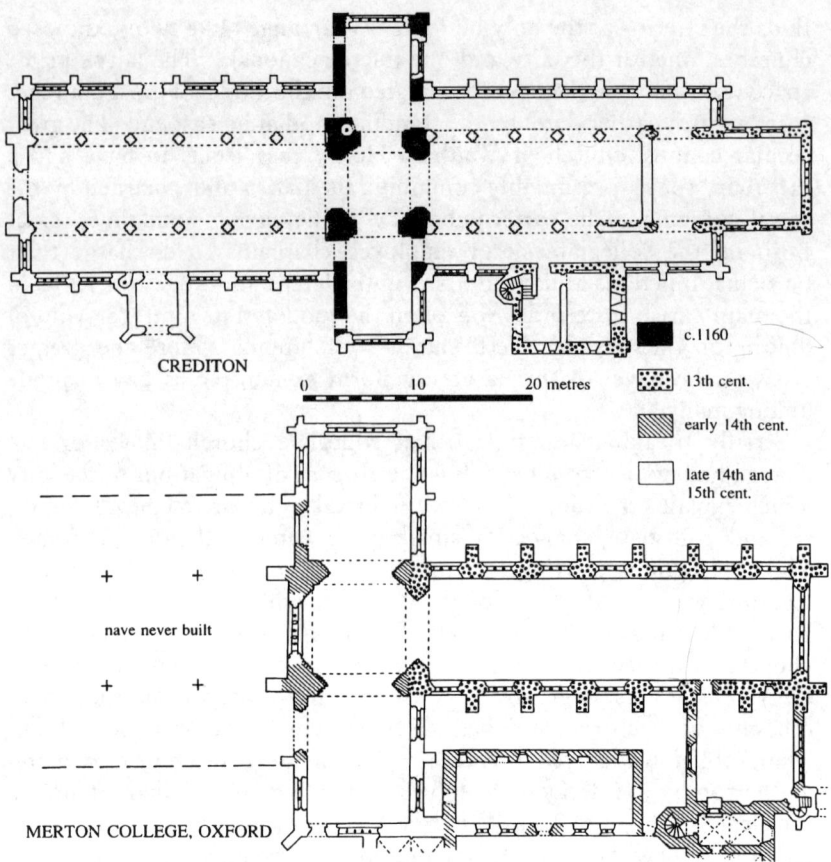

12.5 Two cruciform collegiate churches in their later medieval state: Crediton, Devon (after *Transactions of the Exeter Diocesan Architectural Society 1878*, pl. XIII); Merton College, Oxford (after *RCHM Oxford*, opp. 80)

middle ages some collegiate churches had both rood-screen and choir-screen, respectively west and east of the crossing.[42] In a dispute of 1307 concerning an ordinary parish church, it was adjudged that an axial tower 'in choro seu cancello super ipsum constructum existit', in other words that its floor-space (which could have served literally as the choir) belonged to that part of the church which it was the rector's duty to maintain. The controversy does, however, illustrate the distinct and slightly ambiguous status of the crossing: by the thirteenth century the belfry which it supported had come to be seen as a parish responsibility.[43]

No screenwork before the mid-thirteenth century has survived in English churches, so we have very little idea of how buildings such as those shown in Figure 12.4 functioned east of the rood-screen. Restricted access, perhaps along the lines of the monastic examples described above, seems likely, especially in those ex-minsters where one transept contained the shrine of the local saint,[44] or served as the Lady chapel. The chapels, apses or flat-backed niches in the east walls of transepts were clearly designed to take altars, but were these for the private use of the clergy or for parochial masses? At Beverley Minster the nine vicars had parochial responsibilities which were discharged from specific altars, two of which can probably be located in the transepts.[45] In churches where the laity were excluded from the crossing, were they allowed into the transepts via openings in the east ends of the aisles? At Ripple (Worcestershire) (Figure 12.4), where such openings remain, they are narrow and closed by doors; this church still gives an overwhelming sense of separation between the nave and everything to its east. And was it clergy or laity who used the elaborate Romanesque doorways occasionally found in the end walls of the transepts, as at Newbald (Yorkshire), Shifnal (Shropshire) and Bampton (Oxfordshire)? This remains a very dark area, which needs elucidation through systematic observation and through archaeology above and below ground.

If the laity's access to the crossing and transepts was restricted, they may have had virtually no access to the chancel. In ordinary parish churches the laity could approach the altar at certain points in the mass,[46] and in the 1220s lay patrons were even allowed to sit in the choir with the clergy.[47] It is possible, however, that the grander chancels of collegiate and crypto-collegiate churches were more strictly reserved: there were additional barriers between the choir-screen and the laity, and often the patrons were clergy themselves.

It is a question whether chancels modelled on monastic ones could boast a commensurate liturgy. One might think, for instance, that the two prebendaries and one vicar of Ledbury (Herefordshire) would have felt rather lost in their enormous twelfth-century aisled choir (Figure 12.3). One possibility is that the high altar and reredos stood only two-thirds of the way down the chancel, the eastern bay being screened off as a Lady chapel. This seems especially likely where choir aisles gave access to the east end and allowed a square ambulatory to be formed (as later at Crediton and Wimborne, Figures 12.5 and 12.6), a possible interpretation of some fragmentary Romanesque plans such as Ledbury or Dorchester. But another explanation for large choir spaces is that a staff of three or four beneficed clergy implies a range of lesser people whom we cannot see: each could have had his own deacon, subdeacon and clerk, *capellani* are often mentioned but rarely quantifiable, and clergy attached to the subordinate chapels of mother parishes were

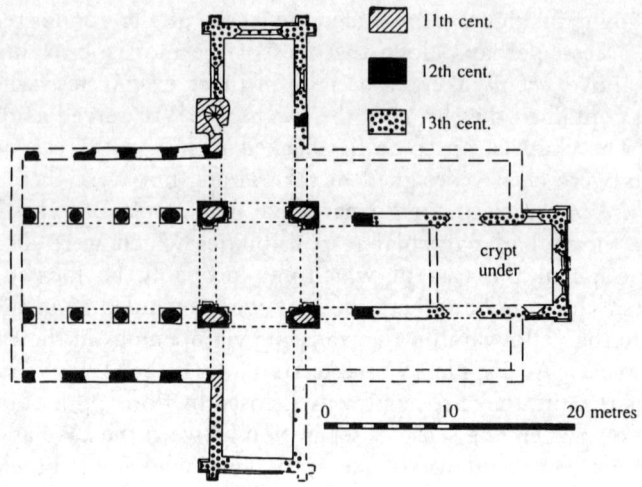

12.6 Wimborne Minster, Dorset (pre-1250 features only). After *RCHM Dorset*, 5, 79

often obliged to attend the main church on certain feasts. However, there is clearly much that we will never know about the personnel, liturgy and musical practice in churches of this kind during the twelfth and early thirteenth centuries.

The chancel which was added to the ex-minster of Faringdon (Berkshire) in the early thirteenth century is unusually well recorded, thanks to a vicarage ordinance, perhaps exactly contemporary, issued by the Bishop of Salisbury in 1227 (see Figure 12.7).[48] A perpetual vicar with three priests or chaplains (*sacerdotes* or *capellani*) served the mother church and its chapel of Little Coxwell, but their pastoral work did not absolve them from exacting liturgical duties. In addition to certain anniversaries and special feasts they were daily to celebrate the canonical hours 'decently standing in suitable places' (*locis convenientibus decenter consistentibus*), the vicar and a chaplain on one side of the choir and the other two chaplains on the other. Following the practice of the clergy of Salisbury Cathedral, they were to wear surplices with closed black copes. On festive days they were to say *Placebo* and *Dirige* 'in a low voice before the altar of the Blessed Virgin [was this in the east bay of the chancel?], where are to be said the offices of St Mary and for the deceased'. In their daily prayers they were to remember their patrons, the clergy of Salisbury, as well as the parishioners of Faringdon and all those buried in Faringdon churchyard. On a miniature scale this church mirrored the mother church of the diocese, combining a cathedral-type liturgy with pastoral care and offices involving the lay community.

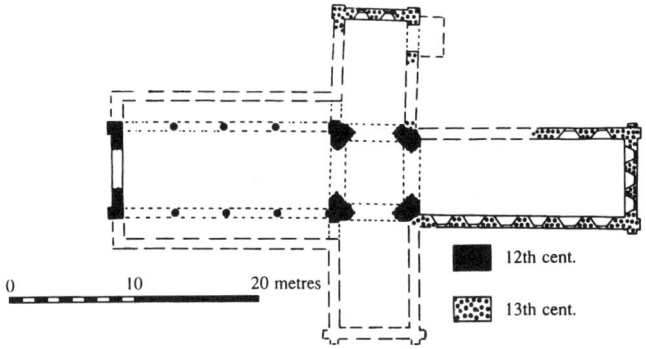

12.7 Faringdon, Berkshire, as existing c.1250. After *VCH Berkshire*, 4, 496

By the fifteenth century there is increasing evidence for liturgical fittings, principally the choir-stalls which survive in many collegiate and quasi-collegiate churches.[49] One factor that must have made the choir liturgy and music of such churches rather special is that their clergy were often career churchmen, of modest background but moving up the ladder and with cathedral experience behind them. At Bampton[50] a high proportion of the late medieval vicars, including all three between 1454 and 1479, were former vicars-choral of Exeter Cathedral. The stalls in this church included six special ones against the west wall, three on either side of the chancel arch. Those on the north bore the initials of the three early sixteenth-century vicars,[51] and the arrangement clearly imitates cathedral choirs (including Exeter) where the western stalls were assigned to dignitaries. Given Bampton's complex parochial arrangements, a dozen or more clergy could have sat in the choir on at least the major feasts.

This runs ahead into the late Middle Ages. By the thirteenth century, we can identify two trends calculated to erode the distinctness between crypto-colleges and ordinary churches. The first was the principle, applied to all parish churches alike by the late 1220s, that the chancel arch marked a frontier between different zones of responsibility – the patron eastwards, the parish westwards.[52] The second was the rising tide of liturgical elaboration and of personal and corporate initiative in devotion. The paintings in the nave of St Alban's epitomize 'a period when lay people have begun more generally to appropriate to themselves types of devotion formerly of monastic origin, in which images played an important part'.[53] When the Faringdon vicarage ordinance was issued in 1227, the rectors of many ordinary parish churches were already rebuilding their chancels on spacious lines, with the liturgical paraphernalia of fixed sedilia and piscina.⁵⁴ During the thirteenth century the new symbolic importance of the altar led to the provision of retables, the proliferation of lights and richer glazing displays, making the east end of the chancel a remote but brightly lit theatre for mass performance.⁵⁵ West of the rood-screen, parishioners would soon embark on the initiatives which created the classic late medieval parish church: the enlargement of naves, the addition of aisles and chapels and the insertion of screens to accommodate the proliferating altars of parish gilds, chantries and cult images.⁵⁶

Thus clerical groups with a collegiate past must have seemed less and less different from the various clergy, themselves multifarious in their functions, who used any substantial parish church. Especially in the major urban churches, liturgy could be a co-operative activity between the official establishment and clergy (notably chantry priests) maintained on lay endowments. The parishioners were now paying for more and more clergy who would make an ever-increasing contribution to liturgy, music and teaching, and their claim on space within the church was correspondingly greater.⁵⁷ It is symptomatic that cruciformity was unfashionable after the mid-fourteenth century: a common feature of the drive to convert the church into a rectangle with aisles was the replacement of the axial with a western tower.⁵⁸ In such cases clerical space tended to retreat as parochial space advanced, and arrangements in newly built churches suited current priorities. In Holy Trinity at Coventry, guild chapels ran up the chancel aisles by 1500, while the rood-screen at Ashburton (Devon) was set well to the east, leaving the quasi-transepts as part of the nave.⁵⁹ Even in ground plans inherited from the past, old forms could assume new functions: transepts were convenient sites for guild and chantry altars, for instance.

Yet there was still life in the old models. Ottery St Mary (Devon) and Tong (Shropshire) show that if a fourteenth- or fifteenth-century patron chose to found a new college of clergy in an existing parish church, the cruciform plan was still thought to be the best way of housing the dual functions.⁶⁰ Even in the much larger number of former minsters transmuted into grand urban churches, the basic layout of the east end and its adjuncts was powerfully influenced by the past. The rood-screen, increasingly emphatic through these very changes, still divided the activities to its west from those to its east. After 1300, rood-lofts started to appear at the ordinary parochial level, offering a powerful and independent visual focus for devotion in the nave and influencing how liturgy and music were structured.⁶¹

This chapter has traced the definition, and then the diffusion, of a pattern which was to influence the layout of major parish churches for the rest of the Middle Ages. The elaboration of the eastern arm, combining a long chancel for the corporate liturgy of a clerical group with transepts for lesser altars served by its members, had been a development principally of collegiate and quasi-collegiate churches during the eleventh and twelfth centuries. The major changes of the thirteenth to fifteenth centuries were the extension of these forms to lesser churches, and a corresponding particularization of the nave and aisles for the benefit of lay groups. The underlying trend is consistently towards a clearer demarcation of devotional space. Gradually overlaid on the old tradition of community life in minsters was the expectation of private daily masses for each priest, and somewhere to perform them. In the nave, the laity who paid for more and more mass-singers came to call the tune: parochial congregations, guilds and chantries expected their own miniature versions of the grand retables and roods, and their own spaces defined by screens.[62] This definition epitomized the range and variety of late medieval lay religion:

> If the roof were lifted from the parish church of Ludlow in the fifteenth century there would be revealed no less than eleven separate sub-groups of the parishioners at their several altars in the nave. Such, in a market town parish, was the variety of linked social and religious associations, in several of which any individual might choose to participate in turn.[63]

There was much that was new about late medieval local religion, and some of the grandest churches of the day had no significant history behind them. Yet practices were conditioned, far more than historians have recognized, by an accommodation between clerical and lay communities which originated well before the Norman Conquest, and which lasted best in small-town society. At the urban ex-minsters, new currents in popular devotion merged with older forms of lay religious life centred on mother churches. After the thirteenth century, parish guilds contributed a flexibility to local religious life which the parochial framework lacked; yet their own roots stretched back to a world in which guilds formed a bridge between the clergy of proto-urban minsters and the scattered lay communities of the mother parishes.[64] By the same token, their late medieval liturgical space had evolved from arrangements designed to serve the dual needs of clergy and laity, who centuries earlier had stimulated urban growth through the co-ordinated rhythms of their social and religious lives.

Acknowledgements

Comments from Paul Binski, Sarah Blair, Clive Burgess, Eric Fernie, David Palliser and Gervase Rosser have improved earlier drafts. I owe a special debt to Christine Peters for her rigorous criticism.

Notes

1. There is a good survey in R. Morris, *Churches in the Landscape* (1989), 198–210.
2. A. Everitt, 'The Banburys of England', *Urban History Yearbook 1974*, 28–38; J. Blair, 'Minster churches in the landscape', in D. Hooke (ed.), *Anglo-Saxon Settlements* (1988), 35–58, at 40–50.
3. For this paragraph and the next see J. Blair, 'Secular minster churches in Domesday Book', in P.H. Sawyer (ed.), *Domesday Book: a Reassessment* (1985), 104–42; J.H. Denton, *English Royal Free Chapels 1100–1300* (1970); *idem*, 'Royal supremacy in ancient demesne churches', *Journal of Ecclesiastical History*, 22 (1971), 289–302; A. Hamilton Thompson, 'Notes on colleges of secular canons in England', *Archaeological Journal*, 74 (1917), 139–239.
4. Thompson, 'Notes on colleges', 192 f, stresses the difference between collegiate and portionary churches, but it is probably anachronistic to apply this to the pre-1200 period.
5. See above all the ordinances of Hugh de Welles, Bishop of Lincoln: A. Gibbons (ed.), *Liber Antiquus de Ordinationibus Vicariarum Tempore Hugonis Wells* (1888).
6. For the early development of the vicarage system see B.R. Kemp, 'Monastic possession of parish churches in England in the twelfth century', *Journal of Ecclesiastical History*, 31 (1980), 133–60.
7. J. Blair, 'St Beornwald of Bampton', *Oxoniensia*, 49 (1984), 47–55. This clerical community is the subject of a detailed study in progress, and is also discussed in *Victoria County History* (hereafter VCH) *Oxfordshire*, vol. 13 (1966), 48–53, so only brief references are given here.
8. *Registrum Antiquissimum Linc.* vol. 3, Lincoln Record Society, 29 (1935), 265; *Rotuli Literarum Patentium*, 1(1), 86, 87; *Rotuli Hugonis de Welles*, vol. 1, Lincoln Record Society, 3 (1912), 129.
9. *Registrum Edmund Lacy*, vol. 2, Canterbury and York Society, 61 (1966), 339–41.
10. *VCH Yorkshire East Riding*, vol. 1, 287–93.
11. R.A. Stalley, 'A twelfth-century patron of architecture', *Journal of British Archaeological Association*, 3rd series, 34 (1971), 62–83; *An Inventory of Archaeological Sites and Churches in Northampton*, Royal Commission on Historical Monuments (hereafter RCHM) (1985), 61–2; S. Woodcock, 'The building history of St Mary de Haura, New Shoreham', *Journal of British Archaeological Association*, 145 (1992), 89–103.
12. Blair, 'Secular minster churches in Domesday Book', 133–7.
13. J. Blair, 'St Frideswide's monastery: problems and possibilities', *Oxoniensia*, 53 (1988), 221–58, at 228.
14. Chester will be discussed by R. Gem in *Medieval Art and Architecture in Chester* (British Archaeological Association, forthcoming), and by A. Thacker in *VCH Chester* (forthcoming). For Waltham see E.C. Fernie, 'The Romanesque Church of Waltham Abbey', *Journal of British Archaeological Association*, 138 (1985), 48–78. The existence of a great Romanesque church at Beverley is well attested, even though virtually nothing survives of it.
15. R.D.H. Gem, 'Holy Trinity Church, Bosham', *Archaeological Journal*, 142 (1985), 32–6.

16. M.J. Franklin, 'The identification of minsters in the Midlands', *Anglo-Norman Studies*, 7 (1985), 69–88. The very sumptuous example at Blockley (Gloucestershire) is discussed by J.K. West, 'Architectural sculpture in parish churches of the 11th- and 12th-century West Midlands', in J. Blair (ed.), *Minsters and Parish Churches* (1988), 159–67, at 164–5.
17. *RCHM Herefordshire*, 3, 100–103; RCHM, *Inventory of Sites in Northampton*, 57–61.
18. I am grateful to a lecture by Richard Gem for this idea.
19. E. Fernie, *The Architecture of the Anglo-Saxons* (1982), ch. 8.
20. Plans in Blair, 'Secular minster churches', 122, Fig. 7.2.
21. Ibid.; Blair, *Minsters and Parish Churches*, 14–15 and references cited there.
22. For this definition see R. Gilyard-Beer, *Abbeys*, 2nd edn (HMSO, 1976), 16–18 and Fig. 6. R. Halsey, 'The earliest architecture of the Cistercians in England', in C. Norton and D. Park (eds), *Cistercian Art and Architecture in the British Isles* (1986), 65–85, considers the wider context and questions (p. 68 etc.) how far the plan-form is distinctively Cistercian.
23. Two useful surveys of Augustinian churches of this type are given by D. Baker in B. Cunliffe (ed.), *Excavations at Portchester Castle*, 3 (1977), 115–20, and P. Greene, *Norton Priory* (1989), ch. 5.
24. The plans in Fig. 12.4 are based on the following sources. Norton: Greene, *Norton Priory*, Fig. 36. Dorchester: *VCH Oxfordshire*, vol. 7, 57. Leonard Stanley: *VCH Gloucestershire*, vol. 10, 265, and *Antiquaries Journal*, 9 (1929), 13–25. Ewenny: C.A.R. Radford, *Ewenny Priory* (HMSO, 1952). Crediton: see Fig. 12.6. Bampton: survey by J. and S. Blair. Shifnal: M. Salter, *The Old Parish Churches of Shropshire* (1988), 62. St Mary's Shrewsbury: ibid., 64. Halesowen: *VCH Worcestershire*, vol. 3, 147. Hemel Hempstead: RCHM, *Hertfordshire*, 111. Cholsey: *VCH Berkshire*, vol. 3, 300. Lambourn: *VCH Berkshire*, vol. 4, 261. Ripple: *VCH Worcestershire*, vol. 3, 492. Bishops Cleeve: *Transactions Bristol and Gloucestershire Archaeological Society*, 4 (1879–80), opp. 250. Hook Norton: survey by J. and S. Blair.
25. D. Parsons, '*Sacrarium*: ablution drains in early medieval churches', in L.A.S. Butler and R.K. Morris (eds), *The Anglo-Saxon Church: Papers on History, Architecture and Archaeology in Honour of Dr. H.M. Taylor*, CBA Research Report, 60 (1986), 105–20, at 106–8, gives an excellent account of this development, emphasizing the connection between the movement of the altar eastwards and the installation of sedilia and piscinae in the south wall.
26. For the choirs of French *collégiales* see J. Hubert, 'La Vie Commune des Clercs et l'Archéologie', in his *Arts et Vie Sociale de la Fin du Monde Antique au Moyen Age* (Geneva, 1977), 125–59, at 153–4.
27. R. and C. Brooke, *Popular Religion in the Middle Ages* (1984), 86–8; J. Blair, 'Anglo-Saxon minsters: a topographical review', in J. Blair and R. Sharpe (eds), *Pastoral Care before the Parish* (1992), 226–66, at 246–58.
28. For what follows see G. Rosser, 'The cure of souls in English towns before 1000', in Blair and Sharpe (eds), *Pastoral Care before the Parish*, 267–84; M. Franklin, 'The cathedral as parish church: the case of southern England', in D. Abulafia, M. Franklin and M. Rubin (eds), *Church and City 1000–1500: Essays in Honour of Christopher Brooke* (1992), 173–98; Blair, 'St. Frideswide's Monastery', 255–8.

29. Franklin, 'Cathedral as parish church', 192–4.
30. Ibid., 178–81.
31. Blair, 'St Frideswide's Monastery', 255–6.
32. Rosser, 'Cure of souls in English towns', 271.
33. P. Binski, 'The murals in the nave of St Alban's Abbey', in Abulafia, Franklin and Rubin, *Church and City 1000–1500*, 249–78.
34. Blair, 'Secular minster churches', 138. For this pattern of endowment at Southwark Priory see J. Blair, *Early Medieval Surrey: Landholding, Church and Settlement before 1300* (1991), 142–8.
35. Greene, *Norton Priory*, 85–6.
36. Hubert, 'La Vie Commune des Clercs', 154 (and 155–9 for the functions of *jubés* and choir-screens).
37. Fernie, 'Romanesque church of Waltham', 61–6 and Fig. 4. Cf. Laon, where the screen was one bay west of the crossing and the next bay westwards contained the nave altar framed betwen four elaborate piers: E. Fernie, 'La Fonction Liturgique des Piliers Cantonnés dans la Nef de la Cathédrale de Laon', *Bulletin Monumental*, 145 (1987), 257–66. For the Anglo-Saxon and Norman background to nave altars and roods see B.C. Raw, *Anglo-Saxon Crucifixion Iconography* (1990), 44–9.
38. *VCH Sussex*, vol. 4, 188.
39. P. Riden and J. Blair (eds), *History of Chesterfield: V: Records of the Borough of Chesterfield* (1980), 169.
40. C.N.L. Brooke, 'The churches of medieval Cambridge', in D. Beales and G. Best (eds), *History, Society and the Churches: Essays in Honour of Owen Chadwick* (1985), 64–6; RCHM, *Cambridge*, 2 (1959), 281; RCHM, *Oxford* (1939), 78–9; N. Pevsner, *The Buildings of England: Cambridgeshire*, 2nd edn (1970), 226–7; J. Sherwood and N. Pevsner, *The Buildings of England: Oxfordshire* (1974), 156–61.
41. Fernie, 'Romanesque church of Waltham', 61, and *idem*, 'Fonction Liturgique ... de Laon', 260–62, argues that the structural hiatus after the building of the two or three easternmost bays of the nave, commonly found in great churches, marks the westward limit of the part used by the monks or clergy. For the antecedents of arrangements involving both nave screen and choir screen see Raw, *Anglo-Saxon Crucifixion Iconography*, 51–2.
42. Aymer Vallance, *Greater English Screens* (1947), 21, 130–79, argues that this arrangement was restricted to monastic churches, but the cases which he cites (notably Ottery St. Mary, pp. 156–8) do not support this view. There is a lengthy discussion of this issue in F.B. Bond and B. Camm, *Roodscreens and Roodlofts*, vol. 1 (1909), 3–58.
43. A. H[amilton] T[hompson], 'The tower of Silkstone Church', *Yorkshire Archaeological Journal*, 28 (1924–26), 342–4. The bells and belfry were defined as a parish responsibility in 1228x56 (Salisbury III, c. 8; *Councils and Synods*, ii.1, 512–13).
44. Blair, 'St Frideswide's Monastery', 250–51.
45. Rosser, 'Cure of souls in English towns', 271 n. 18; *Yorkshire Chantry Certificates*, vol. 2, Surtees Society, 92 (1895), 528–9; *VCH Yorkshire*, vol. 3, 355. For the locations of the altars of St Martin and St Katherine see D. O'Connor, 'The medieval stained glass of Beverley Minster', in C. Wilson (ed.), *Medieval Art and Architecture in the East Riding of Yorkshire*, British Archaeological Association Conference Transactions for 1983

(1989), 67, 71–2; in the Romanesque minster St Martin's altar was on the north side, apparently either in the transept or in the aisle near the crossing. I am grateful to David Palliser for advice on this matter.

46. The 'Canons of Eadgar' (in fact compiled 1005x8), c. 44, prohibit women from approaching the altar during mass, which may possibly imply that male laity were allowed to do so: *Councils and Synods*, i.1, 328–9. A late-medieval woodcut showing parishioners gathering around the priest at mass is reproduced by E. Duffy, *The Stripping of the Altars* (1992), pl. 43.

47. A statute of 1229 enjoins 'ut laici non sedeant in choro inter clericos', but another of ?1239, exempts patrons (Worcester II, c. 23, and Lincoln c. 45; *Councils and Synods*, ii.1, 174, 275).

48. W.R. Jones and W.D. Macray (eds), *Sarum Charters and Documents*, Rolls Series, 97 (1891), 187–9.

49. A.H. Thompson, *The Historical Growth of the English Parish Church* (1911), 118.

50. See n. 7 above.

51. This is inference, since one of the three stalls was destroyed in 1870, but the other two bear the appropriate initials.

52. The first clear evidence for this comes from Winchester diocese in 1224: a rector was obliged to maintain his chancel roof, whereas 'parochiani ... compellantur corpus ecclesie reficere secundum quod tenentur' [the parishioners were compelled to refurbish the body of the church as they were obliged to do] (Winchester I, c. 11; *Councils and Synods*, ii.1, 128). Some 15 years later it was declared that 'onus reficiendi et conservandi chorum seu cancellum ad rectores, ad parochianos vero corpus ecclesie secundum consuetudinem ecclesie Anglicane optentam et approbatam non dubitant pertinere' [they do not doubt that the burden of refurbishing the choir or chancel belongs to rectors, however, the parishioners are obliged to look after the nave of the church according to the customs of the English church as they have been handed down and approved] (Salisbury II, c. 2; *Councils and Synods*, ii.1, 367).

53. Binski, 'Murals in the nave of St Alban's Abbey', 272.

54. Thompson, *Historical Growth*, 37–50, 78–87; Parsons, 'Sacrarium'.

55. P. Binski, 'The thirteenth-century English altarpiece', *Proceedings of the Norwegian Academy in Rome* (forthcoming). I am very grateful to Dr Binski for showing me this paper in advance of publication.

56. Summaries in Morris, *Churches in the Landscape*, ch. 9; C. Platt, *The English Medieval Town* (1976), ch. 6.

57. This has been demonstrated above all in two articles by Clive Burgess: '"For the increase of divine service": chantries in the parish in late medieval Bristol', *Journal of Ecclesiastical History*, 36 (1985), 46–65; and 'A service for the dead: the form and function of the anniversary in late medieval Bristol', *Transactions Bristol and Gloucestershire Archaeological Society*, 105 (1987), 183–211, especially 206.

58. A.H. Thompson, *The Ground Plan of the English Parish Church* (1911), 124–33. In 1307 the archbishop saw the axial tower of Silkstone as anomalous, the siting of towers at the west end being 'communius in hiis partibus' [more common in these areas], and a western tower eventually replaced it: T[hompson], 'Tower of Silkstone'.

59. Morris, *Churches in the Landscape*, 367; N. Orme (ed.), *Unity and Variety: a History of the Church in Devon and Cornwall* (1991), 59.
60. Late medieval 'chantry colleges' are surveyed by Thompson, 'Notes on colleges', 196–9.
61. Bond and Cam, *Roodscreens and Roodlofts*, vol. 1, 78–82. There is an evocative early reference in a visitation of Tillingham Church (Essex) in 1335 (Guildhall Library, MS 25122/ 1112), where it is complained that 'solarium de ligno in navi ecclesie coram cruce inpedit lumen circa altare Beate Virginis, et facit etiam locum obscurum in quo parochiani garrulant, et inpedit etiam quominus stantes in ecclesia possent videre corpus Christi' [the wooden solar in front of the rood in the nave of the church impedes the light around the altar of the Holy Virgin, and it makes a dark space in which the parishioners chatter, and it also prevents those standing in the church from seeing the elevation of the host]. Burgess, 'Increase of divine service', 56, notes that the roodloft of a late medieval town church would often house the organ, organist and choir.
62. I am grateful to Clive Burgess for the last point. Brooke, 'Churches of medieval Cambridge', 67, has evocatively sketched the context of the dual-function college chapels and parish churches:

> The practice of daily mass for priests became normal in the tenth and eleventh centuries; by the fifteenth it had entered so deeply into the religious sentiment of the age that many devout priests evidently coveted their own private place to celebrate it ... [I]n some sense the search for privacy in worship is a crucial explanation of the proliferating private oratories and chapels and pews.

Binski, 'Murals in nave of St Albans', 263, observes that 'each painting, with its two-tiered structure, represents in effect a rood placed upon a beam over a statuesque Marian figure, a smaller counterpart to the grander exalted carved and painted roods by now common in the midst of Benedictine churches, and also over their high altars'.
63. G. Rosser, 'Parochial conformity and voluntary religion in late medieval England', *Transactions Royal Historical Society*, 6th series, 1 (1991), 173–89, at 187–8.
64. G. Rosser, 'Communities of parish and guild in the late Middle Ages', in S.J. Wright (ed.), *Parish, Church and People* (1988), 29–55; idem, 'The Anglo-Saxon gilds', in J. Blair, *Minsters and Parish Churches*, 31–4.

Index

abbot 132–3, 251
Abbots Bromley 160
Abingdon 156
accounts 69, 103
Aethelstan 209
agrarian society 10
aisle 241, 243, 245–6, 248, 250, 256, 259, 288
air photographs 136, 147
Alcester 55, 64, 67, 70
    Abbey 26
    abbot of 70
aldermen 2, 15
ale 62
almoner 168
alms 4
almshouses 170
Alnwick 178
altar 7, 246, 256
    high 279
Amblecote 65
Angevin monarchy 48
Anglo-Norman colonization 131
Annals of Ulster 149
Aquablanca, Peter, Bishop of Hereford 23
apprentices 11
appropriation 4, 103
apse 241
Aragon 45
arbitration 27, 36
archaeological excavations 141, 183, 241, 248
    evidence 6, 156, 160
archaeology 7, 161, 178, 243
archery butts 168
architectural historians 7, 272
archives, mendicant 76
Arden, Forest of 58, 66
aristocracy 4, 21
Aristotle 20
Armagh 144, 146–7
Arras 12
artisans 10–11, 14, 70, 82
Ashburton 288
Atherstone 58, 63, 70
Athlone 142

Attwood, Thomas 260
Augustinians 108, 121, 139, 279
    canons 282
    Priories 274, 282
Austin friars, 83, 85, 87–9, 120
Avignon 13
Avon Valley 66
Aylesford 77

Baltic 111
Bampton 275–6, 280, 285, 287
baptism 210, 212
barons 44
Bath 47, 157, 159
    Abbey 159
Battenhall 60
Battle 158–9
Beauchamp, Lady Margaret 59
    Lady Catherine 67
belfry 284
bell ropes 63
bells 253
Benedictine 5–6, 26, 155
    cathedral priory 16, 18, 104, 182
    monastery 6, 160, 171, 274, 281
    nunnery 238, 263
    Order 156
    town planning 155
benefice 102, 108
    urban 103
Benet of Hulme 16
Berkhampstead 47
Beverley 100, 106
    Minster 278, 285
    St John's 106
bishop 12, 49, 132–3
    suffragan 239
bishopric 132
Bishop's Cleeve 61, 63, 65, 280
    rectory 56
Bishop's Lynn 100, 106–7, 109, 115–18
    All Saints, South Lynn 116
    Holy Trinity 116
        Guild 120
    St James 105, 108, 110, 118–19
    St Margaret's 4, 105, 108–10, 113

296 INDEX

St Mary on the Bridge 108, 116
St Mary on the Mount 108, 117, 119
St Nicholas's 105, 108, 110, 118–19
Black Death 13, 100, 105, 160, 236
Blois 45
Board of Health plans 179, 185, 187–9, 193
Bologna 89
Bonvil, Sir William 32
Bordesley 55, 59
  Abbey 56, 63
borough 155, 159–60, 166, 177
  Anglo-Norman 143
  boundary 167, 169, 263
  courts 70
Brabant
Brakelond, Joscelin of 47
brasses 275
  memorial 259, 275
Breton towns 15
brewers 64
Bridgnorth 47, 67
brine 65
Brinklow 196
Bristol 3, 34, 45, 47, 58, 61–3, 69, 211
  mayor of 15
  merchants 61, 67
  St Augustine's Abbey 34
Bromsgrove 67
Bruton 157
Buckfast 157
Buckler, John 238
building
  materials 4, 65
  trades 11
  works 3
burgage tenure 158, 172, 199
burgesses 14, 64, 163
burh 134, 142, 144, 148, 157, 159, 172, 212, 215–18, 220, 224, 226, 229, 230, 233
burial 210, 212, 221, 262, 282
Burton Dassett 56, 65
Burton on Trent 64, 158, 166, 183, 191
  Abbey 160
Bury St Edmunds 45–6, 100, 158–9
  Abbey 47

butter 62

Caen stone 252
Calais 111
Cambridge 44, 47, 89, 101, 104, 274, 283
  Michaelhouse 283
  Peterhouse 283
  St Mary the Less 283
  Stourbridge fair 61
canons regular 272, 275
Canterbury 13, 34–5, 85, 89, 132, 236
  All Saints 236–8, 241, 246–7, 250, 261–3
  Archbishop of 33, 238, 246, 256, 262, 264
    Lanfranc 163, 191, 199, 265
  Austin Friars 261
  Blackfriars 261–2
  Burgate 34, 250, 262–3
  castle 239, 263–4
    new 239
  Christ Church Cathedral 238, 241, 252, 261–5
    precinct 237
  Greyfriars 261–2
  High Street 246, 255
  Holy Cross 237–9, 249, 256–7, 261–2, 265
  mills 34
  St Alphege's 236, 240, 242, 245–6, 252, 257, 259, 261–4
  St Andrew's 237, 239, 244, 255, 257, 261–3
  St Augustine's Abbey 236, 238–9, 250–51, 261, 264
  St Dunstan's 236, 245–6, 253–4, 260–61, 264–5
  St Edmund Ridingate 238–9, 256
  St George's 236, 238, 241–2, 246, 248, 252, 257, 263
  St Gregory's Priory 238, 241, 260–62, 265
  St Helen's 236
  St Margaret's 236–8, 241, 243, 254–5, 261, 263
  St Martin's 236, 239–40, 245–6, 252, 256, 261, 264
  St Mary Bredin 236, 238–9, 241, 243, 246, 252, 256, 260–63

St Mary Bredman 237, 253, 258, 261–3
St Mary-de-Castro 239, 256, 261–3
St Mary Magdalen 237–8, 244, 258, 261–3
St Mary Northgate 236, 238–9, 241, 244–5, 261–2, 265
St Mary Queningate 237, 261–2
St Michael's Burgate 239, 261–2
St Mildred's 236, 239, 245–6, 249, 252, 257, 259, 261–5
St Pancras's 241, 264
St Paul's 237, 245, 250–52, 261–2, 264
St Peter's 236, 245–7, 252, 257, 260–64
St Sepulcre's Priory 238, 261–4
Watling Street 241
Westgate 239, 256, 265
Whitefriars 262
Carcassonne 134
Carmelites 77, 85, 87–9, 108, 120–21
carnival 15, 17
Carolingian empire 134
carpenter 63
carrier 60, 68
cartwright 59
Cashel 135
Castile 45
castle 12, 134, 142, 150, 277
  bailey 226
  earthwork 148
cathedral 132, 157, 277, 281
  city 2, 15
  close 275
cattle 58
cemetery 116, 141, 224, 226, 238, 261
  chapel 220
central-place functions 7, 157
Chaddesley Corbett 66
chancel 7, 241–2, 246, 248, 250–51, 253, 255–6, 259, 263, 278–9, 285–6
  long 276, 288
chantry 9, 251, 288–9
  chapel 104, 252–3, 259–60, 288
  priests 102, 260, 277, 288
chapel 105, 117, 277
  college 283

dependent 220
Lady 244, 250–51, 253, 255, 259, 285
chaplain 9, 283
chapmen 31
chapter house 81
charters 24, 82, 177
  forged 6
Chartham church 252
Chartres, Bishop of 14
Chateau Narbonnais 147
Chaucer 105
Chester 157, 185, 194, 199
  Bishop of 191, 199
  Earl of 177, 181, 194
  Hugh II 179, 181
  St John's 278
Chesterfield 283
  guild of smiths 283
Chichester 211
  All Saints in the Pallant 211
  Roger of 251
Chipping Campden 67
Cholsey 280
churches 272
  appropriated 155
  Celtic monastic 157
  collegiate 102, 273, 281–2
  cruciform 7, 272–3, 275, 278–9
  parish 4, 6–7, 159, 212, 236, 274
churchwardens 55, 64, 104, 116, 121
  accounts 256, 260
churchyard 34, 102, 167, 275, 287; *see also* burial ground; cemetery
  St Paul's 46
Cirencester, Abbot of 82
Cistercians 56, 155
cité 142, 147–8
civic ceremony 14
civitates 132, 134, 139
Clarisses 80
class conflict 1, 9–12
clergy 3, 9–10, 34, 70–71, 275
Clonard 141
Clonmacnoise 138–9, 143, 147–8
cloth 3, 13, 62, 63, 65
clothing 59
clothmaking 63
  woollen 60
Colchester 46, 79
Coleshill 58, 63

collective memory 28–9
colleges, secular 274
Cologne 89
community 22, 27
  urban 272
conflict 2, 29, 33, 36
convent 4, 155, 157
conventual buildings 81, 183
cook 45
cooper 59
coppice 65
coroner 24
Corpus Christi 14, 16
Coventry 6–7, 14, 16, 56, 58, 61, 63–4, 67, 69, 158, 177, 179
  Bishop of 61, 185, 198
  bishop's palace 183
  Bishop Street 182, 191, 193–4
  Broadgate 185, 187, 190
  Butcher Row 187–9
  cathedral priory 59, 182
  Cook Street 182, 191, 193–4
  Cross Cheaping 187–8
  Earl Street 187, 200
  Holy Trinity 179, 181–3, 185, 191, 198, 288
  Ironmonger Row 187, 191
  Little Butcher Row 185, 188
  Pittancer's Rental 185, 187
  Priory Lane 183
  Priory mill 185
  St Mary's Abbey 159, 177, 199
  St Michael's 179, 181–3, 199
  Smithford Street 187, 189, 190
  West Orchard 189–90
craftsmen 13–16, 63
Crediton 273, 279–80, 284, 285
Cricklade 157
Crowle 60
Crusade, first 44, 77, 238
  Albigensian 146
Cromwell, Thomas 50
Crutched Friars 80
cult, Marian 115

Dean, Forest of 61
debt 22, 70
Deerhurst Priory 225
deer park 59
defences 5, 142, 165; *see also* town walls

demesne 59
Derby 147
Derry 149
Devizes 47, 277
  Richard of 46
Devon 65
  Earl of 32
Dissolution 35, 81, 183, 199, 261–2
ditch 35, 147, 164, 167, 226, 256; *see also vallum*
Domesday 28, 159, 178
  Book 166, 177, 199
Dominican Friars 3, 50, 77, 81–7, 90, 108, 121
Doncaster 115
Doras 141
Dorchester 285
  Abbey 280
Dover 77, 264
Downpatrick 142
drapers 14
drinking houses 32
Droitwich 55, 58, 63–5, 67
Dublin 131, 135, 147
Dudley 58, 64
Duleek 136, 138, 143
Dunmore 142
Durham, New Elvet 159
Durrow 143

East Anglia 16, 157
earthworks 136, 141, 164
ecclesiastical communities 7
  liberty of 2, 21
Edgar, King 156, 209
Edward I, King 2, 43, 47–8, 87, 90
Edward III, King 156, 209
élite 2, 20, 177
  civic 30
  feudal 142
  of Hereford 28
Ely 158, 281
  Holy Cross altar 281
  St Mary's 281
  St Peter's 281
England 11–12, 115, 274
episcopal see 178
Ethelred, King 163
Ethelwold, King of Kent 132, 156
Europe 4–5, 77, 79, 131–2, 142, 274
  Western 133–4

Evesham 58, 63–5, 68–9, 100, 158–9, 166, 183
  Abbey 55, 60, 160
  Vale of 133–4
Ewenny Priory 280
Exeter 31, 33
  Bishop of 31
  canons of 31–2
  cathedral close 32
  Dean and Chapter 31
  mayor Shillingford 31–2
  St Stephen's fee 32
extra-parochial areas 236

fairs 16, 23, 63, 67, 76–7, 133, 166
  St Botolph's 61
  Stourbridge 61
Faringdon 286
Fécamp Abbey 159
Feckenham Forest 58
fee farm 2, 22, 33
fees 27, 36
Feldon 58
Fenagh 149
Ferdinand and Isabella 48
festival, religious 199
feudal 16
  kingdoms 131
  landowning 12
  power 12
  society 4
financial services 44
fines 26
fish 3, 61–2, 65, 109, 187
fisheries 109
fishmongers 14
fish pool 163
Flanders 134
font 226
foodstuffs 55
France 2, 11–12, 48, 79, 89, 279
franchises 30, 33
Franciscans 77, 80–84, 86–7, 90, 108
  Friars 3, 50, 121–2
  Provincial chapter 89
fraternities 9, 55
French towns 13, 15
Friars de Areno 87, 89
Friars of the Holy Cross 79, 84, 87–8
Friars of the Sack 79, 84–5, 87–8, 90
Frome 65

Galway 142
garlic 58
Gascony 48, 111
gate 158, 213, 245, 261
  churches 225, 227
  fortified 147
  priory, 189
  town 17, 224
gentry 9, 14
Germany 89
ghetto 44
Gladman, John 16–17
  insurrection 2, 18
glass, stained 252, 260
Glastonbury 156, 159
glaziers 3, 64
glazing 63, 288
glebe 70, 121
Glendalough 140, 147
Gloucester 6–8, 35, 47, 58, 61, 157, 212–13, 215, 231–2
  Abbot of 35, 228
  All Saints' 224–7
  Barton Street 225
  Duke of 16
  Eastgate Street 225
  gates 35, 224
  great ditch 35
  High Cross 35
  Holy Trinity 226
  Lower Westgate Street 227
  New Inn 228
  Oxbow Lane 225
  parishes of 222
  St Aldate's 225, 232
  St John's 224–5, 227–9
  St Kyneburgh's 224, 227
  St Mary de Crypt 225
  St Mary de Lode 221, 224, 226
  St Mary's Square 227
  St Michael's 224–5, 229
  St Oswald's Priory 224
  St Peter's Abbey 6, 45, 160, 212, 221, 227
  Westgate Street 226
Godgifu (Godiva) 158–9, 181, 198
goldsmiths 3, 60, 64, 68
gold wire 63
goods and services 55
Gough Map 58
Gower, John 10

grange 169
Greyfriars 77, 82
Grimley 60
Grossteste, Robert 47
graveyard 248, 256, 261–3
guild 14–15, 63, 70, 171, 283, 289
  ceremonies 110
  chapel 288
  craft 13–15
  hall 100, 179
  play 16
  of St George 15–16

Halesowen 55, 58–9, 63, 280
  Abbey 56, 61, 63–7
  parish church 56
Hamwic 266
Hanley Castle 67
Hanseatic 111
Hartlebury Castle 64
Haslor 70
Haughmond 279
Hebrew *starrs* 43
Hemel Hempstead 280
Henley in Arden 64–5
Henry I 28
Henry II 9
Henry III 3, 23, 46, 49, 50–51, 79, 80, 87–8, 90
Henry IV 88
Henry VI 116
Henry VII 113, 117
Henry VIII 117
Hereford 2, 13, 21–2, 24, 29, 31, 33–5, 47, 157, 211, 282
  Bailiffs of 23, 25
  Cabbage Lane 31
  Castle Street 21
  cathedral 23–4, 27, 30
    canons 21, 30
    cemetery 21, 24, 29
    clergy 26
    close 22, 26
    fee 24–5, 28
    precinct 23, 28
  coroner 24
  customs of 22
  Dean and Chapter 22–7
  fair 23
  King's fee 22, 24–5, 27
  liberties 25, 27
  mayor of 22, 24–5, 28
  St John's 282
  town hall 24, 30
Hermits of St Augustine 79
Hessle 277
Hiberno–Norse towns 131, 135, 147
high crosses 139, 142
High Wycombe 47
Holy Child of La Guardia 45
Hook Norton 280
hospitals 102, 108, 260, 263
  leper 161
houses of converts 3, 50–51, 90
Howden, Roger of 46
Hull 102
  Holy Trinity 277
Hulne 77
Humbert of Romans 76
Huntingdon 47

images 282
  cult 288
imported products 55
imprisonment 28
incumbent 104
Inishcaltra 141
inn 228, 255
Inquisition 50
Inquisitiones Nonarum 102
Iona 140
Ipswich 115
Ireland 4–5, 44, 131, 133–6, 177
  Anglo-Norman 134, 142, 149
ironmongery 63, 70
Isabel of Bavaria 15
Isabella, Queen 181
Italian bankers 48
Italy 83, 89

Jews 43, 84
  Ashkenazi 44
  expulsion of 2, 45
  in Lincoln 86
  murder of 2, 45, 46, 47
  orthodox 144
Jewish–Christian relationship 48
Jewish
  community 3
  residents 2
Jordan of Saxony 89
journeyman 12–13

justice, administration of 22
Jumièges 136

Kent 157
Kells 136–7, 142
Kidderminster 58, 65
Kildare 133, 139, 144, 148
Killaloe 142
Kilpatrick 141
Kinver 64
Kinwarton 70
Kirkham 282
knight 11, 13, 44, 67

laity 7
Lambourne 280
Lancaster, Edmund of 80, 85
landgable payments 221, 225, 227
landowners 1, 9, 11, 155
    ecclesiastical 16
    monastic 10
landownership 33
Languedoc 11, 13, 79
Lateran Council, Third 50
    Fourth 48, 275
Ledbury 278, 285
legacies 119–20
Leicester 197
Le Mans 134
Lent 17, 49
Leofric of Mercia 6, 158–9, 181–3, 190, 198
Leominster 160
Leonard Stanley Priory 280
Liathmore 141
Lichfield 58, 61, 67, 171, 193
Liège, Bishop of 80
Lilleshall 282
Limerick 135, 147
Lincoln 13, 44–6, 200
    Bishop of 46, 275
    Earl of 87
        Henry de Lacy, 82
    Hugh of 45, 51
    jews in 86
Little Coxwell 286
liturgical arrangements 276
liturgy 278, 286, 288
Llantony Priory 225, 227–8
locksmith 64
London 3–4, 7, 10, 12, 14, 17, 44, 58, 60, 62, 67, 76–7, 80, 89, 104, 115, 164, 166, 179, 194, 210–11, 218, 255, 265
    Aldersgate 84
    Baynard's Castle 85
    Bethlehem Hospital 90
    Bishopsgate 83
    Bridge 90
    chancery 80
    Chancery Lane 50
    City of 46, 86
    city liberties 17
    Colchurch Street 87
    Cornhill 77, 81, 86
    Fleet Prison 82
    Fleet River 82, 85
    Fleet Street 83
    Holborn 85, 87, 89
        Bridge 82
    Holy Trinity, Aldgate 90
    Lincoln's Inn 82
    Ludgate 87
    Montfitchet tower 85
    Newgate 81–2
    St Andrew's, Holborn 81
    St Mary le Strand 84
    St Mary Staining 211
    St Michael Bassishaw 211
    St Nicholas, Shambles 81
    St Olave's, Bread Street 83
    St Olave's, Hart 84
    St Pancras 211
    St Paul's Cathedral 15
        Dean of 46
    St Thomas of Acon Hospital 90
    The Strand 60
    The Temple 90
    Tower of 46, 84
    Wards
        Broad Street 83
        Coleman Street 84
Longbridge Deverill 101
Long Itchington 58
Ludlow 102, 289
Lyon, 13
    Council of 79

malefactors 32
Malmesbury 157
Malvern Chase 58
manor 12, 250, 265

maps, manuscript 179
Margaret, Queen 87
market 26, 62, 67, 101, 142, 160, 163–4, 170–72, 182
  cross 187
  infill 187–9, 193
  place 159–60, 168, 170–71, 181, 185, 187, 189–91, 194, 199, 200
    triangular 6
  tolls 163
marketing 8
Marlborough 47
Marmion, Robert 194
martyrium 161
master craftsman 11, 13, 15
Matilda, Queen 172
Maxstoke Priory 55–6, 58–9, 61, 63–5, 68
mayor 2, 14–15, 17, 22, 24–5, 28, 34, 86, 90, 260
Mendicant Orders 4, 76
mercers 15
merchants 1–2, 4, 9–14, 17, 21, 31, 60–63, 66–7, 69
Mercia, Earls of 199
Merevale 55, 70
  Abbey 56, 59, 63–4
Merovingian 134
metal working 190
Mildenhall 47
mill 34
  water 59
Minoresses 80, 83, 85, 88
minster 212, 272, 274
  Anglo-Saxon 272
  church buildings 7, 272, 279
  old 209, 224, 226, 232
  parishes 209
  secular 157, 160–61
Minster in Thanet 239
mint 80
miracle 162
monastery 4, 8, 12, 102–3, 131, 133, 155, 277, 281
  Anglo-Saxon 136
  Irish 5, 138
monastic
  annals 140
  community 3
  enclosure 136

  houses 3
  institutions 4
  precincts 185
  towns 4–5, 68–9, 132–3, 135, 144, 150, 155
Monmouth, Thomas of 45
Montfort, Simon de 47, 147
moot hall 171
More, Thomas 260
More, William, Prior of Worcester 60, 62, 64, 67, 69
mortuary 106, 109–10, 119
mother church 272, 276
  ancient 212, 272
  parishes 274
Municipal Reform Act, 1835 22
municipium 171

nave 7, 241, 243, 245, 250, 255, 258–9, 276, 278, 281, 288
'nearest church door' principle 7, 211, 213, 218–21, 223–6, 230–33
Newbald 285
Newburgh, Richard of 46
Newbury 47
Newcastle under Lyme 13
Newcastle upon Tyne 47, 104
New Shoreham
  St Mary de Haura 277
Norfolk, Duke of 17
Norman 185
  Conquest 44, 178, 224–6, 236, 239, 241, 264–5, 279, 281, 289
  England 277
  invasion 2, 134
Normandy 44, 136
Northampton 64, 89
  St Giles's 277
  St Peter's 278, 280
Northleach 160
Norton Priory 280
Norwich 2, 15–18, 33, 44–7, 101, 104, 116, 179, 215, 225–6
  Bishop of 108–9
  Cathedral Priory 108
  Dean and Chapter 108
  Magdalen Hospital 16
  St Andrew's 104
  St Bartholomew's 104
  St Clement ad Pontem 104

St Giles's 104
St Gregory's 104
St John, Maddermarket 104
St Michael in Coslany 104
St Peter Mancroft 104
St Stephen's 104
St William of 45
Nottingham 210
novices 85
Nuneaton 58, 64, 70
nuns 161

Offa, King of Mercia 161–2
oligarchy 20
oratory 84
orchard 168, 171
Ordnance Survey plans 178–9
Oswold 156, 220
Ottery St Mary 288
Owston abbey 63
Oxford 3, 44, 49–50, 60, 77, 89, 104, 157, 274, 283
    Earl of 17
    Merton College 283–4
    St Frideswide's 281
        shrine of 282
    University of 89

pageant 14
painters 3, 64
Paris 79, 80, 89, 240–41
    Matthew 45, 79
parish 8–9, 15, 36, 102, 236
    boundary 7, 100–101, 105, 167, 179, 187, 210, 213–15, 218, 228, 264–5
    geography 218, 229–31
    intramural 210, 233
    urban 6, 100–101, 209, 232
parishioners 227, 274
Parliament 60
parochia 209, 224, 226, 229, 230, 232
pastoral care 6, 272, 274
patronage 238
peasant 10, 69, 70
    rebellions 9
peasantry 1, 9, 11
Pensnett 65
Pershore 58, 63–5, 67–8, 158–9
    Abbey 55–6, 60–61, 63–7, 69, 159–60

Peterborough 158–9, 183, 191
    Abbey 45, 63
pilgrimage 85, 115, 122, 162, 198
pilgrims 35, 62, 115–16, 171, 193
Pisa, Albert of 89
plague 7, 113, 256
plan
    analysis 5–6, 142, 156, 178, 180, 182–3, 185
    unit 156, 179, 182, 189, 191, 193–4
plot 182
    pattern 134, 164–6, 178
    series 164, 167, 169
political control 20
power 27
poor 10–11, 88
Pope
    Clement IV 77, 79, 83
    Gregory IX 50
    Innocent III 48–50
    Martin IV 80
    Nicholas IV 102
popular protest 34
porticus 278–9
pottery 190
poverty 105
Powicke 215
prebend 275
precinct 81–4, 86, 155, 163, 183, 200, 227
    wall 140, 211
Preston on Stour 66
priest 106, 209–10, 275, 278
processions 2, 30–31, 199
Prophet, John 26
proto-urban settlements 155
Provence 11, 79, 87
    Eleanor of 47, 49, 87
public
    ceremony 12, 36
    order 31
Purbeck marble 252

Quinton 66

ramparts 140
Ramsay Abbey 160
Reading 158, 160
    Abbey 160
Reask 141

rebellion 11
rector 70, 102
rectory 104, 106, 108, 121
Redditch 66
Reformation 68–9, 100, 102, 105, 119, 212–13, 236, 238, 255, 257, 260, 262–3
relics 116
Rennes, Bishop of 9
rents 59, 70
Rheims 134, 147
Rhineland 44, 161
Richard I 3, 46
Richborough 241
Rickman 246
ringfort 141
Ripon Minster 278
Ripple 280, 285
ritual 2, 29
Rochester 281
  Bishop of 14, 79
Roman 161
  Britain 132
  cemetery 5, 161
  earthwork 218
  Empire 132
  post- 161
  towns 5, 134
Romanesque 276, 279–81, 283, 285
rood 7
  screen 256–7, 283–4, 288–9
Rugby 197
Rye 158–9

saddlery 63
Saint
  Alban 5
  Augustine 239
  Brigit 139
  Columba 138
  Columbanus 136
  Dominic 89
  Dunstan 156
  Edmund 88
  Edward 88
  Ethelbert 29
    feast of 23
  Étienne 147
  Francis 88
  Thomas Cantilupe 29
  Thomas, shrine of 35

St Albans 5, 100, 155, 158–60, 163, 282, 287
  Abbey 282
    Chronicle 163, 171
    precinct 164, 170
  Abbot Wulsin of 158, 163, 166, 168–71
  Dagnal Street 166, 169
  Fraternity of All Saints 171
  French Row 166
  George Street 166, 169
  Holywell Hill 164, 166–8
  Kingsbury 159, 163, 166, 169–72
  market 163
  moot hall 171
  Romland 166, 171
  St Andrew's 167, 169
  St Michael's 163, 167, 170
  St Peter's 163–7, 169
  St Peter's Street 164–5, 167–70
  St Stephen's 163, 166–8
  Sopwell Lane 164, 166–8
  Sopwell Priory 161, 168
  Tonman Ditch 167–9
  Verulamium 161, 162–3, 166, 170–71
  Watling Street 161, 163, 166
St Ives 160
Salisbury 33, 101, 116
  Bishop of 286
    Roger, Bishop of 277
  Cathedral 286
sanctuary 5, 26, 136, 139–40, 144
Sandwich 159, 264
Santiago de Compostella 85
Scarborough 101, 103, 140, 144
Seirkieran 147
Selby 103, 106
  Abbey 107
sergeant 26, 28, 30
servants 13, 49
Severn River 45, 61, 64, 67
Shaftesbury 157
Sherborne River 158, 182, 185, 190–91, 194, 196
Shifnal Priory 280, 285
Shipston on Stour 58, 64, 70
shoemakers 15, 17, 60
shop 27, 31, 165
Shrewsbury 13, 157, 215, 232
  Pride Hill 215

INDEX

St Mary's 279
shrine 115, 117, 282, 285
   Marian 115
Shustoke 58
Siena 82
silk 13
skinner 60
smith 66
Solihull 64–5
Southampton 47
Southwark 3, 50
social
   conflict 9
   hierarchy 9
   structure 20
     of towns 2, 13
Spain 48, 51, 79
Speed, John 183, 185
   plans of 193, 196
spices 3, 59–63, 68
spire 253
stalls 31, 164–6
Stamford 46
Stephen, King 172, 177
Stourbridge 64, 66–7
Stour River 265
Stow, John 77, 79–80
Stow on the Wold 160
Stratford upon Avon 58, 63 70, 100
   Guild of the Holy Cross 56, 60, 63–6
Sturry 265
suburbs 4, 6, 33–4, 82, 84, 90, 134, 146, 160–61, 191, 194, 198, 224–5
Suffolk, Earl of 15–16
sumptuary regulations 13–14
Sutton Coldfield 64–5
synagogue 49, 84

tailor 60
tallow 109
Talmud 50
Tamworth 64, 182, 190
tannery 59
taverner 31
Tavistock 157
taxation 12, 21, 31, 70
Templars 90
Temple Guiting 65
tenement 160, 167

Tewkesbury 59, 64, 105, 107
   Abbey 56
textiles 70
Thames River 85, 157
Thannington Without 265
tithes 58, 65, 69, 101–3, 105–7, 109–11, 118, 209–10, 212, 229
Todi 82
tolls 189
Tong 288
Torah 44
Toulouse 146–7
   Counts of 147
Tours 13
tower 246, 250, 253, 256, 259, 263
   crossing 276, 279, 285
   round 139
   west 278
town
   English 120
   fields 101
   founding 157
   functions of 55
   hall 24
   Irish 139
   multi-parish 4
   new 157
   planning 5–6, 83, 155
   plans 8, 164, 179
   Tuscan 82
   Umbrian 82
   wall 82, 84–5, 90, 100, 134, 136, 143, 147, 196, 221, 229, 232, 245, 256, 264–5
townscape 181, 183
tracery 252–3, 259
transept 276, 279, 283, 285
   chapel 252, 282
Tredington 66, 69
Trent, River 156
   Simon of 45
tribal kingdoms 131
Trier 147
Tuam 149
Tullylish 140
Tysoe 70

university colleges 102
urban
   community 36

decline 104
defences 134, 142
economy 3, 55
government 14, 33
hierarchy 6, 178
  in West Midlands 3, 56, 71
revolt 11–12
society 10–11, 29, 35
topography 178
urbanization 4, 132, 134
'urbs–suburbium' model 5

vagabond 27
vagrancy 31
vallum 136, 140, 142–4, 149; see also ditch
Valor Ecclesiasticus 102, 104–5, 117
venison 63
Ver River 167–8
Verulamium, see St Albans
vestments 60
vicarage 104, 121,
  perpetual 275
vicars 70, 103–4, 286
Vikings 131, 140
vintners 31
Visigothic 134
visitation 260

Wakefield 115
Wales, 177
  North 43–4, 58
Wallingford 172
Walsall 58
Walsingham 115
Waltham Holy Cross 278, 283
wards 211, 263, 265
  boundaries 264
Wareham 157
Warwick 64, 69, 103, 105, 182, 190
  Countess of 85
  Earls of 67
  St Mary's 55, 56, 59, 63, 68–9, 105
Warwickshire 56, 182
water supply 81, 85
wax 63, 106, 109–10
wealth 9, 20
Welles, Hugh de 275
Wessex 157, 172
West Midlands 3, 55, 157

Westminster 14, 80, 83–4, 87–8, 101, 108, 159
  Abbey 87, 89
  Hall 46
West Saxon kings 132
Westwood Priory 55–6, 63, 65–7
Whitby 107
Whittington 220
Wickhamford 66
William the Conqueror 159, 239
Wimborne Minster 285
Winchester 6, 13, 33, 45, 49, 100, 104–5, 132, 156, 172, 177, 210–11, 213, 218, 224, 227, 230–31
  Bishop of 33
  cathedral 278
  Nunnaminster 157
  old and new minsters 157
  Wolvesley 211
windows 246, 253, 258
  lancet 246
  triple 248, 259
wine 3, 60–65, 69
  price of 31
wills 255, 260–61
Wilton 157
Worcester 3, 6, 8, 47, 55, 58, 60, 64, 67–8, 101, 104, 115, 156–7, 159, 171, 210, 212–13, 216–17, 229–30, 233
  All Saints 215, 220, 229
  Anglo-Saxon defences 229
  Birdport 214–15, 218
  Bishop of 3, 60, 65, 100
  bishopric 56, 59
  cathedral priory 56, 59, 61–2, 66, 69, 212, 218
  Greyfriars precinct 213, 220
  High Street 214–15, 218
  merchants 62–3
  Prior of 3, 59
  St Alban's 215, 220, 229
  St Andrew's 213, 215, 218
  St Clements 217
  St Helen's 213, 215, 218, 220–21, 229–30
  St Martin's 217, 220, 229
  St Michael in Bedwardine 220
  St Nicholas's 217, 229
  St Peter the Great 217, 220, 229

St Swithun's 216, 218, 220–21, 229–30
streets 215, 220
Worcestershire 56

Xanten 161

Yarmouth 106–7, 109, 116–17

York 3, 26, 44, 46–7, 49, 101, 104–5, 107, 179
Archbishop of 100
Bootham 159
Duke of 67
massacre at 46
Minster 100
St Mary's Abbey 159